Fighting for Britain?

BRITISH IDENTITIES SINCE 1707
Vol. 7

Series Editors:

Professor Paul Ward
School of Music, Humanities and Media,
University of Huddersfield

Professor Richard Finlay
Department of History, University of Strathclyde

PETER LANG
Oxford · Bern · Berlin · Bruxelles · Frankfurt am Main · New York · Wien

Wendy Ugolini and Juliette Pattinson (eds)

Fighting for Britain?

Negotiating Identities in Britain During the
Second World War

PETER LANG

Oxford · Bern · Berlin · Bruxelles · Frankfurt am Main · New York · Wien

Bibliographic information published by Die Deutsche Nationalbibliothek
Die Deutsche Nationalbibliothek lists this publication in the Deutsche Nationalbibliografie;
detailed bibliographic data is available on the Internet at http://dnb.d-nb.de.

A catalogue record for this book is available from the British Library.

Library of Congress Control Number: 2015932382

ISSN 1664-0284
ISBN 978-3-0343-1824-2 (print)
ISBN 978-3-0353-0704-7 (eBook)

© Peter Lang AG, International Academic Publishers, Bern 2015
Hochfeldstrasse 32, CH-3012 Bern, Switzerland
info@peterlang.com, www.peterlang.com, www.peterlang.net

All rights reserved.
All parts of this publication are protected by copyright.
Any utilisation outside the strict limits of the copyright law, without the
permission of the publisher, is forbidden and liable to prosecution.
This applies in particular to reproductions, translations, microfilming,
and storage and processing in electronic retrieval systems.

This publication has been peer reviewed.

Printed in Germany

Contents

List of Tables — vii

MARTIN FRANCIS
Foreword — ix

WENDY UGOLINI AND JULIETTE PATTINSON
Negotiating identities in multinational Britain during the Second World War — 1

LUCY NOAKES
'Deep England': Britain, the countryside and the English in the Second World War — 25

GARY SHEFFIELD
Englishness in the British army of the Second World War — 49

MARTIN JOHNES
Welshness, Welsh soldiers and the Second World War — 65

BERNARD KELLY
'Excellent Irishmen': Irish volunteers and identities during the Second World War — 89

IAN S. WOOD
Northern Ireland's War — 113

TREVOR GRIFFITHS
Scottish cinema-goers at war: The popular reception of
British and Scottish films during the Second World War — 137

GAVIN BOWD
'Fortify the Cheviots!': The Nazis and the Scottish Nationalists — 161

JESSICA THURLOW
'Total War on Spiritual Issues': English feminists, Christian
national identity and gender equality in wartime Britain — 185

WENDY WEBSTER
Transnational communities of allies — 209

IAIN E. JOHNSTON
Imperial settler-regions in the Second World War:
The case of British air training in southern Africa — 235

STUART ALLAN
'Some idea of our country': Scotland, Wales and
Northern Ireland in early wartime documentary film — 261

LINSEY ROBB
'His Own Weapons to His Own Battlefront':
The civilian working man in British culture 1939–1945 — 287

Notes on contributors — 311

Index — 315

Tables

Table One	Distribution of the Films of Scotland Committee Films, 1939–1943	146
Table Two	Favourite Films of Ms Eileen Crowford, 1944–1945	152–3
Table Three	Output of Training Schemes in the Union of South Africa, Southern Rhodesia, the UK and the BCATP Dominions	256

MARTIN FRANCIS

Foreword

It is now exactly forty years since the appearance of J.G.A. Pocock's famous plea for a self-consciously 'British history' that would recognise not merely the interaction between the four constituent nations of the British Isles, but also how this 'four nations' narrative was framed by the broader contexts of empire and the Atlantic world.[1] In the decades since this pivotal intervention, an extensive historical literature on the topic of Britishness has emerged, although most of it has been dedicated to the internal and multinational, rather than the external and trans-national, dimensions to Pocock's call for a more pluralist understanding of the nation's past. However, there has been relatively little sustained attention to the operation, expression and reception of Britishness during the Second World War. This is despite the significance of both national and regional difference as a category of analysis in Sonya Rose's landmark study of the identity politics of wartime Britain, *Which People's War?*, and the central place held by the Second World War in British national myth and memory, mapped in Lucy Noakes' pioneering *War and the British*.[2] The chapters that constitute *Fighting for Britain* therefore are a welcome addition, not merely to the historical literature concerned with wartime Britain, but to the broader questions of how national identity functioned in Britain throughout the twentieth century.

---

1   J.G.A. Pocock, 'British History: A Plea for a New Subject', *Journal of Modern History* 47/4 (1975), 601–28.
2   Sonya O. Rose, *Which People's War? National Identity and Citizenship in Britain, 1939–1945* (Oxford: Oxford University Press, 2003); Lucy Noakes, *War and the British: Gender and National Identity, 1939–91* (London: IB Tauris, 1998).

Why then has Britishness during the Second World War not received more attention? One answer may lie in the legacy of Linda Colley's highly influential *Britons*, which seemed to suggest that the work of constructing a British national identity was effectively complete by the time of Victoria's accession.[3] Certainly the notion of England, if not Britain, possessing a long history as a nation state, served the British well in the late nineteenth and early twentieth centuries, as they were obliged to confront the challenges of more recent national unifications (notably that of Germany) and to resist the claims of nascent nationalisms (especially Irish and Indian) within the empire. However, such narratives were of course myths or, at the very least, exercises in wishful thinking. In fact, to borrow the conceptual categories deployed by Antoinette Burton, the British nation was essentially a 'performative, rather than a prescriptive' entity. Far from being 'forged' by 1837, Britishness was 'always in the making', and we need to be acutely aware of the fluid, unstable and incomplete status of national identity during the 1940s, and indeed beyond.[4] Similarly, we can dispense with hackneyed clichés, peddled as much on the political Left, as evidenced by Robert Colls' irresponsibly flawed *Identity of England*,[5] as on the intransigent Right, that Britain or any of its constituent nations possessed a common culture and sense of togetherness during the Second World War, which stands in stark contrast to a post-war national history characterised by cultural and political fragmentation and multicultural chaos.

This is not to say that Britishness did not display considerable resilience in both political and emotional registers during the Second World War. This was, of course, a reflection of the relatively light touch that Britain received from the monumentally destructive forces that were unleashed across the European continent between the mid-1930s and mid-1940s.

---

[3] Linda Colley, *Britons: Forging the Nation, 1707–1837* (London: Yale University Press, 1992).

[4] Antoinette Burton, 'Who Needs the Nation? Interrogating "British" History', in Catherine Hall, ed., *Cultures of Empire: Colonizers in Britain and the Empire in the Nineteenth and Twentieth Centuries* (Manchester: Manchester University Press, 2000), 137–53. Here 145.

[5] Robert Colls, *Identity of England* (Oxford: Oxford University Press, 2002).

Britain was saved the massive dislocation and movement of populations, the ethnic cleansing and genocide that characterised the war's impact in the bloodlands of central and eastern Europe. Moreover, it was subsequently immunised from these events, which clearly constituted the paramount trauma of the Second World War, by the onset of the cold war which left the death zone between Berlin and Moscow in a darkness shrouded by the Iron Curtain. In the absence of defeat or occupation (with the exception of the peripheral Channel Islands), Britain's territorial integrity was saved the violent reshaping of borders, and even dismemberment, that befell nations that fell under the sway of either Hitler or Stalin. For large parts of the Second World War, several nation states (notably Czechoslovakia and Poland) were deemed by their new rulers to have literally ceased to exist. Even where sovereignty was re-established in the wake of the collapse of the Axis powers, what amounted to murderous civil wars tore apart Greece, Italy and, to a lesser extent, France. Placed in this broader comparative context, the continued efficacy of Britishness during the war might seem to require little need for sustained examination or explanation.

Moreover national institutions, whether political or cultural, in Britain also fared well during the war. For all the niggling demands for more Welsh language broadcasting on the BBC or for the restoration of the kilt in Scottish regiments, the Union remained secure. The monarchy also had a good war, steadying itself after the embarrassments of the Abdication and George VI's poorly advised public affirmation of Neville Chamberlain during the Munich crisis. A (qualified) degree of accommodation to wartime populism allowed the BBC to establish its reputation as the 'voice of Britain' between 1939 and 1945. The symbolic power of the chimes of Big Ben echoing across a London scarred by the Blitz guaranteed the lionisation of Britain's parliamentary traditions, even if wartime politics had inevitably seen a strengthening of executive power and limited opportunities for legislative initiative. Civil service high-handedness and pettiness, especially in regard to issues such as rationing, was eventually to make a serious contribution to the unravelling of 1940s collectivism, but this was less evident in 1945 than it was to become in 1950. Wartime health and education provision revealed many of the inadequacies of Britain's local government system, but no one was willing to take on reform in this area in earnest until the 1960s. Significantly, the Attlee government, which took power in the closing months of the war, while it pursued a radical agenda in the domains of welfare and the economy, had virtually no interest in constitutional or institutional reform. Indeed some decidedly conservative national institutions continued to thrive in the Attlee years, often drawing on the dividend created by their ostensible contribution to the war effort. In this light, Ernest Bevin's famous defence of the Labour government's unwillingness to trespass on the prerogatives of the elite public schools is worth repeating in full: 'I am not one of those who decry Eton and Harrow. I was very glad of them in the Battle of Britain.'[6]

So, given the absence of the more palpable traumas that afflicted nations and states in continental Europe, how can one go about writing about national identity in wartime Britain in ways that are rewarding and historiographically consequential? A simple resort to discussing the relationship of the Celtic fringe to England, or Englishness, is clearly inadequate to the task of reconstituting understandings of nation and national cultures in wartime Britain. Instead, the historian needs to be both geographically and conceptually more expansive. One fruitful line of enquiry is to relate national identity to other categories of analysis, based on gender, social class, sexuality or memory, especially since the Second World War has already provided a rich terrain for historians interested in issues of femininity and masculinity, and which, in the light of Geoffrey Field's major study, may once again become a significant site for examining questions of class relations, albeit in a more eclectic vein than previously.[7] Indeed several of the contributions to *Fighting for Britain* directly address the intersections between nation and gender, in areas as diverse as the relationship between feminists and religious identity and the masculinities of both fighting men and non-combatants.

---

6   Quoted in Roderick Barclay, *Ernest Bevin and the Foreign Office* (London: Latimer, 1975), 76.
7   Geoffrey G. Field, *Blood, Sweat and Toil: Remaking the British Working Class, 1939–1945* (Oxford: Oxford University Press, 2011).

Foreword

Two other approaches stand out as worthy of consideration, and they both require a willingness to adopt a more globalised perspective. First, there needs to be a more concerted effort to probe beneath the surface of familiar discourses and sites of wartime national identity, in order to register the extraordinary diversity that characterised the range of components involved in their cultural production. In particular, there needs to be recognition of the contribution of elements derived, not merely from all the four constituent nations of the United Kingdom, but from outside of Britain entirely. To take just one example, the 1944 feature film *A Canterbury Tale* has often been cited as an example of the narrow identification of the wartime nation with a conservative, rural vision of 'Deep England.'[8] However, this both ignores the film's larger metaphysical agenda, especially its critique of materialism, and the fact that its director Michael Powell was able to articulate the same celebration of hierarchy, history and custom, not just in wartime Kent, but in the Scottish Highlands that form the dramatic backcloth to his *I Know Where I'm Going* (1945). More significantly, is it not possible that the emphasis in both films on tradition and community is rooted not merely in Powell's personal history, but in the Austrian Jewish past of his émigré co-director Emeric Pressburger? We should also remember that the deployment of the English village as a metaphor for the nation in the 1943 invasion scare drama *Went The Day Well?* did not preclude the film, directed by Alberto Cavalcanti, a Brazilian who had been an avant-garde film-maker in France, from exposing the local Justice of the Peace as a Nazi collaborator and insisting that it might be necessary to resort to a very un-English form of merciless brutality to repel the invader.

At one level, the subordination of most of continental Europe to Nazism obviously reinforced a sense of British distinctiveness, but at the very same time it required Britain to act as a proxy for an often fantasised cosmopolitan European culture that otherwise would be consigned to

---

8   For example, Anthony Aldgate and Jeffrey Richards, 'Why We Fight: *A Canterbury Tale*', in Anthony Aldgate and Jeffrey Richards, *Best of British: Cinema and Society from 1930 to the Present* (London: IB Tauris, 2002), 57–76.

oblivion. It is not merely that London became a shelter for exiled European governments and crowned heads, that the Royal Air Force became a genuinely multinational force or that the BBC broadcast nightly in a variety of languages to occupied Europe. It is that Britishness was regularly aligned, and rendered compatible, with a broader European sensibility, most poignantly in Dame Myra Hess's performance of a Mozart piano concerto in the lobby of the National Gallery, the scene that closes Humphrey Jennings' *Listen to Britain* (1942). In the same vein, the ending of the 1946 movie *The Captive Heart*, in which a Czech POW is finally, and successfully, united with the widow of a British officer whom he has impersonated, suggests either that Englishness is a sufficiently elastic concept that it can encompass sympathetic foreigners, or, more radically still, that national identity, far from being an inherent attribute, is essentially a fictional construction.

Second, there needs to be a full and proper recognition of empire in the formations of wartime British national identity, and as a constitutive, rather than merely additive, presence. Britain not merely fought the war as an imperial power, but most of the army and navy's major campaigns were in defence of Britain's overseas possessions (especially India and Egypt), rather than to protect metropolitan Britain or liberate continental Europe. As Elizabeth Bowen put it, after 1941 the local intimacy of the Blitz disappeared, as 'war moved from the horizon to the map.'[9] How did service overseas impact on the sense of Britishness of men and women during the war? Even more critically, how did the humiliation heaped on notions of imperial hierarchy and white supremacy by the military disasters of the Far East impact on Britain's sense of self? Similarly, the presence of American GIs in British pubs, and bedrooms, was not merely a personal affront to many (especially moralisers and men) in Britain, but was also an encroachment on national sovereignty and a potent symbol of national decline. Given that the ultimate legacy of the war was the eclipse of Britain as a hegemonic world power (an external consequence that was arguably of greater import than the war's significance as a harbinger of internal

---

9   Elizabeth Bowen, *The Heat of the Day* [1949] (New York: Anchor Books, 2002), 100.

social change and the creation of a post-war welfare state), how does the nexus of war and empire oblige a repositioning of the formations of nation and nationalism? Addressing such questions does not mean abandoning attention to the local, the regional and the sub-national in British history. Recent debates about the question of 'scale' in history have suggested that large global patterns can be mapped and comprehended through a careful analysis of the smallest of places. However, it is only by acknowledging those broader global forces that we can write a historical account of Britishness that returns us to a robustly progressive agenda, rooted in the motifs of connectedness, pluralism and hybridity that Pocock first sought to promulgate four decades ago.

WENDY UGOLINI AND JULIETTE PATTINSON

Negotiating identities in multinational Britain during the Second World War

Introduction

The Second World War has been defined by Paul Addison as the 'culminating moment' in the history of Britain, a multinational state which since the eighteenth century 'had drawn the English, the Scots and Welsh into an ever closer union.'[1] The wartime period, in particular 1940 with the signal events of Dunkirk, the Battle of Britain and the Blitz, is acknowledged as constituting the 'high-water mark of Britishness': a time when a sense of common purpose bound together the constituent countries of the United Kingdom and heightened a British consciousness.[2] Since its inception, Britishness has been 'imagined and narrated in interacting dimensions which include regional and internal national borders, class, ethnicity, gender and other notions of communal identity.'[3] Paul Ward suggests that the period from 1870 onwards has essentially been about 'the continuing definition' of Britishness and that the active and ongoing

---

1   Paul Addison, 'The Impact of the Second World War' in Paul Addison and Harriet Jones, eds, *A Companion to Contemporary Britain, 1939–2000* (Oxford: Blackwell Publishing, 2005), 3–22. Here 12. He adds the proviso, 'and the Irish into rebellion.'
2   Paul Addison, 'National Identity and the Battle of Britain' in Barbara Korte and Ralf Schneider, eds, *War and the Cultural Construction of Identities in Britain* (Amsterdam: Rodopi BV, 2002), 225–40. Here 235.
3   Barbara Korte, 'Wars and "British" Identities – From Norman Conquerors to Bosnian Warriors: An Overview of Cultural Representations' in Korte and Schneider, eds, *War and the Cultural Construction*, 9–24. Here 9.

engagement of the people in the construction of British national identity has, in itself, 'made Britishness a resilient force.'[4] As he writes, identities of place have also frequently been multiple, 'combining allegiance to street, neighbourhood, locality, town, county, region, nation(s) and even a global empire.'[5] This volume contributes to our understanding of how hybrid and multiple identities within the multinational state of Britain and within the constituent countries informed the functioning of Britishness during the Second World War.[6] With a primary focus on military identity formation, underpinned by an examination of civilian identities, this book explores the multinational character of the United Kingdom in wartime as well as the individual identities of its constituent countries: England, Scotland, Wales and Northern Ireland. It also examines the relationship between Ireland and Britain, addressing those Irish citizens who volunteered to serve in the British armed forces. This collection contributes to the 'four nations' approach to British history and follows R.R. Davies in its aim 'to enrich our understanding by considering the connection, comparison and contrasts between them.'[7] It aims to explore the complex ways in which the citizens of Wales, Scotland, England and Northern Ireland interacted with an overarching concept of Britishness during the wartime period. It also addresses the imperial and transnational dimension of wartime Britishness and addresses those who did not fight, for religious, nationalistic or occupational reasons.

As well as adopting a 'four nations' approach, this volume also pursues the question set by scholars such as Krishan Kumar and Paul Ward as

---

[4] Paul Ward, *Britishness Since 1870* (London: Routledge, 2004), 7–9.
[5] Ward, *Britishness Since 1870*, 4.
[6] See also Lucy Noakes, *War and the British: Gender and National Identity, 1939–91* (London: IB Tauris, 1998); Steven Caunce, Ewa Mazierska, Susan Sydney-Smith and John K. Walton, eds, *Relocating Britishness* (Manchester: Manchester University Press, 2004); Helen Brocklehurst and Robert Phillips, eds, *History, Nationhood and the Question of Britain* (Basingstoke: Palgrave, 2004).
[7] R.R. Davies, 'In Praise of British History', in R.R. Davies, ed., *The British Isles, 1100–1500: Comparisons, Contrasts and Connections* (Edinburgh: J. Donald, 1988), 9–26. Here 23.

to whether Britishness functions as a mode of unifying identity, with the sum of Britain being greater than its parts.[8] It also builds on the work of Lawrence Brockliss and David Eastwood who argue that, in the eighteenth and nineteenth centuries, Britons possessed a 'composite identity', thus underlining the need to explore the development of Britishness as a 'lived identity.'[9] Kumar and Ward both counter the arguments of those who focus on notions of Britishness as, historically, a largely pragmatic relationship with a wider state identity and instead, posit the extent and possible existence of a more 'emotional' commitment and allegiance to Britishness from the citizens of the constituent nations.[10] Thus, Ward argues that, rather than being artificially imposed from above, for much of the twentieth century Britishness was an identity accepted, put together and lived by the majority of the people within the United Kingdom.[11] However, there has been remarkably little scrutiny of Britishness during the Second World War. As Martin Johnes notes for the post-1939 period, 'the whole concept of what Britishness meant beyond the realms of the state ... is fumbled with or just ignored.'[12] He calls for the 'populism of Britishness' and the links between Welsh and Scottish identities and the pillars of Britishness – capitalism, Protestantism and empire – to be revisited.[13] This edited collection attempts to interrogate and examine the expressions and reception of Britishness in the twentieth century more closely, using the Second World War as a case study.[14]

---

[8] Krishan Kumar, *The Making of English National Identity* (Cambridge: Cambridge University Press, 2003); Ward, *Britishness Since 1870*.

[9] Laurence Brockliss and David Eastwood, 'Introduction: A Union of Multiple Identities' in Lawrence Brockliss and David Eastwood, eds, *A Union of Multiple Identities: The British Isles, c.1750–c.1850* (Manchester: Manchester University Press, 1997), 1–8. Here 4.

[10] Kumar, *The Making of English National Identity*, 147; Ward, *Britishness Since 1870*.

[11] Ward, *Britishnness Since 1870*, 7.

[12] Martin Johnes, 'Wales, History and Britishness', *Welsh History Review* 25/4 (2011), 596–619. Here 600.

[13] *Ibid.*, 601.

[14] Kumar, *The Making of English National Identity*; Ward, *Britishness Since 1870*.

Constructions of Britishness

In 1975, J.G.A. Pocock famously made his plea for an explicitly 'British history', a term which he used to denote 'the plural history of a group of cultures situated along an Anglo-Celtic frontier.'[15] Calling for the adoption of a pluralist and multicultural approach to the study of British history – or the Atlantic 'archipelago' – Pocock subsequently insisted that British history should be understood as 'the interaction of several peoples and several histories.'[16] He referred not just to the four nations but also their broader connections with North America and the rest of Britain's 'white' empire.[17] From the moment of Pocock's intervention, British history, notes Raphael Samuel, became 'alive to the importance of dual allegiances and multiple identities' and began to be conceptualised 'in the spatial dualisms of core and periphery, metropole and provinces.'[18] Another landmark contribution was Linda Colley's *Britons: Forging the Nation 1707–1837* which argued that a new sense of British identity was constructed in the long eighteenth century through a shared common Protestantism contrasted with the Catholicism of Continental Europe.[19] Britons, she asserts, 'defined themselves ... not just through an internal and domestic dialogue but in conscious opposition to the Other beyond their shores.'[20] In particular, they constructed themselves against France through a series of major wars and

---

15 J.G.A. Pocock, 'British History: A Plea for a New Subject', *Journal of Modern History* 47:4 (1975), 601–28. Here 605.
16 *Ibid.*, 616; J.G.A. Pocock, 'The Limits and Divisions of British History: In Search of the Unknown Subject', *American Historical Review* 87/2 (1982), 311–36. Here 313.
17 Linda Colley, 'Britishness and Otherness: An Argument', *Journal of British Studies* 31/4 (1992), 309–29. Here 312.
18 Raphael Samuel, *Island Stories: Unravelling Britain. Theatres of Memory, Volume II* (London: Verso, 1999), 24–5. This included works such as Hugh Kearney, *The British Isles: A History of Four Nations* (1989) and Norman Davies, *The Isles: A History* (1999).
19 Linda Colley, *Britons: Forging the Nation, 1707–1837* (London: Yale University Press, 1992).
20 Colley, 'Britishness and Otherness', 316.

against the global empire attained through military prowess. The creation of an overseas empire enabled all constituent nations to profit; the Scots, in particular, were incorporated into the British imperial project, as 'the arsenal of the Empire.'[21] Overall, Colley argues, there developed both a language of Britishness and a recognisable unit called Britain which constituted 'a workmanlike nation of sorts', albeit one that encompassed other, smaller nations.[22]

In relation to the nineteenth century, Keith Robbins has called for an exploration of the relationship *between* England, Scotland, and Wales on the one hand, and the internal dynamics *within* England, Scotland, and Wales on the other. He refers to this as the blending of 'the English', 'the Scots', and 'the Welsh' to produce 'the British', although this does not automatically imply the existence of a monolithic British entity.[23] Addressing the twentieth century, Kumar points to the fundamental importance of the British Empire, a tightly knit British economy and industrial system buttressed by a British labour movement which, in turn, was integrated by trade unionism and the Labour Party. He also highlights the significance of the BBC, a 'determinedly British' institution, as another of these cohesive factors linking all parts of the United Kingdom.[24] Trevor Griffiths concurs, stating that throughout the first half of the twentieth century, 'the trend across the period was for a growing range of organisations to be structured and to function on a British canvas.' Between the wars, he notes, radio broadcasting acquired a 'self-consciously "British" character', while the growth of 'British' influence was also in evidence at the cinema.[25]

---

21   Colley, *Britons*, xv; 120.
22   *Ibid.*, xi–xii.
23   Keith Robbins, *Nineteenth-Century Britain: England, Scotland and Wales. The Making of a Nation* (Oxford: Oxford University Press, 1989), 2.
24   Kumar, *The Making of English National Identity*, 235–7. For more on the role of the BBC in constructing a pluralistic British national identity in the first half of the twentieth century, see Thomas Hajkowski, *The BBC and National Identity in Britain, 1922–53* (Manchester: Manchester University Press, 2010).
25   Trevor Griffiths, *The Cinema and Cinema-Going in Scotland, 1896–c.1950* (Edinburgh: Edinburgh University Press, 2012), 6.

Essentially therefore, as Kumar argues, Britishness has 'over the centuries developed a set of institutions, symbols and traditions that can lead to a form of emotional identification remarkably similar to that evoked by ethnic nationhood.'[26]

The Second World War and Britishness

Historically, war has acted as a buttress to British national identity. Judy Giles and Tim Middleton note how wars are 'obvious occasions when ideas about national identity become particularly visible.'[27] In the twentieth century, war forced people to think about what they were fighting for, thus reinforcing ideas of Britishness defined against enemies both abroad and at home.[28] Furthermore, as Barbara Korte and Ralph Schneider indicate, the idea of national unity needs to be sustained particularly after a war has ended, to justify the nation's involvement in it or to console the survivors by providing them with a motivation for the losses they have suffered.[29] The Second World War holds a central place in the British national narrative and, notes Korte, 'has engendered its own myths of Britishness', including 'standing alone' against Hitler's Germany during its Churchillian 'finest hour.'[30] As Samuel puts it, wartime Britain became, 'a beacon of hope to

26 Kumar, *The Making of English National Identity*, 239.
27 Judy Giles and Tim Middleton, *Writing Englishness: An Introductory Sourcebook* (London: Routledge, 1995), 110.
28 Max Jones, 'War and National Identity Since 1914' in Francesca Carnevali and Julie-Marie Strange, eds, *20th Century Britain: Economic, Cultural and Social Change* (London: Longman, 2007), 79–94. Here 81.
29 Barbara Korte and Ralf Schneider, 'Introduction' in Korte and Schneider, *War*, 1–8. Here 3.
30 Korte, 'Wars and British Identities', 12. For books which interrogate the mythic dimension of Britain's Second World War narrative, see Angus Calder, *The People's War: Britain 1939–1945* (London: Jonathan Cape, 1969); Angus Calder, *The Myth of the Blitz* (London: Jonathan Cape, 1991); Robert Mackay, *Half the Battle: Civilian*

occupied Europe, standing up to the Nazis where others had capitulated or collaborated. The BBC, starched accents and all, was "the voice of Britain". Westminster was thought of as an example to the world, "the mother of parliaments".[31] London, as the principal target of enemy attack, had a special place in the nation's esteem with its projection of 'Cockney heroism and good humour – the stoical indifference of the air-raid shelter crowd, cocking a snook at "Jerry"' and 'the "business as usual" of the cabbies, clippies and bobbies.'[32]

The Second World War 'heightened national consciousness in Britain by creating the potentially inclusive, democratic sentiment of the "People's War" and in doing so, it prompted a thorough examination of what constituted British national identity.'[33] Ken Lunn notes how both world wars witnessed formal attempts by the British state to create a propaganda of unity to better implement the war effort.[34] In the Second World War, in particular, the state played a more active role than ever before in mobilising the people behind an inclusive vision of Britishness.[35] The Ministry of Information, in its 'Programme for Film Propaganda', stressed the need for films to convey 'British life and character' and 'British ideas and institutions'; there was also strong urging of the need for 'publicity about the British Empire.'[36] Wartime regional broadcasting saw the BBC, for the first time, project a truly multinational image of Britain as regional productions

---

    Morale in Britain during the Second World War (Manchester: Manchester University Press, 2002); Mark Connelly, *We Can Take It! Britain and the Memory of the Second World War* (Harlow: Pearson, 2004).

31 Samuel, *Island Stories*, 41.
32 Ibid., 41–2.
33 Richard Weight and Abigail Beach, 'Introduction' in Richard Weight and Abigail Beach, eds, *The Right to Belong: Citizenship and National Identity in Britain, 1930–1960* (London: I.B. Tauris, 1998), 1–18. Here 8.
34 Kenneth Lunn, 'Reconsidering "Britishness": The Construction and Significance of National Identity in Twentieth Century Britain,' in Brian Jenkins and Spyros A. Sofos, eds, *Nation and Identity in Contemporary Europe* (London: Routledge, 1996), 83–100. Here 88.
35 Jones, 'War and National Identity Since 1914', 87.
36 Kumar, *The Making of English National Identity*, 234.

had to be carried by either the Home Service or Forces Programme.[37] The Second World War thus highlighted what it meant to 'be British.' There was not one solitary, unified way that Britishness was constructed however. Rather, myriad forms were presented by different commentators. Prime Minister Winston Churchill, for example, looked to Britain's past to articulate what it meant to be British, using heroic rhetoric to construct a national 'linguistic community' engaged in an epic struggle for 'Britain' and the 'British Empire',[38] while the literary intelligentsia, who were 'enlisted as state-sponsored patriots', emphasised the everyday heroism of the ordinary British public.[39] Left-wing commentators such as J.B. Priestley in his *Postscripts* radio programme, documentary film-maker Humphrey Jennings in his body of work and author George Orwell focused on, and celebrated, the 'national character.'[40] In his wartime essay 'The Lion and the Unicorn', Orwell described the British people as 'a nation of stamp-collectors, pigeon-fanciers, amateur carpenters, coupon-snippers, darts-players, crossword-puzzle fans' and defined British culture as 'somehow bound up with solid breakfasts and gloomy Sundays, smoky towns and winding roads, green fields and red pillar-boxes.'[41] Such portraits of national unity, notes Sonya Rose, suggested that 'those who best represented Britain at war were not exceptional individuals but rather were everyday, ordinary people; those who were "doing their bit".'[42] Whilst putting forward a similar argument,

37   Hajkowski, *The BBC and National Identity in Britain*, 14.
38   John Baxendale, '"You and I – All of Us Ordinary People": Renegotiating "Britishness" in Wartime' in Nick Hayes and Jeff Hill, eds, *'Millions Like Us'? British Culture in the Second World War* (Liverpool: Liverpool University Press, 1999), 295–322. Here 308; Kumar, *The Making of English National Identity*, 234.
39   Addison, 'Impact of the Second World War', 11.
40   Sonya O. Rose, *Which People's War?: National Identity and Citizenship in Britain 1939–1945* (Oxford: Oxford University Press, 2003), 153; Sonya O. Rose, 'Sex, Citizenship, and the Nation in World War II Britain', *American Historical Review*, 103/4 (1998), 1147–76. Here 1148.
41   George Orwell, *The Lion and the Unicorn: Socialism and the English Genius* (London: Searchlight Books, 1941), 15. This essay was entitled 'England Your England' and Orwell acknowledged his propensity to use 'England' to represent 'Britain'.
42   Rose, *Which People's War?* 5.

John Baxendale also argues for recognition of a 'discursive field crossed by many different and conflicting ideas.'[43] Thus, whilst a sense of 'sameness' was culturally 'evoked in innumerable wartime celebrations of familiar British things – a cup of tea or a radio catchphrase', 'sameness' essentially resided in the daily lived experience of the British people. This focus on the ordinariness of everyday lives became 'all the more precious' during the destructive and disruptive chaos of wartime, and increasingly, a source of national pride.[44] During the war, argues Baxendale, it was this shared experience and the related impulse 'not to have a familiar way of life destroyed by an alien political force' that gave people a stronger feeling of national identity or 'belonging.'[45]

Within this context, much of British national character was also being constructed in opposition to the humourless and militaristic Nazi, with the perceived British characteristics of tolerance, cheerfulness and stoicism being widely celebrated. This depiction assumed a gendered dimension: it was British men, not women, who were drawn culturally as the polar opposites of brutish German soldiers. This form of ordinary British martial masculinity, which merged heroism and brawn with humour and the enjoyment of cosy pleasures such as a pint of beer or a cup of tea, is termed 'temperate' masculinity by Sonya Rose.[46] This is at the heart of Linsey Robb's chapter in this edited collection which applies Rose's concept to civilian masculinities. She amasses an array of cultural sources, including film, cartoons and newspaper evidence surrounding the wartime civilian man to argue that there was a continuum of British masculinities predicated upon occupational status that extended from the home front to the battlefront. Popular memory has regarded the British home front as a domain populated solely by women, the young, the elderly and the medically unfit. Programmes such as *Dad's Army* (1968–77), *We'll Meet Again* (1982), *Goodnight Sweetheart* (1993–9) and *Foyle's War* (2002–current)

43 Baxendale, 'You and I', 299.
44 *Ibid.*, 300.
45 *Ibid.*, 322.
46 Rose, *Which People's War?*, 2, 153.

have cemented this notion. Yet millions of physically fit men within the call-up age range were retained in 'essential work' considered by the state to be essential to the prosecution of war and were thereby precluded from service in the armed forces. Twice as many men (over ten million) remained in their reserved occupations, both blue-collar trades (such as agricultural labourer and docker) and white-collar professions (such as medicine and dentistry), as were enlisted into the armed forces (4.6 million) and yet historians to date have not examined this aspect of the People's War.[47] In 2007, Matthew Cragoe and Chris Williams noted that the reserved occupations would 'repay exploration in the Welsh context.'[48] With a high proportion of Welsh men employed in the mining and agricultural industries, the home front in Wales was certainly no feminised space. But neither were industrial heartlands such as Clydeside, Tyneside and Merseyside, as Juliette Pattinson, Arthur McIvor and Linsey Robb illustrate in their forthcoming nationwide study of reserved occupations.[49]

While Rose asserts that the British nation was 'masculine',[50] a key aspect of the People's War was the contribution made by women. Britain was unique in the extent to which it conscripted 'womanpower', compelling at first young single women to serve in December 1941, and then as the war evolved into a protracted war, older and married women and finally even mothers of older children. Over seven million women worked in industry or civil defence, with a further half a million serving in the auxiliary services, the WAAF, the ATS and the WRNS.[51] State-funded nurseries, canteens

47 Peter Howlett, *Fighting with Figures: A Statistical Digest of the Second World War Statistical Digest of the War* (London: HMSO, 1951), 8.
48 Matthew Cragoe and Chris Williams, 'Introduction' in Matthew Cragoe and Chris Williams, eds, *Wales and War: Society, Politics and Religion in the Nineteenth and Twentieth Centuries* (Cardiff: University of Wales Press, 2007), 1–14. Here 9.
49 Juliette Pattinson, Arthur McIvor and Linsey Robb, *Men in Reserve: British Civilian Masculinity in the Second World War*. Forthcoming.
50 Rose, *Which People's War?*, 153.
51 Penny Summerfield, *Women Workers in the Second World War: Production and Patriarchy in Conflict* (London: Croom Helm, 1984); Penny Summerfield, *Reconstructing Women's Wartime Lives: Discourse and Subjectivity in Oral Histories of the Second World War* (Manchester: Manchester University Press, 1998).

and restaurants and the implementation of shopping time to facilitate female workers with domestic responsibilities enabled the state to effectively harness womanpower. Nevertheless, the relocation by the state of young single 'mobile women' from one region to another provoked considerable hostility; Scottish women for example were reported as greatly resenting their transferral to English factories.[52]

The conscription of large numbers of women into the auxiliary services prompted the creation in 1942 of a female 'chaplaincy' to oversee their spiritual needs. This is the subject of Jessica Thurlow's chapter in this volume. She foregrounds the intersection of gender and nation with religious identities through an examination of English Christian feminist activism in the English-based Churches Work for Women in the Forces. She asserts that the female chaplaincy's desire for equal ministry was not realised and that, like women generally, they were excluded from full involvement in all spheres and regarded as second-class citizens.

A range of identities, including gender, religion, class, marital status and sexuality intersected with nation. The gendering of national identity is a theme foregrounded by Lucy Noakes in her examination of the British at war in the twentieth century.[53] During the Second World War, when both national identity and gender roles became visibly marked, men and women were expected to serve their country and had definite roles to play. They were 'encouraged to identify themselves as members of the nation in very gendered ways: man as soldier and woman as wife, mother and war-worker.'[54] Active citizenship was promoted through army education texts such as those produced by the Army Bureau of Current Affairs and the Army Education Corps, which depicted servicemen as a unified group bound together by masculinity and shared experience, while women's magazines largely constructed women as individuals defined by their association with the home, despite their war work.

52 Rose, *Which People's War?*, 224.
53 Noakes, *War and the British*.
54 Ibid., 52.

There was of course not one home front but several. As Graham Dawson and Bob West assert, 'feeling British' could be experienced differently within the four nations – the sense of feeling Scottish, Welsh, English or Northern Irish, for example, could interact with a sense of Britishness in distinct ways.[55] Despite emphasis upon a united community fighting the Nazis as witnessed in so many wartime films and projected by a number of social commentators, sub-national allegiances to Scotland, Wales, England and Northern Ireland undoubtedly, and unsurprisingly, lingered. Nationalism continued to be an important issue during wartime by-elections in Scotland, for example as Chris Harvie notes.[56] Gavin Bowd's chapter in this volume foregrounds the existence of Scottish Nationalism, tracing pre-war Fascist sympathies, a half-hearted wartime fight against Nazism and a reawakening of anti-English feeling. The Scottish National Party (SNP), argues Bowd, was ultimately strengthened by the war. This would suggest that some Scots on the home front did not automatically regard themselves as part of the same 'imagined community' as the English, even in wartime.

Fighting for Britain?

While the home front(s) were an important site for the incubation of national identities, the battle front was even more so. War and military action 'have remained contexts in which "the nation" is habitually evoked.'[57] Indeed, in terms of either regular members of the British Army, volunteers or conscripts in a time of war, the ultimate signifier of national allegiance

---

[55] Graham Dawson and Bob West, 'Our Finest Hour: The Popular Memory of World War Two and the Struggle Over National Identity' in Geoff Hurd, ed., *Nationalising Fictions: World War Two in British Films and Television* (London: BFI, 1984), 7–13. Here 8.

[56] Chris Harvie, 'Labour in Scotland During the Second World War', *Historical Journal* XXVI, 4 (1988), 921–44. Here 934–7.

[57] Korte and Schneider, 'Introduction', 4.

is men's willingness to fight and die for their country.[58] It has been argued that the experience of fighting in the First World War had a cohesive effect for members of the constituent territories of Britain. Keith Robbins concludes that, despite internal divisions, the Great War demonstrated that a British nation did authentically exist.[59] In relation to Wales, the historian John Davies concurs: 'By suffering alongside Geordies and Brummies, Cockneys and Scousers, Micks, Jocks and Aussies, the Taffs became part of a new brotherhood; to become a soldier was to assume a new nationality.'[60] Angela Gaffney confirms that memorialisation in post-war Wales consistently situated loss within a wider British and imperial identity, although Jenny Macleod makes the point that the Scots, in the form of their national war memorial, used imperial sentiment to assert a separate, but equal Scottish identity within Britishness.[61] In Northern Ireland, the specificity of Ulster's sacrifice at the Somme was foregrounded within a wider British commemoration.[62]

This edited collection explores the experiences of soldiers from across the United Kingdom within the British Forces and investigates the meanings which men of a multinational state attached to their military service during the Second World War. It also aims to track the Government's negotiation of the 'mixing of multiple identities into a unified military structure.'[63] Many of the contributors examine the ways in which the War

---

58   Anne-Marie Fortier, *Migrant Belongings: Memory, Space, Identity* (Oxford: Berg, 2000), 91.
59   Keith Robbins, *Nineteenth-Century Britain: Integration and Diversity* (Oxford: Clarendon Press, 1988), 174–5.
60   John Davies, *A History of Wales* (London: Penguin, 1994), 514.
61   Angela Gaffney, *Aftermath: Remembering the Great War in Wales* (Cardiff: University of Wales Press, 2000); Jenny Macleod, 'Britishness and Commemoration: National Memorials to the First World War in Britain and Ireland', *Journal of Contemporary History*, 48/4 (2013), 647–65. Here 651.
62   Catherine Switzer, *Unionists and Great War Commemoration in the North of Ireland, 1914–1939* (Co. Kildare: Irish Academic Press, 2007).
63   Steve Murdoch and Andrew Mackillop, 'Introduction: Military Identity and Multiple Identities' in Andrew Mackillop and Steve Murdoch, eds, *Fighting for Identity: Scottish Military Experience c.1550–1900* (Leiden: Brill, 2002), xxiii–xliii. Here xxv.

Office utilised national identities to foster regimental *esprit de corps* and the extent to which national cultural and religious differences were accommodated or denied. Service in the army has been viewed as central to the forging of a distinct Scottish identity within Britain, particularly since the eighteenth century. Heather Streets has shown how the powerful iconography surrounding the Scottish military tradition, embodied in the image of the Highlander, influenced how Scottish soldiers approached military service in the nineteenth century, acting as both an inspirational model and emotive device.[64] Indeed, this martial ideal became integral to the Scottish soldier's self-image throughout subsequent generations. Jeremy Crang shows how, even though the policy of cross posting undermined the links between the Scottish regiments and their traditional recruiting areas during the Second World War, the 51st (Highland) Infantry Division still became one of the most celebrated divisions.[65] Alvin Jackson confirms the centrality of this famous Division as a vehicle for Scottish military identity during the war although he points out that, 'the universal aspects of the experience of the Division, and of other Scots in military service, were probably no less significant than the distinctively Caledonian.'[66]

The War Office attempted to ensure that Englishmen, Welshmen, Scotsmen and Irishmen were posted to units of their own nationality but in light of the policy of cross posting, this was not always successful.[67] The fact that conscripted Welshmen were perceived as being 'scattered among other national regiments' caused national resentment as did the banning of the kilt from Scottish regiments on active service.[68] There

---

[64] Heather Streets, 'Identity in the Highland Regiments in the Nineteenth Century: Soldier, Region, Nation' in Mackillop and Murdoch, eds, *Fighting for Identity*, 213–36.

[65] Jeremy Crang, 'The Second World War', in Edward M. Spiers, Jeremy A. Crang and Matthew J. Strickland, eds, *A Military History of Scotland* (Edinburgh University Press, 2012), 559–99.

[66] Alvin Jackson, *The Two Unions: Ireland, Scotland and the Survival of the United Kingdom, 1707–2007* (Oxford: Oxford University Press, 2012), 169.

[67] David French, *Military Identities: The Regimental System, the British Army and the British People, c.1870–2000* (Oxford: Oxford University Press, 2005), 281.

[68] Rose, *Which Peoples War?*, 231–8.

were also apparent tensions with the Welsh press expressing resentment at 'Scotsmania' on the BBC which credited Scots forces for all the victories in North Africa.[69] The specific political and geographical circumstances which set Northern Ireland apart also impacted on their interaction with the army during the Second World War: levels of volunteers during the war 'rarely surpassed the unimpressive monthly figure of 1,000.'[70] The concept of Englishness during the Second World War remains relatively unexamined,[71] especially within a military context but here regional loyalties and territorial associations could also play their part. Gary Sheffield, in his chapter in this collection on the British Army, argues that regimental or other unit identities were assiduously cultivated in units that were based in England, and this identity often had a regional dimension. He points out that, in the era of a unitary state, when the dominant ideology was unionism, there was little incentive to promote Englishness in an army in which Celtic units were 'exotic additions' to an organisation that was largely English.

Martin Johnes has made a significant contribution to our understanding of where Wales sits in relation to constructions of Britishness in the twentieth century.[72] Addressing Wales since 1939, his work critically develops the key argument of historian Gwyn A. Williams that 'Welsh identity has constantly renewed itself by anchoring itself in variant forms

69   Rose, *Which Peoples War?*, 230.
70   Brian Barton, 'Northern Ireland: the Impact of War, 1939–45' in Brian Girvin and Geoffrey Roberts, eds, *Ireland and the Second World War: Politics, Society and Remembrance* (Dublin: Four Courts Press, 2000), 47–75. Here 68. See also Brian Barton, *Northern Ireland in the Second World War* (Belfast: Ulster Historical Foundation, 1995).
71   There is a growing historiography on wider notions of Englishness. See Robert Colls and Philip Dodd, eds, *Englishness: Politics and Culture 1880–1920* (London: Croom Helm, 1986); Judy Giles and Tim Middleton, *Writing Englishness 1900–1950: An Introductory Sourcebook on National Identity* (London: Routledge, 1995); Robert Colls, *Identity of England* (Oxford: Oxford University Press, 2002); Kumar, *The Making of English National Identity*.
72   Johnes, 'Wales, History'; Martin Johnes, *Wales Since 1939* (Manchester: Manchester University Press, 2012).

of Britishness.'[73] In this volume, Johnes shows how the plurality of British identity meant that a sense of Welshness was neither lost nor subsumed during the Second World War. In particular, he argues that the traditional language and cultural divisions within Wales itself – loosely between the west and north and the more industrialised, largely English-speaking south-eastern counties – meant that the Welsh 'could actually find it easier to embrace Britishness than the English' because they had always had to negotiate two nations.

Colley notes that, mainly for religious reasons, in Ireland between 1800 and 1920, 'the bulk of the population was never swept into a British identity to the degree that proved possible among the Welsh, the Scots and the English.'[74] Bernard Kelly's chapter in this collection shows how Irish volunteer service in the British forces during the Second World War generated a specific sense of Irishness. Indeed, by incorporating uncontroversial and easily recognisable signifiers of Irish identity, and going to great lengths to accommodate the religious differences of Irish recruits, the British forces managed to fashion 'a composite Irish identity within which sectarian and political divisions were erased.' Kelly also tracks the recent political willingness in Ireland to connect the histories of Eire volunteers to the idea of an overlapping Irish-British identity.

As with Eire, British conscription did not apply to Northern Ireland and thus the Ulstermen who served in the British forces did so as volunteers. In his chapter on Northern Ireland in this edited collection Ian Wood examines the Ulster Unionists and nationalists who served in the forces, both in Irish regiments and in English ones, as well as those who joined uniformed civil defence organisations on the home front such as Air Raid Precautions and the Home Guard, participation in which subjected many to hostility. The war did little to soothe ethnic, religious, cultural and political tensions between Northern Ireland's two communities as sectarianism and IRA activity were ongoing. Wood concludes that for the Catholic and nationalist volunteers, Britishness was largely irrelevant

---

73   Gwyn A. Williams, *The Welsh in Their History* (London: Croom Helm, 1982), 194.
74   Colley, 'Britishness and Otherness?', 314.

to their motivations to enlist, while for Protestant loyalists, service was a proud avowal of their Britishness.

Four Nations?

'England', 'the English', 'we', 'us' 'the nation' and 'the country' were all terms deployed during wartime to draw together disparate groups of people divided by class, region and nation, to elide those differences and unite them around a sense of belonging to an 'imagined community' in opposition to a common enemy. A unified communality then was imagined as the very essence of Britishness. The dominant discourse of Britishness was privileged by both radio and film. The BBC, which had been under the direction of John Reith, a Scot, until 1938, broadcast programmes during the war that promoted solidarity and cut across national lines, while also promoting the Britishness of the Empire. The song 'Merrie England' for example, was replaced by 'The Motherland' in a programme celebrating Empire Day 1941 as it was recognised that 'it would raise a storm from our friends across the Scottish and Welsh borders.'[75] With the appointment of J.B. Priestley and Wilfred Pickles, northern regional English dialects also began to be heard on the BBC. Similarly, filmmakers who were projecting on screen the People's War repeatedly emphasised the theme of communality by including Scottish, Welsh, northern English and west country characters.[76] The casting of, among others, Gordon Jackson, Mervyn Johns, Frank Randle and Bernard Miles expanded understandings about what constituted Britishness and as Wendy Webster notes, friendships and

---

75   Thomas Hajkowski, 'The BBC, the Empire and the Second World War, 1939–1945', *Historical Journal of Film, Radio and Television*, 22/2 (2002), 135–55. Here 141.
76   See, for example, *In Which We Serve* (1942), *One of Our Aircraft is Missing* (1942), *The Gentle Sex* (1943), *Millions Like Us* (1943), *San Demetrio, London* (1943), *We Dive at Dawn* (1943), *The Way Ahead* (1944), *Two Thousand Women* (1944) and *Western Approaches* (1944).

romances often crossed the boundaries between Englishness, Scottishness and Welshness in wartime films.[77] Dave Russell notes how, exceptionally, during the People's War, 'the North was warmly embraced for its distinctive contribution to a wider Englishness or Britishness.' This was not merely a matter of propaganda or manipulation, he argues, but rather reflects the fact that attitudes were briefly changed in both North and South. One Yorkshire commentator, for example, saw 'a new, half-envious respect for southern England' emerge from the North from 1940 onwards.[78]

Nevertheless, the wartime drive for unity was also subject to contestation on the grounds of national, gender and geographic difference as Sonya Rose has highlighted.[79] Certainly, as Johnes asserts, 'if a plural identity like Britishness is to be fully understood then it has to be studied from all its peripheries.'[80] For a long period myths about Englishness dominated the conceptualisation of British identity.[81] Indeed, the use of the term 'English' as a synonym for 'British' during the war represented what Ken Lunn defines as 'a series of assumptions about the natural right of England to speak for Britain and ... the inability of Welsh, Irish and Scottish voices to challenge effectively those assumptions.'[82] The myriad ways in which the cultural wartime representations in which Britishness was often predicated upon Englishness was continually contested, negotiated and challenged is a theme which is addressed by some of our contributors. Trevor Griffiths' chapter addressing Scottish wartime cinema goers, for example, demonstrates that whilst UK films successfully promoted an integrated vision of the British nation on celluloid, there was also continued sensitivity to points of internal difference. A particular point of contention was the tendency in films and their

77 Wendy Webster, 'Rose Tinted Blighty: Gender and Genre in Land Girls' in Mike Paris, ed., *Repicturing the Second World War: Representations in Film and Television* (London: Palgrave Macmillan, 2007), 12–25. Here 16.
78 Dave Russell, *Looking North: Northern England and the National Imagination* (Manchester: Manchester University Press, 2004), 33.
79 Rose, *Which People's War?*
80 Johnes, 'Wales, History', 603.
81 Korte, 'Wars and British Identities', 9.
82 Lunn, 'Reconsidering "Britishness"', 81.

attendant publicity to conflate Britain with England, a wartime practice which irritated Scottish audiences. Ultimately, Griffiths concludes, the success of Britain's wartime film industry rested on its ability to offer a sufficiently diverse product to satisfy the needs of audiences whose tastes often varied markedly. Yet the interchangeable terms 'English' and 'British' are, according to Linda Colley, a consequence of a vagueness about boundaries and identity, rather than arrogance.[83] Lucy Noakes in her chapter in this collection studies a 1941 Mass Observation Directive which asked respondents to reflect upon what Britain meant to them. She notes how the panellists, the majority of whom were from the south of England, 'either unproblematically conflated Englishness with Britishness or went to great lengths to explain that they *felt* and identified as English, not as British.' They also, overwhelmingly, understood the England they felt this emotional attachment to as being best symbolised by the countryside, especially the rural areas of Southern England.

One of the ways in which Englishness came to stand for Britishness was, then, through the celebration of the southern English countryside. Rural England had been perceived as the spiritual core of British national identity since the 1880s and became central to constructions of Britishness in the inter-war era.[84] The wartime depiction of a pastoral idyll functioning as a visual shorthand for 'Britain' can be seen in the 'Your Britain. Fight for it now' series, in documentary films such as *The Dawn Guard* (1940) which depicted thatched cottages and country characters and in films such as *Went the Day Well?* (1942) and *A Canterbury Tale* (1944). These evocations of Englishness sit uneasily with the fact that Britain was the first nation to urbanise and without its industrial power would have been unable to sustain the waging of total war. But at a largely imaginative level, the Southern English countryside was a pervasive wartime image of Britishness, nostalgically reaffirming unchanging values.[85]

---

83 Linda Colley, *Acts of Union, Acts of Disunion: What Has Held the UK Together – And What is Dividing It?* (London: Profile Books, 2014).
84 Weight and Beach, 'Introduction', 14.
85 John Stevenson, 'The Countryside, Planning and Civil Society in Britain, 1926–1947', in Jose Harris, ed., *Civil Society in British History: Ideas, Identities, Institutions* (Oxford: Oxford University Press, 2003), 191–211. Here 192.

While the English countryside featured heavily in propaganda, there are glimpses of the varied landscapes of the other nations in wartime culture. *The Silent Village* (1943), for example, was Humphrey Jennings' tribute to Lidice, a mining community in Czechoslovakia whose inhabitants were massacred following the assassination of Reinhard Heydrich. Daily life in the mining community of Cwmgiedd in West Wales is presented, with the Welsh language being heard without sub-titles to assist non-Welsh speakers. In a letter to his wife whilst working with Welsh miners on the film, Jennings highlighted a perceived continuity between past and present cultural representations of British identities, writing:

> I never thought to live to see the honest Christian and Communist principles daily acted on as a matter of course by a large number of British – I won't say English – people living together. Not merely honesty, culture, manners, practical Socialism, but real life, with passion and tenderness and comradeship and heartiness all combined. From these people one can really understand Cromwell's New Model Army and the defenders of many places at the beginning of the Industrial Revolution.[86]

Stuart Allan in his chapter here examines three documentary films, all of which feature footage of the countryside: *Scotland Speaks*, *Wales – Green Mountain, Black Mountain* and *Ulster*. He notes that they all engage with the concept of wartime Britain as a multinational state and whilst the explicit purpose of the films was to present an image of these parts of the United Kingdom as full and equal partners in the British war effort, they still managed to introduce their own distinct messages into each film, which arguably subverted the primary objectives of the Ministry of Information.

Overall, however, the impact of the Second World War was cohesive. Paul Addison notes how the Second World War tended to undermine nationalism by restoring jobs and prosperity to the previously depressed areas of Scotland and Wales. Paul Ward agrees that out of the conflict 'emerged a new form of Britishness that entered into people's everyday

---

86 Letter dated 10 September 1942, cited in Antony Aldgate and Jeffrey Richards, *Britain Can Take It: British Cinema in the Second World War* (London: Tauris, 2007) 228.

Negotiating identities in multinational Britain during the Second World War 21

lives through a national welfare state.'⁸⁷ This conclusion is also confirmed by Richard Finlay and by Andrew Edwards and Wil Griffith.⁸⁸

This book also addresses the intersections between war, identities and belonging within imperial 'Greater' Britain. As Krishan Kumar notes, the Second World War was fought not just by British nationals from the British Isles, but also British citizens from the Dominions of Canada, Australia, New Zealand and South Africa; and by British subjects from the colonies and dependences of Asia, Africa and the West Indies.⁸⁹ Up to and throughout the Second World War, 'empire remained an important symbol of British prominence and an exemplar of the achievements of the British character.'⁹⁰ Indeed, Robbins cautions that when addressing the relationship between the constituent 'territories' of the United Kingdom, we need to be wary of stripping them of 'that imperial destiny which in the first fifty years arguably still served ... to subdue centrifugal forces.'⁹¹ The close relationship felt by Britain's external dominions towards the mainland can be illustrated by examining the material culture of the latter. An Australian magazine for example featured in 1941 a fabric patterned with small crowns spelling 'England.'⁹² In this volume, Wendy Webster

87   Ward, *Britishness Since 1870*, 7.
88   Richard Finlay, 'Scotland and Devolution, 1880–1945' in Duncan Tanner, Chris Williams, Wil Griffith and Andrew Edwards, eds, *Debating Nationhood and Governance in Britain, 1885–1939: Perspectives From the Four Nations* (Manchester: Manchester University Press, 2006) 27–44; Andrew Edwards and Wil Griffith, 'Welsh National Identity and Governance, 1918–45' in *Debating Nationhood*, 118–45.
89   Kumar, *The Making of English National Identity*, 233. See Gavin Schaffer, 'Fighting Racism: Black Soldiers and Workers in Britain During the Second World War', *Immigrants and Minorities*, 28/2–3 (2010), 246–65; Wendy Webster, *Englishness and Empire 1939–1965* (Oxford: Oxford University Press, 2005).
90   Hajkowski, *The BBC and National Identity in Britain*, 13.
91   Keith Robbins, 'Introduction: Halfway House – Isles and Empire over half a century' in Keith Robbins, ed., *The British Isles 1901–1951* (Oxford: Oxford University Press, 2002), 1–10. Here 6.
92   BP Magazine, 1 December 1941, 36–7, cited in Peter McNeil, '"Put Your Best Face Forward": The Impact of the Second World War on British Dress', *Journal of Design History*, 6/4 (1993), 283–99. Here 292.

considers the experiences of Britain's 'transnational communities of allies.' Addressing the wartime presence of Dominion troops, East European exiles and American GIs, amongst others, Webster highlights the prominence of the propaganda idea of the 'allies war' which associated Britishness with an expansive transnational community. Iain Johnston's chapter in this collection underlines how membership in the 'British World' was a key factor that played into wartime geopolitical and strategic decision-making. He uses case studies of southern Africa's two settler-regions, the Dominion of South Africa and the colony of Southern Rhodesia, to show how the shared experience of training airmen for the RAF can act as a framework through which to analyse evolving imperial bonds in this period.

Overall, this volume aims to draw attention to the existence of the fluidity and multiplicity of identities in the first half of the twentieth century, underpinning a pluralistic Britishness. In recent years a number of studies have emerged which address the questions of ethnicities in wartime Britain: work on the Jewish, Japanese and Italian communities have underlined the diversity of the British population at war, while Thomas Hajkowski's work illustrates the existence of 'hybrid "dual identities"' in wartime Britain.[93] This volume endorses Paul Ward's call for using hybridity as a useful concept for understanding twentieth-century Britain in terms of the range of identities adopted by migrant groups and their descendants within Britain, including internal migration.[94]

---

93 Tony Kushner, *The Persistence of Prejudice* (Manchester: Manchester University Press, 1989); Keiko Itoh, *The Japanese Community in Pre-War Britain: From Integration to Disintegration* (London: Routledge, 2001); Wendy Ugolini, *Experiencing War as the 'Enemy Other': Italian Scottish Experience in World War II* (Manchester: Manchester University Press, 2011). See also Gavin Schaffer, ed., *Racializing the Soldier* (London: Routledge, 2013); Hajkowski, *The BBC and National Identity in Britain*, 2.

94 Wendy Ugolini, 'An English-Welsh Odyssey? Exploring Hybridity in the Wartime Self-Representations of a "Desert Rat"', Warwick University conference, 'Formations and Representations of British National Identity' (2013); Jackson, *The Two Unions*, 168.

Conclusion

Since the late twentieth century there has been a tendency to present Britishness as an identity in terminal decline.[95] Works such as Tom Nairn's *The Break of Britain* (1977) projected a sense of uncertainty surrounding the future of Britain, in the context of the Northern Ireland Troubles, the energy crisis, the question of Scottish devolution and the growth of the Welsh language movement.[96] These anxieties have been further reinforced by the decline of Protestant Christianity, the end of Britain's imperial role and the increasingly fractious relationship with Europe, alongside political devolution in Scotland, Wales and Northern Ireland.[97] Writing in 1999, Samuel, who prophesised that 'Britain is a term which has a very uncertain future',[98] predicted 'the unravelling of any unitary idea of national character.'[99] He identified fiftieth anniversary celebrations of VE day on 8 May 1995 as a visible indicator of the collapse of British power largely because Scotland gave commemorative events 'the cold shoulder.' According to Samuel, there were more VE Day events in Hampshire than the whole of Scotland with the then Lothian Regional Council refusing to recognise 8 May as a public holiday.[100] However, as Jodie Matthews and Daniel Travers assert, Britishness is also fundamentally dynamic: 'it can be transplanted or absorbed into the daily life of a society, it can be used pragmatically, and importantly, it can be rejected.'[101]

---

95 Ward, *Britishness Since 1870*, 1.
96 Samuel, *Island Stories*, 22.
97 Jeffrey Richards, 'Foreword' in Caunce, Mazierska, Sydney-Smith and Walton, eds, *Relocating Britishness*, xii.
98 Samuel, *Island Stories*, 41.
99 *Ibid.*, 43.
100 *Ibid.*, 42–3.
101 Jodie Matthews and Daniel Travers, 'Introduction' in Jodie Matthews and Daniel Travers, eds, *Islands and Britishness: A Global Perspective* (Newcastle: Cambridge Scholars Publishing, 2012), 1–11. Here 4.

The Second World War was a point where what Hajkowsji terms 'the "we feeling" of belonging to a particular nation' was fully illuminated.[102] Indeed, during this period, Britishness could be defined as residing in Samuel's realm of 'the taken-for-granted', providing a prime site for one of the 'shared, interlinked and over-arching stories' of British society.[103] This edited collection confirms the Second World War as a key example of what Krishan Kumar identifies as 'the potential for a powerful British identity that was fully capable of matching and at times surpassing other identities.'[104] It also supports the notion that Britishness is potentially more than 'simply a civic or political identity that overlay deeper cultural differences.'[105] Martin Johnes posits the question of whether the British consciousness experienced and articulated during the Second World War was a 'moment of genuine British sympathies' or was also largely formed by state control, a bombardment of propaganda and an external military threat.[106] Only by interrogating the multiple meanings of Britishness during iconic events such as the Second World War can we begin to achieve a fuller understanding of its meaning, its vulnerabilities and its endurance. It is hoped that this volume will promote and encourage fresh understandings of the pluralistic Britishness which functioned during the Second World War.

102   Hajkowski, *The BBC and National Identity in Britain*, 5.
103   Samuel, *Island Stories*, 37; Colley, *Britons*, xii.
104   Kumar, *The Making of English National Identity*, 147.
105   *Ibid.*, 200.
106   Johnes, 'Wales, History', 600.

LUCY NOAKES

'Deep England': Britain, the countryside and the English in the Second World War

In September 1941, two years after the outbreak of war, the British social survey organisation Mass Observation (MO) asked its panel of writers to 'let yourself run with pen or pencil' and reflect on what Britain meant to them.[1] The key issue that came through in what remains of the responses from the MO National Panel (much of the material from 1941 being lost) was that Britain, largely, meant very little to them. Very few of the panellists identified themselves as British – the majority were English and either unproblematically conflated Englishness with Britishness or went to great lengths to explain that they *felt* and identified as English, not as British. They also, overwhelmingly, understood the England they felt this emotional attachment to as being best symbolised by the countryside, especially the rural areas of Southern England. Many of the respondents were from the South of England, with approximately 50% of those recorded as writing for MO at the end of its first year living in the Home Counties. A substantial minority however came from other regions and nations of Britain.[2] This chapter draws on the surviving material collected by MO, together with contemporary representations of the nation, to explore two, interlinked, questions: why did so many of the English respondents to the MO Directive identify themselves as English rather than British, and why did they largely articulate this Englishness through an attachment to a particular version of rural England?

1   Mass Observation (henceforth MO), Panel Directive, September 1941.
2   James Hinton, *The Mass Observers: A History 1937–1949* (Oxford: Oxford University Press, 2013), 62.

At the heart of these questions is what appears to be a profound contradiction. The Second World War was the most modern of wars: building on the First World War's experiments with industrial warfare, the Second World War saw the development and use of a whole new range of technologies designed to kill, maim and to utterly destroy previously unimaginable numbers of people and the cities in which they lived. It was also a war fought for and against the self-consciously modern ideologies and political systems of democracy, fascism and communism. It was a war that mobilised 'the masses', perhaps the key social grouping of modernity, as never before and which drew on modern systems of communication to not only record, but to fight. Propaganda, in both its official forms, created and issued by the Ministry of Information (MoI), and in its multiple unofficial texts, such as films, radio programmes and magazines, emphasised the war as a British and even an imperial venture; one fought in defence of a greater Britain, rather than its constituent parts. In Britain, it prepared the ground for the egalitarian, modernising, reformist impulses of the post-war Labour government and put the urban working class, as the social grouping that best embodied the collectivist notion of democracy that was foregrounded during the war, at the heart of the nation.[3] At the same time however, it was widely represented in Britain as being fought in defence of established values and a 'natural', organic national community, seen as existing in opposition to the regimented and mindless masses of Nazi Germany.[4] Many of the wartime representations of the nation, whilst giving a voice to the urban working class, 'the people' of the People's War, situated the nation in the 'deep England' that Angus Calder argues 'stretched from Hardy's Wessex to Tennyson's Lincolnshire, from Kipling's Sussex to Elgar's Worcestershire.' It excluded, self evidently, the 'Black Country of the industrial Midlands and the north with its factories and windswept moors.'[5] In its emphasis on the centrality of the rural, southern English regions, this construction of

---

3   Ross McKibbin, *Classes and Cultures: England 1918–1951* (Oxford: Oxford University Press, 1998), 69.
4   For an example of these contrasting views of Britain and Germany see the film scripted and narrated by J.B. Priestley, *Britain at Bay* (1940).
5   Angus Calder, *The Myth of the Blitz* (London: Pimlico, 1991) 182.

national identity also, of course, excluded Wales, Scotland and Northern Ireland.

It is against this backdrop that the MO Directive of 1941 was carried out. According to Tom Harrisson, the war bought MO 'into its own' with the particular, detailed and subjective material it collected bringing it to the attention of the MoI, which employed MO to survey public opinion, thoughts and feelings about the war.[6] MO sent out numerous Directives during the war years, asking its panellists to keep diaries, sending observers to report on life in blitzed towns and evacuation areas, and collecting information on morale through twice weekly random street surveys.[7] The numbers of those who formed the national panel expanded in the first years of the war, reaching about one thousand at its peak. Observers were no doubt attracted by the thought of living through a period of historical significance and of playing an active role in this, contributing to a national project by recording their thoughts, feelings and experiences in wartime, a period when notions of both active citizenship and nationhood were foregrounded.[8] Although the identities of most of those who responded to the 1941 Directive are lost, we can assume that many of them shared this desire to record their lives and to participate in what Ben Highmore has argued was a project established with the aim of creating a democratic, participatory bulwark against the threat of fascism.[9] Whilst, as Peter Mandler has shown, stories about an enduring national character often appear at times of rapid social and political change, the specific historical conditions and public debates of wartime Britain, make their very visibility at

---

6   Tom Harrisson, *World Within: A Borneo Story* (London: Cresset Press, 1959) 162.
7   Hinton, *The Mass Observers*, 167.
8   Ben Lander and Stephen Brooke, 'Mass Observation: An Historical Introduction', *Mass Observation Online*, n.p., <http://www.massobservation.amdigital.co.uk.ezproxy.sussex.ac.uk/essays/content/historicalintroduction.aspx>.
9   Ben Highmore, 'Everyday Life and the Birth of Mass Observation', *Mass Observation Online*, n.p. <http://www.massobservation.amdigital.co.uk.ezproxy.sussex.ac.uk/essays/content/everydaylife.aspx>.

this juncture worthy of close investigation.[10] The responses of those who answered the Directive on what Britain meant to them need to be read alongside the wide range of cultural texts that they were both informed by, and informed. As Janet Watson has argued, literary and historical texts are 'constructions of experience that simultaneously respond to, and contribute to, social perceptions.'[11] Cultural forms and experiences act to inform and to shape one another; cultural forms draw on the dominant beliefs of a period, themselves shaped in part by experience, whilst these beliefs find their articulation in, and are in turn shaped and limited by, the cultural forms of the time. Raymond Williams, whose influential theorisation of 'structures of feeling' as a means of approaching this relationship between text and experience, drew on the cultural forms that he saw as dominant in a historical period to understand the structures of feeling of the age. However, a careful reading of the subjective accounts collected by MO can deepen our understanding of the structures of feeling of wartime Britain.[12] These though, need to be read in conjunction with the cultural forms representing the nation back to itself at the time, and it is to these that this chapter now turns.

England and Britain in wartime

In 1975 the historian J.G.A. Pocock instigated a debate about how to write British history and, by implication, how to understand the relationship between the different nations that make up the United Kingdom. Presciently suggesting that future historians may write of the United

---

[10] Peter Mandler, "Against 'Englishness": English Culture and the Limits to Rural Nostalgia 1850–1940', *Transactions of the Royal Historical Society* 7 (1997), 155–75.

[11] Janet K. Watson, *Fighting Different Wars: Experience, Memory and the First World War in Britain* (Cambridge: Cambridge University Press, 2004) 10.

[12] Raymond Williams, *Marxism and Literature* (Oxford: Oxford University Press, 1977), 128–37.

Kingdom as an entity that existed between the seventeenth and twenty first centuries, Pocock urged historians to both disentangle the histories of the different British nations and to study British history by bringing these national narratives together. Pocock hoped historians would write British history as a history of different kingdoms, with different but interlinked subcultures; a pluralist approach that nonetheless recognised that 'the pattern of "British history" is one of the steadily increasing dominance of England as a political and cultural entity.'[13] Concepts of nationhood become highly visible in wartime as a time when the need for a sense of a united nation is more important than ever, but this visibility, at the same time, makes differences and ruptures more apparent. One of these ruptures was the overarching emphasis on England in discussions of the wartime nation.

In the popular imagination the nation is a 'natural' grouping – something separate from the state, a collective of people brought together by a shared identity, a shared history, shared beliefs and experience. This concept of the nation, of a shared national identity, is particularly important in wartime, when people need to be bound together as far as possible; to feel that the dangers and deprivations they are facing are for a set of vaguely defined yet widely shared, historically grounded aims and beliefs unique to that nation and finding its opposite in the enemy. The British nation at the outset of the Second World War faced deep economic, social, political and regional divisions – the people so effectively scrutinised in Calder's *The People's War* were never the unified imagined community so beloved of political leaders then and now.[14] Wartime conditions effectively levelled out some of these rifts – full employment re-invigorated the old industrial regions of the North and the West while the reforms of the Labour government at the war's end contributed towards a redistribution of wealth. Rationing and conscription during the war went some way to narrowing the gap between rich and poor whilst evacuation made some of the effects of urban poverty and deprivation painfully apparent to those in the reception

13 J.G.A. Pocock, 'British History: A Plea for a New Subject', *Journal of Modern History*, 4/47, (1975), 601–28.
14 Angus Calder, *The People's War* (London: Jonathan Cape, 1969).

areas. But deep divisions remained and shaped the wartime experience – divisions of class, gender, political belief and income, but also of region, both within England and more widely between the four nations of Britain.

Famously, when Leo Amery called on Arthur Greenwood to 'speak for England' in a Parliamentary debate on National Service in September 1939, other MPs quickly implored him to instead 'speak for Britain.'[15] Despite this evidence of a political awareness of the need not to conflate England with Britain, numerous wartime texts nonetheless did precisely that: Orwell's *The Lion and the Unicorn* acknowledged that 'a Scotsman ... does not thank you if you call him an Englishman' but saw divisions of class as greater than those of national identity, whilst J.H. Massingham evoked a nostalgic vision of the English countryside in his patriotic *The English Countryman*, situating what was being fought for in the heart of the English, not British, countryside.[16] Arthur Mee's *Nineteen Forty: Our Finest Hour*, a popular piece of contemporary myth-making written in 1941 and reprinted four times in two years, conflated Christianity and the maintenance of Empire in its depiction of British war aims. It similarly conflated England and Britain in its claim that 'never has the English spirit knit our people so closely into one', describing 'the fair play of the English spirit that has ruled our land for a thousand years.'[17] This use of England to represent Britain, whilst it may have been problematic to many from Wales, Scotland and Northern Ireland, was a view of the nation state also held outside of the British Isles. A German pamphlet written in 1940 for use by the planned invasion forces advised that while 'the English national character may have the flaw of putting tradition above all ... in an emergency the British would

---

15 Hansard, House of Commons Debates, National Service (Armed Forces), Volume 351, 2 September 1939, Col. 224.
16 George Orwell, *The Lion and the Unicorn: Socialism and the English Genius* (London: Secker and Warburg, 1941), <http://orwell.ru/library/essays/lion/english/e_ter> accessed 24 May 2014; H.J. Massingham, *The English Countryman* (London: Batsford, 1942).
17 Arthur Mee, *Nineteen Forty: Our Finest Hour* (London: Hodder and Stoughton, 1941), 37.

be capable of letting everything go and becoming surprisingly modern.'[18] Attempts to represent the different nations within Britain in wartime film almost always situated England at the centre of cinematic representations of the British at war. The 1943 film *Millions Like Us* self consciously set out to be as inclusive as possible in its appeal to women to take up industrial work, including characters from across the classes, across political divides and across the regions and nations of Britain, but Celia Crowson, played by Patricia Roc, the figure at the heart of the drama, was not only a lower middle class English woman, she was from the South of England, holidaying and then honeymooning on the South Coast after her marriage to Fred, an RAF Tail Gunner played by the Scottish actor Gordon Jackson. In common with the majority of his wartime roles, Jackson's character is killed, his fate embodying the marginality of the non-English nations in Britain to dominant representations of the war effort. Scotland and Wales, and to a lesser extent Northern Ireland, were often represented, but the characters who came from these nations were largely marginal to the plot and very often expendable, the nations themselves functioning as sites for the romantic and the uncanny.[19]

In his influential text *Imagined Communities*, Benedict Anderson wrote that the nation 'is imagined because even the members of the smallest nation will never know most of their fellow members, meet them, or even hear of them, yet in the minds of each lives the image of their communion.'[20] As Britain faced the military power and ruthlessness of Nazi Germany a variety of commentators and media texts attempted to provide a picture of Britain which as many members of the nation as possible could identify with. To a remarkably large extent, given that the majority of British people lived in towns and cities, the unifying picture of the nation that was represented was a rural one – not just any part of rural Britain, but in particular

---

18 Cited in Richard Weight, *Patriots: National Identity in Britain 1940–2000* (London: Pan Books, 2002), 25–6.
19 For examples of this see *I Know Where I'm Going* (1945) and *The Halfway House* (1944).
20 Benedict Anderson, *Imagined Communities: Reflections on the Origin and Spread of Nationalism* (London: Verso, 1983), 6.

the gentle, tamed, rolling countryside of Southern England. When *Picture Post* published a pictorial essay describing what was being fought for at the height of the Battle of Britain in 1940, it was not the Scottish mountains, the lakes and fells of Northern England or the mining valleys of South Wales that were pictured, it was the countryside of Southern England that was juxtaposed with modern, mass, militarised Germany.[21] Although the blitzed cities, especially London, also took their place as symbols of the nation a few months later, the gentle countryside of the Southern counties remained central to the wartime vision of nationhood. This, of course, was not anything new. Alun Howkins has vividly described how a 'ruralist version of a specifically English culture' took root in the late nineteenth century, representing a sense of continuity and stability that was set against the perceived upheavals, instability and crises of modernity in the late nineteenth and early twentieth centuries, and culminating in Arthur Quiller Couch's First World War edition of the *Oxford Book of English Verse*; a paean to pastoral England in the midst of industrial warfare.[22] Although representations of the nation being fought for in the Second World War were not entirely southern or rural, the popular wartime films of George Formby, for example, foregrounding the archetypally cheerful, down-to-earth stereotype of the northern working class, while Tommy, the fire-fighting cockney hero of the 1943 film *The Bells Go Down* sacrifices himself in a doomed attempt to save his Fire Chief during the London Blitz, numerous portrayals of Britain chose to focus on rural southern England.[23] The next section examines some of these.

21 *Picture Post*, 13 July 1940, 10–11.
22 Alun Howkins, 'The Discovery of Rural England' in Robert Colls and Philip Dodd, eds, *Englishness: Politics and Culture 1880–1920* (Kent: Croom Helm, 1986), 63.
23 See, for example, *Let George Do It!* (1940) in which Formby accidentally travels to Germany where he punches Hitler; *The Bells Go Down* (1943).

Deep England

The centrality of Southern England to this vision was not accidental but at the heart of the meanings of England that were being produced by writers across the political spectrum in the inter-war years. H.V. Morton's *In Search of England* (1927), Ivor Brown's *The Heart of England* (1935) and Clough William-Ellis' *England and the Octopus* (1928) all saw rural Southern England as the site of an authentic Englishness, something that linked the past and the present and which was threatened by the various encroachments of modernity. Self-consciously modernist, *avantgarde* artists too took to painting Southern England – Eric Ravilious and Ivon Hitchens perhaps most famously in their depictions of the coasts and landscapes of the South such as Ravilious' 'The Vale of the White Horse' and Hitchens' 'Lavington Common.' Southern England, with its small, 'closed' villages, with their paternalistic class structure and traditional agricultural lifestyle, provided a conservative, nostalgic image of English life that was effectively mobilised as an enduring image of 'home' in the 1940s, seen, famously, in Powell and Pressburger's filmic paean to the Kentish countryside *A Canterbury Tale* (1944) and in Frank Newbould's *Your Britain Fight for it Now* series of four wartime posters, which featured images of a village green, the South Downs at Birling Gap, Sussex, Salisbury Cathedral and the village fair at Alfriston, Sussex, a particularly picturesque example of a Southern village.[24]

This very countryside was, of course, a site of contestation and conflict in the inter-war years, and, as Williams suggests, this conflict was articulated through a variety of cultural texts, which in turn helped to shape the experience of life in Britain at this time.[25] The representation of a rural ideal

---

24 On Englishness and landscape in the inter-war period, see Alex Potts, '"Constable Country" Between the Wars', in Raphael Samuel, ed., *Patriotism: The Making and Unmaking of British National Identity. Volume III: National Fictions* (London: Routledge, 1989), 160–88. *A Canterbury Tale* (1944).

25 Raymond Williams, *The Country and the City* (Oxford: Oxford University Press, 1973).

during and preceding the First World War contributed to a 'back to the land' movement amongst the urban working and middle classes in the inter-war years, seen in the establishment of working class communities in places such as Peacehaven on the Sussex coast, symbolic of the ribbon developments of the time held in such disdain by authors such as Clough Williams-Ellis, the popularity of day trips by charabanc and railway to the countryside, and the growth of cycling and rambling as widely shared leisure pursuits. As the town planner Thomas Sharp wrote in 1932: 'People have lived too long in dreary streets. They had seen too few trees and too little grass in their sordid towns. They were tired of the squalid paved back yards. They wanted gardens of their own, back and front, with a space between their house and the next.'[26] In the inter-war years the appeal of the countryside as a site of tranquillity and continuity, the heart of an authentic and unchanging nation, was understood by many of its defenders to be threatened by its very popularity, and by the movement of the urban populations into rural areas. At times, as in the 1932 Mass Trespass of Kinder Scout in the Peak District, this led to violent clashes in the very countryside desired because of its perceived qualities of peacefulness and permanence.[27] Whilst these antagonisms no doubt continued to be felt in the social relations of village and country town during the war, they largely disappeared from public view as the rural idyll was mobilised, as it had been in the First World War, as a powerful symbol of national community and continuity.[28]

In part, this was because the countryside really did represent peace and tranquillity for many from the bombed towns and cities. The rural idyll came to be a place of sanctuary for evacuees and others, even when,

26 Thomas Sharp, *Town and Countryside: Some Aspects of Urban and Rural Development* (Oxford: Oxford University Press, 1932) 6–7, cited in Alun Howkins, *The Death of Rural England: A Social History of the Countryside Since 1900* (London: Routledge, 2003), 96.
27 Ben Harker, '"The Manchester Rambler": Ewan MacColl and the 1932 Mass Trespass', *History Workshop Journal* 59, (2005), 219–28.
28 On these social relations, see Howkins, *The Death of Rural England*. For an example of one place where these divisions very much *continued* to be felt, see MO, FR475 'Worcester', 31 October 1940, 20, 43.

as Maggie Andrews and Sonya O. Rose have both demonstrated, it was not always a very welcoming one.[29] But it was also due to the importance of the countryside, and of farming, to the war effort. The demands of the war economy bought about increased demand for, and debate about, state intervention, land nationalisation, centralised planning and the protection of the countryside, bringing about what Alun Howkins has called 'the second agricultural revolution.'[30] The 'Land Question' was widely debated by politicians and policy makers, keen to ensure that the British agricultural industries were able to reach their maximum levels of production, a priority given that Britain only produced about 40 per cent of the food consumed by the nation in 1939, the remainder being imported via newly vulnerable shipping routes.[31] A number of government reports, including The Barlow Commission (1940), The Scott Report (1942), The Uthwatt Report (1942) and the Dower Report on National Parks (1945) examined various aspects of 'the Land Question', ensuring that the politics of rural reform, and countryside preservation, remained in the public eye throughout the war years.[32] In some important ways, the countryside had, together with the Navy, gone to war before the rest of the country: County War Agricultural Committees were established to oversee food production in 1939 and large areas of grazing and grassland went under the plough from the first days of the war, with the twelve million acres of arable land available in 1939 increasing to eighteen million by the war's end.[33] Agriculture, which had been one of the long list of depressed industries in the 1930s, was modernised and mechanised early on in the war, with

29 Maggie Andrews, *The Acceptable Face of Feminism: the Women's Institute as a Social Movement* (London: Lawrence and Wishart, 1997), 100–22; Sonya O. Rose, *Which People's War? National Identity and Citizenship in Wartime Britain 1939–1945* (Oxford: Oxford University Press, 2003), 207–14.
30 Howkins, *The Death of Rural England*, 113.
31 Geoffrey G. Field, *Blood, Sweat and Toil: Remaking the British Working Class, 1939–1945* (Oxford: Oxford University Press, 2011), 169.
32 Michael Ticheler, 'The Labour Party, Agricultural Policy and The Retreat From Rural Land Nationalisation During the Second World War', *British Agricultural History Review* 51/2, (2003) 209–25. Here 211.
33 Calder, *The People's War*, 418.

tractors replacing farm horses in large numbers, and newly rationed fertilisers being used to increase production levels for the foodstuffs no longer being imported. Town and city dwellers moved to the countryside in the first wave of evacuation that was triggered by the declaration of war and new workers appeared on the farms: the 87,000 members of the Women's Land Army being joined by nearly 40,000 Italian prisoners of war and, in the school summer holidays, numerous children and adults who took working holidays on farms.[34] War thus modernised the countryside alongside other facets of Britain's society, culture and economy.

Nonetheless, the countryside remained a symbol of continuity, tradition and stability. The English village as a microcosm of the nation, a place where representatives of the different social classes came together united by their desire to defend England against an aggressive and alien enemy, can be seen in a range of wartime texts. Famously, these include Cavalcanti's 1942 film *Went the Day Well?*, itself based on Graham Greene's short story of 1940 *The Lieutenant Died Last*. It is set in Bramley End, a small southern village described in *The Times* film review as 'as lovely and sleepy as any English village.'[35] Its inhabitants, including the poacher, the lady of the manor and urban evacuees, but not the local squire who is, revealed as a Nazi sympathiser, band together to defeat German invaders.[36] Cavalcanti's film juxtaposed the violence enacted on and by the villagers with the peaceful and eternal nature of the Southern English countryside. The Local Defence Volunteers, cycling home through country lanes in an early evening full of birdsong, are gunned down by the German soldiers. The vicar is shot in the back whilst ringing the church bells to try and raise the alarm while the postmistress is bayoneted when caught attempting to telephone for help. As the village shrinks to an embattled manor house, representative of the nation as the sole remaining opponent of Nazism in Europe, where men and women of all social classes band together to defeat

---

34 Field, *Blood, Sweat and Toil*, 170.
35 'The Battle of Bramley', *The Times*, 29 October 1942, 6.
36 Graham Greene, 'The Lieutenant Died Last', *Collier's Weekly*, 29 June 1940, 9–10, 24.

the invaders, the key roles fall to two outsiders: the poacher and a young evacuee. United by their social class and lack of respect for established authority, but representing the different worlds of the country and the city, these two succeed in alerting the authorities outside of the village to the crisis, and the invaders are defeated by the British army. Country and city, rich and poor, civilian and military, men and women, young and old; almost all are united in the defence of an immemorial England.

The journalist C. Henry Warren's 1941 book *England is a Village* conveyed this sense of continuity well in its claim that 'England's might is still in her fields and villages and though the whole weight of mechanised armies roll over them ... in the end they will triumph.'[37] Written at the height of the invasion crisis of 1940, but not published until 1941, the book begins, like Cavalcanti's film, by juxtaposing the peacefulness of English rural life with the brutal realities of war: when the only son of a village woman dies at sea the previously distant war 'became a dreadful reality' which 'killed a man we knew and left a weeping mother in our midst.'[38] The opening chapter describes a village cut off by a snowstorm, as Britain was isolated in 1940 by the rapid Nazi advances in Western Europe, and where 'We are even more closely united. If there was kindness among us before, it is more than trebled now. If there was envy, hatred or malice, it seems for the moment to have been forgotten. Perhaps there is an element of fear compelling us to this unstinting kindness ... or perhaps it is nothing other than excitement, engendered by a spectacle in which, whether we will or no, we are all compelled to play our part.'[39] Whilst the book functions on one level as a nostalgic, 'golden age' representation of an organic community, mobilised rather heavy-handedly as a symbol for Britain in the summer of 1940, it is also gently critical of a class stratified society, and suggests that, in the modernising conditions of wartime 'even the remotest villages ... are slowly shaking themselves free of servility.'[40] Warren looked both backwards

---

37   C. Henry Warren, *England is a Village* (London: Dutton, 1941).
38   Ibid., 3.
39   Ibid., 4–5.
40   Ibid., 44.

and forwards, drawing a comforting and nostalgic picture for an audience shaken by the uncertainties of war while reminding them that the national community his village of 'Larkfield' symbolised was itself changing, driven by the modernising forces of total war towards a more democratic future.

In this, *England is a Village* bears comparison with the work of J.B. Priestley, one of the best known producers of wartime propaganda. Priestley's work combines an assertion of an eternal Englishness with a critique of the iniquities of inter-war Britain, a viewpoint that had shaped his account of economic and regional divides in his 1934 book *English Journey*.[41] This version of Englishness combined a sense of historical continuity, symbolised largely by a peaceful rural England, with a repeated assertion that, if the war were to be won, the divisions of the inter-war years had to be fought as well as the Axis powers. His script for the morale boosting 1940 Ministry of Information film *Britain at Bay* contrasted a timeless England with a mechanised and soulless Germany, but insisted as well that the dirty and cramped urban cities were a part of the nation; the eradication of poverty being a key war aim.[42] Priestley's popular *Postscripts* radio programmes drew on the imagery of life in a romanticised southern village as a means of conveying both a sense of historical continuity and of inevitable victory at a time of great uncertainty and anxiety. In his broadcast of Sunday 16 June 1940, just after the fall of France and the Low countries, and the evacuation of the remains of the BEF from Dunkirk, Priestley described a night with his Local Defence Volunteers, later to become the Home Guard. In this short piece, he skilfully interwove a sense of place, describing the 'high down, with a view over a dozen wide parishes', with a sense of tradition, listing the hurdle maker, the woodman and the shepherd who were serving alongside him, which, he said, made him feel as if he had 'wandered into one of those rich chapters of Thomas Hardy's fiction in which his rustics meet in the gathering darkness on some Wessex hillside', contrasting these with 'half crazy German youths, in whose empty eyes the idea of honour and glory seems to include every form of beastliness.'

---

41   J.B. Priestley, *English Journey* (London: Victor Gollancz, 1934).
42   *Britain at Bay* (1940).

Priestley conveyed a sense of timelessness, describing how, on top of the Downs at night, he felt at one with those who had watched there for the Armada in the sixteenth century, and for Napoleon 150 years earlier, concluding that this was 'merely our particular testing time; what we must face, as our forefathers faced such things, in order to enjoy our own again.' But he also has something of the future here. Priestley mustered his rural idyll not only in defence of what was worth preserving about England, but also to highlight what had to be changed, a broadcast the following month emphasising that the war was an opportunity to 'really plan and build up a nobler world in which ordinary decent folk can not only find justice and security but also beauty and delight.'[43]

Even the imperialist and evangelist Arthur Mee, discussed above, combined this sense of an Englishness, rooted in a rural past that was worth defending, with a desire for reform. While *Nineteen Forty: Our Finest Hour* situated an essential Englishness in a description of 'the sunlight ... passing across the valley. The golden harvest hidden in the hills and the daffies ... peeping through in the wood', he ended the book with a call for a future in which life was to be 'nobler, broader, fairer for the common folk who are our brothers and our sisters everywhere.'[44] This contrast, between the values symbolised by the countryside, and the social conditions that demanded reform as a key war aim, were made apparent in the short MOI film *The Dawn Guard*, scripted by the exiled Austrian author Anna Gmeyner, under her pen name Anne Reiner, and directed by the Boulting Brothers in 1941. This drew on these same tropes of rural England – continuity, stability, pastoralism – but used them to make some of the divisions of wartime Britain, and potential solutions, even clearer. Bernard Miles, playing a rural member of the Home Guard patrolling a quiet and peaceful, almost timeless, Southern English landscape, tells his elderly companion that after the war 'there mustn't be no more dirty filthy back streets and no more half starved kids with no room to play in ... We can't go back to the old ways

---

43 J.B. Priestley, *Postscripts* (London: Heinemann, 1940), 16 June 1940, 9–12, 21 July 1940, 36.
44 Mee, *Nineteen Forty*, 32, 218.

of living, leastways not all of it, that's gorn forever, and the sooner we all make up our minds about that the better. We got to all pull together.' As he speaks, the scene changes from the countryside to a factory, then to an urban slum and finally to new flats and houses.[45] By trying to contain and represent the different regions of England, and demonstrate that they were united in their determination not to go back to these 'old ways', the film makes the existing divisions and fractures more visible. These divisions and fractures, the structures of feeling which underpinned these cultural texts, and the enduring centrality of 'Deep England' to a widely shared sense of English national identity, can be read through the MO material examined in the next section of this chapter.

Observing the Nation: Mass observation and Englishness

The very existence of MO can, in itself, be seen as integral to and indicative of the structures of feeling of mid twentieth-century Britain. Formed in 1937 by Tom Harrisson, Humphrey Jennings and Charles Madge, MO was at one and the same time a social survey organisation, an artistic experiment and a social movement, driven by the desires of its founders to make socially progressive, political interventions.[46] MO was both a means of observing and recording thoughts and feelings regarding national identity in mid-century Britain, and an integral part of reflections and arguments about what it meant to be British at this historical juncture. In contrast to established models of social research that had been used to examine and make visible the impact of the economic depression of the inter-war years on British towns and cities, MO did not conduct statistically based quantitative

---

45   Robert Murphy, *Realism and Tinsel: Cinema and Society 1939–1948* (London: Routledge, 1989), 18.
46   Tom Jeffery, *Mass Observation: A Short History* (Birmingham: Centre for Contemporary Cultural Studies, 1978).

surveys. Rather, it sought to make visible the 'social consciousness of the time' by collecting detailed, subjective material that would provide insights into the lived experience of everyday life.[47] Formed in 1937 following the abdication crisis of the previous year, MO was created as a means to create 'an anthropology of ourselves', using some of the same techniques that were then being developed in the relatively new academic discipline of anthropology, and which Harrisson had used in *Savage Civilisation*, his study of tribal life in the New Hebrides.[48] This was to be achieved, firstly, through the recruitment of a 'National Panel' of observers, who would submit written answers to a series of Directives, many of whom in addition kept diaries for MO, and secondly, through the application of ethnographic methods to the study of the inhabitants of Bolton, or 'Worktown' as it was referred to by MO. The triumvirate of Madge, Jennings and Harrisson wanted to use these different methods to both 'observe' the British, to gain a deeper understanding of the interplay between private lives and public events, and by so doing, to intervene in what they saw as a divided nation, using the material that they collected and published to bridge the multiple social, economic, political and cultural divisions of inter-war Britain.

So how did the respondents to MO's 1941 Directive define their identity? The first aspect of the panel's responses that MO thought worthy of note was the widespread dislike of the word Britain expressed by many of the respondents. Naomi Mitchinson, the Scottish author brought up in England, wrote 'Britain as a word means damn all, England means things I love and hate' while a Civil Servant replied 'I don't think in terms of Britain but of England', aptly giving expression to Pocock's ideas about the different national narratives that make up Britain by continuing: 'although of course I should without hesitation go and help turn out the Germans from

---

47 Penny Summerfield, 'Mass Observation: Social Research or Social Movement?', *Journal of Contemporary History* 20/3,(1985), 439–52. Here 440. For a discussion of contemporaneous Social Survey reports and approaches, see Jon Lawrence, 'Class, "Affluence" and the Study of Everyday Life in Britain c.1930–64', *Journal of Cultural and Social History*, 10/2 (2013), 273–99.

48 Charles Madge and Tom Harrisson, *Mass Observation* (Letchworth: Frederick Muller Ltd, 1937), 10; Tom Harrisson, *Savage Civilisation* (London: Victor Gollancz, 1937).

Caithness as readily as I would from Kent, I consider the Scots a separate and unsympathetic race and the Welsh a peculiar people.'[49] The very word 'Britain', Calder has suggested, was problematic in the construction of the myth of the British at war: redolent of ideas of Empire, of superiority and of power and thus could not be opposed to a mechanised, powerful and expansionist Germany in the way that an England, widely represented in inter-war and wartime texts as timeless, calm and peaceful, could be.[50] Many of the MO contributors, in common with many of the cultural texts discussed above, simply replaced or interchanged Britain with England in their responses. For example, one man wrote 'England means home and ... that's what Britain means to me.' This tendency was replicated in the MO Report on the Directive which despite stating its intention to 'refer to Britain throughout for clarity', frequently substituted England for Britain.[51]

Britain, when it was desegregated from England, was seen as an impersonal and external institution, one respondent commenting that 'Britain is a word that I hardly ever use for my country. I am an Englishman and my country is England', though even here England and Britain were conflated as the respondent continued to explain that England 'in my mind includes all of Great Britain except when I particularly want to distinguish England from Scotland and Wales.'[52] Others were critical of Britain but not of England seeing it as responsible for the iniquities of Empire and of the pre-war social order, a government worker contrasting Britain as a 'land of hope and glory, hope for capitalist exploiters, and glory for reactionary governments and muddling, self serving politicians' with an England that he loved for 'her fields, her woods, her homes, her Wordsworth.'[53] In this respondent's construction of the nation, while 'Britain' stood for Empire, for class divisions and for a political system mired in outdated convention, 'England', situated in the countryside, stood outside of this. Tom Harrisson, in a draft of an article written for the journal *World Review* in 1941, argued

---

49 MO, File Report (FR) 878, 'Report on What Does Britain Mean to You?', 1941, 2.
50 Calder, *The Myth of the Blitz*, 196.
51 MO, FR 878, 5, 3.
52 *Ibid.*, 8.
53 *Ibid.*, 3.

that 'Britain is felt to be somewhat symbolic and rather more impersonal, whereas England ... is more personal (and) intimate.'[54] Harrisson thought he had spotted a wartime trend for an upsurge in English nationalism, stating that 'the English seem just as ready to be English Nationalists as the Welsh or Scotch' (sic).[55] He over-extended this argument when he went on to suggest that an English nationalism might be comparable to Scottish or Welsh nationalist movements, with their desire for the break up of the United Kingdom and independence for the different nations contained therein, but it is noticeable that many respondents saw 'England' in a positive light, expressing an emotional attachment, a sense of national identity as English, while seeing 'Britain' as embodying and being responsible for, their more negative feelings about the nation.

Given the emphasis in so much wartime propaganda on England, and on a romanticised southern rural England at that, in some ways it should not be surprising that so many respondents conflated England with Britain, or that they identified as English rather than British. Images of rural England come up again and again in the Directive replies and the countryside was mentioned more often than anything else. A 54-year-old man wrote that 'England ... means Devonshire chess-board fields and red cliffs – the country back of the Sussex Downs, and above all the little village of Salcombe in Devon which is the most beautiful place I know', while a 35-year-old engineer described 'certain views and villages, Poole Harbour from the Purbecks, of the Duddon from about half way up.' Another echoed part of Orwell's famous description of England in *The Lion and the Unicorn* in his definition of the nation as 'Cotswold villages and village green cricket, late September mists filling the valleys in the Surrey Downs; quiet backwaters on the river and winding country lanes.'[56] Britain, as well as England, was situated in the rural by one respondent who replied:

54 MO, FR 904, Tom Harrisson, 'What Britain Means to Me' Draft of article for *World Review*, 8 October 1941, 5.
55 *Ibid.*, 6.
56 Orwell, *The Lion and the Unicorn*, 10.

> This question floods my mind with memories of many happy hours spent cycling in all the countries of these islands and most of the counties of England. The pleasant English scene then, I record first. The leafy lanes of Warwickshire and Worcestershire, the peacefulness of the Cotswold country, the hills and mountains of the Lake District, of North Wales, the romance of the Cornish coast, the splendour of the Scottish Highlands and the almost frightening loneliness of the Western coast of Ireland.[57]

This pastoral vision of the nation, seen here as uniting the British regions and, even the Republic of Ireland, provided a sense of continuity and stability missing from reflections on the cities which, as Martin Wiener has argued with regard to the nineteenth century, were, with the exception of representations of stoicism beneath bombardment, excluded from a celebration of national character and national strength.[58] While cities could be blitzed and bombed, the countryside remained, timeless and indestructible, a fitting symbol, alongside representations of London during the Blitz of 1940–1, for British endurance in arguably the darkest war years of 1940–1.[59]

However, this emphasis on the rural invited contrasts with the urban. The cities were, with the exception of London during the Blitz, rarely seen as embodying Englishness and instead appear again and again in the MO material as symbols of what had to change if the war was to be truly won.[60] If England appeared in many of the responses as a home, it was a home in which all was not well. One compared an idealised countryside with 'horrible roads plastered with advertisements each side of places like Sheffield on a wet gloomy day', while another dismissed the urban with the comment that 'many of (the) cities and towns depress me but they are easy to escape.'

---

57 MO, FR 878, 6.
58 Martin Wiener, *English Culture and the Decline of the Industrial Spirit* (Cambridge: Cambridge University Press, 1981).
59 See, for example, the MoI film, *London Can Take It!* (1940). The film, originally intended for release in the USA, was released as *Britain Can Take It!* on its British release.
60 For a detailed discussion of the contrast between the rural and the urban in British culture see Williams, *The Country and the City*.

In responses such as these, MO's class bias perhaps becomes apparent: the majority of those who wrote for the National Panel were middle class, only 19 per cent self identifying as working class in 1937, at a time when the urban working class constituted about 75 per cent of the population, and even fewer, about 10 per cent in 1948.[61] Although many respondents positioned themselves politically on the left, perhaps participating in the MO project because of its progressive credentials and the sense of 'transcendence' that James Hinton has claimed writing for MO offered, this does not necessarily translate into an understanding of the lives of the urban working class.[62] Others were more overtly political and critical in their responses; one respondent, who lived in the countryside, asserted 'we should not be content to let the peaceful green fields, the woods, and the delightful lazy rivers contrast themselves with the industrially denuded countryside or the depressed areas ... we ought not to allow poverty among the richness of Britain.'[63] Underlying much of the description of the beauties of the English countryside was a widespread unease about the perceived ugliness and poverty of many of the towns, especially those of Priestley's 'second England' described in his *English Journey*, the depressed, congested districts of the industrial North and West.[64] A sense, echoing Wiener, that these areas were somehow not really 'English' was underpinned in the MO material by a commonly expressed belief that life in these cities would have to change; that the war was not being fought for the continuation of such disparities but for a more egalitarian future.

---

61   James Hinton, 'The "Class" Complex: Mass-Observation and Cultural Distinction in Pre-war Britain', *Past and Present*, 199/1 (2008), 207–36. Here 210–11; Mike Savage, 'Mass Observation and Social Class', *Mass Observation Online*, n.p. <http://www.massobservation.amdigital.co.uk.ezproxy.sussex.ac.uk/essays/content/socialclass.aspx>.
62   James Hinton, *Nine Wartime Lives: Mass-Observation and the Making of the Modern Self* (Oxford: Oxford University Press, 2010), 16.
63   MO, FR 878, 6.
64   Priestley, *English Journey*.

Conclusion

For the majority of those who responded to the MO Directive on Britain, together with many cultural and political commentators, it was England, not Britain, that formed the basis for the imagined nation that many were fighting for. As the MO Report concluded, 'England remains a known quantity, the tangible soil and countryside and the people met in the streets. These are the things that are inspiring feelings of patriotism in people now.'[65] This should not be surprising. 'Britain' was a far more abstract concept than 'England', one that was often, unthinkingly, conflated with England in a manner that infuriated many from Scotland, Wales and Northern Ireland. But for the largely middle class, and broadly left-wing contributors to MO, England could evidently be distinguished from the imperial and conservative values that were associated with Britain. Drawing on the range of cultural texts celebrating a rural, Southern England as the site of an 'authentic' Englishness that preceded the war, many of those who responded to this Directive expressed their sense of national identity by articulating a love of this landscape.

The strength of this notion of an essentially rural, Southern Englishness as a focus for national identity appeared remarkably unaffected by the war, despite the role of the towns and cities, especially of course London, as the epicentre of the People's War during the Blitz, which just preceded the 1941 Directive. Rural England stood in English culture for a timelessness, a continuity and a sense of tradition, meanings which had been laid down over many years and which account for its centrality to much wartime propaganda and for its appeal for many of the Mass Observers. The emphasis on a shared past embodied in notions of the rural acted as a means to bind people together – the English might live in a highly stratified, class-based society, with different political beliefs, leisure activities and levels of income, but they could agree that whether they lived in the city or the country, it was rural England that somehow defined them. However, the emphasis on the

---

65   MO, FR 878, 13.

beauty of the English countryside could not help but bring into focus the differences between the countryside and the city, seen by so many as the site of inequalities which the war was being fought to overcome. The English countryside then, stood for the authentic nation and for continuity, but also reminded many that much needed to change. In reply to MO's question 'What Does Britain mean To You', the answer appeared to be 'very little'; it was an England best represented by the countryside that the respondents identified with and believed they were fighting for.

At the same time however, the demands of this most modernising of wars were changing the countryside irrecoverably. Large areas of grassland, like the South Downs in the heart of Calder's 'deep England', were ploughed up to produce food for the nation, while some 20,000 acres of Essex was drained and ditched to improve food production and the Somerset Levels were drained to make them into more productive arable land.[66] Large areas, especially in East Anglia, were requisitioned for use as Air Force bases used by the Royal Air Force and the United States Air Force for their bombing campaign from 1942 onwards. In the South East the Battle of Britain of 1940 and the V1 campaign of 1944 and 1945 visibly and sometimes viscerally brought the war home. New workers and new inhabitants, fleeing the cities, arrived in the countryside, and their very presence, at times, led to misunderstanding and conflict. More widely, increased mechanisation and the opportunities for better paid employment in the towns and cities in the aftermath of war, meant that between 1945 and 1960, the number of agricultural workers fell from 865,000 to 678,000, while the numbers of those living in the countryside but not working in agriculture, increased.[67] Whilst the uncertainties and disruptions of the war years made the perceived 'authenticity' of rural England appealing to many, these same forces were, at the same time, irrevocably changing the landscape and the ways of life that so many identified with Englishness.

---

66 Sadie Ward, *War in the Countryside 1939–45* (London: Cameron Books, 1988), 26–7.
67 Howkins, *The Death of Rural England*, 164.

GARY SHEFFIELD

Englishness in the British army of the Second World War

The concept of 'Englishness' was of little importance in the British army of the Second World War except in very specific circumstances. In the era of a unitary state, when dominant ideology was unionism and England could still be used as a synonym for the United Kingdom, there was little incentive to promote Englishness or an English identity in an army in which Celtic units were exotic additions to an organisation that was largely English.[1] Instead of Englishness, regimental or other unit identities were assiduously cultivated in units that were based in England, and this identity often had a regional dimension. 'Englishness' is a slippery term. I am not concerned here with the myth that the essence of England is 'rural, agricultural, tranquil and unchanging' rather than urban and industrialised.[2] Rather, 'Englishness' here is defined as a combination of 'values, traits and stereotypes that are held to be intrinsic and unique to English people, and are measured against perceived *external* and *internal* significant "others".'[3] At the risk of tautology, Englishness is at its core an individual's or group's sense of being English. The British national community, paradoxically, is both one nation and at least four nations, but the English

---

[1] English in terms of numbers that is. For the army as a genuinely 'British' organisation, see below.
[2] Michael Bartholomew, 'Englishness: The Case of H.V. Morton (1892–1979)', in Keith Dockray and Keith Laybourn, eds, *The Representation and Reality of War: The British Experience* (Stroud: Sutton Publishing, 1995), 203.
[3] Rebecca Langlands, 'Britishness or Englishness? The Historical Problem of National Identity in Britain', *Nations and Nationalism*, 5/1 (1999), 55–69. Here 57.

often conflate 'Britain' and 'England.'⁴ At the time of the Second World War, English nationalism was largely subsumed in a wider British identity, with the rest of the UK being seen as, in effect, Greater England. In the Second World War, the Union Flag (or 'Union Jack' as it is popularly but inaccurately known) was regarded by the vast majority of the English as their national flag; this remained the case long after the end of the war. With VE-Day twenty-one years in the past, during the symbolically laden 1966 World Cup Final when England played West Germany at Wembley Stadium, England fans waved the Union Jack, not the English national flag. Likewise, the tournament mascot, World Cup Willie, a cartoon lion, wore a Union Jack waistcoat.⁵ By contrast, thirty years later, during Euro 96, the European football championship held in England in 1996, 'Wembley was a sea of St George's crosses and red-and-white painted faces.'⁶ The reasons for the rise of English nationalism and identity are complex and beyond the scope of this piece.⁷

This chapter examines identity in English units of the British army of the Second World War, placing the subject in the wider history of the army. It draws largely upon the writings of individual soldiers of the period, who occasionally mused on their identity or (more likely) made throwaway comments germane to this topic. Another useful source proved to be unit and formation histories, which tend to be unjustly neglected by historians but are sometimes highly informative. The piece is located in broader studies of identity and Englishness, especially David French's pioneering work on British military identities.⁸ I argue that while 'Englishness' *per se* was

---

4   Hugh Kearney, *The British Isles: A History of Four Nations* (Cambridge: Cambridge University Press, 2006), xv; Langlands, 'Britishness or Englishness?', 53.
5   See the official film of the tournament, *Goal! World Cup 1966* (1967).
6   Richard Weight, *Patriots: National Identity in Britain 1940–2000* (London: Pan, 2003 [2002]), 709.
7   See Weight, *Patriots*; Ben Wellings, 'Rump Britain: Britishness and Englishness, 1992–2001', *National Identities* 9/4 (2007), 395–412.
8   David French, *Military Identities: The Regimental System, the British Army, and the British People c.1870–2000* (Oxford: Oxford University Press, 2005).

unimportant to regiments and corps, some English units had a very strong regional identity which played a roughly similar role to 'Scottishness' in regiments recruited from north of the border. English soldiers, however, sometimes developed a sense of their Englishness while serving in non-English units, especially if they faced hostility.

Englishness in the British army

To my knowledge, there was no regiment, brigade or division in the British army in the era of the Second World War that had the words 'England' or 'English' in their titles. The same is true of the post-1945 army. The present day Royal Anglian Regiment derives its name from East Anglia, not from England. It was formed in 1964 from the 1st, 2nd and 3rd East Anglian Regiments, themselves recent amalgamations of county regiments such as the Royal Norfolks, Essex and Suffolks. The 1939–45 order of battle of the Brigade of Guards included separate regiments of Scots, Irish and Welsh Guards (the latter two formed in 1900 and 1915 respectively to recognise the military contributions of these two nations in major wars), but there were no 'English Guards'; instead there were two regiments, the Grenadier and Coldstream Guards, which recruited in England. Whereas the British army of 1939–45 included the 15th (Scottish) and 53rd (Welsh) Divisions, and the 38 (Irish) Brigade, other divisions had regional English subtitles, such as 43rd (Wessex), 44th (Home Counties) and the 50th (Northumbrian), the latter with its 'TT' (for Tyne-Tees) insignia. This reflects the fact that the military authorities were keen to emphasise English regional identit*ies* (plural), rather than an English national identit*y* (singular). Such a regional emphasis was not unique to England, as the subtitles of two Scottish divisions, 51st (Highland) and 52nd (Lowland), indicate.

The army, from the late eighteenth century onwards, was an important vehicle for creating a British identity. This had never been monolithic, and Scottish, and to some extent Irish and Welsh units, were distinctive in terms of dress and customs, although this was overlaid with other peculiarities of the British regimental system. To take one example, Fusilier regiments, which had originally been armed with a particular type of musket, the 'fuzil', to guard artillery, had some distinctive items of uniform. In addition to six Fusilier regiments with regional English and Irish titles, there were Welsh, Scottish and Irish regiments of Fusiliers.[9] British infantry regiments were fiercely individual, jealous of their reputation, engaged in rivalries with other regiments and thrived on eccentricities of uniform and behaviour. The distinctiveness of, say, Highland Regiments can be usefully compared with that of the two English Rifle (Green Jacket) Regiments. The former had the kilt and sword-dancing; the latter wore black buttons and marched at a fast pace. Highland regiments were a distinctive part of the army, but so were Rifle, and for that matter Fusilier and Light Infantry regiments.

One historian has referred to the existence of 'quintessentially English regiments' in the mid-Victorian army. This term reflected adherence to Anglicanism, and the ranks being filled overwhelmingly by Englishmen.[10] English regiments of the era of the Second World War were likely to be more religiously diverse, but also possessed a vague sense of Englishness meaning recognition of an English identity within a wider British identity and expressed, for instance, in the playing of the epitome of English sports, cricket.[11] Active uses of Englishness were rare. One came on the

---

9 The following were fusilier regiments: Royal Northumberland Fusiliers (5th Foot); Royal Fusiliers (City of London Regiment, or 7th Foot); Lancashire Fusiliers (20th Foot) Royal Scots Fusiliers (21st Foot); Royal Welch Fusiliers (23rd Foot); Royal Irish Fusiliers (87th and 89th Foot); Royal Inniskilling Fusiliers (27th and 108th Foot); Royal Munster Fusiliers (101st and 104th Foot); and Royal Dublin Fusiliers (102nd and 103rd Foot).
10 H.J. Hanham, 'Religion and Nationality in the Mid-Victorian Army', in M.R.D. Foot, ed., *War and Society: Historical Essays in Honour and Memory of J.R. Western 1928–1971* (London: Paul Elek, 1973), 164.
11 For examples of cricket in the Grenadier Guards, see Brian Johnson to mother 25 August 1940, 18 May 1941, 26 May 1942, in Brian Johnson [Barry Johnson, ed.], *Letters Home 1926–1945* (London: Weidenfeld & Nicolson, 1998), 246, 259, 284, for 2nd Beds and Herts, see R.H. Medley, *Five Days to Live: France 1939–40* (Privately published, 1990), 50.

eve of the Second World War, when British cavalry regiments were in the process of mechanisation. General Sir Ernest Makins, Colonel of the Royal Dragoons, in 1937 argued that since the Royal Scots Greys were lobbying to keep its horses, the Royals, the senior English cavalry regiment, should have the same privilege. Both regiments were granted their wish; it proved to be merely a stay of execution.[12] With such rare exceptions, no regiment fostered 'Englishness' *per se*, but every regiment promoted its identity, based on its history and traditions, which may have had a regional or local English dimension.

The Regiment

When discussing the importance of the regiment, however, we need to be aware of certain things. First, not every part of the army was organised on a regimental basis, and a soldier serving in the Royal Engineers (RE) or Royal Electrical and Mechanical Engineers (REME), or a large logistic corps like the Royal Army Service Corps (RASC) or the Royal Army Ordnance Corps (RAOC), would have had a different experience from an infantry battalion. There were large numbers of such men in units other than the 'teeth arms' of the infantry, armour or artillery. Some 44 per cent of British soldiers in Normandy served on the lines of communications.[13] Moreover, many units recruited from across the UK. One such was D Troop, H Battery, 13th (HAC) Regiment Royal Horse Artillery. Although the Honourable Artillery Company, the parent unit, was London-based, Ernest Powdrill, 'Don' Troop's Battery Sergeant Major, commented that four of the nine sergeants he commanded led 'a gun subsection, and like their

---

12   Barney White-Spunner, *Horse Guards* (London: Macmillan, 2006), 495–6.
13   Gary Sheffield, 'Dead Cows and Tigers: Some Aspects of the Experience of the British Soldier in Normandy, 1944', in John Buckley, ed., *The Normandy Campaign Sixty Years On* (Abingdon: Routledge, 2006), 119.

men, they came from all parts of the country ... In my Troop there was the never ending repartee whereby anyone who did not live in, say, London, Manchester, Liverpool, Cardiff, Newcastle or Glasgow had been deprived of the decencies of a civilized culture.'[14]

Even in peacetime it was far from the case that all units with a specific territorial designation actually recruited exclusively from that area. As David French has shown, the ideal behind the nineteenth-century Cardwell and Childers reforms that created the County regimental system from numbered regiments of foot, that regiments would become so deeply rooted in local communities that the bulk of recruits would come from them, was not realised.[15] Unsurprisingly, large urban conurbations provided recruits for regiments with thinly populated recruiting districts. Even after the first stage of territorialisation, in 1878 the Cameronians (26th Foot) could muster only 190 Scottish Other Ranks, along with 138 Irish and 143 English.[16] The raising of a mass volunteer army in 1914–15 exacerbated this trend away from localised recruitment. One West Country English battalion, the 9th Devons, was nicknamed the '9th London and Lancs' because of its personnel.[17] If anything, the trend away from truly local recruiting grew stronger after the First World War, perhaps in reaction to the heavy casualties suffered by local communities in 1914–18. In 1921, recruiting for the infantry was placed on a national basis. During the period 1920 to 1937, only around 28 per cent of recruits to the Regular army actually found their way to their local regiment.[18]

During the Second World War, it was more of the same. Local recruitment was struck a further blow in July 1942, when recruits began to be posted to a General Service Corps, and after basic training were transferred to regiments and corps. The 'need for fostering the county, T.A. and regimental spirit' was ranked fourth out of four criteria for posting. A sample

14   Ernest Powdrill, *In The Face of the Enemy: A Battery Sergeant Major in Action in the Second World War* (Barnsley: Pen and Sword, 2008), 42–3.
15   French, *Military Identities*, 58.
16   Hanham, 'Religion and Nationality', 166.
17   Martin Middlebrook, *The First Day on the Somme* (London: Allen Lane, 1971), 11.
18   French, *Military Identities*, 47.

of the dead of one Welsh and five English regiments in 1944–5 revealed that a mere '34 per cent were serving with their "local regiment."'[19] George Coulthard's experience was not untypical. Hailing from Birmingham, he acquired the nickname 'Brum' in the army, but was posted to the Somerset Light Infantry and later the 10th Glosters, which became 159 Regiment Royal Armoured Corps (RAC).[20] Under the pressure of replacing casualties, reinforcements (both officers and Other Ranks) tended to be sent wherever they were needed regardless of their nominal cap badge. It was entirely possible for an Englishman to end up in a non-English unit. One North Country battalion, 6th Borders, was disbanded in August 1944 and twenty five officers and 550 men sent to 15th (Scottish) Division were they were spread across nine different Scottish battalions.[21] According to an Other Rank of 6th Royal Welch Fusiliers, only one-third of the battalion was Welsh; we can safely assume that a large part of the unit was English.[22] In mid-June 1944, just before going into battle for the first time, 30 per cent of the officers and men of 7th Seaforth Highlanders were highlanders, 49 per cent lowland Scots, and 21 per cent hailed from outside Scotland, six of whom were Irish; again, we can assume that the bulk of the other members of this group were English.[23] Significantly, in the context of the arrival of a new draft for 1st Queen's (Royal West Surreys) during the Burma campaign, an officer thought it worthy to mention that his batman (unlike, it is implied, many of the draft) was a Surrey native with previous combat experience in a Territorial battalion of the regiment.[24] Similarly, 2/4 King's Own Yorkshire Light Infantry (KOYLI) in Italy in 1944 were pleased to

19 French, Military *Identities*, 279–81.
20 George (Brum) Coulthard, *From Private to Trooper Back to Private* (Bishop Auckland: The Pentland Press, 1994), 12, 99, 103.
21 Douglas Sutherland, *Tried and Valiant: The Story of the Border Regiment 1702–1959* (London: Leo Cooper, 1972), 179.
22 Imperial War Museum, Dept of Documents, 92/37/1, D. Evans, ts account, 9.
23 Ian Daglish, *Over the Battlefield: Operation Epsom* (Barnsley: Pen and Sword, 2007), 243.
24 Michael Lowry, *Fighting Through to Kohima* (Barnsley: Pen and Sword, 2008 [2003]), 189. This memoir is based on contemporary notes.

welcome drafts from the 9th Battalion of the regiment. As the 9th had started the war as a Yeomanry (Territorial) unit, the Yorkshire Dragoons, the drafts were likely to contain at least some local men.[25]

Whatever the nominal territorial designation of a unit, the officers were likely to be drawn from a wide geographical area. Murray Walker, who was later to achieve fame as a motor racing commentator, joined a smart cavalry regiment (by this stage equipped with tanks), the Royal Scots Greys, as a newly commissioned Second Lieutenant in 1944. From a middle class Birmingham family – he described himself as 'a proud Brummie'– Walker was 'immensely proud' of being an officer in the Greys 'but I certainly felt as though I was in a club of which I was not a natural member.' However in Walker's case it seems that social class, rather than being an Englishman in a Scots regiment (his father was a Scot), was the cause of him feeling 'rather a round peg in a square hole.' His fellow officers were wealthy, 'County gentry'; not necessarily Scots, but many had 'Scottish connections.' Although Walker had attended a public school, Highgate, he was in awe of his fellow officers educated 'at the very best and most expensive schools.' He gravitated towards the company of the Regimental Quartermaster, who is likely to have been promoted from the ranks, and the commander of the Regiment's Light Aid Detachment, a REME officer. Walker's case underlines the complex nature of military identity.[26]

At divisional level, the idea of self-contained formations composed solely of individual nationalities from within the UK is something of a myth. The order of battle of two of the most self-consciously Scottish formations, 51st (Highland) and 15th (Scottish) Divisions, included specifically English units. At El Alamein in October 1942, the former had 1/7 Middlesex, a Machine Gun battalion; while during Operation Epsom in Normandy in June 1944 the latter included another Machine Gun battalion of the Middlesex Regiment, the 1st. During this action, 15th (Scottish) Division was supported by, among others, two English armoured regiments, 141st

---

25   Ellenburger, *King's Own Yorkshire Light Infantry*, 6, 109.
26   Murray Walker, *Unless I'm Very Much Mistaken* (London: CollinsWillow, 2003 [2002]), 21, 43, 44–5.

RAC (The Buffs [East Kent Regiment]) and the Westminster Dragoons.[27] 53rd (Welsh) Division's order of battle in the Northwest Europe campaign of 1944–45 included three non-Welsh battalions, two English and one Scots (1st East Lancashires, 1st Oxfordshire and Buckinghamshire Light Infantry, 1st Highland Light Infantry), in addition to an English Machine Gun battalion, 1st Manchesters. The Divisional History claimed that all members of the division, regardless of background, 'were quickly assimilated and became good "Welshmen" for the duration of their stay.'[28]

Regionalism and localism were important factors in mid-twentieth-century England. For example, working class men from Liverpool, London, Birmingham and Tyneside were instantly recognisable by their accents as 'Scousers', 'Cockneys', 'Brummies', and 'Geordies', and had strong regional identities. These affected the character of some locally recruited units. A good example is found in the war memoir of the historical novelist George MacDonald Fraser. He served in a battalion of the Border Regiment in Burma, and as a semi-outsider – being both a Scot and middle class – brilliantly captured the distinct atmosphere, including the local dialect and local cultural references.[29] It would be unwise indeed to assume that his portrait could be taken as representative of English units as a whole, of battalions from London, or Lancashire, or Cornwall.

Units of the Territorial Army, by their very nature, had a local identity, although as the war progressed this became increasingly watered down as original members were replaced by incomers. With the doubling of the TA in March 1939, some new units were raised. One, which became 2/106th Regiment Royal Horse Artillery (TA), which had its roots in the Lancashire Yeomanry, was raised in the Hoylake area of Cheshire in little more than a week in April 1939. By the end of the war, when the Regiment

---

27   J.B. Salmond, *The History of the 51st Highland Division 1939–1945* (Bishop Auckland: Pentland Press, 1994 [1953]), 274; Daglish, *Epsom*, 242. An officer claimed that the 'corporate spirit' of 15th Division was 'expressed by the Divisional pipes and drums', Robert Woollcombe, *Lion Rampant* (London: Leo Cooper, 1970 [1955]), 21.
28   C.N. Barclay, *The History of the 53rd (Welsh) Division in the Second World War* (London: William Clowes, 1956), 25, 201–2.
29   George MacDonald Fraser, *Quartered Safe Out Here* (London: Harvill, 1992).

(renumbered as 149th RHA (TA)) was serving in the Mediterranean, fewer than 'one-third of the men who had left England' four years earlier were left.[30] Actually, in the circumstances, this was a respectable number of 'originals' remaining with the unit. A Territorial infantry battalion, 4th Lincolns, was before the war typically 'local', with companies recruited in the areas of Lincoln, Boston, Horncastle, and Spilsby and Alford. On the eve of the Battalion's deployment to the Normandy campaign, a 'large proportion' of the pre-war Lincolnshire Territorials, including 'many' officers, remained on the strength. Subsequently the Battalion took heavy casualties and lost some key leaders; Major Don Stokes, killed in August 1944 *'was the 4th Lincolns and somehow things would never seem the same again.'* Thus by October 1944 the Battalion's local identity had been considerably diluted. However it does not seem to have vanished entirely: some men wounded early in the campaign eventually returned to the 4th Lincolns, and there was some promotion from within the Battalion.[31]

The vast majority of British soldiers in the Second World War were non-professional civilians in uniform, and links with home were important factors in maintaining morale. Letters telling of mundane doings of friends and family and local news were often treasured. So were local newspapers: a soldier of 6th Cheshires serving with Eighth Army in North Africa thought it worth recording that amongst the reading matter sent from home was the *Stockport Express*.[32] A sense of the importance of localism comes from the memoirs of Don Clark, a pre-war Territorial from Dewsbury. His battalion, 2/4 KOYLI, during the 1940 campaign in France, came across the Duke of Wellington's Regiment (almost certainly either the Territorial 2/6 or 2/7

---

30 E.W. Capleton, *Shabash – 149: The War Story of the 149th Regiment RA* (Privately published, 1963), xv, 261.
31 John Benson, *Saturday Night Soldiers: the 4th Lincolns in World War II* (Privately published, 2002), 7, 75, 111, 119, 124, 149.
32 Cheshire Military Museum, 0066.01, Pte. S. C. Brooks, transcribed diary, 2 Nov. 1942. For a detailed unit study of First World War troops that emphasises the importance of localism and links with home, see Helen B. McCartney, *Citizen Soldiers: The Liverpool Territorials in the First World War* (Cambridge: Cambridge University Press, 2005).

Battalions), which he called by the nickname 'the Dirty Dukes.' This was also a Yorkshire unit, being recruited from the area of Halifax area, 'so we were fellow countrymen of sorts.' There was friendly rivalry between the two units, and the fact that the KOYLI had already been under fire '[i]n some way gave us temporary status over [their fellow Yorkshire Territorials].'[33]

Depictions of the twentieth-century British armed forces had frequent recourse to a number of archetypes: the dour Scot, the 'quick-witted, resourceful and cheerful cockney'[34] and so on. These archetypes can be found in contemporary writings of soldiers of 1939–45. Troops of 51st (Highland) Division had a reputation as hard men. In 1942, an English soldier in Egypt commented that while native bootblacks usually swarmed around and had to be physically repelled, it was different with the Highland Division: they knew better than to attempt to clean the boots of a Jock.[35] In reporting this stereotype, the Englishman was of course unconsciously defining his own identity against the 'other.' Such an overarching English identity allowed diverse English regionalism to flourish.

Regiments attempted to pass on their ethos and traditions to their soldiers, no matter where they came from. It was not, of course, only English units that prioritised the maintenance of a distinctive identity. The Royal Monmouth Royal Engineers, the senior Reserve unit of the army whose origins dated back to the sixteenth century, fought a tenacious and successful bureaucratic battle to be allowed to wear distinctive regimental insignia: 'although the original officers and men [of 1939] were long since dispersed the newcomers of 1944–45 were provided with a constant reminder of the ancestry and traditions of the Regiment.' In the view of the modern historian of the unit, '[T]he arguments over the badges were important not only for the continuation of the Regiment's identity but also for personal and Regimental pride and motivation.'[36] Similarly, on 1 August 1944 2/4

---

33 Don Clark, *Cede Nullis: A Personal History of the 1940 Normandy Campaign* (Edinburgh: The Pentland Press, 2000), 24–5.
34 Andrew Robertshaw, '"Irrepressible chirpy cockney chappies?" Humour as an aid to survival', *Journal of European Studies*, xxxi (2001), 277–87.
35 Cheshire Military Museum, 0066.01, Brooks diary, 9 Dec. 1942.
36 Graham Watson, *Militiamen and Sappers* (Privately published, 1996), 115–17.

KOYLI, on campaign in Italy, celebrated Minden Day, commemorating the battle of 1759 when British infantry had supposedly plucked roses to wear in their hats. A tradition was established by which the six 'Minden regiments' wore roses on Minden Day, in the course of other celebrations.[37]

Jack McManners, an Oxford DPhil student, whilst in basic Other Ranks' training with the Royal Northumberland Fusiliers in late 1939 was indoctrinated by NCOs into the history and culture of the Regiment: 'battle honours, why we wear red and white roses in our hats on St George's Day.' At least in McManners' case, the NCOs were building on a predisposition to belong: 'In 1939 we didn't think of dying for our country, just about stopping Hitler; but we wanted to identify with the Royal Northumberland Fusiliers; more and more the regiment became a tangible intermediary for patriotism, even, in the last resort, something we might die for.' For McManners, a County Durham vicar's son, allegiance to Kipling's 'Tyneside Tail-Twisters' was also about local pride.[38] Other men might lack local roots, but still identified with the regiment or corps in which they found themselves serving.

It is possible that a soldier of the Black Watch or the Seaforth Highlanders might perhaps feel more Scottish as a result of his military service, but even though the rose is the emblem of England, it is very doubtful whether soldiers of the KOYLI or the Royal Northumberland Fusiliers would feel more English. However, they would certainly be aware of their identity as members of these regiments, and very many internalised and took pride in it. There is ample evidence of ordinary English soldiers closely identifying with their regiment. 'Brum' Coulthard, by his own account something of a rough diamond, when posted to a tank unit, surprised a

---

37 G.F. Ellenburger, *History of the King's Own Yorkshire Light Infantry Vol. VI 1939–1948* (Aldershot: Gale and Polden, 1961), 102. For the importance of Minden Day to this regiment (celebrated in Minden itself in 1945–7 when the regiment formed part of the British Army on the Rhine) see *Ibid.*, 168–9, 173–4. For the Minden tradition see R. Money Barnes, *A History of the Regiments and Uniforms of the British Army* (London: Sphere, 1972 [1950]), 43–4.

38 John McManners, *Fusilier: Recollections and Reflections 1939–1945* (Norwich: Michael Russell, 2002), 29.

staff sergeant by marching at a blistering pace. 'We lot, Staff, are from the Somerset Light Infantry ... and this is how we march.'[39] In a particularly moving example, the mother of one soldier of 1st Battalion Loyal Regiment (North Lancashire) took the trouble to reply to a letter of condolence sent by his divisional commander, Major-General W.R.C. Penney after her son's death. In the letter she stressed her son's pride, and hers, in the regiment.[40] By contrast, I have yet to come across a single reference to a soldier taking pride in being English (in the narrow sense) as a result of military service in the Second World War.

An exception? Englishmen in non-English units

Evidence suggests that one circumstance in which English soldiers might feel a sense of Englishness is when they were made to feel an outsider while serving in a non-English unit. Cyril Poffley, a south Londoner, briefly spent time in the ranks of Royal Ulster Rifles before the war. As an Englishman he felt something of an outsider in this Irish regiment, particularly given the Protestant/Catholic divide in the battalion, but only on one occasion did he experience personal hostility, although he was unsure whether this was because he was an Englishman or an Anglican.[41] Poffley later enlisted in the East Surreys, a regiment which recruited from the environs of London and here he 'felt as though I was a member of the same tribe and not living in the slightly alien surroundings where people not only spoke with an unfamiliar accent but whose interests when they conversed, bore little relation to one's own.'[42] Here, we might say, is an example of a soldier who

---

39 Coulthard, *From Private*, 99.
40 Liddell Hart Centre for Military Archives, PENNEY 7/34, Penney papers, Mrs Clitheroe to Major General Penney, 21 July 1944.
41 Cyril Poffley, *Remembering My Twentieth Century* (Ringwood: Navigator Books, 1994), 89–91.
42 *Ibid.*, 94.

felt English when serving in Ulster, in the sense that he was made aware that his regiment and fellow soldiers had a culture very different from that to which he was familiar. However, once in the East Surreys, Private Poffley, by now a square peg in a square hole, adopted the English *regional* identity of his regiment.

Englishmen serving in Scots units were constantly reminded of their identity as the 'other.' For English officers, dialect, or to be more precise the inability to understand what Other Ranks were saying, might place a barrier between an officer and the troops under his command in addition to the usual factor of class. Peter White, a Southern English ex-public schoolboy served as an officer with 4th King's Own Scottish Borderers. Initially he found it difficult to integrate into this cohesive community, which as a Territorial unit had a very local identity; the fact that he found the men incomprehensible did not help matters.[43] An Englishman on joining 78th (City of Edinburgh) Field Regiment Royal Artillery suffered a culture shock. In his memoirs he commented on the plight of the English recruits being 'Sassenachs in a Scottish mob, with no liking for kilts, haggis and the bagpipes – although we have to hide it.'[44] One of the most vivid descriptions of the experience of being an Englishman in the ranks of a Scots regiment appears in the testimony of Cyril James, a Yorkshire-born member of the Royal Scots Fusiliers.[45] A working class man born in Leeds in 1918, James was conscripted as a militiaman shortly before the outbreak of war in September 1939. Posted to the depot in Ayr – a place of which he was vaguely aware because of the local football team – he had no

---

43 Peter White, *With The Jocks: A Soldier's Struggle for Europe 1944–45* (Stroud: Sutton Publishing, 2002 [2001]), xiv. Officers posted to English units with large numbers of men who spoke in strong regional accents could also experience problems of comprehension.

44 Tom Roe, *Anzio Beachhead: Diary of a Signaller* (Privately published, 1988), 17, 71. Roe puts the quotation into the mouth of a fellow English soldier. Although there is a suspicious amount of verbatim quotation in Roe's memoir, there is no reason to doubt that it reflects the views that he held during his wartime service.

45 James' reminiscences appear in Dave Foxton, *Born at the Wrong Time: The Biography of Cyril James* (Privately published, 2012), which is based on extensive interviews with the subject.

strong objections to being posted to a Scottish regiment. He was a gregarious, liberal-minded man who liked Scots, and was horrified to be referred often as a 'fucking Sassenach.' James believed that he, and the only other Englishman in the batch of a hundred conscripts, were bullied more than their Scottish fellows by the NCOs. One of their insults passed him by: he had no idea of the significance of Bannockburn. However, he also records how other conscripts, Scots, joined in the bullying and when, inevitably, fights ensued, the Scots NCOs turned a blind eye. By no means all the Jocks behaved like this, and James made friends with some Scottish fellow soldiers. He learned to ignore those Scots who were prejudiced against the English. On one occasion later in the war, while travelling on a bus in Glasgow, James was verbally abused by three privates in the Royal Scots Fusiliers because he was English: he was rescued by a 'formidable couple of [middle-aged] women.' While at the Depot, James was also exposed to some 'hard men of the industrial Clyde.' Leeds was a rough city, but James had always stayed away from the hard men. However, the religious sectarianism he now witnessed was something quite new to him.[46]

After completing Basic Training, in March 1940 Cyril James was transferred to a holding battalion. There, too, there were stark divisions between English and Scots. Reaching 4/5 Royal Scots Fusiliers in June 1940, the by now Lance-Corporal James found himself in a close-knit Territorial battalion which had a brief and chaotic spell in France as part of the Second British Expeditionary Force. Back in the UK to rebuild, the threat of a German invasion had the effect of enhancing unit solidarity: '[T]here was no talk about the Scots and English divide now.' For all that, in 1941 the complexion of 4/5 RSF changed as increasing numbers of Englishmen, both officers and Other Ranks, were drafted in to the Battalion as replacements. Thus the 4/5 RSF followed the pattern of many other Territorial units. The influx of Sassenachs caused the balance of power within the Battalion to shift. English soldiers responded to Scottish antipathy by insulting them, and deciding to 'have a go' at their tormentors, but eventually things settled down. James found it ironic that the only soldier of the Battalion to

46 Foxton, *Born at the Wrong Time*, 81–3, 90, 95, 143.

win the Victoria Cross, Dennis Donnini, who thus entered the pantheon of heroes of the Royal Scots Fusiliers, was an outsider. Donnini was the County Durham-born son of an Italian immigrant, thus an Englishman whose father was an 'enemy alien.' James commented that 'it made a farce of all regimental pride stuff.'[47] Less pejoratively, it can also be said to illustrate the fluidity of regimental identity in the British army of the Second World War.

Conclusion

It is an exaggeration to say that the British army of the Second World War was an English organisation, with Scottish, Welsh and Irish units as exotic parts of it, but it is not entirely wide of the mark. This was a time when most English people viewed their national identity as British, and when Britishness and Englishness were regarded as being much the same thing. The one exception was when Englishmen wanted to define themselves as being different from their fellow Britons. Lacking an overarching concept such as Scottishness, English units stressed regimental rather than national identity. These identities might also have a regional dimension, although given the decline in localised recruiting it might be the case that a number of the soldiers in a country regiment originally came from a very different part of England. Englishness was thus of little relevance to the British army of the Second World War.

---

47 Foxton, *Born at the Wrong Time*, 120, 104, 204, John Frayn Turner, *VCs of the Second World War* (Barnsley: Pen and Sword, 2004), 269–70, Wendy Ugolini, 'The Embodiment of British Italian War Memory? The Curious Marginalization of Dennis Donnini, VC', *Patterns of Prejudice*, 46/3–4 (2012) 397–415.

MARTIN JOHNES

Welshness, Welsh soldiers and the Second World War

> On the heights of El Rhorab, looking out through the Fondouk gap, and on the rocky hill that stands over Hammam Lif facing blue distances across the sea, two marble stones were raised later bearing the names of those who fell in battle, with the Regimental crest and motto 'Cymru am Byth.' Rupert Brooke wrote that where he fell would be 'for ever England.' So to the 3rd Battalion the hill tops by Fondouk and Hamman Lif are marked as 'Wales for ever.'
> — MAJ. L.F. ELLIS, *Welsh Guards at War* (1946)[1]

The Second World War is often thought of as a time when Britishness peaked. Some historians have argued that propaganda, bombing, the threat of invasion, the shared sacrifices of serving in the forces and enduring rationing all created a common sense of purpose amongst the British people, bringing together its different nations and regions. That sense of solidarity also cut across gender and class lines in a war where everyone was 'in it' together. This was a feeling that the state was only too keen to encourage and it helped ensure that the news and popular entertainment were dominated by the 'shared national predicament.'[2] Such perspectives

---

1   Maj. L.F. Ellis, *Welsh Guards at War* (Aldershot: Gale & Polden, 1946), 36.
2   Richard Weight, *Patriots: National Identity in Britain 1940–2000* (London: Pan, 2003); John Baxendale, '"You and I – All of Us Ordinary People": Renegotiating "Britishness" in Wartime', in Nick Hayes and Jeff Hill, eds, *'Millions like Us'? British Culture in the Second World War* (Liverpool: Liverpool University Press, 1999), 295–322. On the role of cinema in this, see Jeffrey Richards, 'National Identity in British Wartime Films', in Philip M. Taylor, ed., *Britain and the Cinema in the Second World War* (London: Macmillan, 1988).

have also been adopted by Welsh historians. John Davies' seminal history of Wales argues that the war 'did much to strengthen Britishness. At the same time, it seemed to be a death blow to Welshness.'³ Similarly, K.O. Morgan suggests that 'Culturally the second world war seems largely to have passed the Welsh and Scots by. The quintessential images of the war, and of what the country felt it was defending, were essentially timeless English concepts.'⁴

There is little reason to doubt the argument that, just as the shared experience and fear of mass unemployment had sustained a powerful consciousness of class that cut across local, regional and national identities within inter-war Britain, the shared experience of war did much the same for a British identity. The Welsh people probably did feel more British during the Second World War than at any other time during their history. Moreover, war meant people in Wales travelled more, listened to the radio more and had more contact with the English; even the most remote Welsh villages gained inhabitants from elsewhere in Britain. Psychologically and physically, the British nation came closer together. The war thus, as Morgan puts it, further integrated Wales into Britain.⁵

Yet the idea of a united Britain is not quite as straightforward as is often imagined and other historians have emphasised the disunity that also existed. Angus Calder, in particular, has questioned the extent of British

3   John Davies, A *History of Wales* (London: Penguin, 1993), 602. The Second World War in Wales awaits its definitive history but for an overview see Martin Johnes, *Wales since 1939* (Manchester: Manchester University Press, 2012), ch. 1. For Welsh-language responses to the war see Gerwyn Wiliams, *Tir Newydd: Agweddau at Llenyddiaeth Gymraeg a'r Ail Rhyfel Byd* (Cardiff: University of Wales Press, 2005). For commemoration of the war see Angela Gaffney, '"The Second Armageddon": Remembering the Second World War in Wales', in Matthew Cragoe and Chris Williams, eds, *Wales and War: Society, Politics and Religion in the Nineteenth and Twentieth Centuries* (Cardiff: University of Wales Press, 2007), 184–203. On munitions workers see Mari A. Williams, *A Forgotten Army: The Female Munitions Workers of South Wales, 1939–45* (Cardiff: University of Wales Press, 2002).
4   K.O. Morgan, 'England, Britain and the Audit of War', *Transactions of the Royal Historical Society*, sixth series, VII (1997), 151.
5   Ibid., 150–1.

national unity, arguing that beneath the propaganda were low morale and ongoing social conflict and inequalities.⁶ Building on Calder's work, Sonya Rose has emphasised the difficulties women, ethnic groups and colonial peoples had fitting into dominant ideas of British national identity. She also highlights the ongoing potency of Welsh and Scottish identities, arguing that 'The very existence of these "regional" nations, and the continuing issue of national/cultural difference, suggested that "Britain" both historically and contemporaneously was less a nation and more an empire.'⁷ Neither Rose nor Calder go as far as saying there was no British national unity or identity but they do demonstrate that there was no single notion of a British national identity that people united behind. Britishness was subject to different meanings and it was read and constructed differently by different regions, sexes, races and classes.

The plurality of British identity meant that a sense of Welshness was neither lost nor subsumed during this period of heightened Britishness. More contact with England made people more aware of not just what they had in common but also their differences, especially in the context of a war that was being fought over issues of national identity and self determination. With national identity being discussed in pubs, papers, pulpits and programmes on the radio, it is unsurprising that at least some of Wales reflected on what it meant to be Welsh. Central to this question was the sense of difference engendered by the popularity of Nonconformity and the Welsh language. Both, however, were in clear retreat and struggling against the influences of mass education, class-based politics, the wireless and cinema, and the economic and demographic upheavals brought first by inward migration from England before 1914 and then, between the wars, by outward migration to England. By the 1931 census, just 36.8 per cent of the population spoke Welsh and that figure was as low as 30.5 per cent in

---

6   Angus Calder, *The Myth of the Blitz* (London: Pimlico, 1991); Angus Calder, *The People's War, 1939–45* (London: Jonathan Cape, 1969).
7   Sonya O. Rose, *Which People's War? National Identity and Citizenship in Wartime Britain, 1939–45* (Oxford: Oxford University Press, 2003), 238. Also on the gendered nature of national identity see Lucy Noakes, *War and the British: Gender, Memory and National Identity* (London: I.B. Tauris, 1998).

Glamorgan, by far the most populous county in Wales. The cultural and economic pull of both England and working-class consciousness did not, however, mean that Welsh people who could not speak Welsh did not feel Welsh, something only too evident in sport.[8] Thus what war did was sharpen Wales' faltering sense of its own identity, particularly amongst those for whom it was generally a rather unfocused and diffuse feeling. Rose is quite right that the war activated expressions of cultural distinctiveness. Its challenges, its opportunities to debate what was being fought for, and the way it increased the role of the state and the state's interest in what its people thought, all created a space for Wales to have a public profile. Moreover, she suggests, 'It seemed almost as though the very efforts on the part of the Government to recognise Britain's cultural heterogeneity in order not to antagonise those who felt themselves to be equally Welsh or Scottish and British fostered identity politics.'[9] This chapter explores how these themes played out for men who served in the armed forces. It embraces the argument that national identity during the war was a plural concept but it adds that this was as true of Wales as it was of Britain. Just as there was no single understanding of Britain, nor was there a single understanding of Wales. Moreover, the Welsh could actually find it easier to embrace Britishness than the English because they had always had to balance and react to two nations, whereas for the English there had been traditionally little understanding of the nuances of nationality within the mainland of the United Kingdom.

---

8   On sport and nationhood before the war see Martin Johnes, *Soccer and Society: South Wales, 1900–39* (Cardiff: University of Wales Press, 2002). On the wider relationship between class and nation see Chris Williams, 'The Dilemmas of Nation and Class in Wales, 1914–1945', in Duncan Tanner, Chris Williams, W.P. Griffith and Andrew Edwards, eds, *Debating Nationhood and Government in Britain, 1885–1945: Perspectives from the 'Four Nations'* (Manchester: Manchester University Press, 2006), 146–68.
9   Rose, *Which People's War?*, 231, 286.

Welshness and the war

The continuing power of Welsh identity during the war was only too evident in the names, traditions and insignia of Welsh regiments, all of which were examples of what social scientist Michael Billig called banal nationalism, the subconscious but influential flagging and reminder of the existence of the nation.[10] The Royal Welch Fusiliers' emblem, for example, was a red dragon; it had choirs that sang Welsh hymns and a tradition where men ate a raw leek on St David's Day (although shallots sometimes had to be substituted when the regiment was on active service aboard). Such was the power of these traditions that part of the regiment even wore leeks in their hats when fighting on St David's Day 1945.[11] Their pride in Wales was further evident in a notice in *The Times* in memory of the soldiers of the 6th battalion killed in northwest Europe in 1944; it finished with the words 'Cymru am Byth' [Wales forever].[12] Welsh regiments also had a keen sense of history, despite the way that history could emphasise disunity between Wales and England. David Lloyd George addressed the Royal Welch Fusiliers' 250th anniversary celebrations at Caernarfon castle in August 1939, claiming 'It is a source of confidence to us that we know that this Regiment will once more face its responsibilities in a way which will be worthy of its glorious past and which will uphold that reputation for bravery which the Welsh people won in their age-long struggle for freedom.'[13] Similarly, the official history of the Welsh Guards, whose emblem was a leek, began by making connections between the regiment and Celts fighting the Romans and medieval Welsh princes fighting the Normans.[14]

The regiments were very proud of their identities and traditions and, like all parts of the army, promoted them to ensure men felt they belonged

---

10   Michael Billig, *Banal Nationalism* (London: Sage, 1995).
11   Lt-Com. P.K. Kemp and John Graves, *The Red Dragon: The Story of the Royal Welch Fusiliers, 1919–45* (Aldershot: Gale and Polden, 1960), 46–7, 258.
12   *The Times*, 1 August 1945.
13   Quoted in Kemp and Graves, *Red Dragon*, 9.
14   John Retallack, *The Welsh Guards* (London: Frederick Warne, 1981), xi.

to a unit of consequence.¹⁵ By St David's Day 1943, part of the Royal Welch Fusiliers was in North Africa and its men celebrated with leeks, beer and a 'Wales versus the Rest' soccer match, in which one Sergeant-Major 'carried an enormous leek with which he belaboured opponents foolish enough to come within reach.'¹⁶ The needs of military operation however were complicating the identities of regional and national units by leading to relatively frequent reorganisations. When, in November 1938, the 5th (Flintshire) battalion of the Royal Welch Fusiliers was converted into an anti-tank unit and made part of the Royal Artillery, there was some resentment and senior officers secured the right to continue wearing Royal Welch Fusiliers' uniforms. The regiment's official history claimed 'These units and their offshoots, although part of the Royal Regiment of Artillery, and despite numerous drafts of replacements from every corner of the British Isles, clung tenaciously to the old Royal Welch traditions, customs, and memories.' A merger with two other units from London regiments to create the 101st Light Anti-Aircraft and Anti-Regiment RA led to the Royal Artillery uniform being worn in the battalion but Welsh traditions continued and St David's Day 1940 was celebrated 'with, if possible, even greater fervour than usual.'¹⁷

Military needs and a growing policy of cross posting personnel to where they were needed also meant there was no guarantee that Welshmen would end up in Welsh units. The records (or indeed official definitions of Welshness) do not exist to know how often this happened but the issue was a matter of periodic public and private concern. For Glyn Ifans, a trainee teacher from Carmarthenshire, being in the RAF led to a feeling of being detached from his comrades and superiors and it fed his growing sense of political nationalism. With no units existing just for Welsh troops, he exclaimed 'Are we a nation? Certainly the authorities running this war do

---

15 David French, *Raising Churchill's Army: The British Army and the War Against Germany, 1919–1945* (Oxford: Oxford University Press, 2000), 124.
16 Kemp and Graves, *Red Dragon*, 287.
17 Ibid., 279–81.

not believe so.'[18] Great War veteran Sir Henry Morris Jones, a Liberal MP and chairman of the Welsh Parliamentary Party in 1941–2, was the leading voice of such concerns. Accusing the War Office of broken promises, he told the House of Commons in 1941: 'Judging from my correspondence and the feeling expressed in the Principality there is a very distinct and a justifiable grievance that the War Office has not met them' on the issue of keeping Welshmen in Welsh units.[19] Part of the blame for this was thought to be the issue of whether Welsh was used in recruitment processes and in 1940 a question was raised in Parliament about how many recruiting officers actually spoke Welsh.[20] In 1941, Wyn Griffith, a civil servant, broadcaster and former captain in the Royal Welch Fusiliers, noted:

> That young Welshmen should join the armed forces is, of course, only right and proper. They have no wish to shelter behind the sacrifices of others, and they are proud of the fighting qualities of their race. They remember their fathers. All they ask is that they should be allowed to serve in Welsh units, as Welshmen. But this is denied to them, not out of malevolence, but out of sheer indifference: it does not seem important enough for any great trouble to be taken to contrive it.[21]

Whether it actually did so or not, the War Office always maintained that those who volunteered and expressed a desire to serve in a Welsh unit were posted to one where vacancies existed. It also claimed that territorial connections were taken into account in allocating conscripts but this was always subject to the vague proviso 'where possible.' The government was not, however, willing to repeat what had happened in the Great War and form a separate Welsh division of the army.[22] Similarly, in 1943, a request from Sir Henry Morris-Jones that Welsh soldiers be allowed to wear a

---

18   Glyn Ifans, *Coron ar Fotwm* (Denbigh: Gee and Sons, 1960). Quoted in translation in Gerwyn Wiliams, 'Continental excursions', *Planet*, 129 (1998), 85.
19   Hansard, House of Commons Debates, 18 March 1941 vol 370, cc84, 93–5, 108–9. Also see Hansard, House of Commons Debates, 23 January 1940 vol 356, cc360–1.
20   The answer was one out of the nine recruiting officers in Wales. Hansard, House of Commons Debates, 12 November 1940 vol 365, cc1606–7W.
21   Wyn Griffith, *Word from Wales* (London: George Allen Unwin, 1941), 33.
22   Hansard, House of Lords Debates, 14 August 1940, vol 117, cc237–8.

distinctive mark on their uniform was turned down by the Secretary of State for War because it would be too complicated to administer.[23] How many Welshmen were actually concerned about such issues is a different matter. The likes of Wyn Griffith were what might be called cultural nationalists, people deeply committed to the identity of Wales. In contrast, one Welsh-speaking Meirionnydd man, who found himself in the South Lancashire Regiment, wrote in his memoirs, 'this did not really bother me: the army was the army, and it hardly made any difference which badge I was given.'[24] With comrades sharing the same experiences, hardships and routines, other Welsh speakers also described their wartime experience in terms that centralised a common bond with their English comrades over any sense of national difference.[25]

It was not just Welshmen who were being posted to English units; the reverse was happening too. In 1940, after hearing that some Welsh units drew as much as 40 per cent of their strength from outside Wales, a military correspondent at the *Western Mail* visited one unit with the permission of the War Office to investigate. He found a 'mixed bag. B.A.s, M.A.s, bakers, butchers and candlestickmakers. Cambridge University men rubbed shoulders with miners in this democratic army.' But the unit was 99.5 per cent Welsh.[26] Yet this was far from typical and there was a long history of Welsh regiments recruiting from England. Between 1883 and 1900, just 28 per cent of men in Welsh regiments were from their regimental districts.[27] The recruitment patterns of the Great War intensified the locality of regiments but casualties and reorganisations still led to Welsh units

---

23 Hansard, House of Commons Debates, 19 January 1943, vol 386, c19.
24 Selyf Roberts, *Tocyn Dwyffordd* (1984). Quoted in translation in Williams, 'Continental Excursions', 87.
25 For example, Caradog Prichard, *Rwyf Innau'n Filwr Bychan* (Dinbych: Llyfrau Pawb, 1943).
26 *Western Mail*, 23 December 1940.
27 David French, *Military Identities: The Regimental System, the British Army, and the British People c.1870–2000* (Oxford: Oxford University Press, 2005), 46.

drawing on men from across Britain.[28] Unable to rely on local or national identities to bond regiments, there was instead an emphasis on teaching men regimental traditions and using associated rituals to enhance a sense of togetherness and regimental loyalty. Thus what on the surface might appear to be national symbols were in practice driven more by the need to create personal relationships and a common bond between diverse sets of men. This does not mean that national pride played no role for soldiers who were Welsh in their personal sense of regimental identity but it did mean that Englishmen also partook in the first of March tradition of 'eating the leek.'[29] Non-Welsh servicemen thus do appear to have been assimilated easily into Welsh regiments. This was made easier by the fact that the Welsh Guards were actually based in London. One of its sergeants recalled recruits from outside Wales were made to feel part of the regiment:

> They are Welsh Guardsmen and once they joined us they were treated equally, the same as if they had been born and bred in Wales. They also learned that the family spirit is more binding in the Welsh Guards than in any other regiment ... I think it's just the way we are in Wales.[30]

But it happened in other regiments too. A man, who in 1939 was allocated to the 81st (Welsh) Field Regt RA, recalled 'the Welsh boys were extremely friendly and gave us a genuine warm welcome, sharing their food parcels, mainly of Welsh cakes.'[31]

The experience of fighting together in combat tends to produce a powerful bond between men so the lack of influence of cultural differences

---

28   For a discussion of this and an attempt to quantify the trends see Chris Williams, 'Taffs in the Trenches: Welsh National Identity and Military Service, 1914–1918', in Williams and Cragoe, eds, *Wales and War*.

29   Kemp and Graves, *Red Dragon*, 305, 334.

30   Trevor Royle, *Anatomy of a Regiment: Ceremony and Soldiering in the Welsh Guards* (London: Penguin, 1990), 87.

31   Patrick Delaforce, *Red Crown and Dragon: 53rd Welsh Division in North-West Europe, 1944–45* (Stroud: Amberley, 2009), 10.

should not be surprising.³² An officer who served with the Welsh Guards argued that he had a very close relationship with his men from their time training together and that he knew many of them better than his own family. The pride in themselves and the fear they might let their comrades and friends down intensified that and led, in his opinion, to many of the acts of bravery. One of his sergeants similarly argued 'We developed an obsession to help each other, sharing ourselves without expecting reward.'³³ Thus the war certainly developed a sense of group consciousness amongst troops in Welsh units but it was not necessarily based on the nation. This is further evidenced by the fact that battalions from Welsh regiments were put in the same brigades as battalions from English regiments without any problems. A history of the Welsh Guards noted,

> No Welsh Guardsman who fought in the Second World War would like this account to close without special mention of the Leicestershire Yeomanry, the Lothian and Border Horde, the Ayrshire Yeomanry, or the Light Aid Detachment from REME, which gave such unstinted backing to the 2nd Battalion.³⁴

Of course, this does not mean there were not tensions and army morale reports suggested that the cross posting of men and officers across units detracted from the development of an *esprit de corps*.³⁵ Yet, on the whole, the sense of unity within and between units that had fought together was strong.

---

32 As Keegan notes, the esteem of comrades was an important motivation in combat. John Keegan 'Towards a Theory of Combat Motivation', in Paul Addison and Angus Calder, eds, *Time to Kill: The Soldier's Experience of War in the West* (London: Pimlico, 1997), 3–11. Reading the citations of VC winners, it is hard not to think that these men were reckless in their concern for personal safety and willing to sacrifice themselves for their comrades. W. Alister Williams, *The VCs of Wales and the Welsh Regiments* (Wrexham: Bridge Books, 1984).

33 That sense of belonging continued after the war too. A Welsh Guards NCO injured at Normandy in 1944 recalled with pride the importance of wearing the regimental tie after the war: 'You're never alone when you wear this. You can be anywhere in the world and soon as they see it someone will talk to you.' Royle, *Anatomy of a Regiment*, 90, 92.

34 Retallack, *Welsh Guards*, 151.

35 National Archives (hereafter TNA), WO 163/51, Morale report, February-May 1942, 10.

This was not down to the experience of combat alone. Most of a serviceman's time was not spent in the frontline and the dominant experience was preparing for war rather than fighting. Indeed, perhaps only a fifth to a quarter of the army actually directly experienced combat during the war.[36] As Jeremy Crang has summed up, for most soldiers 'the experience of war was not one of daring deeds at the sharp end, but rather of a sedentary existence in camps and depots across the country polishing their brasses and wondering why they were there.'[37] The hardships, sacrifices and monotonies of military service pulled men from different parts of Britain together. One Welsh Guardsman thus recalled that the talk in the military huts ranged from:

> sex to the absolute bloody awful life of the British Soldier and then inevitably to the schemes for 'working your ticket', i.e. being thrown out as unfit for duty. Schemes like holding the little finger of the right hand just over the barrel of a 2" mortar and getting it blown off were discussed and discarded, the impact might blow the lot off, and in any case, the loss of a little finger was considered too trivial, there were many cases of soldiers with three fingers. Threatening the Sergeant Major with a bayonet, and many similar enterprises were all discarded. Surprisingly all this talk did no harm at all to the general moral[e] and discipline. Quite the opposite in fact, it kept the dream alive to beat the system, now that would be something![38]

When people were thinking along such lines, rather than serving first and foremost from a strong sense of patriotism or ideology, it is unsurprising that different backgrounds and understandings of nationality could be easily assimilated. Indeed, many soldiers were acutely aware that their sense of individuality was actually being eroded by their experiences of military life.[39]

---

36 John Ellis, *World War II: The Sharp End* (London: Windrow and Greene, 1990), 157–8. There are, of course, issues of how experience of combat is defined.

37 J.A. Crang, 'The British Soldier on the Home Front: Army Morale Reports, 1940–45', in Paul Addison and Angus Calder, eds, *Time to Kill: The Soldier's Experience of War in the West* (London: Pimlico, 1997), 60–74. Here 60.

38 A.R. Lewis, *Working His Ticket*, <http://www.proprose.co.uk> accessed 23 June 2014.

39 Ellis, *World War II*, 14.

However, the boredom and discomforts of camp life also gave opportunities for pre-existing tensions and cultural tensions to fester, especially when mixed with alcohol and the nerves and tensions of battles been or forthcoming.[40] Raymond Williams, the son of a Welsh railway worker and an officer in the Guards Armoured Division, never felt comfortable with the English officers that he mixed with in the mess, although that probably owed more to class than nationality.[41] Others objected to being referred to as the 'bloody Welsh.'[42] Those from strict Nonconformist backgrounds could feel uneasy with the drinking and swearing of their comrades. Even when the powerful bonds that existed between comrades did transcend any differences arising from different cultural backgrounds, individuals' Welshness or personal beliefs were not completely subsumed beneath a wider Britishness and loyalty to one's comrades. Servicemen and women for whom English was a second language were hardly going to forget they were Welsh. But for English-monoglot Welshmen and women too, being surrounded by people from other parts of the UK, probably for the first time in their lives, could make them more aware of their own Welshness and the diversity of Britain. A Welsh member of the Women's Royal Naval Service recalled: 'I don't think I'd ever heard of a Scouse person or a Geordie until I joined up. Then, suddenly, all these different accents all around you. A lot of people didn't know my accent. I'd be asked what part of Scotland I came from. Or Ireland – was I north or south?'[43] The unfamiliarity of the accent of one nurse from west Wales, together with her white cap and long uniform, even made some men regaining consciousness after anaesthetic think she was an angel.[44] Whether others initially knew the accent or not, many men and women spent their war being known by everyone as Taff or Taffy, making their nationality central to who they were, even if this did not make for a distinct Welsh experience of military service. One result was that when Welshmen outside Welsh units met they often quickly felt

---

40   Ellis, *World War II*, 327–8.
41   Dai Smith, *Raymond Williams: A Warrior's Tale* (Cardigan: Parthian, 2008), 161.
42   Wiliams, *Tir Newydd*, p. 7.
43   Quoted in Phil Carradice, *Wales at War* (Llandysul: Gomer, 2003), 98.
44   *Lleisau Ail Rhyfel Byd: 1939*, Episode 1, S4C, 16 September 2012.

something in common, regardless of where in Wales they were from.[45] The autobiography of a Welsh-speaking Royal Engineer from Caernarfonshire records that the small crew from Wales in his unit would come together to swap news. Such encounters were a link back to home but they also reinforced differences within Wales too, reminding those from the north in particular that not everyone spoke Welsh. This Royal Engineer found he was called Taff by everyone except men from south Wales who called him Ianto, an archetypal Welsh-language name.[46]

With around a third of the Welsh population able to speak Welsh, it was unsurprising that the language was spoken and, by and large, tolerated in the forces. In October 1939, a Welsh-speaking censor was posted to the British Expeditionary Force to deal with soldiers' writing home in Welsh and in May 1940 it was reported to the House of Commons that there had only been one known case of a letter being returned to a soldier because it was written in Welsh.[47] Welsh was included in BBC broadcasts to the forces and the secretary of the National Eisteddfod organised *Cofion Cymru* (Memories of Wales), a newsletter with stories, poems and the like, which was distributed with official support to Welsh speakers in the forces between 1941 and 1946.[48] In Cairo, another Welsh-language paper was set up, *Seren y Dwyrain* (The Star of the East). The toleration of Welsh was further evidence of how the state was aware that while all the men were fighting for Britain, their conception of what Britain actually was could be very different. Welsh had practical uses too. The *Western Mail* told readers in 1945 that Welsh had been used to 'deceive the Germans on the Western Front and confound the Japanese in the swamps and jungle of Burma.'[49] There was some truth to such claims. In 1943, for example, the Royal Welch Fusiliers were able to re-establish contact with a company that had been cut off during fighting in Burma by asking them in Welsh over loudspeakers to

45   For memories of such encounters amongst POWs see Sydney Pritchard, *Life in the Welsh Guards, 1939–46* (Talybont: Y Lolfa, 2007), 50, 63.
46   Ifan G. Morris, *Atgofion Hen Filwr* (Caernarfon: Wasg y Bwthyn, 2005), 73, 63.
47   Hansard, House of Commons Debates, 28 May 1940, vol 361, c397.
48   Wiliams, *Tir Newydd*, 27–33.
49   *Western Mail*, 9 May 1945.

fire rifles to indicate their position and strength. During the ensuing battle, further orders were given in Welsh over the loudspeakers. This lesson led to it becoming standard practice in the regiment that one wireless operator in every company be Welsh speaking.[50] Such actions could be rather confusing for the enemy. After the Welsh Guards used Welsh in radio communications at Cassino in 1944, the Germans responded twenty four hours later with propaganda leaflets in Urdu.[51] There were other occasional military advantages to Welshness too. One battalion of the Royal Welch Fusiliers spent some of the war stationed in Northern Ireland and the regiment's official history claimed that it was probable that the Welsh nationality of soldiers had helped keep the peace amidst tensions on the border and poor relations with the police.[52]

Yet the British authorities could also be rather perplexed or just indifferent to the needs of Welsh-speaking soldiers. In November 1939, the government was worrying that Welsh might be used to leak information to Germany via Eire.[53] In 1941, the Minister of Information was asked in Parliament why a telephone conversation in Welsh between a parent in north Wales and his soldier son in Northern Ireland had been prohibited by the Liverpool Telephone Exchange.[54] Such cases owed much to misunderstandings and were never the result of official policy but they happened repeatedly and added to the sense that Wales was not being treated fairly. In 1942, a deputation of Welsh MPs saw the Secretary of State for Dominion Affairs to complain of a general failure to recognise that Wales was a distinct nation. Amongst the issues raised was the placing of Welsh men and women in Welsh units, especially when they did not speak English, and the issue of being allowed to write home in Welsh. Attlee recommended to Cabinet that 'care should be taken' to see that Welsh men and women were posted to Welsh units and that 'Unless security grounds

50 Kemp and Graves, *The Red Dragon*, 51–3, 54.
51 Morris, *Atgofion*, 126; Ellis, *Welsh Guards at War*, 144.
52 Kemp and Graves, *Red Dragon*, 160.
53 TNA, CAB/65/4/2, Confidential annex by Minister without portfolio, 2 November 1939.
54 Hansard, House of Commons Debates, 18 December 1941, vol 376, c2067.

render it undesirable, they should be allowed to send and receive letters in the Welsh language.'⁵⁵ Cabinet agreed that it 'was desirable to avoid action which might foster the growth of an extreme Welsh Nationalist movement' but it was pointed out that 'the Ministry of Labour and National Service and the Fighting Services went to great trouble to ensure that Welsh-speaking men were posted to Welsh-speaking units.' A reminder was sent to all departments on the need to recognise Welsh nationality.⁵⁶ The greater importance given to placing Welsh-speaking soldiers in Welsh units than was attached to where English-monoglot Welsh soldiers was sent owed much to the practicalities of censoring Welsh letters in English units. A Royal Engineer in Egypt found himself summoned before one of his officers and asked to write home in English because the difficulties in censoring his letters was causing delays in getting them sent. Because he saw the officer as a gentleman who had taken the time to explain the situation to him, the soldier agreed, although he noted it felt repugnant to write to his parents in English. He did continue to write the occasional letter or passage in Welsh and sometimes they would be crossed out.⁵⁷ He was not the only one to find it strange but still accept the situation with the resignation that characterised so much of military life. Meurig Evans, of the 31st East Africa Infantry Brigade, recalled that it was 'strange' to write to his parents in English 'but that's how it was.'⁵⁸ In contrast, one RAF serviceman felt insulted when a Welsh-language telegram he sent to his parents was returned to him. For him, this was part of a wider process of politicisation and alienation caused by his feeling that his nationality was not recognised.⁵⁹

Yet not everyone was able to write or even speak English. The 1931 census reported that there were 97,932 Welsh monoglots, 8,831 of whom

55 TNA, CAB 66/23/3, 'Welsh representation', Memorandum by the Secretary of State for Dominion Affairs, 15 March 1942.
56 TNA, CAB/65/25/34, Cabinet minutes, 16 March 1942.
57 Morris, *Atgofion Hen Filwr*, 95.
58 *Lleisau Ail Rhyfel Byd: 1939*, Episode 1, S4C, 16 September 2012.
59 Wiliams, 'Continental Excursions', 85.

were males between the ages of ten and twenty four.[60] It is thus unlikely that there were no Welsh monoglots in the armed forces. The census did not define language ability and it was up to people to classify themselves. Compulsory education meant there cannot have been people of service age who were completely unversed in English but if they recorded themselves as Welsh monoglots their English skills must have been very rudimentary and many others who returned themselves as bilingual may also have had relatively limited commands of English. There are no records of any official discussion of the implications of this but this does not mean there were not problems. In 1955, the Council for Wales and Monmouthshire set up a committee to investigate whether Welshmen faced any special problems in their national service. It found that the army's personnel dossiers did not record Welsh-language ability and that recruits were told that Welsh should not be recorded in the section on foreign languages spoken. It also found that Welsh-monoglot recruits and those with a poor command of English suffered in the intelligence tests. This affected where they were posted and it may be that in the Second World War too those with poor skills in English found themselves sent to service units where the emphasis was on manual labour.[61]

These interactions between the Welsh and British authorities were thus creating a situation where some people at least contemplated their place in the world and the meaning and relevance of where they came from. In 1943, one soldier wrote in a journal entitled *Wales*:

> This is a time when members of the fighting generation everywhere should be expressing themselves and their opinions strongly – without cynicism – and nowhere more forcibly than in our small green oblong country. For the war has made the Welsh realise that they are a nation with a country, a people, a culture and a tradition *different* from England's to fight for. There is a new wave of national feeling about among our people. There is, in truth, a Welsh renaissance.[62]

---

60   *Digest of Welsh Historical Statistics*, table 1.18. Data refers to people aged 3+.
61   The Council for Wales and Monmouthshire, *Third Memorandum by the Council on its Activities 1956–57* Cmnd. 53 (London: HMSO, 1957), 118–30. The report recommended against sending those with poor command of English to such units.
62   Keidrych Rhys, 'Editorial', *Wales*, 3/1, July 1943, 4.

Another even suggested that the experiences of Welshmen in military service would lead to a growth in Welsh nationalism.[63] Nor was it just Welsh soldiers who were becoming more conscious of Welsh identity. Back home too, that intensifying awareness of Welsh difference was beginning to be felt through greater contact with people from other parts of the UK. As in the forces, this simultaneously led to a sense of a common interest and difference. The isolation that had kept Welsh strong in the west and north was being eroded, not just physically but psychologically too, as more people took an interest in global affairs and listened to the wireless.[64] Some 110,000 children were evacuated to Wales and they were received with both a sense of horror at their different manners and hygiene but also love and care.[65] Children were not the only ones arriving, as government departments and even the BBC's Variety Department were moved to the safety of Wales. *National Geographic Magazine* thought that children, government officials and civil servants had 'taken possession of Wales.' Its correspondent was told by one man that Wales had become 'little old England's refuge room.'[66] It is unlikely that they followed the example of some evacuees and learnt Welsh, but it was impossible to live in rural Wales without being aware that Welsh was a genuine community language. Indeed, even in the industrialised valleys, American GIs could become aware enough of the differences between Wales and England to write home about it.[67] Some civilians went

63 N. Hughes, 'Effaith galwad i'r caci', in J.E. Jones, ed., *Llais y Cymry yn Lluoedd Lloegr: Dyfyniadau o'u Llythyrau* (Caernarfon: Plaid Cymru, 1944), 3. The membership of Plaid Cymru grew from 3,750 to 6,050 over the course of the war. Wiliams, *Tir Newydd*, 37.
64 Between 1939 and 1945, the number of radio licenses in Wales increased from 406,000 to 490,000. John Davies, *Broadcasting and the BBC in Wales* (Cardiff: University of Wales Press, 2004), 138–9.
65 Some of these evacuees came from other parts of Wales. For an overview of their reception see Johnes, *Wales since 1939*, 14–16.
66 Isobel Wylie Hutchinson, 'Wales in Wartime', *National Geographic Magazine*, 85/6 (1944), 751–68.
67 See the reproduced letter in Bryan Morse, *A Moment in History: The Story of the American Army in the Rhondda in 1944* (Llandysul: Y Lolfa, 2001), 94–5.

the other way too, especially conscripted young women who were sent to factories wherever in Britain needed their labour.

Quite how all this interaction played out was no doubt an individualised experience that varied by personality and outlook; but there were certainly some tensions. Mass Observation reported that there was frequent resentment of the Welsh, the Irish and other foreigners in English towns.[68] Another Mass Observation report recorded being told that the Welsh were rather 'peculiar', while someone else reported that he saw the Welsh as a different race.[69] Similarly, there was resentment amongst nationalists about the influx of English people into Wales, not so much at an individual level but in terms of their collective impact on what was already a fragile traditional Welsh-speaking culture.[70] W.J. Gruffydd, a professor of Celtic languages and the Liberal MP for the University of Wales, remarked that 'England can win the war and Wales can lose.'[71] The requisition of land by the military was the strongest cause of nationalist concern, because for many the landscape was an embodiment of the Welsh nation. This was evident in the powerful verses of Pembrokeshire poet Waldo Williams that bemoaned the loss of community land to the cause of the British state's war.[72]

But nationalists also resented the loss of people to the war and parts of the nationalist party Plaid Cymru complained that the 'English government' did not have the right to conscript Welshmen.[73] Not many shared this concern though. There were 2,920 registered conscientious objectors

68 Mass Observation (MO), File Report (FR) 332, 'Public opinion and the refugee', August 1940.
69 'What Britain means to me', Mass Observation file report 904 (October 1941).
70 For contemporary concerns about evacuation see R.I. Aaron, 'A Modern Dispersion', *University of Wales Guild of Graduates: The Guild Annual 1940* (Cardiff: University of Wales Press, 1940), 2–6.
71 Quoted in translation in J. Graham Jones, 'The attitude of the political parties towards the Welsh language', in Geraint H. Jenkins and Mari Williams, eds, *'Let's Do Our Best for the Ancient Tongue': The Welsh Language in the Twentieth Century* (Cardiff: University of Wales Press, 2000), 262.
72 For a discussion of these poems see Robert Rhys, 'Poetry 1939–1970', in Dafydd Johnston, ed., *A Guide to Welsh Literature* (Cardiff: University of Wales Press, 1998), 89–116.
73 See, for example, the 1939 editions of *Welsh Nationalist*.

in Wales, a proportion significantly higher than in any other part of Britain but one which owed more to religion than nationalism or politics. A 1940 Mass Observation report thought that Welsh nationalism was too marginal and its members too old to have much impact on conscientious objector numbers. It noted that there were only six cases where conscientious objection was based on Welsh nationalism alone. The English Appellate Tribunal did recognise Welsh nationalism as grounds for conscientious objection. While tribunals in England followed this ruling, the two tribunals that covered Wales refused to allow nationalism as a sole basis for conscientious objection, arguing that the objection had to be to military service rather than the issue of the governance of Wales. Thus nationalists who did not cite pacifism or religion could be imprisoned for refusing conscription, although Caernarfon magistrates preferred to fine them. But such cases were few and far between. Over the course of the war, perhaps as few as two dozen members of Plaid Cymru ended up in court for making political objections to conscription.[74]

In 1945 one Welsh writer complained of Plaid Cymru:

> This was the party that saw more peril to Wales from English evacuee children than from Hitler's hordes. They were 'neutral' in the greatest war for human freedom. They, a handful of fanatics, presumed to speak for Wales from their safe jobs and safe hide-holes when 250,000 Welshmen were risking their lives to resist the greatest military despotism the world has ever seen.[75]

In fact, many Welsh nationalists were deeply hostile to Nazism and members of Plaid Cymru did serve in the armed forces.[76] Although conscription limited their options, not all nationalists resisted enlistment and some believed that the war was ultimately a just cause. In this, they reflected a

---

74   K.O. Morgan, 'Peace Movements in Wales, 1899–1945', *Welsh History Review*, 10/4 (1981), 398–43; MO, FR 312, 'Conscientious Objectors', June 1940; A.O.H. Jarman, 'Plaid Cymru in the Second World War', *Planet*, 48 (1979), 21–30. For the recollections of nationalist objectors, see John Griffith Williams, *Maes Mihangel* (Dinbych: Gwasg Gee 1974).
75   *Western Mail*, 21 April 1945.
76   Jarman, 'Plaid Cymru', 24.

much broader feeling amongst their compatriots. People may have joined up with a strong sense of resignation rather than British patriotism but there was a widespread acceptance that war was inevitable and that ultimately the British cause was morally sound, even if a clear ideological commitment to it was often rather lacking.[77] One Welsh writer, who gave speeches in favour of the war effort, noted in his 1946 autobiography of his officer son and others like him:

> These were free men ready to defend our freedom. They had not been driven or bamboozled into the uniforms they were wearing, or hypnotized into a state in which they did not know what they were doing. They knew they were fighting for something really worthwhile, whilst well aware that Britain had been no garden of paradise between the wars. The main thing was that they still had minds of their own.[78]

That was rather a romantic view of military service that belied how the conscript's existence was dominated by getting by but it indicated a feeling that could be found if military researchers dug deep enough and in this there is no evidence that Wales was any different to anywhere else in Britain. People may have been conscious at some level or other that Wales was different to England but that did not mean that they did not also feel part of Britain and its war effort.

Two interwoven nations

It was because people served with minds of their own that Welshness and Britishness were interwoven in the minds and experiences of both military personnel and civilians. These twin national identities were clearly evident

---

77 On the lack of ideological commitment see French, *Raising Churchill's Army*, 126 and Ellis, *World War II*, ch. 8.
78 Jack Jones, *Me and Mine: Further Chapters in the Autobiography of Jack Jones* (London: Hamish Hamilton, 1946), 124–5.

in the *Western Mail*'s celebrations of VE day. At one level, the newspaper celebrated how the British had contributed something very real to the future of the world, telling its readers that they had served a 'humane and righteous cause.' But it also published a page looking proudly at what the Welsh had contributed to the victory at home and abroad.[79] To readers of the article, it was evident that the Welsh had fought, worked and died for a greater cause, and many had sung while doing it. That same month Megan Lloyd George told an Anglesey eisteddfod that the Welshmen who had fought were 'worthy successors of the [medieval] heroes of Wales, such as Llewelyn and Owain Glyndwr, and others who fought not only for the independence of Wales, but of nations as well.'[80] In the aftermath of the war, even the London press occasionally celebrated Welshness. The *Daily Mirror*, for example, proudly told the story of POWs in Thailand, who, each week, held a meeting of a Welsh society, singing hymns and the Welsh national anthem. Some of them, it claimed, died singing.[81]

There was nothing surprising in any of this; war or no war, the Welsh were a people that belonged to two nations. Yet which took precedence was something that varied significantly. There was not even any straightforward link between language and the balance that individuals struck. There were Welsh speakers who were content to see their Britishness predominate, and there were English monoglots who clearly saw themselves as Welsh before British. Rose is thus right when she uses Wales to illustrate that while the British did pull together, they did not agree on what Britain meant.[82] But it also has to be remembered that there was no singular definition or understanding of Wales either. The war did not change the fact that what Welshness meant remained as problematic as ever. For a relatively small number of nationalists, it was about defending Welsh-language culture through some kind of self-government. For parts of the labour movement, it was about preventing a return to economic catastrophe through stronger

---

79   *Western Mail*, 8 May 1945.
80   *Caernarvon and Denbigh Herald and North Wales Observer*, 11 and 25 May 1945.
81   *Daily Mirror*, 13 September 1945.
82   Rose, *Which People's War?*, 290, 286.

Welsh representation in London government. For probably many more, it was just a simple pride in where they were from, something that was only enflamed when ignored or not recognised.

The government was aware of that and made efforts to ensure Welsh nationality was recognised. This extended beyond how it treated Welsh soldiers to passing legislation giving people the right to speak Welsh in court, to reminding the BBC to not say England when it meant Britain, and to pushing for propaganda that displayed the plurality of Britain, even if the results could actually annoy Welsh listeners who felt a narrow and overly traditional image of Wales was being portrayed.[83] The state even advertised in Welsh-language papers hostile to the war. This did not mean there were not tensions and the odd civil servant or military official who did not understand or recognise Welsh difference.[84] But it is not unreasonable to conclude that there was a greater sensitivity to Welsh identity in London government during the Second World War than there had been at any previous time.

If anything, the government worried too much about Wales. Nationalists were in a minority, not all were against the war, and there was nothing to suggest that their numbers might grow significantly. The Germans had tried to exploit the sense of Welsh national identity but got nowhere. In April 1940, for example, Wales was given special prominence in Nazi propaganda broadcasts which claimed that the Welsh were as different from the English as the Poles or Czechs were from the Germans. 'Anyone who has heard 80,000 Welshmen singing "Land of My Fathers" knows what a spirit these people have. Will that spirit be broken in grinding poverty,

---

83 On the 1942 Welsh Courts Act, see J. Graham Jones, 'The National Petition on the Legal Status of the Welsh Language, 1938–1942', *Welsh History Review*, 18/1 (1996), 92–124. For a wider view of official responses to Welsh identity in the war, see Johnes, *Wales since 1939*, ch. 1. For resentment of Welsh clichés, see Rose, *Which People's War?*, 221. On the BBC, see Davies, *Broadcasting and the BBC*, ch. 3.

84 There were periodic concerns, for example, that Wales was not properly represented on bodies such as the Ministry of Information. See *Western Mail*, 21 December 1940.

or will it burst forth in revolt?' one broadcast asked.[85] Yet there was nothing to suggest that the Welsh as a whole were not as behind the war effort as any other part of Britain, even if they had their own understandings of what Britain meant. Indeed, the Welsh might even have a stronger sense of British identity than the English. A 1941 Mass Observation report claimed 'Britain is felt to be somehow symbolic and rather impersonal, whereas England (or whichever other country the person lives in) is more personal, intimate. ... [A]n astonishing number of people, irrespective of education and politics, talk about Britain as if it were a unit of four countries, the one in which they live and three others, all foreigners.'[86] Their research was concentrated in England and there was actually little to suggest that there was the same remoteness from Britain in Wales, whether amongst civilians or soldiers. The state might be remote but that was not the same as the British nation. Most memoirs by Welsh servicemen do not make any sustained reference to their sense of Welshness, while civilians could also happily speak of themselves as British. This was perhaps because to the Welsh the difference between Britain and Wales were much clearer than the differences between England and Britain were to the English. The Welsh, or at least those that listened to the radio or worked in the cosmopolitan communities of the south, were used to thinking of the complexities of their nationality and their position within a multinational state.[87] Before the war, the English, in contrast, tended to simply conflate the two. Thus while the war certainly reinforced a sense of Welshness amongst the Welsh, this was just a case of building on what was already there. It was perhaps the English that had a bigger task in facing up to the existence of Wales and the plurality of Britain.

85   TNA, CAB/18/6/8, Analysis of German propaganda, April 1–15, 1940. For memories of a Welsh Guardsman POW who the Germans tried to entice into doing radio propaganda broadcasts by appealing to his Welshness, see Pritchard, *Life in the Welsh Guards*, 30–1.
86   MO, FR 904, 'What Britain means to me', October 1941.
87   For a wider consideration of British in Wales, see Martin Johnes, 'Wales, History and Britishness', *Welsh History Review*, 25/4 (2011), 596–61.

Yet the fact that nationality is not a pervasive theme in the memoirs of so many soldiers from all parts of the United Kingdom is because, for the majority, the experience of military service, like all everyday existences, was not, by and large, a reflective one. Military service could be dangerous and frightening, adventurous and exciting, tedious and monotonous, enlightening and educational. Patriotism or ideology rarely had much to do with everyday service, even when it came to what led men to fight, kill and die.[88] Thus while at an abstract level people may have been fighting for Britain and Wales, whatever they might mean by those terms, those abstract concepts actually had little impact on their everyday existence, an existence dominated by making do and survival. The world of the Welsh soldier was thus not Wales or Britain but their immediate unit, their mates, comrades, superiors and subordinates.

---

88 French notes that the lack of personal commitment to the war did not mean a lack of morale or combat effectiveness. French, *Raising Churchill's Army*, 134.

BERNARD KELLY

'Excellent Irishmen': Irish volunteers and identities during the Second World War

In one of the first examinations of Irish volunteer identity during the Second World War, Geoffrey Roberts argued that the estimated 70,000 men and women who left neutral Eire to join the British forces during the conflict[1] represented a shared Irish-British identity, which existed in the middle ground between the two competing ideologies on the island: unionism in Northern Ireland and nationalism in Eire. Northern Ireland, still within the UK, participated in the war while Eire, under the leadership of Eamon de Valera, remained neutral. The unionist leadership in Belfast used the conflict as a demonstration of their loyalty to the Crown, while de Valera's policy of neutrality was partially driven by his wish to demonstrate Eire's independence from Britain. Throughout the war, the Fianna Fáil government took the opportunity to promote its own vision of Irish history and identity, one that emphasised Eire's distinctiveness from Britain. The contrasting experiences of the war drove the two Irelands further apart and partition of the island became entrenched. However, Irish service in the British forces during the conflict generated a specific sense of Irishness, one that contradicted de Valera's nationalist narrative of the war. By incorporating uncontroversial and easily recognisable signifiers of Irish identity, such as harps, shamrocks and wolfhounds, into Irish units, going to great lengths to accommodate the religious differences of Irish recruits and the use of Irish nicknames, the British forces created a space for Eire volunteers to express their nationalism, but also fashioned a composite Irish identity

[1] Geoffrey Roberts, 'Neutrality, Identity and the Challenge of the "Irish Volunteers"' in Dermot Keogh and Mervyn O'Driscoll, eds, *Ireland in World War Two: Diplomacy and Survival* (Cork: Mercier Press, 2004), 274.

within which sectarian and political divisions were erased. Many volunteers themselves were able within this context to simultaneously support Irish neutrality while fighting for the Allies. Roberts' second major point, that the volunteers were at least partially sympathetic to the Allied cause and were less hostile towards Britain than other Irish citizens, can be tested by analysis of the testimony of Irish volunteers held at the Volunteers Project Oral History Archive at University of Cork. This reveals that, while a significant proportion of Eire volunteers joined the British forces either to assist the Allied war effort or because of empathy for Britain, their motivations for enlisting were a complex mixture of personal, economic and ideological reasons. The process of volunteer identity formation has continued until the present day: their contribution to Allied victory was not acknowledged by the Irish state until the 1990s, when the Northern Ireland peace process began to take shape. As obvious examples of a shared Irish-British identity, Irish veterans of the Second World War have come to play a central role in Dublin's engagement with the unionist community in Northern Ireland and are consistently cited as representing the ideal modern, mature and pluralist Irish identity.

Identity in neutral Eire

During the war, the de Valera government promoted what Roberts has termed a 'nationalistic neutralistic narrative': a combination of 'strict political neutrality with a moral distancing of Ireland from both sides of the conflict.'[2] Since being elected in 1932, de Valera had gradually removed the diplomatic and constitutional links between the Irish Free State and Britain, a process that culminated in the introduction of the 1937 constitution. In it, de Valera engaged in what Brian Girvin described as the 'republicanisation of Irish society': removing the recognisably British elements of the

2   Ibid., 275.

state while also shifting towards an Irish identity based on the Gaelic past and Catholicism.[3] Diarmaid Ferriter suggested that de Valera's insistence on emphasising these two aspects of Irish identity was a defensive reaction to the fact that Eire and Britain existed in close symbiosis with each other; that by 'exaggerating the relatively minor differences', the Fianna Fáil leader hoped to 'mask obvious similarities.'[4]

Evidence of this is seen in the new constitution. De Valera retained the British two-tier parliamentary system inherited in 1922, as well as the cabinet of ministers, but the head of government was renamed Taoiseach and his deputy Tánaiste. The Irish language was established as the first official language of the state, while English was downgraded to 'a second official language.' Although not installed as the state religion, Catholicism was afforded a special position. The new constitution also created the office of president, replacing the British monarch as head of state, and contained an official claim to both the physical and abstract limits of the island. Article two stated that the 'national territory consists of the whole island of Ireland', claiming both the territory and inhabitants of Northern Ireland, while Article four altered the official title from the Irish Free State to Eire, 'or in the English language, *Ireland*.'[5] By making these bold claims, de Valera displayed an utter lack of consideration for any alternate Irish identity, and particularly alienated unionists with his attempted monopolisation of the term 'Ireland.'[6]

De Valera's decision to remain neutral in September 1939 was motivated by a mixture of a lack of military resources, public support for non-participation and a desire to express Dublin's freedom of action from Britain. Neutrality was rapidly assimilated into the Irish public's sense of identity.

---

3 Brian Girvin, 'The Republicanisation of Irish Society, 1932–48' in J.R. Hill, ed., *A New History of Ireland VII: Ireland, 1921–84* (Oxford: Oxford University Press, 2003), 138.
4 Diarmaid Ferriter, *The Transformation of Ireland, 1900–2000* (London: Profile Books, 2005), 364.
5 *Bunreacht na hÉireann* (Constitution of Ireland), 4, italics in original.
6 Garret FitzGerald, *Reflections on the Irish State* (Dublin: Irish Academic Press, 2003), 42.

By July 1940, Joseph Walshe, the secretary of the Department of External Affairs, noted that neutrality had become 'just as much a part of the national position as the desire to remain Irish, and we can no more abandon it than we can everything that constitutes our national distinctiveness.'[7] In April 1941, the twenty-fifth anniversary celebrations of the Easter Rising offered the government the chance to repeat and reinforce this message. In 1916, de Valera had been one of a small group of rebels who had seized control of parts of Dublin city centre for almost a week and proclaimed an Irish republic; most of the city centre was reduced to ruins in the subsequent fighting, and fourteen of the leaders were executed by firing squad. De Valera himself had been sentenced to death but had been reprieved, and his status as a surviving commander of the Rising was of huge benefit to him once he launched his political career. In his April 1941 speech to the nation he made a determined effort to link the Easter Rising to neutrality and pointed out that the independence to remain neutral in the war was a direct result of the actions of the 1916 rebels. Furthermore, de Valera declared that the 'freedom we now enjoy is the direct fruit of the courage and sacrifices of the leaders of Easter Week.'[8] This reductive and overly simplistic interpretation of Irish history was clearly not flexible enough to accommodate those who felt they were serving Ireland by fighting in British uniform. During the war, de Valera was willing to go to great lengths to highlight Eire's independence from Britain. Daniel Leach has observed that de Valera even accepted short-term breaches in relations with the Allies if his actions demonstrated Dublin's sovereignty: for instance, when the government refused to hand over German diplomats to the Allies in 1945.[9] De Valera's visit to the German Legation in May 1945 to express his condolences to the German representative in Ireland upon the death of Hitler can also be placed in this bracket.

7   Thomas E. Hachey, ed., *Turning Points in Twentieth-Century Irish History* (Dublin: Irish Academic Press, 2011), 82.
8   University College Dublin Archives, de Valera papers, P150/2618, de Valera speech, Easter Sunday 1941.
9   Daniel Leach, *Fugitive Ireland: European minority nationalists and Irish political asylum, 1937–2008* (Dublin: Four Courts Press, 2009), 68.

During the conflict, de Valera assiduously suppressed anything that challenged his and his government's interpretation of the war. The scale of Irish enlistments in the British forces was concealed by requiring Irish volunteers returning on leave from the British forces come home in civilian clothes, and the British military obligingly stockpiled suits and coats at departure ports for Irish troops on leave. An aggressive and partial censorship regime[10] consistently removed any mention of Irish involvement in the war. Instructions sent to the press in August 1941 prohibited 'Matter consisting of references to, letters from, or statements made by or purporting to have been made by any person of Irish nationality serving in the forces of any of the belligerents.'[11] Promotions, decorations and death notices of Irish volunteers in the belligerent forces were also banned from appearing in Irish newspapers. All of these measures can plausibly be explained as maintaining the façade of Irish neutrality, but their side effect was to effectively reinforce the identity narrative that the Dublin government was anxious to present.

Irish identity in the British forces

The Second World War was the final highpoint of Irish recruitment in the British forces, a tradition that dates back several centuries. Modern Irish enlistments began in 1793, when penal law statutes were reversed and the ban on Catholic recruitment was lifted. From then until the 1830s, Irish recruits flooded into the Crown forces and the scale of Irish enlistments is illustrated by the number of Irish regiments which were created: the Connaught Rangers, the Royal Irish Regiment, the Leinster Regiment, the Royal Munster Fusiliers, the Royal Dublin Fusiliers, the Royal Irish

---

10   Donal Ó Drisceoil, *Censorship in Ireland, 1939–1945: Neutrality, Politics and Society* (Cork: Cork University Press, 1996), 291.
11   *Ibid.*, 319.

Fusiliers, the Royal Irish Lancers, the Royal Irish Rifles and the Irish Guards. The formation of such regiments in the nineteenth century were part of a deliberate strategy of localisation; creating army units with strong regional identities in order to raise the profile of the British army and to stimulate recruitment.[12] In the case of the Irish regiments, each was heavily laden with Irish symbols and iconography. For instance, the dress uniform of the Irish Guards (still in existence) contains a shamrock on each collar[13] and a harp embossed on the buttons;[14] the coat buttons of the Royal Irish Rifles displayed both a harp and a shamrock.[15] Most of the regiments had an Irish wolfhound as a mascot and their regimental songs were generally sentimental Irish ballads such as 'St Patrick's Day', 'Let Erin Remember' or 'The Wearing of the Green.' The Irish Guards regimental marching tunes in 1918 were 'St Patrick's Day in the Morning' and 'Father O'Flynn.'[16] In addition, from 1900 onwards, Irish regiments wore sprigs of shamrock in their headgear on St Patrick's Day.[17] Jan Rüger has noted that the Royal Navy, an iconic symbol of Britishness which had traditionally ignored the regional identity of its members, also made an effort to accommodate Irish identity. From 1901 onwards, new classes of cruisers were named after various parts of the UK and the empire. When HMS *Hibernia* was launched in 1905, it was decorated in shamrocks, launched by Irish nobles and the bows were christened with a bottle of Irish whiskey, rather than the traditional bottle of wine. In addition, the navy joined the army in allowing Irish recruits to wear shamrock on St. Patrick's Day.[18]

---

12   Nicholas Perry, 'Nationality in the Irish Infantry Regiments in the First World War', *War & Society*, 12/1 (1994), 65–95.
13   R.G. Harris, *The Irish Regiments, 1683–1999* (Staplehurst: Spellmount, 1999), 91.
14   Ibid., 106.
15   Ibid., 153.
16   Ernest Hart, 'British Regimental Marches: Their History and Romance', *The Musical Quarterly*, 4/4, (1918), 579–86.
17   Harris, *The Irish Regiments*, 89.
18   Jan Rüger, 'Nation, Empire and Navy: Identity Politics in the United Kingdom, 1887–1914', *Past and Present*, 185 (2004), 159–88.

Irish volunteers and identities during the Second World War 95

The wider issue of what constituted Irish identity was never solved during the long road towards Irish independence, and this had a direct effect on the pattern of Irish participation in the British forces. Paul Bew has suggested that until the late eighteenth century, Protestants in Ireland could still self-identify as Irish.[19] However, by 1886 Conservative politician Joseph Chamberlain felt able to tell the House of Commons that 'Ireland is not a homogenous community ... it is a nation that comprises two nations and two religions.'[20] During the Second World War, George Marshall, the director of the BBC in Northern Ireland, expressed similar sentiments. He dismissed the idea of single-identity 'Irishmen' serving in the British forces, saying that 'there is no such thing as an Irishman ... Irishmen as such ceased to exist after partition.'[21] This was reflected in Irish recruitment during the First World War, in which three Irish divisions were raised for the British army: the 10th (Irish), 16th (Irish) and 36th (Ulster) divisions. The 10th and 16th were largely recruited from the Irish Volunteers, the pro-Home Rule paramilitary force founded in 1913. The 36th was composed mostly of the Ulster Volunteer Force, the anti-Home Rule force that was established in 1912. In total, 200,000 Irishmen volunteered for the British forces,[22] of which between 27,000 and 35,000 died.[23] Because conscription was never implemented in Ireland, all Irish enlistments were volunteers. The fracturing of Irish recruitment along sectarian and political lines between 1914 and 1918 quickly became a political issue and was carefully avoided by the British government during the Second World War.

In an attempt to solve the Irish Question, in 1922 Ireland was divided by the British government into two self-governing units: the six counties of

---

19   Paul Bew, *Ireland: The Politics of Enmity 1789–2006* (Oxford: Oxford University Press, 2007), 368.
20   Ronan Fanning, *Fatal Path: British Government and Irish Revolution, 1910–1922* (London: Faber and Faber, 2013), 13.
21   Alan F. Parkinson and Eamon Phoenix, eds, *Conflicts in the North of Ireland, 1900–2000* (Dublin: Four Courts Press, 2010), 12.
22   Philip Orr, '200,000 volunteer soldiers' in John Horne, ed., *Our War: Ireland and the Great War* (Dublin: Royal Irish Academy, 2008), 65.
23   John Horne, 'Our War, Our History' in Horne, ed., *Our War*, 6.

Northern Ireland, which contained a majority of Protestants and remained within the UK, and the Irish Free State, which was granted Dominion status. As part of the independence settlement, the British forces evacuated the Free State, leaving behind only small garrisons at the so-called 'Treaty Ports' in Cork and Donegal. In addition, five of the famous Irish infantry regiments which were associated with the south of the island were disbanded: the Connaught Rangers, the Royal Irish Regiment, the Leinster Regiment, the Royal Munster Fusiliers and the Royal Dublin Fusiliers. Four infantry regiments survived the process: the Irish Guards, the Royal Inniskilling Fusiliers, the Royal Irish Fusiliers and the Royal Irish Rifles, which was subsequently renamed the Royal Ulster Rifles.[24] All these units retained their distinctive Irish identities and traditions during the Second World War and continued to attract recruits from both parts of Ireland throughout the conflict.

One of the major concessions made by the Crown forces towards its Irish recruits was the freedom of religion and from the early nineteenth century, it was recognised that provision needed to be made for Irish Catholic volunteers. In 1802 Catholic chaplains were permitted in the forces and Catholic soldiers were exempted from church parades.[25] During the Second World War, the removal of any sectarian tension remained the policy of the British forces and, in February 1941, instructions were sent to chaplains stating that 'no officer or soldier will be obliged to attend the service of any religious denomination other than his own.'[26] Throughout the conflict, the British Army Senior Catholic Chaplain recruited Jesuit priests directly from Eire. In total, twenty one Jesuits served as chaplains, all but two in the British army,[27] where the bulk of Eire volunteers served, and Ireland contributed 161 chaplains in total to the forces during the

---

24   Richard Doherty, *Clear the Way! A History of the 38th (Irish) Brigade, 1941–1947* (Dublin: Irish Academic Press, 1993), 5.
25   Terence Denman, 'The Catholic Irish Soldier in the First World War: The "Racial Environment"', *Irish Historical Studies* 27/108 (1991), 352–65.
26   Jesuit archives, CHP 25/7, *Memorandum for Catholic Army Chaplains and officiating chaplains to the Forces*, February 1941.
27   *Interfuse: Irish Province Communicating*, 41, (1986), 5.

war,[28] although it is not known how many were recruited specifically for Irish units. However, it is clear that concessions for Catholic volunteers were sanctioned at the highest level, as all British army chaplains were officially appointed by the Permanent Under-Secretary of War, on the nomination of a bishop and the recommendation of 'the Catholic Bishop-in-Ordinary to H.M. Forces.'[29]

Complementing the use of Irish iconography and allowances made for religion was the informal practice of applying nicknames to Irish recruits. Since large-scale Irish enlistments began in the 1790s, 'Paddy' or 'Mick' was the standard nickname issued to all recruits from Ireland, and was applied regardless of their religious or political background or their branch of service. It was probably rooted in the fact that their British comrades could not distinguish between the various Irish accents. Brian Inglis, a Dubliner who joined the RAF, wrote in his memoirs that to his 'mess colleagues every Irishman was Paddy, whether he came from Bantry or Belfast, as long as he spoke with an Irish accent.'[30] The indiscriminate use of the nickname served to erase differences between recruits from the differing traditions on the island, signifying that the sectarian or political divisions within Irish society would not be tolerated within the British forces. Submerged in a composite Irish identity, volunteers could express themselves much more freely than at home. For example, Paddy Brabazon, an RAF volunteer from Cork, recalled that he would joke with his Northern Irish comrades, saying 'To Hell with King Billy!' to which the northerners would reply jovially 'to hell with the Pope!'[31] Similarly, Jack Harte, a British army recruit from Dublin who was a keen boxer, recalled in his memoirs that when he was fighting in the ring, '... all the boys from the Belfast Shankill and Sandy Row, Republican Derry, Dublin and Kerry ... turn out and support the lad from their own regiment. Whatever your politics, there was no divide between

28   Tom Johnstone and James Hagerty, *The Cross and the Sword: Catholic Chaplains in the Forces* (London: Geoffrey Chapman, 2006), 195.
29   Jesuit archives, CHP 25/7, *Memorandum for Catholic Army Chaplains and officiating chaplains to the Forces*, February 1941.
30   Brian Inglis, *West Briton* (London: Faber & Faber, 1962), 65.
31   Volunteers Project Oral History Archive, Tape A, Paddy Brabazon.

us.'³² However, being rebranded a 'Paddy' was not universally welcomed and another RAF recruit remembered Northern Irish volunteers rebelling against the nickname, declaring 'We're British subjects!'³³ It was not just individual Irish recruits who were labelled: the Royal Irish Dragoon Guards were known before their abolition in 1922 as the 'Mounted Micks'³⁴ and the Irish Guards have long been referred to as 'the Micks.'³⁵

The British military practice of creating a unique space in which Irish recruits could express their identity was not only maintained during the Second World War, it was accelerated. In October 1941, Winston Churchill mooted the idea of grouping together existing Irish units to form an Irish infantry brigade. This provoked strong opposition from political leaders in Belfast, where the unionist administration resisted the absorption of any Ulster-based regiments into any formation that would be classified as 'Irish.' This mirrored almost exactly the situation during the First World War when, as a result of a sharp decline in Irish enlistments, the British military authorities suggested that the 16th (Irish) Division and the 36th (Ulster) Division be merged. Edward Carson, leader of the Ulster unionists, was aghast at the possibility of the separate Ulster identity of the 36th being submerged within an Irish formation, and requested instead that if the 36th had to be amalgamated with another unit, it be incorporated into the 51st Highland division.³⁶ He no doubt hoped that the strong economic, migratory and religious connections between Ulster and Scotland would prevent the 36th from losing its unionist ethos. Faced with such resistance, in 1916 the British government backed down. However, it did not do so during the Second World War and despite unionist protests, the 38th (Irish) infantry brigade was formed in January 1942. Composed of elements of the Royal Inniskilling Fusiliers, the Royal Irish Fusiliers and the London Irish

---

32 Jack Harte, *To the Limits of Endurance: One Irishman's War* (Dublin: Liberties Press, 2007), 61.
33 Volunteers Project Oral History Archive, Tape A15, Denis Murnane.
34 David Murphy, *The Irish Brigades, 1685–2006: A Gazetteer of Irish Military Service, Past and Present* (Dublin: Four Courts Press, 2007), 120.
35 *Ibid.*, 226.
36 Perry, 'Nationality in the Irish Infantry Regiments', 81.

Rifles, the new brigade was, like the original Irish regiments, saturated in symbols of Irishness. It had the usual complement of pipers clad in kilts, and the headdress was the caubeen, a large and distinctively Irish form of beret.

The concessions on identity offered to Irish units by the British forces represented a two-way exchange: in return for loyalty to the British forces and their units, volunteers were offered a space in which to express their own pluralist identity. However, this process had to be carefully controlled. Because of the antagonism between the unionist/Protestant and nationalist/republican/Catholic communities on the island of Ireland, neutral and non-partisan symbols were chosen to represent the units. Both before the Second World War and during it, shamrock, harps and wolfhounds were prevalent as they were familiar to both communities and neither side had a monopoly over their use. The emphasis on respect for religion was also crucial in this context. Catholics, Anglicans or Presbyterians from Ireland would doubtlessly have resisted the imposition of a standard religion upon them and allowing them the freedom to practice their faith was a key element in ensuring their loyalty to their regiments.

On a more practical level, Irish iconography also maintained discipline and raised morale. The creation of a strong central identity helped to weld together recruits from disparate backgrounds into a cohesive whole and any non-Irish recruits were required to put aside their personal feelings and buy into the regimental ethos. Their distinctive appearance generated a sense of *esprit de corps* and made each regiment unique, engendering pride in the unit. The regiment served as a substitute home for many recruits, particularly on long overseas postings, and reminders of home were crucial to keep troops' spirits up and stifle dissent. All of this ensured that these regiments maintained a high level of combat readiness, which even Catholic chaplains were expected to contribute towards: directives issued by the United Services Catholic Association to army chaplains in February 1941 instructed them to 'be living examples of the moral qualities expressed by the word MORALE, viz: – DISCIPLINE, THE FIGHTING SPIRIT AND THE WILL TO WIN.'[37]

---

37 Jesuit archives, CHP 25/7, *Memorandum for Catholic Army Chaplains and officiating chaplains to the Forces*, February 1941, 5. Capitals in the original.

There are strong parallels between Irish regiments and Scottish units in the British forces at this time. By creating Scottish regiments with strong Highland identities in the mid-nineteenth century, the British army assimilated the once-banned symbolism of Jacobite individualism. Festooned with overt manifestations of Highland Scottishness, such as kilts, tartans and pipers, Highland regiments assumed the physical appearance of the Jacobite forces of the eighteenth century and thus also laid claim to the fighting prowess of the Highland clans, representing the ideal image of the fierce but loyal Celt.[38] This also proved to be an effective way of attracting recruits. As one Scot said after joining the Argyll and Sutherland Highlanders in 1940, 'The Army was one service I had sworn I would never join ... but, I told myself, a Scottish regiment would be different, more glamorous.'[39] Similarly, the creation of Irish units drew in more Irish recruits which then absorbed some of the anti-British aspects of Irish identity; for instance, the motto of the 64th Lancashire Rifle Volunteer Corps (Liverpool Irish) was the nineteenth-century nationalist-emigrant cry *'Erin go Bragh'* (Ireland forever).[40]

Volunteer reactions

Recent research into the Volunteers Project Oral History Archive at University College Cork has shed new light onto how Eire volunteers viewed themselves when joining the British forces, and what identity they carried with them when they enlisted. After the war, Northern Ireland Prime Minister Basil Brooke claimed that volunteers from Eire were 'our

---

38 Heather Streets, *Martial Races: The Military, Race and Masculinity in British Imperial Culture, 1857–1914* (Manchester: Manchester University Press, 2004), 167.
39 Charles Glass, *Deserter: The Last Untold Story of the Second World War* (London: HarperCollins, 2013), 11.
40 Murphy, *The Irish Brigades*, 218.

men, they were our people who thought as we did',[41] suggesting that they were either Protestants or were motivated by loyalty to Britain. However, analysis of the fifty-five Irish veteran testimonies in the Volunteer Archive tells a different story. Jeremy Jenkins has found that thirty-four per cent of the interviewees listed 'adventure' as their reason for enlisting, while only nine per cent mentioned 'affiliation to Britain' and a further two per cent giving 'help Britain' as their motivation for volunteering.[42] Ideological recruits comprised nineteen per cent of the total, partly confirming Roberts' assertion that the volunteers were 'not unsympathetic to the cause they were fighting for.'[43] When broken down into branches of service, the majority of those Eire volunteers who sought adventure in the British forces joined the RAF; those who were following a family tradition of service tended to join the army. The Royal Navy consistently lagged behind the other two services, except among recruits who self-identified as being ideologically motivated. In this group the RAF came first, the Royal Navy second and the army was the least popular destination. Further disproving Brooke's point, fifty-seven per cent of the interviewees were Catholic, with twenty-five per cent Church of Ireland, and the rest a combination of 'mixed faith', 'other faith' or provided no data.

One of the most remarkable facts about the volunteers was their ability to comfortably assimilate Irish neutrality with their service in British uniform. Of the fifty-five interviewees, twenty-two supported Eire's neutrality, thirteen disagreed while another sixteen ventured no opinion.[44] One RAF recruit from Clontarf in Dublin remarked that the destruction of town and villages he witnessed on the continent made him fully agree with Irish neutrality, as he did not wish to see the same fate befall his home city.[45]

---

41 Roberts, 'Neutrality, Identity', 279.
42 Jeremy Jenkins, '"This a private shindy or can any bloke join in?" Why neutral Irish volunteered for service in the British Forces during the Second World War', *The Irish Sword* XXVII/114 (2012), 419–54. Here 443.
43 Roberts, 'Neutrality, Identity', 280.
44 University College Cork Volunteer Archive Tape Summaries.
45 Bernard Kelly, *Returning Home: Irish Ex-servicemen After The Second World War* (Dublin: Merrion Press, 2012), 62.

Such convictions were probably strengthened by the extensive damage done by air attacks on Belfast and Dublin during the war. Four air attacks killed 1100 people in Belfast,[46] while thirty-four people died and three hundred dwellings were destroyed or damaged when German bombs hit Dublin's North Strand in May 1941.[47] As David Baynham, a Dublin-born volunteer in the Royal Engineers, said neutrality 'kept friends and relations safe when I was away.'[48] Ian Wood has quoted a volunteer as saying that southern Irish were 'keen to get into the fight while applauding de Valera's astuteness in keeping them out of the war.'[49] Eire volunteers consistently differentiated between Eire's neutrality from their own personal attitude towards the war. This attitude was perfectly summed up by Romie Lambkin, a Dublin woman who joined the ATS in 1941, who wrote in her diary regarding her enlistment that 'Even if Eire is staying neutral, I am not.'[50] Dermot Clarke, another Dubliner and a Merchant Navy seaman, declared that he was 'delighted' with neutrality, and that whereas de Valera may have kept Eire neutral, 'he didn't keep me out of the war.'[51] They may have supported Irish neutrality, but many were not personally neutral.

It was this combination of individual reasons for enlisting and their reaction to the manifestations of Irishness they encountered in the British forces that generated the unique sense of identity experienced by Irish volunteers in the Second World War. This had a profound effect on Irish recruits, particularly those who did not self-identify as Irish. Sam McAughtry, a self-described 'Protestant Loyalist, reared in the orange and purple'[52] from

---

46 Brian Barton, 'Northern Ireland: The Impact of War, 1939–45' in Brian Girvin and Geoffrey Roberts, eds, *Ireland in the Second World War: Politics, Society and Remembrance* (Dublin: Four Courts Press, 2000), 52.
47 Ian Wood, *Britain, Ireland and the Second World War* (Edinburgh: Edinburgh University Press, 2010), 151.
48 Volunteer Project Oral History Archive, Tape reference 3L, David Baynham.
49 Wood, *Britain, Ireland and the Second World* War, 152.
50 Romie Lambkin, *My Time in the War: An Irishwoman's Diary* (Dublin: Wolfhound Press, 1992), 5.
51 Volunteer Project Oral History Archive, Tape Reference S11, Dermot Clarke.
52 Sam McAughtry, *McAughtry's War* (Belfast: The Blackstaff Press, Belfast, 1985), 39. For more discussion of McAughtry's experiences, see Ian Wood's chapter in this collection.

Belfast who joined the RAF, recorded in his memoirs the culture shock he felt, particularly at being named 'Paddy': where he grew up 'Paddies tended to be as rare as crucifixes at the Presbyterian General Assembly.'[53] His book is an insightful and self-conscious account of his journey from a strong Ulster Protestant identity to a multi-polar sense of Irishness. McAughtry's world-view was transformed by 'the warm discovery of my Irishness' while training in England.[54] He went so far as to draw a red hand, the symbol of the ancient province of Ulster, on his helmet, in order to attract other Irish recruits to him: 'Drawn by the emblem of Ulster, people from home came up to me on station platforms and in transit camps halfway around the world, and introduced themselves to me as Irish.'[55] The full extent of McAughtry's acceptance of his Irishness can be seen in his use of the word 'home' to describe, not just Belfast or Northern Ireland, but the island of Ireland as a whole.

In another example, a Dublin-born Protestant volunteer, whose unionist family 'waved a Union Jack over my cot', was so delighted at suddenly being Irish that he sewed the words 'Southern Ireland' onto his Royal Engineers uniform.[56] But the process also worked the other way. In 1943, Dubliner Jack Harte was part of a British unit captured by the Germans on the Mediterranean island of Leros. While under guard on the Greek mainland, a German colonel addressed Jack and his other Irish comrades, saying that Germany had no quarrel with Ireland and asking for volunteers to partake in propaganda radio broadcasts. He was interrupted by the senior NCO, a Northern Irishman named 'Ducksy' Traynor, who 'told the colonel in his strongest Belfast accent to address us as *British* soldiers. Ducksy then walked among the ranks, reminding us that, Irish or not, we were enlisted British soldiers.'[57] Despite being hungry and dispirited, morale in the unit remained solid and they refused to cooperate. Jack displayed a remarkable ability to integrate the two sides of his military

---

53   McAughtry, *McAughtry's War*, 6.
54   Ibid., 7.
55   Ibid., 7.
56   Kelly, *Returning Home*, 46.
57   Harte, *To the Limits of Endurance*, 168.

identity: a proud Irishman, he made no secret of his nationality, but he also remained loyal to his British regiment when under pressure. Rather than diluting their sense of Irish identity, being surrounded by such overt symbols of Irishness served to concentrate it. As Brian Inglis pointed out in his memoirs, by the end of the war he felt 'more Irish – in the sense of thinking of myself as Irish – than when it began.'[58]

However, one stereotype which Irish volunteers consistently encountered was the supposed natural affinity of the Irish for war. James Corkery from Longford, who joined the RAF medical corps, remembered that his British colleagues occasionally remarked that 'Paddys [sic] like a fight'[59] and an American officer informed Sam McAughtry that 'The Irish have a special dispensation in this world, because they're good scrappers.'[60] In his victory broadcast to the nation in May 1945, Churchill also referred to this, mentioning the 'temper and instinct of thousands of Southern Irishmen who hastened to the battlefront to prove their ancient valour.'[61] The fact that men and women voluntarily left neutral Eire and chose to join the armed forces of a belligerent seemed to confirm the view that the Irish enjoyed soldiering. Cork-born author Paddy Galvin, who joined the RAF, was asked by his conscripted English friend 'I sometimes wonder why you joined this lot. Ireland is neutral, isn't it? ... I wouldn't join my hands, let alone the Armed Forces.'[62] Similarly, Dubliner Thomas Meehan, who served with the Royal Ulster Rifles, found that his British comrades thought he was 'mad' to volunteer for the war, while they were doing their best to avoid it.[63] Kilkenny native John Kelly was asked by some American troops he encountered if he was 'goddamn mad or something?' when he informed

58 Inglis, *West Briton*, 67.
59 Volunteers Project Oral History Archive, Tape A8, James Corkery.
60 McAughtry, *McAughtry's War*, 139.
61 Robert Fisk, *In Time of War: Ireland, Ulster and the Price of Neutrality* (Dublin: Gill & MacMillan, 1985), 538.
62 Patrick Galvin, *The Raggy Boy Trilogy* (Dublin: New Island, 2002), 283.
63 Volunteer Project Oral History Archive, no tape reference, Thomas Meehan.

them that he had left Ireland to enlist in the Irish Guards.[64] The Irish were not the only troops to be pigeonholed like this. As Terence Denman has observed, during the First World War Dominion soldiers were regarded as shock troops[65] and in the run-up to the battle of El Alamein, Bernard Montgomery remarked that Scottish and Dominion troops were compatible because 'both of them are slightly uncivilized.'[66]

Volunteer identity in post-war Ireland

The most obvious vehicle for Eire veterans to express their identity in Ireland after 1945 were commemorative ceremonies, which were largely coordinated by the British Legion. During the war, all public parades were banned and needed government permission to proceed, which was also the situation in Northern Ireland.[67] The annual Dublin Armistice Day parade from Smithfield market to the Islandbridge memorial park was not permitted during the war, although the commemoration ceremonies themselves were allowed to go ahead. The de Valera government also restricted the flying of British flags, the use of the 'V for Victory' sign[68] and curbed newspaper reports on the ceremonies.[69] The Minister for the Co-ordination of Defensive Measures, who also had responsibility for censorship, Frank Aiken justified a ban on newspaper advertisement for the poppy appeal by saying that it was prohibited 'in order to prevent the

---

64   Bernard Kelly, 'Prisoners of History: Irish Ex-Servicemen, Irish Society and the de Valera Government, 1945–1948', (PhD thesis, NUI Galway, 2009), 134.
65   Denman, 'Irish Catholic Soldiers', 363.
66   Glass, *Deserter*, 29.
67   Adrian Gregory, *The Silence of Memory: Armistice Day, 1919–1946* (Oxford: Berg, 1994), 191.
68   National Archives of Ireland, Department of the Taoiseach s3370D, Summary of restrictions on parades, 23 October 1948.
69   Ó Drisceoil, *Censorship in Ireland*, 109.

growth and development of such competitive organisations ... to the detriment of national unity.'[70] Dublin argued that the display of British symbols would breach neutrality, but after the war the Eire government remained deeply suspicious of ex-service organisations and their capacity to subvert de Valera's nationalist interpretation of Irish identity.

Controversially, in November 1945, the veteran's parade from Smithfield was once again prohibited. Minister for Justice Gerald Boland stated in the Dáil that the government was acting on police advice and feared an outbreak of violence similar to VE Day, which was marked in Dublin by riots centred on Trinity College where a group of students partially burned an Irish tricolour.[71] The next day, the windows of the British Representative's office and those of the US Consulate-General were smashed, leading the Secretary of External Affairs Joseph Walshe to apologise to both the British and American governments. Further flag-burning occurred in Sligo on VJ day.[72] The government dreaded a repeat of the violence and the international embarrassment which had followed. However, during the parliamentary debate on the 1945 parade ban, Boland's true attitude was inadvertently revealed when he stated that he was not 'trying to prevent these people honouring their dead',[73] a telling phrase which suggests that he viewed Irish veterans as outsiders. From 1946 to 1948, restrictions on the flying of flags and the singing of the British anthem at the Remembrance Sunday ceremonies continued. Often, the veterans themselves ignored the prohibitions. In December 1946, the Legion removed the British anthem from the ceremony, but the participants defiantly sang it anyway.[74] In addition, throughout his tenure as Taoiseach from 1932 to 1948 de Valera refused to send a government representative to Armistice ceremonies, despite being invited.

The de Valera government also remained extremely wary of the British Legion itself both during and after the war. G2, Irish military intelligence,

---

70   *Dáil Debates*, vol. 95, 9 November 1944, col. 797.
71   *Irish Press*, 8 May 1945.
72   *Evening Mail*, 21 August 1945.
73   *Dáil Debates*, vol. 98, 15 November 1945, col. 1247.
74   *British Legion Journal*, 26, 12, Irish Supplement, December 1946.

investigated the Legion in 1941 on the suspicion that it was assisting members of the Irish Defence Force to desert to the British forces.[75] In February 1946, Frank Aiken, by then Minister for Finance, forced the chairman of the Legion in Eire, A.P. Connolly, to resign from his post as a civil servant in the Revenue Commissioners, after Connolly had criticised the Irish government at a Legion conference in Belfast.[76] Surveying the position of the British Legion in Eire after the war, an anonymous official wrote that the government

> should not be too unhappy at the very defective manner in which the Legion is organised in this country. While not suggesting for a moment that Irish members of the Legion cannot be excellent Irishmen, the very raison d'etre of their membership rather suggests a qualification to their national sense and must, if only to a minute extent, act as a brake. To assume that those in charge of the British Legion will ever entirely abandon an effort to maintain alive some sense of loyalty to either Britain or the British Crown would be naïve and even a reformed Legion in this country would therefore always be somewhat of an exception to the ordinary course of national life. In so far as the Legion is a British influence here, the less active and effective it is, perhaps the better.[77]

Added to this was a note from John A Belton, the legal advisor to the Irish High Commission in London, expressing his view that 'It is, if course, a well-known but nonetheless deplorable fact that the administration of the British Legion in Ireland is entirely in the hands of a small Protestant and Freemason minority',[78] a dismissive attitude that mirrored Boland's.

From the 1940s until the mid-1990s, Irish veterans of the Second World War remained on the margins of Irish politics and society. Their position was complicated by the Northern Ireland conflict from 1968–69 onwards. Events such as Bloody Sunday, when British paratroopers killed thirteen

---

75   Maurice Walsh, *G2 In Defence of Ireland: Irish Military Intelligence 1918–45* (Cork: Collins Press, 2010), 268.
76   Kelly, *Returning Home*, 138.
77   National Archives of Ireland, Department of Foreign Affairs, 365/30 'The British Legion' unsigned memo, 4 September 1946.
78   National Archives of Ireland, Department of Foreign Affairs, 365/30 'The British Legion' letter from Belton to Walshe, undated.

civilians in Derry in 1972, made it difficult for veterans to celebrate British service during the war, or for the Irish public to commemorate Irish dead in either of the world wars. As a result, it became increasingly complicated for Irish veterans to openly express their identity. As one Dublin-born RAF recruit put it, in the aftermath of Blood Sunday, those fund-raising for the British Legion on the streets ran the risk of 'getting a firebomb or something thrown at you.'[79] However, once the Northern Ireland peace process began to gather momentum in the 1990s, the situation changed. Part of the process was a promise from the Dublin government to engage with the unionist/Protestant population of Northern Ireland and to acknowledge that there existed a legitimate British element to Irish identity. As a result of this, Irish participation in both world wars quickly became part of political discourse and was chosen by the Irish government as a way of demonstrating its commitment to the peace process.

In a groundbreaking speech at the Islandbridge war memorial in Dublin on 28 April 1995, Taoiseach John Bruton was the first Irish political leader to officially acknowledge the involvement of Irish citizens in the British forces during the Second World War. He estimated that 10,000 Irish volunteers had died during the conflict and he felt that 'In recalling their bravery, we are recalling a shared experience of Irish and British people ... We remember a British part of the inheritance of all who live in Ireland.'[80] During a Dáil debate on Northern Ireland in May 1995, Bruton explicitly placed his Islandbridge speech in the context of other measures his government was taking to drive the peace process forward, including the release of republican prisoners and talks with Sinn Fein.[81] In 1998, Irish president Mary McAleese and Queen Elizabeth unveiled a memorial at Messines, near Ypres, to the Irish dead of the First World War. Casualties from both North and South were included on the memorial and, significantly, the centrepiece of the monument was a round tower; like the shamrock and

---

79 Kelly, *Returning Home*, 143.
80 Geoffrey Roberts and Brian Girvin, 'The Forgotten Volunteers of World War II', *History Ireland*, 6/1 (Spring 1998), 46–51.
81 *Dáil Debates*, vol. 453, 17 May 1995, col. 82.

harps of the Irish regiments, the round tower is an uncontroversial but very recognisable symbol from Irish history.

The most remarkable step by the Irish government to rehabilitate Irish veterans of the Second World War was taken in June 2012 by the then Minister for Justice and Defence, Alan Shatter, when he announced that the government was issuing a pardon and apology to all Irish military personnel who had deserted from the Irish Defence Forces during the Second World War and joined the British forces. Approximately 6000 members of the Irish Defence Forces left their posts during the Second World War and an unknown number of these subsequently joined the British forces. In August 1945, under Emergency Powers Order no. 362, de Valera summarily dismissed all Irish military deserters who had been absent from 180 days or more, stripping them of their pay, allowances and gratuity from the day they deserted. They were also barred from government-funded employment for seven years. Public reaction to this in 1945 was muted and it remained a forgotten issue until a public campaign was started in 2006 to overturn it.

Like John Bruton, Shatter explicitly connected Eire volunteers to the idea of an overlapping Irish-British identity. Speaking in the Dáil, he said that 'at a time of greater insight and understanding of the shared history and experiences of Ireland and Britain, it is right that the role played by Irish veterans who fought on the Allied side be recognized.' Significantly, in a complete reversal of the de Valera government's attitude, Shatter noted that 'Those who fought on the Allied side also contributed to protecting this State's sovereignty and independence and our democratic values';[82] an official acknowledgement that Irish volunteers in the British forces felt they were defending Ireland while in British uniform, which mirrored the attitude to those volunteers who supported Irish neutrality. The widespread political and public approval of this demonstrates that the Irish veteran narrative of the Second World War, once so marginalised, has been fully assimilated into the Irish public's sense of self.

82   *Dáil Debates*, vol. 768, 12 June 2012, col.57.

Conclusion

Both before and during the Second World War, the British practice of allowing Irish volunteers to express their identity proved to be a successful tactic. The evidence suggests that Irish recruits embraced the concept, sometimes with great enthusiasm. The three-tiered approach of using neutral Irish symbols, acceptance of religious difference and the use of nicknames removed any tensions which may have existed between Irish volunteers. Allowing Irish recruits to express their identity was a potentially risky option, particularly seeing as Ireland has a consistent history of rebellion against British rule. As late as 1921, Irish rebels were in conflict with the British army in southern Ireland, yet the British military authorities were confident that their carefully calibrated Irish identity would function effectively. Moreover, it was recognised that the wholesale Anglicisation of Irish volunteers was liable to cause more problems than it solved. Imposing unfamiliar traditions, symbols or religion on Irish recruits would undoubtedly have proved to be counter-productive and would have resulted in far less Irish enlistments. The consistently high level of volunteers from Eire is testament to the success of the practice.

As for the volunteers themselves, the British forces provided an environment in which they could enjoy an Irish identity free of sectarian and political connotations. Veteran testimony shows that volunteers from Northern Ireland and Eire mixed with minimal problems. For instance, it allowed a Protestant from Belfast to rescue a Dublin-born RAF pilot from being attacked by two English soldiers; when the two soldiers informed the Belfast man that the target of their anger was a southern Catholic, he said 'It doesn't matter a damn, he's Irish.'[83]

From the perspective of the Dublin government, volunteers from Eire threatened the facade of Irish identity erected by de Valera during the war. The constant flow of men and women out of Eire to the British

---

83   Myles Dungan, *Distant Drums: Irish Soldiers in Foreign Armies* (Belfast: Appletree Press, 1993), 106.

forces, estimated by Irish military intelligence as 200 a week,[84] undermined Dublin's claims to be neutral, and the de Valera government went to great lengths to conceal just how many citizens had left to join the war. De Valera's version of Irish history, emphasising Irish distinctiveness from Britain and drawing an implausibly straight line from the 1916 rebellion to neutrality in 1939, was contradicted by the fact that Irish volunteers could comfortably express their identity while in the British forces. In addition, that some volunteers could both support neutrality and take an active part in the war made de Valera's formula for neutrality seem very parochial and narrow-minded.

The conflict in Northern Ireland and the subsequent peace process forced a reappraisal of Dublin's attitudes towards Irish veterans of both world wars. The policy of ignoring Irish service in the British forces was unsustainable, as it completely sidelined an important aspect of Irish military history and identity-making. The government was committed to the concept of recognising and engaging with the unionist tradition in Ireland – a complete reversal from the provisions of the 1937 constitution – and acknowledging Irish veterans of the Second World War was a perfect opportunity to do so. The lack of public resistance to government moves in this direction, the deserters' pardon in particular, shows that Irish veterans of the Second World War have completed a remarkable journey from the margins of Irish society to the very heart of Irish modern self-image.

---

84   National Archives of Ireland, Department of Foreign Affairs P81, 'Recruiting of Irishmen for the British Forces and Position re deserters from the Irish Army', Dan Bryan to Joseph Walshe, 12 January 1944.

IAN S. WOOD

Northern Ireland's War*

The Belfast writer Sam McAughtry was prompt to volunteer for military service when war came in 1939. He grew up in a fiercely Loyalist working class district, Tiger Bay, in the north of the city where there was a strong local tradition of joining the British forces and also the Merchant Navy. 'There were no pacifists in Cosgrave Street', he wrote later. 'We thought highly of the Crown forces. When World War Two was more than a year off the men of my district joined the Territorial Army in hundreds. The annual bounty of eight pounds or so helped, of course, but the men would have joined anyway.'[1] Sam McAughtry had 'a good war' and saw active aircrew service over North Africa and the Mediterranean but he also encountered what often seemed to him unthinking prejudice about where he was from at some of his postings in England: 'Oddly, coming from a district which had provided so many men for the King's colours, nobody had ever mentioned the fact that in the armed forces all Irishmen were Paddies, all the way up to and including officers.'[2] He learned to shrug this off but at one point a fellow Belfast recruit called Burgess was wrongly blamed for a fire in an aircraft hanger. A court martial loomed and McAughtry made it known he was willing to be a witness for his comrade. A Squadron Leader assigned to investigate the charge ascertained their origins and then put a question to them which enraged McAughtry. He asked them: 'Are your hearts in this war?' Just a month before, McAughtry's older brother, whom he idolised,

---

* The author would like to thank the staff of the Public Record Office of Northern Ireland in Belfast and the National Library of Scotland in Edinburgh for their invaluable help in accessing material for this chapter.
1 Sam M. McAughtry, *McAughtry's War* (Belfast: Blackstaff, 1985), 3.
2 *Ibid.*, 6.

had been lost at sea when his merchant vessel was torpedoed in the North Atlantic and his father was still serving there on convoy duty. He recalled telling his interlocutor: 'There's no conscription in Ireland, but we're here and there's not all that many English volunteers alongside Burgess and me, let me tell you.'[3] By no means all of the Loyalist community were as ready for military service as Sam McAughtry. Some of them thought the Irish Republican Army (henceforth IRA), with its commitment to an armed struggle to end the partition of Ireland, was as great an enemy as the Third Reich. When he returned to Belfast after his demobilisation McAughtry was approached by an acquaintance in a North Belfast pub who had seen out the war at home in the Royal Ulster Constabulary (henceforth RUC). After a drink he handed McAughtry an application form for the force's B-Special Reserve, with the words 'That's in case there's a real war.'[4]

Answering the Call

Twenty years into the existence of the devolved mini-state of Northern Ireland, sectarian fault-lines ran deep. They were endemic to the very nature of the devolved mini-state brought to birth in 1920 amidst a bloodbath of communal violence when the Government of Ireland Act enacted a partitionist settlement in which a six-county northern statelet, along with the rest of the island, was accorded internal self-government. This violence returned to Belfast's streets in July 1935 when the army had to be deployed there in support of the RUC to control riots which took twelve lives and left many hundreds of people injured and homeless. The IRA also re-appeared,

---

3   *Ibid.*, 22.
4   *Ibid.*, 170, also quoted in Maurice Goldring, *Belfast: From Loyalty to Rebellion* (London: Lawrence and Wishart, 1991), 97.

claiming to be acting in defence of nationalist areas of the city.⁵ 1935 in economic terms was Northern Ireland's lowest point, with over 100,000 of its insured workforce registered as unemployed. Three years earlier many of them had marched in protest at the starvation rates of outdoor relief paid by Belfast's Board of Guardians. Catholics and Protestants united briefly in this campaign but the Stormont government's response was to rely on the guns, batons and armoured cars of the RUC.⁶ When war came in 1939 the working class population of Belfast and elsewhere was still ravaged by unemployment, substandard housing and tuberculosis.

Serving members of the RUC were, it must be said, forbidden at the outbreak of war to enlist in the armed forces. This was a decision taken by the Stormont government at a time when the IRA had already declared war against Britain and was setting off bombs in English cities while its active membership across Northern Ireland had been placed on a war footing. The Public Security Ministry took the view that: 'in total war sentiment and prestige must give way to the National Interest and that trained members of the Royal Ulster Constabulary would be giving greater service to the war effort by remaining at their posts and ensuring peace and security at home than by joining the fighting services.'⁷ The Ministry backed its decision with the assertion that 'A large number of the younger and more active officers and men would have joined the services had this been permitted. It would have left a depleted force of elderly men excellent in every way but not so suitable for dealing with armed aggression [from the IRA] as the younger men.'⁸ These reflections by the Ministry date to late in the war and its assertions or indeed assumptions about the readiness of RUC men to enlist of course cannot be tested. There certainly seems to be no record of those who resigned from the force in order to do so.

---

5   Conor Foley, *Legion of the Rearguard: The IRA and the Modern Irish State* (London: Pluto, 1992), 156.
6   Ronald Munck and William Rolston, *Belfast in the Thirties: an Oral History* (Belfast: Blackstaff, 1987), 27–40.
7   Public Record Office of Northern Ireland (PRONI), CAB 3A/77.
8   *Ibid.*

Enlistment in Northern Ireland in 1939 was a choice since the Chamberlain government's conscription legislation did not apply there. Lord Craigavon, the Stormont Prime Minister, however saw the adoption of conscription as a necessary proof of the province's loyalty to the Crown. He was strongly supported by a ministerial colleague, Sir Basil Brooke, who blamed the Chamberlain government for overruling his own leader on the issue. Writing in his constituency newspaper he attributed London's weakness to 'the presence in our midst of a minority who, whilst prepared to share in the benefits of empire were either afraid or too despicable to take a hand in the defence of the country who defended them and were prepared to go to any length to prevent loyal and brave men from doing their duty.'[9] Brooke had served with distinction in the First World War and his family's military reputation was legendary but when he became Prime Minister of Northern Ireland in April 1943 there was still no prospect of conscription in the province. As his predecessor put it in a press interview the year before: 'Our view remains unchanged but we accepted the decision [by the Churchill government] as we were constitutionally bound to.'[10]

Tensions over enlistment

Not all Ulster Unionists were like Sir Basil Brooke or his sons, two of whom were killed in action during the war. For example, Brian Faulkner, who became the province's last Prime Minister prior to the imposition of direct rule by Britain in March 1972, did not even consider joining up in 1940 when he gave up his law degree at Queen's University. Instead, he became a manager in his father's shirt factory as it went over to seven days a week working to meet lucrative wartime contracts for the forces. Years later

---

9 Brian Barton, *Northern Ireland in the Second World War* (Belfast: Ulster Historical Foundation, 1995), 118–19.
10 *Glasgow Herald*, 29 January 1942; see also PRONI, CAB 3/C/1A.

and with some cynicism, he sought to justify his action: 'It was of course my own decision to stay in the family factory and, in retrospect, it was a foolish one. The only service to the country that many people recognised was service in the armed forces. So medals and military rank were valuable assets for political advancement in the post-war world and lack of either was a serious obstacle to overcome.'[11]

No such self-serving considerations seemed to figure in the readiness to enlist of Sam McAughtry and his neighbours in Tiger Bay, but their enthusiasm was not replicated across the Unionist and Loyalist community. Even in what was then the Unionist citadel of Queen's University, its Vice-Chancellor Sir David Lindsay Keir felt the need to send out to all staff and undergraduates a letter urging them to join up. The Mass Observation diarist, Belfast-based Moya Woodside reported, in March 1940, that this appeal was resented by friends who taught at Queen's. She quotes one of them saying to her that 'if the Vice-Chancellor wished to turn the university into a recruiting station it would have been better to close the place down altogether and refuse to accept male students for the duration.'[12] This view had some logic but Woodside also quoted others voicing their preference for conscription which would place their university on the same footing as others in the rest of the United Kingdom. These students could either volunteer for an early call-up or pursue their studies over a period of deferment until their turn came.[13] Conscription, however, was never going to happen. Both the Chamberlain and Churchill governments had already decided against it because of the resentment it would cause within the province's nationalist community, a resentment both fuelled and given voice by their church leaders and by the de Valera government in Dublin.

Even enlisting in the Air Raid Precautions service, the ARP, could expose people in the nationalist community to real hostility. The novelist Brian Moore captured this perfectly when he later wrote about the 1941

---

11   Brian Faulkner, *Memoirs of a Statesman*, ed. J. Houston (London: Weidenfeld and Nicolson, 1978), 13–14.
12   Mass Observation (MO), Moya Woodside, *Diaries*, 10 March 1940.
13   *Ibid.*

Belfast blitz. His young hero, Gavin Burke, appeared at his middle class Catholic home in his ARP uniform only to be at once berated by an aunt: 'Gracious God, did I ever think I'd live to see the day when my own nephew would stand in this room dressed up like a Black and Tan.' The aunt then appealed to his mother: 'Surely you realise that these ARP places will be filled with the scum of the Orange Lodges. Are those the sort of companions you want for a boy of his age?'[14]

Home Guard service was also affected by Northern Ireland's deep ethno-political divisions. The 1940 Order in Council authorising the formation of the precursor of the Home Guard, the Local Defence Volunteers, did not apply to the province, though the Stormont authorities were urged to follow the London government's example. When it did so, the Prime Minister, Lord Craigavon, insisted that the new force be based on the RUC's B Special reserve, a body distrusted by the nationalist community. This could only make the Ulster Home Guard seem a sectarian force and Moya Woodside stressed in her diary how few Catholics were joining it. She claimed that the original Queen's University LDV was discouraging Catholics from joining: 'Craigavon and co prefer to play the party game and continue to cold-shoulder Catholics, many of whom are anxious and willing to undertake National Service, while at the same time reproaching them with lack of interest and non-cooperation.'[15] The following year, the new Stormont Prime Minister told critics of Home Guard recruitment that 'the force had not been raised on a political basis or a religious basis but on a basis of loyalty.'[16] Jack Beattie, a Labour member of the Stormont parliament argued that the only way the force could represent both communities would be to transfer responsibility for it from the B-Specials to the army.[17] His case cut no ice with the Unionists and when the British Home Secretary, Sir John Anderson, looked into the matter he concluded that no action by Whitehall was worthwhile and that most of the minority

---

14 Brian Moore, *The Emperor of Ice Cream* (London: Andre Deutsch, 1966), 165–6.
15 MO, Moya Woodside, *Diaries*, 20 October 1940.
16 *Irish News*, 26 February 1941.
17 *Ibid.*

community would distrust the Home Guard however it was formed and recruited.

Recruitment to the fire service, known as the Auxiliary Fire Service, also came under sectarian scrutiny after the decision was taken to expand it rapidly in anticipation of a repetition of the Luftwaffe's Easter 1941 blitz on Belfast. The Public Security Ministry came under pressure in Parliament over the need to exclude 'undesirables' and to recruit 'loyal Ulstermen.' In June 1943 it admitted it had been accepting 'men of good character even though they had not been born and bred in Ulster' but it agreed to try from then on to maximise the intake of loyal elements from within the six counties.[18]

A full eight months before Britain's declaration of war the IRA itself had gone on to a war footing and on 12 January 1939 its army council wrote to the Foreign Office in London demanding a final British withdrawal from Ireland. Four days later it launched its first bomb attacks on targets in English cities. The organisation had its own Northern Command with jurisdiction over its units in the six counties and Donegal and it claimed to have five hundred active volunteers in Belfast alone,[19] despite years of surveillance and arrests by the RUC. They launched attacks on police and army targets at a level which they proved unable to sustain once war came but as Hitler's armies swept through the Low Countries and France in the spring of 1940, Northern Command issued a call to the 'Men of Ireland' to resist conscription. They claimed recruitment in the north to be at a standstill and that Lord Craigavon was putting to Churchill the case for the call-up to be extended to Northern Ireland. This was close enough to the truth and the statement finished by declaring that 'Only the strength of the IRA stands between you and conscription.'[20]

Conscription, as we have seen, was not on Churchill's agenda, even though voluntary enlistment drew only a minority response within the nationalist community and did not over-enthuse the Unionist majority

18 Ibid., 5 June 1943.
19 Ibid., 193.
20 PRONI, HA/20A/1/24.

either. For many there was still the long shadow of the Somme and Ulster's dramatic loss of life there in 1916 as well as the bitter memory of sacrifice rewarded only by the unemployment and poverty of the inter-war years. Even a generation earlier, doubts had been there among some of them about 'the other side taking over' if they gave up secure jobs to enlist. The reality of such fear was still accepted by Ulster Unionists late on in the Second World War[21] and for many Orangemen the best bet seemed to remain loyally at home. The fact that they did this was of course seized on by commentators hostile to Loyalism. They pointed out that the suspension early on in the war of Orange Order parades like the iconic commemoration of King William of Orange's July 1690 victory at the Boyne, served to conceal just how many Orangemen of military age were still at home.[22] Later on, as parades resumed, the nationalist press was quick to make exactly the same point.[23]

Going to war

None of this takes anything from the contribution to Britain's war effort made by those from Northern Ireland who did choose to enlist in its forces. Partition in 1920 dealt a potentially serious blow to a long tradition of all-Ireland recruitment to the British army. Historic regiments recruited from, and based in, what became the new Free State were disbanded. Those that remained were ones based in what became Northern Ireland, among them the Royal Ulster Rifles, the Royal Irish Fusiliers and the Royal Inniskilling Fusiliers and the Dragoon Guards regiment raised from the area around

---

21 PRONI, DL327/7, Minutes of Ulster Unionist Party Standing Committee, 11 April, 10 November 1944, 9 February 1945.
22 Barton, *Northern Ireland in the Second World War*, 13.
23 *Irish News*, 10 July 1944.

the same town of Enniskillen.²⁴ The Irish Guards, raised only in 1900, were based in or near London.

Economies after the First World War affected the army as a whole and the Royal Inniskilling and Royal Irish Fusiliers as well as the Irish Guards were reduced to single battalion strength. Recruitment in Northern Ireland suffered initially from the effects of partition but it recovered, almost certainly helped by the level of unemployment. In March 1936 the War Office's Adjutant-General was able to report that the annual average intake of infantry recruits in Northern Ireland, which numbered 690 men, was enough to man six battalions instead of four.²⁵ Following upon this, the Royal Inniskilling and Royal Irish Fusiliers had their second battalions reconstituted the following year, as did the Irish Guards in 1939.

Not all this recruitment was from Northern Ireland. The Irish Free State, or Eire, as it became under the 1937 constitution, remained part of a Common Travel Area within the British Commonwealth and movement across the border to seek work or to enlist in the British forces was never a problem. Before and during the war army depots in Northern Ireland simply could not accept all the young men from across the border who offered themselves for service. Recruiting sergeants with the Royal Ulster Rifles and the Royal Inniskillings indeed could take pity on some of those they had to interview: 'Each day there were four, five, six boys from the South of Ireland came over the border, some of them literally in their bare feet, because at that time there was very little work in the South.' One of them recalled some of the hopeful recruits as being 'small, under-nourished, with a hint of desperation.'²⁶

Many from Northern Ireland also made the decision to cross the water in order to enlist and some when they joined up in Belfast were, like Sam McAughtry, at once assigned to units based in England. This all complicates

---

24 The army always used Inniskilling which was how the town was known when the regiments were raised.
25 Thomas S. Bartlett and Keith Jeffery, *A Military History of Ireland* (Cambridge: Cambridge University Press, 1996), 437.
26 Richard Doherty, *Irish Men and Women in the Second World War* (Dublin: Four Courts Press, 1989), 42–3.

immensely the whole issue of recruitment in Northern Ireland and demands caution in response to claims from Loyalist and Unionist sources about the province's response to the call for volunteers from 1939 onwards. As mentioned already, some army battalions were reconstituted there as war approached, recruitment began for an anti-aircraft artillery brigade in 1939, two new battalions of the Royal Ulster Rifles were raised for home defence in September of that year and in 1940 a new battalion of the Royal Inniskilling Fusiliers started to recruit.[27]

Early in 1942 the *Belfast Telegraph* sent one of its staff to report under a headline called 'Ulster Tommies serving in England.'[28] The unit he visited was one of two new battalions of the Royal Ulster Rifles raised after the outbreak of war. He found them at an unnamed location, training hard under a commanding officer who had served in the ranks before being commissioned. He was from an old Cork family and was a fluent Irish speaker: 'As his new command contains a good proportion of men from over the border the ranker CO is in the happy position of knowing all the answers in both languages.' The report went on to describe Lurgan as the best represented town in the unit, with Newry, Derry City, Ballymoney and the Shankill 'well to the fore.'[29] Even so enlistment never went anywhere near First World War levels. There was an initial spurt in September and October 1939 and again after Dunkirk the following year but over the whole of 1941 and 1942 it only exceeded the figure of a thousand a month three times.[30] This leaves out those born in Northern Ireland who had moved to mainland Britain before the war and thus became liable for conscription there, or indeed those of Ulster parentage born in England or Scotland.

Churchill was much given to rhetoric about the ancient valour of the Irish in Britain's cause and in 1942 he threw his weight behind the formation of a designated Irish brigade though John Andrews, the Stormont Prime Minister, sensed a sinister all-Ireland agenda was involved. Indeed, he wrote

27 Bartlett and Jeffery, *A Military History of Ireland*, 437–8.
28 *Belfast Telegraph*, 4 February 1942; also PRONI CAB 3/1/C/1.
29 Ibid.
30 Bartlett and Jeffery, *A Military History of Ireland*, 438.

to Clement Attlee, Churchill's deputy, condemning what he claimed was a move 'calculated to obliterate or blur the distinction between the belligerency of Northern Ireland and the neutrality of Eire.'[31] He was overruled and an existing brigade was simply re-numbered as the 38th Irish Brigade, comprising, apart from logistic and support troops, battalions of the Royal Ulster Rifles, the Royal Inniskilling Fusiliers and the London Irish Rifles, the latter a Territorial unit which recruited among young Irishmen living and working in London.[32]

How Irish were Irish regiments?

By the time that this new brigade was assigned to the British First Army in Tunisia, the Irish and Ulster composition of the units which comprised it was already being substantially diluted. Assigning to them conscripts with no connections to either Northern Ireland or Eire was a matter of necessity in order to bring them up to combat strength but the strong nucleus of Eire and Ulster volunteers in each of the brigade's battalions contributed to the high morale they showed during some brutal fighting amongst the almost impassable tracks and razor-back ridges around Medjez-el-Bab. This, in the eyes of Rommel's Afrika Korps, was Tunisia's Siegfried Line which had to be breached before the Allies could advance on Tunis itself. It was in the midst of this bloodbath that a member of the First Battalion of the Irish Guards won the Victoria Cross. This was Lance Corporal John Kenneally, a bren-gunner who, on 29 April 1943, despite already being wounded in the battle for Hill 212, refused to hand over his weapon and fought on.

---

31 PRONI, CAB 9CD/85/8, Andrews to Attlee, 23 January 1942. See also Robert Fisk, *In Time of War, Ireland, Ulster and the Price of Neutrality* (London: Paladin, 1983), 525.
32 Ian S. Wood, ''Twas England Bade Our Wild Geese Go: Soldiers of Ireland in the Second World War', in Paul Addison and Angus Calder, eds, *Time to Kill: The Soldiers' Experience of War in the West 1939–1945* (London: Pimlico, 1997), 82.

A regimental history later described how 'His extraordinary gallantry in attacking single-handed a massed body of the enemy and breaking up an attack on two occasions was an achievement that can seldom have been equalled.'[33]

Late on in the war the Stormont government published a booklet entitled *Volunteers from Eire Who Have Won Distinctions Serving With the British Force*.[34] It was very likely a calculated attempt to embarrass a Dublin government which was and remained in denial about its own citizens who had chosen to join in Britain's war while their state was neutral. One of the names it included was that of Lance Corporal Kenneally, but in fact there was nothing Irish about him. He was born out of wedlock in Birmingham in 1921, the son of a Jewish father, and was brought up in a tough area of the city by his mother, who changed her surname to Jackson. In 1939 he joined the Honourable Artillery Company but as a result of overstaying his leave he found himself serving a spell of detention at Wellington Barracks in London where the Irish Guards were based. He was so impressed by them that he tried to join them. On being refused a transfer he deserted temporarily and found work with a group of Irish building labourers. One of them gave him the identity card and National Insurance number of John Patrick Kenneally, a fellow worker who had returned home. With this documentation and a new name he was in due course accepted by the Irish Guards. He later recalled joining a training quad of twenty one recruits: 'We came from all points of the compass, Southern and Northern Irish, Liverpool, Manchester, Geordies, Londoners and one young Welshman from the valley by the name of Bryn Morris. How he ever came to join the Irish Guards I never knew but he turned out to be as good a Mick as any of us.'[35] By early 1943 Kenneally was in the regiment's First Battalion on a troopship sailing for Tunisia. The battalion left all too many crosses behind them there, inscribed with the words *Quis Seperabit*,

---

33 Desmond J.L. Fitzgerald, *A History of the Irish Guards in the Second World War* (Aldershot: Gale and Polden, 1949), 183.
34 PRONI, CAB 3F/1/5.
35 John P. Kenneally, *Kenneally VC: the True Story of a Remarkable Life* (Huddersfield: Kenwood, 1991), 44–5. See also *Times* obituary, 28 September 2000.

the regimental motto. The 38th Brigade's losses had been so heavy that, even as new drafts arrived from home, there was talk within the British command of disbanding one of its battalions, the Second London Irish Rifles. The Commanding Officer, Brigadier Nelson Russell, opposed this, urging the case for his brigade's identity to be maintained even if it meant bringing in replacements from non-Irish units, preferably men with some Irish ancestry. As he put it, an Irish stepfather would be good enough and the spirit of his three battalions would do the rest.[36]

Even as the intakes of non-Irish recruits grew, so did the preoccupation on the part of regiments with the symbols of their Irishness. The Irish Guards First Battalion, unlike the 38th Brigade, were not deployed in the attritional fighting which was needed to clear the Germans from Sicily but in January 1944 they were part of the invasion force that sailed for Anzio, piped on to their landing craft with martial Irish airs like *The Minstrel Boy* and *The Wearing of the Green*. Among them was former Lance Corporal Kenneally, who had been made a sergeant after the award of his Victoria Cross, and Father J.R. Brookes, Catholic chaplain to the battalion.

The latter was a legendary figure who had served with the regiment as a junior officer in the 1914–18 war prior to entering the priesthood in 1925. His bonhomie and seemingly imperturbable courage under fire earned him the esteem of the whole battalion, Catholics and non-Catholics alike. What he experienced at Anzio, he later said, was worse than anything he saw on the Western Front a generation earlier.[37] The rationale for the landing had been to breach the Germans' Gustav Line, thus isolating their stronghold at Monte Cassino in order to open the road north to Rome. With bolder leadership and more resources this might have been achieved. Instead the British and American landing force found itself besieged within a confined and vulnerable beachhead from which it took four months to break out at appalling cost. Anzio, and especially an area eight miles inland, known on

---

36 Richard Doherty, *Clear the Way: a History of the 38th (Irish) Brigade 1941–7* (Dublin: Blackrock, 1993), 42.
37 Carlo D'Este, *Fatal Decision: Anzio and the Battle for Rome* (London: HarperCollins, 1991), 150. See also Fitzgerald, *History of the Irish Guards*, 243.

unit maps as the Gullies, a confusing complex of deep, overgrown channels and ravines perfect for defence by the Germans, virtually destroyed the battalion. What was left of it was finally relieved after seven weeks by another battalion whose commanding officer watched in awe as ragged and gaunt survivors stumbled past him on their way to the rear: 'As the tall Guardsmen filed out', he later wrote, 'leaving us the heritage of death and desolation they had borne so long, a peculiar sense of isolation struck us. In all the long crucifixion of the beach-head, no positions saw such sublime self-sacrifice and such hideous slaughter as was perpetrated in the overgrown foliage that sprouted in the deep gullies.'[38]

When the Guards landed at Anzio their battalion strength had been 1,080 officers and other ranks but when they were shipped out on 7 March 1944 there were just 267 left. Many of them were too drained physically and mentally for further combat and the battalion was disbanded. Some recovered sufficiently to form a composite company which, after the liberation of Rome in June, was received by the Pope at the Vatican for a special blessing.[39] A significant number of them, including the indestructible Sergeant Kenneally, got transfers to the regiment's two other battalions and saw more action in France and Germany in 1944 and 1945.

In tandem with the protracted struggle to achieve a breakout from Anzio was the onslaught on the tenaciously held German position on Monastery Hill above the town of Monte Cassino. The 38th Brigade, which had seen fierce fighting in Sicily, was at least rested out of the line before being committed to battle. This gave time for all ranks, whether Irish or not, to celebrate St Patrick's Day. The 6th Inniskilling Fusiliers led the way with a party and ceilidh that took on a life of its own. The battalion war diary records a flow of St Patrick's Day greetings being sent out by telegram to King George VI, the Duke of Gloucester, the regiment's Colonel-in-Chief,

---

38   Fitzgerald, *History of the Irish Guards*, 356.
39   Peter Verney, *The Micks: the Story of the Irish Guards* (London: Peter Davies, 1970), 138.

the Catholic and Church of Ireland Primates of Ireland, numerous generals and not least the Irish Taoiseach, Eamon de Valera.[40]

Monte Cassino was a season in hell for all who endured it. Digging in on rock-hard ground was almost impossible and survival could depend on improvised sangers or stone shelters which, if well enough camouflaged, might deceive enemy gunners. Nonetheless, the pressure that the Irish battalions put on the Germans in relentless close quarter fighting helped make their position untenable, though it fell to the Polish Corps to storm the monastery itself, or what was left of it. One of the brigade's Catholic chaplains, Father Don Kelleher, from Kerry, won a Military Cross for the selfless help he gave under fire to the wounded.[41] Victory at Cassino opened the way to Rome's liberation on 4 June and a representative 38th Brigade group paraded six days later on St Peter's Square for a Papal blessing. This may well have been received by some loyal Orangeman, for Ulster sectarianism had arguably come to mean little to soldiers recruited from both sides of the border, as well as to expatriate Irishmen recruited in Britain, along with those who were not Irish at all. At the Pope's request the brigade's pipers and drummers in their distinctive caubeens and saffron kilts then formed up in the square to entertain him and some Irish priests with traditional airs and marches.[42]

---

40 Doherty, *Clear the Way*, 116. See also 'War Diaries of 6 Royal Inniskilling Fusiliers', *Irish Brigade. The Story of the 38th (Irish) Brigade in the Second World War*, <http://www.irishbrigade.co.uk/pages/original-war-diaries---1942-to-1945/war-diaries-of-6-royal-inniskilling-fusiliers.php> accessed 24 May 2014.
41 Colin Gunner, *Front of the Line: Adventures with the Irish Brigade* (Antrim: Greystone Books, 1991), 81.
42 Doherty, *Clear the Way*, 159–60.

Eire and Ulster: Who gave more?

By 1944, therefore, the brigade was an integral part of Britain's Eighth Army in its grinding and bloody advance up Italy to the plains of Lombardy and the river Po. There the Germans prepared well for one of their last major defensive battles in the West. A Church of Ireland rector's son, Brian Harpur, born in Dublin but educated at Portora school in Northern Ireland, was there to observe the preparations for a battle in which he played a full part. Though commissioned in the Middlesex Regiment he later wrote of how 'The Irish turned up in force. Not only were there battalions of the Royal Inniskilling Fusiliers and the London Irish Rifles carrying the fighting traditions of the historic Irish brigade but there were the North Irish Horse and thousands of Irishmen from the 'neutral' South who had infiltrated every unit in the country – all keen to get into the fight while applauding de Valera's astuteness in keeping them out of the war.'[43] The Irish 'turned up' on other fronts, like Normandy where the Irish Guards were represented by two battalions as were the Royal Ulster Rifles. Its Second Battalion fought its way ashore on D-Day as part of the 3rd Division and suffered heavy losses in the fighting needed to open the road to Caen. Prior to D-Day it had been inspected by King George VI who commented on the number of Eire men serving in an Ulster battalion.[44] He could equally have commented on the number who had neither Irish nor Ulster connections.

Path-breaking research by Yvonne McEwen into the composition of these battalions has cast important new light on Northern Ireland's war where the still contentious issue of recruitment is concerned. She shows that in fact there was not a significant difference in army recruitment from Northern Ireland and Eire to recognisably Irish and/or Ulster regiments and to regiments based in England like the Irish Guards, the London Irish

---

43 Brian Harpur, *The Impossible Victory: a Personal Account of the Battle for the River Po* (London: Granada Books, 1980), 169.
44 Alexander E.C. Bredin, *A History of the Irish Soldier* (Belfast: Century Books, 1978), 510.

Rifles and the 8th Battalion of the King's (Liverpool) Regiment. In total, her figures show that there were 38,000 enlistments from Northern Ireland, including 7000 women, and of this total there were those who opted for and were accepted by the Royal Navy and the Royal Air Force. She has estimated that between 38,000 and 42,000 Eire volunteers joined the British forces though it may of course have included those resident in Northern Ireland or on mainland Britain when they joined up.[45] Equally, her figures have not covered those of Irish or Ulster parentage already living and working in Britain when war came in 1939, such as Brian Harpur, whose graphic account of the Eighth Army's storming of the Germans' River Po defences in April 1945 has already been referred to.

At the end of hostilities in 1945 the Irish consulate in New York concocted a recruitment figure more than five times larger than the total now generally accepted for those from Eire who served in the British forces. Over time these claims were discredited yet even the possibility that Eire might have provided as many or even more volunteers than 'loyal Ulster' became a matter of obsessive anxiety to some Unionist politicians. With the war still on the Stormont government asked all the service departments in London to work through their files to quantify the national origins of those serving. It was always a mean-minded and sterile argument and one unworthy of those who enlisted in or were called up to the Irish and Ulster regiments and paid the ultimate price. As McEwen demonstrates, in not a single one of the ten regiments whose fatalities in the war she has examined was even half the number killed Irish. In the case of the Royal Inniskilling Fusiliers, the regiment with the largest death toll in the war, a total of 1152 men killed, 509 came from Eire and Northern Ireland. This in fact was easily the highest figure. All of the regiments had to dilute their Irish and Ulster recruitment just as Scottish regiments had to reach out beyond the border as the war took its toll. Her research shows that from the island of Ireland as a whole 4543 were killed on service with the British army, 2302 from what had become Eire and 2241 from Northern

---

45 Yvonne McEwen, 'Deaths in Irish Regiments 1939–1945 and the Extent of Irish Volunteering for the British Army', *Irish Sword*, XXIV/95, (2004), 84.

Ireland.⁴⁶ This, like those who survived, included men who opted to serve with units which had no obvious Irish or Ulster connection. Some, like the legendary and much decorated Robert Blair Mayne, or Paddy Mayne as he came to be known, joined up with local regiments and then moved elsewhere. Mayne, a Protestant born and brought up in Newtonards in County Down would, even without the war, have been remembered as a sportsman and Irish rugby internationalist. When war came he joined the Royal Ulster Rifles and then transferred into what became the Special Air Service. His daring exploits behind enemy lines in North Africa targeted at German airfields destroyed more aircraft then any single allied pilot in the whole war. He also served with distinction in Sicily, Italy and North-West Europe, finishing the war as a lieutenant-colonel with three bars to the DSO medal awarded him for his part in operations in Sicily.⁴⁷ There were others like him, from both sides of the border, who volunteered for aircrew duty with the RAF. Brian Moore, in his novel set in wartime Belfast, gives us the case of one optimistic recruit to the RAF, a product of the city's nationalist middle class. At a school reunion he asks the novel's narrator, 'So you think anyone ever joins up for purely patriotic reasons, even the English? Fellows join up because they want to leave home, have some excitement, stuff girls, and so on.' Becoming more eloquent at the bar, he goes on to tell his listeners that women in England are as 'hot as coals' and that 'at least I won't die wrestling to get my man between the thighs of some cold Irish virgin. This uniform is going to liberate me.'⁴⁸

The first RAF pilot to be killed in the war was Edmund Sorley from South Armagh. He was shot down on 4 September 1939, the second day of the war, during an attack on German ships at Brunsbuttel.⁴⁹ Another recruit from Northern Ireland was James Molyneaux, later to become leader of the Ulster Unionist Party. He was motivated to join the RAF

---

46 *Ibid.*, 88.
47 Roy Bradford and Martin Dillon, *Rogue Warrior of the SAS: Lt.Col 'Paddy' Blair Mayne DSO* (London: Murray, 1987).
48 Moore, *The Emperor of Ice Cream*, 169.
49 Doherty, *Irish Men and Women*, 104.

in response to the 1941 blitz on Belfast and in April 1945 he was with one of its ground units which entered Belsen after the camp's liberation, the memory of which never left him.⁵⁰ Over a thousand men and women from Northern Ireland were killed on active service with the RAF which maintained a substantial presence there because of the strategic and tactical requirements of the Battle of the Atlantic. So, of course, did the Royal Navy from whose ranks emerged Northern Ireland's best-known hero of the war, Leading Seaman James Magennis, VC. He was a Catholic from West Belfast who attended St Finian's boys' school where the Sinn Fein president Gerry Adams would later be a pupil. He joined the navy as a boy recruit in 1935 when work in the area was hard to get. A friend later recalled that in his street and two others close to it a dozen other boys also joined the navy before and during the war.⁵¹ As an ordinary seaman Magennis saw major action on destroyers in the North Sea and in the Mediterranean before transferring to the submarine service. Once in it he volunteered for training on midget submarines and in July 1945 he was a crew member of one of these vessels on a hazardous operation in Singapore harbour. In a display of extraordinary courage he helped fit limpet mines to a Japanese battle cruiser, disabling it and earning himself the Victoria Cross. Usually VC winners were awarded the freedom of the town or city from which they came but the then permanent majority on Belfast's city council avoided doing this because Magennis was a Catholic. Instead they held a civic reception for Magennis on his return to Belfast on leave and set up an appeal for him, or 'shilling fund' as they called it, to which citizens were invited to contribute rather than the council as a corporate body. As Magennis's biographer later put it in a newspaper article: 'They might as well have attended Mass at St Peter's on the Falls Road as award the Freedom [of the city] to a Catholic from West Belfast.'⁵²

50   Ann Purdie, *James Molyneaux: The Long View* (Antrim: Greystone, 1989), 29–30.
51   George Fleming, *Magennis VC: the Story of Northern Ireland's Only Winner of the Victoria Cross* (Dublin: History Ireland, 1998), 40.
52   *Irish News*, 2 June 2004.

Coolness to Leading Seaman Magennis went beyond official and Unionist Northern Ireland. He soon encountered it in the area where he had grown up in nationalist West Belfast just off the Falls Road. A pupil at St Finian's recalled the scene when the uniformed hero arrived at his old school accompanied by his mother, a naval officer and council representatives. When the teacher opened the door for the visitors:

> Nobody rose: we sat and we watched in awe as the naval officer told us in a swanky English accent what we already knew. Young Magennis smiled inoffensively and said he was glad to be back in his old school and the party left to visit another class ... I remember feeling proud that I was Irish and that I hadn't honoured King and country by standing up, but there lingered an uneasy feeling inside me that I had hurt the poor young lad Magennis in some way and for years afterwards I could still see his kind, smiling face and his elderly mother by his side as we sat stubbornly in our seats.[53]

James Magennis left the navy in 1949 and returned to Belfast but there was no welcome for him in his native city. He was resented within his own community for his service in the British forces and when he moved to predominantly Loyalist East Belfast he was resented for being a Catholic. As his biographer put it, the unease towards him manifested in his old school 'was hardening into something else, as attitudes in Northern Ireland themselves hardened.'[54] He left for good with his family, settling in Bradford, Yorkshire, and dying in Halifax in 1986. His passing and his bravery was marked by a large memorial service in Bradford's cathedral. A small photograph of Magennis was displayed in Belfast City Hall, overshadowed by large portraits of mostly Unionist dignitaries but in 1999 a proper memorial to him, funded from National Lottery money, was finally dedicated in the grounds of the city hall. There was a large attendance but, five years into the Provisional IRA's ceasefire, Sinn Fein declined to be present. One of its spokesmen told the press: 'The current political situation would not allow us to attend the ceremony. He was a member of the British forces.'[55]

53 Fleming, *Magennis VC*, 181–2.
54 *Ibid.*, 199–200.
55 *Irish News*, 9 October 1999.

The war and Northern Ireland's experience of it was and has remained politically contested territory. Despite Churchill's glowing tribute in his 1945 victory broadcast to the province's part in the war, Unionists are still accused of claiming too much for the majority community's contribution. The level of enlistment within it disappointed the Stormont government although in mainland Britain no chances were taken by a coalition government which legislated comprehensively for national service in the armed forces and in war industries. The war brought badly needed work back to both communities in Northern Ireland but, as always, Protestants were accused of monopolising the best-paid jobs in the shipyards and engineering plants. As in England and Scotland, workers became more militant as the war went on. The official history of Northern Ireland at war gives just one paragraph to strikes,[56] yet during six years of hostilities, the province accounted for 10 per cent of total working days lost through strikes in Britain as a whole, though its workforce constituted only 2 per cent of the British total.[57]

Strikes were proof that class was still a major fault-line in Northern Ireland as a society but even in time of war sectarianism was always there. In March 1944, when five shop stewards were arrested under emergency legislation during a major engineering workers' strike, police questioned them about whether or not they were Catholics. Robert Morrow, secretary to the Belfast Trades Council, wrote in protest to the Stormont Prime Minister that 'whenever industrial trouble breaks out in Belfast, the danger of the importation into the dispute of a sectarian element is never far away. Some interested party or parties was or were sedulously spreading the report that the shop stewards movement was manned almost exclusively by persons of the Roman Catholic faith who were natives of Eire.'[58]

Sectarianism abated at least for a time amidst Belfast's experience of the blitz in April 1941 which was brutal and traumatic. The Luftwaffe's bombs

---

56   John W. Blake, *Northern Ireland in the Second World War* (Belfast: Her Majesty's Stationery Office, 1956), 425–6.
57   PRONI, CAB 9C/22/2, RR Bowman to the Cabinet Secretary, 6 April 1945.
58   *Ibid.*, Robert Morrow to Sir Basil Brooke, 1 May 1944.

spared neither Catholics nor Protestants but arguably the attacks were not sustained long enough to create the kind of social solidarity which some accounts claim to have been a product of the blitz in other British cities. What it quickly revealed was the shocking truth of Stormont's inadequate measures to give shelter to the population and the appalling poverty of so many of those who fled the city or were evacuated from it. For the IRA, the blitz seemed simply another opportunity. Its Northern Command hoped for a repetition and at an army convention in March 1942 those present voted for concerted attacks on police and emergency services to help the Germans if they struck again.[59]

Conclusion

By 1945 the IRA's sporadic but vicious war on both sides of the border was over. The execution in Belfast's Crumlin Road prison in September 1942 of one of their volunteers, the nineteen-year-old Tom Williams, raised sectarian tension to a dangerous level and many IRA members and sympathisers were still interned when the war ended. Neither the majority nor the minority community seemed to have anything to offer that would help to reduce ancient hatreds. For those returning from war service with its bonding around larger loyalties there could be something close to a culture shock. Even as cinema newsreels were showing appalling footage from Belsen and Auschwitz, at the 1945 Stormont election the nationalist electorate of South Armagh returned as their member Malachy Conlon, a republican who was also a blood and soil fascist and anti-Semite.[60] It would need more than a world war to make Northern Ireland try to resolve its corrosive internal divisions.

---

59 PRONI, HA/20/A/1/24.
60 Graham Walker, *A History of the Ulster Unionist Party: Protest, Pragmatism and Pessimism* (Manchester: Manchester University Press, 2004), 100–2.

These divisions were the product of a deep-seated conflict arising from the different ethnic, religious, cultural and political identities of Northern Ireland's two communities. This conflict long pre-dated the partition of Ireland in 1920 but in many ways it became more entrenched after the creation of the Stormont state. When war came in 1939 those of the Catholic and nationalist population who enlisted in the Crown forces could identify with the justness of Britain's cause while also supporting the Irish state's right to be neutral. Their motivation did not have to incorporate any strong sense of Britishness and they could also resent the existence of a Stormont mini-state whose discriminatory policies Britain seemed either to endorse or quietly ignore.

Conversely, for the minority within the Unionist population who were ready to give up secure work often in reserved occupations in order to enlist, doing so was an important affirmation of their Britishness. To this day their decision remains central to the self-image of 'loyal Ulster.' The IRA's atrocities after 1969 were seen as an attack on that self-image, particularly the November 1987 massacre at the Enniskillen war memorial. Even so, Britishness for Unionist and Loyalist Ulster was then, and has remained, a complex and indeed conditional allegiance despite the drum-beating and rhetoric of annual Orange walks. Unionists and Orangemen revelled in Churchill's praise for Northern Ireland's war effort in his May 1945 victory broadcast. Many of them, however, shared the lingering reservations of Lord Craigavon, that Britain's secret talks in the summer of 1940 over the potential terms on which Eire might join the war, were proof of Churchill's wartime readiness to betray them.[61] There are still those who think he would have done had Eire accepted his terms but once the crisis of 1940 and of the war itself was past, Churchill himself was ready to take on trust the Britishness of Unionist Ulster. Once Northern Ireland's latent sectarian tensions erupted into open conflict in 1969, his successors in office, like Harold Wilson and Margaret Thatcher, had to confront the venom of Unionists who saw betrayal in any British initiatives to resolve

---

61 Ian S. Wood, *Britain, Ireland and the Second World War* (Edinburgh: Edinburgh University Press, 2010), 27–30.

politically Ulster's 'Troubles.' One of these, Peter Robinson, now First Minister of Northern Ireland, famously told a huge Unionist and Loyalist rally in Belfast in November 1985 that the province was sitting 'on the window ledge of the Union.'[62] This was his way of dramatising the extent of Unionist and Loyalist disaffection caused by British policies, which he saw as appeasing armed republicanism. More than two decades later he would agree to take office with republicans in the power-sharing executive created by the 1998 Belfast Agreement; he leads what is now the province's biggest single party. Yet many who voted for it and other smaller Unionist parties, the children and grandchildren of those who fought in the Second World War, now feel they are loyal to a Britain which no longer cares much about being loyal to them.

---

62   *News Letter*, 18 November 1985.

TREVOR GRIFFITHS

Scottish cinema-goers at war: The popular reception of British and Scottish films during the Second World War

The Second World War is often identified as the point at which British film acquired cultural significance. While a sizeable production industry had developed from the late 1920s, assisted by the protection afforded by legislation which required exhibitors to screen a growing proportion of footage that was 'British' in origin, its output had rarely enjoyed either commercial success or critical acceptance.[1] Such problems would be overcome in the altered circumstances of wartime. While film production fell in volume to levels not seen since the mid 1920s, this smaller output offered, it has been argued, a more coherent view of a nation united by the stresses of war and which resonated with a cinema-going population close to its numerical peak.[2] In Robert Murphy's words the war placed film at 'The Heart of Britain', while for Charles Drazin, these were, for a cinematic few, unquestionably *The Finest Years*.[3] Nor is this an interpretation bestowed by posterity. Speaking in September 1944 at a lunch to mark the press preview in Edinburgh of Michael Powell and Emeric Pressburger's

---

1   Rachael Low, *The History of the British Film: Film Making in 1930s Britain* (London: Allen & Unwin, 1985).
2   For the war's place in the long-run pattern of British film production, see BFI, Screenonline: UK Feature Films Produced, 1912–2003, <http://www.screenonline.org.uk/film/facts/fact2.html> accessed 17 December 2014.
3   Robert Murphy, 'The Heart of Britain: British Cinema at War', in Robert Murphy, ed., *The British Cinema Book* (London: Palgrave Macmillan, 2008), 223–31; Charles Drazin, *The Finest Years: British Cinema of the 1940s* (London: Andre Deutsch, 2007).

A Canterbury Tale (1944), Ritson Bennell, Divisional Superintendent of the Gaumont-British Picture Corporation in Scotland, remarked on the enhanced standing of British films in wartime. Justifying his claim, Bennell pointed to titles which have subsequently secured acceptance as part of a critical canon of culturally meaningful films, including *49th Parallel* (1941), *In Which We Serve* (1942), *The First of the Few* (1942), *The Life and Death of Colonel Blimp* (1943), and *The Way Ahead* (1944).[4] Here was an integrated vision of the nation on celluloid, one founded on a narrative of collective solidarity in the face of external threat. By this view, the cinema appears as an uncomplicated agent of a united sense of Britishness, in which differences of nation, region, class, and gender were largely set to one side. Of late, however, another interpretation has emerged which explains the continued traction of the 'British' idea by reference to its continued sensitivity to points of internal difference. This chapter will explore the latter phenomenon by examining the popular Scottish take on cinematic expressions of Britishness during the years of war.

Ideas of Britishness were, indeed, shifting and variable, capable of adjusting to altered conditions in a manner that ensured its sustained and enhanced importance in wartime. In this chapter, such arguments are assessed by means of an extended consideration of the view from Scotland, where the notion of 'Unionist Nationalism' had long emphasised specifically national characteristics within a broadly British, imperial framework.[5] These rested on a distinctive set of civic institutions, covering legal, educational and religious life, to which, in the first half of the twentieth century could be added the cinema industry. As the trade publication *Kinematograph Weekly* remarked towards the war's end, while Scotland lacked a significant production capability, its screens were its own. In 1927, the Cinematograph Films or Quota Act, aiming to protect the British film industry, had introduced a requirement for cinemas to show a quota of British films. The growth of UK-wide cinema circuits in the wake of this legislation had

---

4 *Scotsman*, 20 September 1944, 3.
5 Graeme Morton, *Unionist-Nationalism: Governing Urban Scotland, 1830–1860* (East Linton: Tuckwell Press, 1999).

not left Scotland untouched, but proportionately their presence was less marked north than south of the Tweed, so that in cinematic terms Scotland was 'the land of Independents.'[6] Thus, it could be said with confidence, in 1945, that those running the trade across Scotland 'with few exceptions, are first and foremost, Scotsmen.'[7] Among these figures, primarily exhibitors and local cinema managers, representations of the nation which sought to over-ride internal differences were to be resisted. Particularly contentious was the tendency in films and their attendant publicity to conflate Britain with England, a practice which thrived in the patriotic effusions of wartime. Such had been the case twenty years earlier as, within weeks of the declaration of war in 1914, the Scottish correspondent of *The Bioscope* could observe that: 'At the present moment Scotland is suffering from too much England. Its "England's Army", "England's Navy" and "England's Honour" and the patriotic Scot has got his back up.'[8] Given this, the growth in British output following the Quota Act was not unequivocally welcomed north of the border. The cinema correspondent of the Glasgow *Evening Times*, 'Kinoman', detected an underlying antipathy to the British product among local audiences, and was irritated by the repeated use of English points of reference to underscore filmic depictions of Britain, including 'repeated views of the Thames, the Embankment, Piccadilly, the Changing of the Guard, 'Ampstead 'Eath, Hyde Park Corner, and "John Peel" being sung in a pub.'[9] Letters from readers added force to such criticisms. A series of exchanges published in September 1930 gave vent to views that subsequently acquired the weight of orthodoxy. One correspondent to the *Evening Times*, 'Lex', was particularly forthright in declaring that 'British films are the worst in the world', a claim bolstered by the observation that 'When a third-rate American film is shown it means standing room only, and when a first-rate British film is shown there are sure to be plenty of seats everywhere.'[10] The perspective of those within the trade, suggesting that

6   *Kinematograph Weekly*, 11 January 1945, 58.
7   Ibid., 56.
8   *The Bioscope*, 17 September 1914, 1049.
9   *Evening Times*, 27 October 1932, 3.
10 Ibid., 12 September 1930, 6.

the presence of a British subject in a programme could depress takings by between 40 and 100 per cent, confirmed the view that the quota worked against Scottish interests, by obliging exhibitors to book material that was not commercially attractive.[11] Such arguments re-emerged in the 1940s. Summarising its overview of the Scottish industry, *Kinematograph Weekly* noted how 'Ordinary English pictures do not do well in Scotland. English comedies of the boisterous type are useless.'[12] To the same end, if expressed in rather more reserved terms, the Conservative MP for Edinburgh West remarked during the Committee stage of the 1948 bill to increase the quota 'that relatively few British films enjoyed a good run in Scotland because the majority of them, however good they might be, had an English background and they did not appeal to the majority of Scottish people.'[13] The persistence of such views raises questions as to the degree to which opinion was altered through the stresses of conflict. That question is considered here in relation to all aspects of Scottish cinematic activity, from production, which had secured for itself a small but viable existence in the years to 1939, to an exhibition sector that in terms of density for both cinemas and cinema seats outranked that of its larger neighbour to the south. For that part of the industry, box-office data, while fragmentary in nature, allow for a sustained investigation of the popular Scottish take on Britishness during the years of war.

Scottish 'taste communities'

A monopoly provider such as the BBC, technically capable of transmitting the same content simultaneously across the island of Great Britain, was also obliged to acknowledge variations in audience preference. This

11 *Ibid.*, 3 November 1932, 3.
12 *Kinematograph Weekly*, 11 January 1945, 17.
13 *Scotsman*, 5 February 1948, 5.

was achieved in the 1930s through the provision of regional programming alongside the national and although, with the outbreak of war, the regional voice was silenced for a time, the Corporation soon moved to embed these perspectives into its schedules. It did this in part out of a growing recognition that its audience, far from being uniform, comprised a diversity of 'taste-communities.'[14] A comparable idea had long informed the production, distribution and exhibition of film in Britain.[15] Although studios were overwhelmingly centred in the south and east of England, their output endeavoured to harness talent from across the British Isles. If the regional was often employed for its comedic potential, it was an approach justified by financial returns, so that the two leading British box-office stars of the 1930s were both Lancastrian popular entertainers, George Formby and Gracie Fields.[16] Their appeal was not, however, uniform, an important reminder that audience preferences differed significantly across the country, a point to which cinema managers were obliged to be sensitive if their businesses were to thrive.[17]

If the fragmented nature of the cinema audience has been extensively documented for the 1930s, its nature in wartime remains less closely studied. It is known that in aggregate terms cinema attendances increased markedly, rising by some sixty per cent over the duration of the war. Yet the few

---

14 Thomas Hajkowski, *The B.B.C. and National Identity in Britain, 1922–53* (Manchester: Manchester University Press, 2010), 51–82, 109–34; Ross I. McKibbin, *Classes and Cultures: England, 1918–51* (Oxford: Oxford University Press, 1998), 457–76; the term 'taste community' is employed in Sue Harper, 'A Lower Middle-Class Taste-Community in the 1930s: Admissions Figures at the Regent Cinema, Portsmouth, UK', *Historical Journal of Film, Radio and Television*, 24 (2004), 565–87.

15 See Robert James, *Popular Culture and Working-Class Taste in Britain, 1930–39: A Round of Cheap Diversions?* (Manchester: Manchester University Press, 2010).

16 David R. Sutton, *A Chorus of Raspberries: British Film Comedy, 1929–39* (Exeter: University of Exeter Press, 2000); Jeffrey Richards, *The Age of the Dream Palace: Cinema and Society in Britain, 1930–9* (London: Routledge and Kegan Paul, 1984), 11–88; Jeffrey Richards, *Films and British National Identity: From Dickens to Dad's Army* (Manchester: Manchester University Press, 1997).

17 John Sedgwick, *Popular Filmgoing in 1930s Britain: A Choice of Pleasures* (Exeter: Exeter University Press, 2000).

detailed investigations into cinema-goers' preferences, measured through available box-office returns suggest that points of difference remained apparent. In consecutive years at the height of the conflict, the most popular British films at the Majestic Cinema in the Cheshire town of Macclesfield, measured by levels of attendance were *Somewhere in Camp* (1942) and *Somewhere on Leave* (1943). They both starred the unequivocally and aggressively northern comedian Frank Randle and were only outscored each year by prestigious American productions, *Mrs Miniver* and *Holiday Inn* respectively.[18] As far as can be judged, Randle's appeal was, and remained, substantially regional. How far differences in taste became more or less pronounced in wartime is difficult to judge, given the absence of extensive returns from the Majestic for the years before 1939. Nevertheless, the work of Sue Harper on the Regent Cinema in Portsmouth suggests that taste-communities were subject to change over time. Indeed, a comparison of preferences among the Regent's patrons in the 1930s and early 1940s suggests shifts in taste linked to the greater preponderance of women in audiences denuded by the absence of a significant number of men on active service.[19]

Initially, at least, the Second World War cinematically, as in much else, was conducted along the lines of 'business as usual.' Resolutely refusing to learn the lessons of the Great War, film producers deployed the language and imageries of 'Englishness' in a manner guaranteed to give offence to many Scots. By December 1939, Edinburgh exhibitors were sufficiently exasperated to complain of the use of 'England' and 'English' in newsreels, which extended, it was claimed, so far as to describe a Glasgow airman as an 'English hero.'[20] Similar sensitivities would see the titles of some features changed, not always with results that might be judged felicitous. The adaptation of Guy du Maurier's *An Englishman's Home*, released in the first weeks

---

18   Julian Poole, 'British Cinema Attendance in Wartime: Audience Preference at the Majestic, Macclesfield, 1939–46', *Historical Journal of Film, Radio and Television*, 7 (1987), 15–34. Here 22, 24.
19   Harper, 'A Lower Middle-Class Taste-Community'; Sue Harper, 'Fragmentation and Crisis: 1940s Admission Figures at the Regent Cinema, Portsmouth, UK', *Historical Journal of Film, Radio and Television*, 26 (2006), 361–84.
20   *Kinematograph Weekly*, 21 December 1939, 15.

of the war, was re-branded *A Britisher's Home* for Scottish consumption, a change pressed by Charles R. Young of the Paramount Cinema, Glasgow, himself of unimpeachably British character, being Welsh by birth, English by training in the industry, before becoming as the trade press had it an 'ardent Scottish Nationalist.'[21] In 1941, *This England*, a depiction of popular responses to the threat of foreign invasion over the ages, was stripped of its Shakespearian associations and its title rendered as the more inclusive *Our Heritage*.[22] A view of Britain was thus encouraged which saw it as a means of drawing together while still respecting national differences. It received vocal expression each evening early in the war at the Regal Cinema, Glasgow, when the organist Alan Kennedy concluded his performance with a variation on a familiar patriotic air:

> There'll always be a Scotland,
> And England shall be free,
> If England means as much to you
> As Scotland means to me.[23]

At times, the pressures of war appeared to work against such diversity. Scottish film production which had developed an organised presence in the immediate pre-war years, ceased promptly on the outbreak of hostilities. Activity had centred most obviously on the work of the Films of Scotland Committee, formed at the prompting of documentary film pioneer, John Grierson to provide a filmic representation of the nation at the Glasgow Empire Exhibition of 1938. A slate of seven films was prepared, covering many aspects of modern Scottish life, including economic well-being, education, sport and health.[24] The results impressed documentary film-maker

---

21 *Kinematograph Weekly*, 28 September 1939, 11; 18 January 1940, 38.
22 National Records of Scotland (hereafter NRS), GD289/1/1, Playhouse Cinema, Profit and Loss Ledger, 1929–68, week beginning 2 June 1941; for the film, *Scotsman*, 3 June 1941, 6; <http://explore.bfi.org.uk/4ce2b6b82eb1c> accessed 19 December 2014.
23 *Kinematograph Weekly*, 14 December 1939, 25.
24 Trevor Griffiths, *The Cinema and Cinema-going in Scotland, 1896–1950* (Edinburgh: Edinburgh University Press, 2012), 298–9; Andrew Blaikie, *The Scots Imagination and Modern Memory* (Edinburgh: Edinburgh University Press, 2010), 53–94.

Paul Rotha, who regarded it as 'the first time in the history of the cinema [that] film has been used to present a complete picture of a country to the world.'[25] In spite of such judgments, the films' standing appeared to be called into question when the British Council refused to allow them to be shown as part of Britain's contribution to the New York World Fair of 1939, the chairman of the selection committee Philip Guedella declaring that their subject matter was not 'large enough or important enough to include in Britain's official picture.' The refusal to incorporate Scotland into officially sanctioned views of Britishness attracted outspoken criticism from Grierson, who asserted that 'our national identity has been ignored, and our right to express ourselves in our own Scottish way has been denied.'[26] In the end, Films of Scotland productions secured screenings in New York outside the British Pavilion.[27]

The outbreak of war posed a more fundamental obstacle to Scotland's ability to express itself cinematically. With private sponsorship in abeyance due to the restrictions placed on the production of film for advertising purposes, film-makers turned to government as the one reliable source of funding. Production thus became subject to sanction by officials based largely in London. These developments had two consequences for activity north of the border: first, the Films of Scotland Committee, as a privately funded body, was unable to access public moneys and so production plans were suspended for the duration.[28] Secondly, although the Ministry of Information commissioned films from small producers in Scotland, to cover such subjects as the Clydebank Blitz of March 1941, it also insisted that post-production dubbing be carried out in London, the existing sound installation in Glasgow being deemed inadequate. Writing in 1942, Stanley Russell, himself active in film production since the later 1920s, considered it 'a tragic commentary on the state of affairs when a

25 *Scotsman*, 8 November 1938, 13.
26 *Ibid.*, 20 February 1939, 9, for both Guedella's statement and Grierson's response.
27 *Ibid.*, 24 February 1939, 7.
28 NRS, D10/141, Scottish Home Dept, Cinematograph Acts, Films of Scotland Committee, Note, 21 February 1942; Minute of Meeting, Under Secretary of State with Mr Milne and Mr Ballantine, 8 January 1943.

country the size of Scotland has no method of recording her voice except by recourse to London.'[29] That voice remained mute throughout the war and although productions were mounted in Scotland, they were largely overseen by English companies.[30]

The conviction that Scotland lacked an effective outlet for its views both in broadcasting and on the cinema screen gained ground in the later years of the war, encouraging calls for measures to support and sustain a viable film industry. Film producer Stanley Russell thought it was essential if it was 'to revive her individuality, and not become merely a "region".'[31] Yet the degree to which the war can be credited with inhibiting production in Scotland may be questioned. Grierson's proud boast that the efforts of the Films of Scotland Committee laid 'The foundations of a Scottish cinema' overlooked the uncomfortable fact that six of the seven films had been produced in England.[32] *The Face of Scotland* (1938), for example, an overview of Scotland's history which celebrated the tenacity and initiative of a people capable of claiming a living from infertile Highland soils, qualities seen to translate readily into industrial inventiveness and success, was fashioned by Basil Wright, English-born stalwart of the Empire Marketing Board and the GPO Film Unit.[33] What is more, circumstances enabled these films to secure wider British exposure during the war. For most of the 1930s, the absence of a shorts quota under the legislation of 1927 limited the exploitation of these films by commercial cinemas. The revision of the Quota Act in 1938 extended protection to short subjects,

29 Scottish Screen Archive (hereafter SSA), 4/1/13, Scottish Films Productions (1928) Ltd., Memorandum and Proposed Schedule of Production of Scottish Films Productions (1928) Ltd, 26 India Street, Glasgow, C2, December 1942, 2–3.
30 SSA, 4/12/15, Russell Productions Ltd/ Thames and Clyde Films Co. Ltd, cutting from *Glasgow Herald*, 29 February 1944; *Kinematograph Weekly*, 10 February 1944, 19.
31 SSA, Scottish Films Productions (1928) Ltd, Russell to editor of *Glasgow Herald*, 15 February 1944; see also *Kinematograph Weekly*, 10 February 1944, 8, for the views of Major Lloyd, Unionist M.P. for east Renfrewshire; *Evening Telegraph, Angus*, 7 January 1944, letter by JCD.
32 *Scotsman*, 5 April 1938, 15.
33 *Scotland Calling at the Empire Exhibition 1938* (Newton: Panamint Cinema and the National Library of Scotland, DVD Collection, 2008).

ensuring that their audiences were no longer confined to non-commercial outlets such as schools and film societies. The Films of Scotland were early beneficiaries of this change, four of the films being acquired by MGM, and the remaining three by the Associated British Picture Corporation. By early 1943, over 5000 screenings had been secured across Britain, three quarters taking place in England. In all, just short of 24 million cinema-goers had the opportunity of seeing productions devoted to Scotland.[34]

Table One: Distribution of the Films of Scotland Committee Films, 1939–1943

Title	English Bookings	Scottish Bookings	Attendances
Scotland for Fitness	166	124	1,002,000
Sport in Scotland	188	117	1,092,000
Sea Food	386	133	2,075,000
They Made the Land	897	245	5,814,000
Children's Story	669	179	4,228,500
Wealth of a Nation	818	201	5,110,500
Face of Scotland	742	192	4,675,500

Source: NRS, DD/10/141, Scottish Home Dept, 21 Jan. 1943, A.B. King to Steven Bisland.

Although representing a fraction of the total audience for film, such figures at least demonstrate that cinematic representations of Britain were not narrowly Anglocentric. Yet this change was less a consequence of a shift in audience taste as a consequence of wartime, and more a result of legislative initiatives taken before the war, which altered considerably the market viability of such productions.

How such films were received remains to be determined. In the absence of extensive box-office returns, we are often thrown back on responses to particular genres or specific titles. One such, which claimed strong Scottish associations, had been a source of much controversy before the outbreak of war. *Shipyard Sally* (1939) was the latest vehicle for Gracie Fields, in which

---

34 NRS, DD10/141, 27 May 1943, W. Kirkwood to J. Anderson, Scottish Home Dept; 21 January 1943, A.B. King to Steven Bisland.

her solid Lancastrian common sense and unquenchable good humour was applied in the service of the depressed shipbuilding industry of the Clyde. Running a pub in conjunction with her father, played by Leeds-born Sydney Howard, Gracie is sufficiently concerned at the lack of work in the local shipyards following completion of a major order to mount a campaign in London to have the yard reopened. If the film ended on a note of optimism, with activity fully restored, it had, in the process worked to offend local opinion. Concern centred on a sequence early in the piece, which pre-publicity described as being set in a 'typical' Glasgow pub on the evening of the launch of the *Queen Mary*. Here were gathered 'One hundred and fifty extras, varying from bedraggled Clydeside workers to Scots pipers attired in full ceremonial regalia.'[35] Police records of the time were drawn on to refute the imputation of drunken excess levelled against local workers. In response, the film's producers, Twentieth Century Fox, conceded the force of such arguments, but defended the production as a whole, claiming it to represent 'the finest tribute ever paid to Scotland.'[36] While such assertions could be set to one side as standard studio puffery, criticism was more muted when the film went on general release in the weeks leading up to war. Fields' illness in the summer of 1939 evoked widespread sympathy and at screenings in Glasgow in July the main feature was preceded by newsreel footage of her leaving hospital. If Fields herself could not be criticised, the subject matter continued to provoke negative comment: *The Scotsman*'s cinema correspondent was of the view that '*Shipyard Sally* may be a bright and lively diversion; but one would be blind not to recognise that a superb opportunity for a film of some significance has been light-heartedly thrown away.'[37]

With the war in progress, however, such judgments were largely set to one side. When the film arrived in Edinburgh in November 1939, Fields' 'infectious good spirits' were unequivocally welcomed and attention centred

---

35 *Evening Times*, 6 April, 9; 27 July 1939, 9, for Kinoman's less than favourable review; *Scotsman*, 11 April 1939, 13.
36 *Evening Times*, 20 April, 9; 27 July 1939, 9.
37 *Scotsman*, 25 July 1939, 13.

on the production's big musical number, 'Wish Me Luck as You Wave Me Goodbye', which was judged especially suited to the mood of the moment.³⁸ Even the usual doubts about vocal mannerisms were for the time being stilled, the *Aberdeen Journal* remarking that 'the Scottish accents are so natural they won't even make "Bridgeton" cross!'³⁹ For all the hostile pre-publicity it had attracted, *Shipyard Sally* appears to have scored well in box-office terms across Scotland. High audiences at the turn of the year justified its retention for a second week at Dundee's Kinnaird Hall,⁴⁰ while the *Evening Telegraph, Angus*, noted the film's conscious appeal to Britishness in the round, noting that 'there are no "aspidistras". There's "Danny Boy", "Annie Laurie", "Land of Hope and Glory" – all sung straight and with captivating sincerity.'⁴¹ If not the finest, the film could be accepted without reserve as a worthy tribute to Scotland and its place within the Union.

Other productions fared less well, indicating that Scottish audiences continued to exercise discretion in their choice of viewing. Re-branding failed to save *A Britisher's Home* when it appeared in Scotland early in 1940, despite a largely favourable reception south of the border on its initial release. *Kinematograph Weekly* had expressed doubts about the subject, as its theme of the 'Enemy in our Midst' had been rendered obsolete by the fact of war. On the whole, its 'spectacular speculation' about a possible invasion was seen to offer 'a crude reminder of that which all types of audience will be looking to the pictures to forget.'⁴² Despite initially unpromising notices, the film did excellent business at the London Pavilion, the depiction of Britain's armed forces at the climax generating spontaneous applause.⁴³ Further success followed at Oxford, Reading, Bristol, and Blackpool.⁴⁴

---

38 *Scotsman*, 28 November 1939, 9. The film's failure to reflect fully the human drama of the shipyards remained a matter for critical comment.
39 *Aberdeen Journal*, 3 August 1939, 1.
40 *Dundee Courier*, 12 January, 1; 16 January 1940, 1.
41 *Evening Telegraph, Angus*, 9 January 1940.
42 *Kinematograph Weekly*, 28 September 1939, 11, 17.
43 *Ibid.*, 19 October 1939, 19.
44 *Ibid.*, 14 December 1939, 11.

However, critical reaction in Scotland echoed that of the trade press. *The Scotsman* judged it 'a most unfortunate film', encumbered by what was judged to be an implausible scenario, as well as a distinctly clumsy title: 'The Englishman who resents the issue of gas masks refuses to have his lawn dug up for trenches, and does not bother to look in the attic to see what kind of wireless set has been built by the handsome alien is a character from a never-never world.'[45] Such implausibilities did not unduly deter audiences at the film's first run in Edinburgh at the Playhouse; the week's attendance of 22,407 was only slightly below the wartime average for March. Three weeks later, however, its reappearance at the Playhouse's twin house, the Palace, drew only 4946, just over fifty per cent of the wartime mean and generating a loss on the week's business of £24.[46] The reception accorded the blandly re-packaged *Our Heritage* conveyed a comparable indifference to subjects of an openly 'English' character. Its appearance at all three cinemas for which complete box-office data exist generated responses that were consistently below par: at the Playhouse, an audience of 19,488 in June 1941 was some seventeen per cent below the average, while at the Palace in the same month, the attendance of 6035 was fully twenty eight per cent shy of the mean. Cinema-goers in Aberdeen were no more enamoured of the feature, its appearance in May 1941 attracting 11,811, almost thirty two per cent below what could be considered normal.[47]

45 *Scotsman*, 19 March 1940, 9.
46 NRS, GD289/1/1, Playhouse Cinema, Profit and Loss Ledger, 1929–68, week ending 23 March 1940; GD289/1/3, Palace Cinema, Profit and Loss Ledger, 1925–55, week ending 13 April 1940.
47 NRS, GD289/1/1, Playhouse Ledger, week commencing 2 June 1941; GD289/1/3, Palace Ledger, week commencing 23 June 1941; Cinema Museum, Lambeth (hereafter CM), Capitol Cinema, Takings Book, 1941–2, week commencing 12 May 1941.

A Scottish case study: Eileen Crowford's cinema diary

It is rare to have the personal insights of cinema-goers to supplement these bare statistics. However, a series of diaries, maintained by an Edinburgh typist named Eileen Crowford, exists for this period and are deposited at the National Museum of Scotland.[48] They are not the most reflective of documents; Ms Crowford, while assiduous in listing all the films attended, chose not to record her reactions to what she saw. Nevertheless, the rankings provided of both stars and films does offer some insight into her preferences. For Ms Crowford, aged twenty six when the war broke out, going to the pictures ranked second among a range of recreational activities that encapsulate a sober and serious-minded approach to leisure: ranging from reading, to visiting a library (especially Reference and Art Departments), and then visiting museums, art galleries, bookshops, and churches. Among films, her favoured genres were 'Historical Adventure, Romance, Historical Biography, Cartoon and Fantasy, and Travel.' Westerns, a favourite among many Scottish audiences, figured in her top ten, but only 'if out of the rut.'[49] If not wholly representative in terms of her tastes, Ms Crowford reflected the broader trend in favour of higher attendance in wartime by visiting the cinema more often in these years. Her twenty seven visits in 1939 contrasted with an average of just under forty five per year from 1942.[50] Over that time, a shift in film preferences can be detected. In the pre-war diaries, the films listed are mostly mainstream productions, with the exception of *The Legend of Prague*, a Czech production screened in March, the same month that Czech independence was extinguished.[51] By 1942, her film-going had acquired an overtly political dimension, with Soviet productions *In the Rear of the Enemy*, *Defeat of the Germans near*

48 National Museum of Scotland, Scottish Life Archive (hereafter NMS), Eileen Crowford Collection.
49 NMS, Eileen Crowford Collection, Diary 1950; Griffiths, *Cinema and Cinema-going*, 205.
50 NMS, Crowford Collection, Diaries for 1939, 1942–5.
51 *Ibid.*, Diary for 1939, 15 March 1939.

Moscow, and the war drama *The Red Flyer* (support for the American flag-waver *To the Shores of Tripoli*) featuring in her itinerary.[52] Russian subjects figured in two of the three years that followed and significantly her list of preferences in 1945 was headed by the drama *Baltic Deputy*, which figured alongside the historical romance *Adventures in Bokhara*.[53] This politicised outlook continued beyond VE Day, the 1950 Diary recording payments to the Scottish USSR Society, while a list of Favourite Political Figures was headed by Joseph Stalin and USSR President Mikhail Kalinin, the leading British politician being, unsurprisingly, Harry Pollitt of the Communist Party of Great Britain.[54]

Yet on most of her visits to the cinema, Ms Crowford was most likely to encounter more mainstream fare, including some of the key British productions of wartime. So, in 1942, fifty visits to the cinema exposed her to thirteen programmes in which British films featured. These included such standards as Powell and Pressburger's *49th Parallel* and *One of Our Aircraft is Missing* and Ealing's *The Foreman Went to France*.[55] The following year, British programmes accounted for twelve out of forty five attendances, and included another Powell and Pressburger production, *The Life and Death of Colonel Blimp*.[56] War subjects in 1944 included *The Way Ahead* and a celebration of the British tendency to muddle through, *The Demi-Paradise*, contributing to nine British programmes out of forty seen across the year.[57] Although diligent in her attendance at some key British productions of the war years, Ms Crowford's response to them appeared muted. Among the stars favoured in 1942, the only British artiste to figure in a war feature was Googie Withers for *One of Our Aircraft is Missing*. Deborah Kerr also featured for the A.J. Cronin adaptation *Hatter's Castle*, but did not receive a nomination the following year for her multiple roles in *Colonel*

---

52 *Ibid.*, Diary for 1942, 23 February, 15 June, 12 November 1942.
53 *Ibid.*, Diary for 1945, 13 May 1945; the list of favourite films for the year is in the Diary for 1939.
54 *Ibid.*, Diary for 1950.
55 *Ibid.*, Diary for 1942.
56 *Ibid.*, Diary for 1943.
57 *Ibid.*, Diary for 1944.

Blimp.[58] The pattern did not alter in the remaining years of the war. Two war documentaries figured among the favourite films of 1944, both part of the Frank Capra series produced in Hollywood, *Why We Fight*. No British production featured in her personal top ten, headed by the musical *Sweet Rosie O'Grady*. Other films receiving an endorsement reflected Ms Crowford's preference for historical romance, as Table Two indicates. The following year, Russian subjects were favoured, along with another Capra documentary, *The Battle of Russia*. The British industry was represented by Olivier's *Henry V*, a subject explicitly linked to the war effort, but seen at the end of the year some months into the peace.[59] Ms Crowford's political persuasion did not preclude an enthusiasm for standard Hollywood fare.

Table Two: Favourite films of Ms Eileen Crowford, 1944–1945

	Top Ten Films of 1944		
1	*Sweet Rosie O'Grady*	USA	Musical
2	*Lassie Come Home*	USA	Adventure/ Drama
3	*Jane Eyre*	USA	Drama/ Romance
4	*The Phantom of the Opera*	USA	Drama/ Horror
5	*Divide and Conquer*	USA	Documentary
6	*The Cross of Lorraine*	USA	War/ Drama
7	*Buffalo Bill*	USA	Biography/ Western
8	*The Nazis Strike*	USA	Documentary
9	*In Our Time*	USA	Drama
10	*The Song of Bernadette*	USA	Biography/ Drama
	Top Films of 1945		
1	*Adventures in Bokhara*	USSR	History/ Romance
2	*Baltic Deputy*	USSR	Drama
3	*The Hitler Gang*	USA	Biography/ Drama
4	*Dragon Seed*	USA	Drama/ History

58 *Ibid.*, list of favourite stars of 1942 in Diary for 1945; those for 1943 in Diary for 1939.
59 *Ibid.*, Diaries for 1945 (list of attendances) and 1939 (list of favourite films).

5	*A Song to Remember*	USA	Biography/ Drama
6	*The Battle of Russia*	USA	Documentary
7	*Sudan*	USA	Action/ Adventure
8	*Henry V*	UK	Biography/ Drama

Source: NMS, Eileen Crawford Collection, Diary for 1939.

What is more, the 'British' stars favoured, including Greer Garson, Charles Laughton, and Errol Flynn were artistes whose careers flourished across the Atlantic. In her qualified enthusiasm for British films but continued support for the American product, Ms Crawford seems wholly representative of Scottish cinema-goers more generally.

Case studies: Edinburgh and Aberdeen box office returns

Their preferences were measured daily at the box office. Yet such material survives for only three of the 600 or so halls active across Scotland during the war: two city-centre cinemas in Edinburgh, the Palace and the Playhouse, the former opened in 1914 which had become a second-run house by 1939, and the Playhouse, the largest of the capital's thirty seven cinemas, which opened with the coming of sound in 1929; and the Capitol in Aberdeen, another city-centre cinema which opened in 1933.[60] Within this limited sample, differences in the capacities of each hall make it inappropriate to infer popularity from audience size alone. So, the lowest attendance at the Playhouse in 1943, exceeded the highest for the year at the Palace (19,275 compared to 15,179).[61] Growth in the national audience of some sixty per cent between 1939 and 1945 poses a further problem, as audience size might be as much a function of the point in the war at which a film

---

60   Details on the three cinemas can be found on the Scottish Cinemas and Theatres Project website, see <http://www.scottishcinemas.org.uk> accessed 20 December 2014.

61   NRS, GD289/1/1, Playhouse Ledger; GD289/1/3, Palace Ledger.

played as it was a reflection of the attraction of that particular subject. To allow for both variables, popularity is here calculated by comparing the audience achieved by a programme with the mean attendance for that month across the war. This enables the popular response – or popularity score – to be expressed in terms of the degree of variation from 'expected' levels of support suggested by the average. To allow for variations in cinema-going across the war, the average popularity score achieved by all films shown in a year was calculated and then compared to the popularity of programmes in which British films topped the bill and then of all programmes in which British subjects played. The popularity rating of each would indicate the comparative standing of that programme compared to others at the same cinema at a similar point in the war.

If attention is initially confined to weeks in which British films topped the bill, war subjects scored well at both Edinburgh halls from the earliest days of the conflict. At a time when attendances generally were depressed by concerns over public safety, two films drew cinema-goers in higher than anticipated numbers.[62] The espionage thriller, set during the Great War, *The Spy in Black* (1939), directed by Michael Powell, secured comfortably the highest audience at the Palace in the latter months of 1939 (8237; the next highest was 7775 in Christmas week).[63] At the Playhouse, the film's success was only exceeded by Alexander Korda's hastily produced propaganda vehicle, *The Lion Has Wings*. In each case, the programme secured audiences that exceeded the wartime average, two of only four weeks to do so in the first four months of the war.[64] That a film's performance was not entirely related to its subject matter is suggested by the indifference which greeted another war feature: the Gaumont production, *I Was a Spy*. A reissue of a 1933 film, it drew fewer than 4000 to the Palace in December 1939, below

---

62 Early meetings of the Scottish branch of the Cinematograph Exhibitors' Association noted the problem of reduced takings due to the black-out, *Kinematograph Weekly*, 21 September, 8; 28 September, 9; 26 October 1939, 8.
63 NRS, GD289/1/3, Palace Ledger, weeks ending 18 November, 30 December 1939. The average weekly attendance across the last fifteen weeks of the year was 4922.
64 NRS, GD289/1/1, Playhouse Ledger, weeks ending 28 October and 9 December 1939.

half the wartime average. This was despite the presence of Madeleine Carroll and the star of *The Spy in Black*, Conrad Veidt, suggesting that the audience had little appetite for repeat screenings from an earlier era which lacked the production values of later films.[65] Thereafter, as audiences rose overall, British first features initially shared fully in the upswing. Indeed, between 1940 and 1943, 'British' programmes (with a British film billed first) outscored the generality of films on show in three years at the Playhouse and in two at the Palace. Leading the charge were films which centred their treatments on the war, so that in successive years at the Playhouse the most popular British features were: *Contraband*, with an audience of 28,704 and a popularity score of +three per cent in July 1940; *Pimpernel Smith*, attendance of 30,459 and popularity score of +41 per cent in November 1941; *49th Parallel*, audience of 37,461 and popularity score of +51 per cent in January 1942; and *The Life and Death of Colonel Blimp*, audience of 37,658 and popularity score of +44 per cent in its first week in August 1943.[66] At the Palace, which shared many of its programmes with the Playhouse, there was considerable overlap in the ranking of films, the only variation coming in 1943 when *Blimp* was outscored by the Gainsborough production *We Dive At Dawn*, audience of 11,101 and popularity score of +25.4 per cent in September, and the Two Cities film *The Gentle Sex*, which in the preceding week drew 12,463, securing a popularity score of +40.8 per cent.[67] Further north in Aberdeen, war subjects figured less frequently on the bill, but notable successes were scored by *The Lion Has Wings*, with an audience of 19,496 and a popularity score of +18.5 per cent in January 1940, and Noel Coward's exercise in naval heroics, *In Which We Serve*,

---

65 NRS, GD289/1/3, Palace Ledger, week ending 9 December 1939.
66 NRS, GD289/1/1, Playhouse Ledger, week ending 27 July 1940; weeks commencing 17 November 1941; 12 January 1942; 23 August 1943.
67 NRS, GD289/1/3, Palace Ledger, weeks commencing 13 and 20 Sept.; 8 Nov. 1943. In 1940, *Contraband* attracted 8417 in its first week, ending 10 August 1940; *Pimpernel Smith* drew 12,367 in its second week, commencing 24 November 1941; and *49th Parallel* attracted 13,532 in its first week, commencing 16 February 1942.

with an attendance of 27,874 and a popularity score of +72.4 per cent in December 1942.[68]

This preliminary survey would tend to suggest that Scottish audiences marched in step with British cinema-goers more generally, favouring as did their counterparts elsewhere pictures attuned to the rhythms of war. Yet any attempt to view this as evidence of the purchase of officially endorsed versions of Britishness locally should be resisted. The close approximation of the support accorded British programmes with that given to films more generally had been evident at both Edinburgh houses before 1939, so that the war marked more continuity than any change in behaviour. Similarly, the lower performance of British subjects at the Capitol maintained a pattern observed before the war, when a gap of between seven and fourteen per cent in favour of non-British features had been observed.[69] Further evidence of continuity in taste is provided by the success of films in which particular stars featured. To begin with Edinburgh, Leslie Howard figured prominently in both *49th Parallel* and *Pimpernel Smith*, and had a production role in *The Gentle Sex*. Similarly, he played a leading role in many of the most popular productions at the Playhouse before 1939, including the MGM romantic drama *Smilin' Through* (with an audience of 46,581 in March 1933), the British production of *Pygmalion* (43,680 in February 1939), and most notably as the lead in Alexander Korda's dramatisation of *The Scarlet Pimpernel*, the attendance for which at 48,714 in one week in 1935 was the highest at the Playhouse for any pre-war year.[70]

Other stars also enjoyed box-office success either side of 1939. A favourite with patrons of the Capitol was Arthur Lucan in his guise as the Irish charwoman Old Mother Riley. His/her second cinematic outing

---

68   CM, Capitol Cinema, Takings Book, 1939–40, week commencing 8 January 1940; 1942–3, week commencing 21 December 1942. It should be noted that the book for the year from February 1940 to January 1941 and so coverage is less than complete.
69   Griffiths, *The Cinema and Cinema-going*, 201–3. The variation at the Capitol is between weeks when British films topped the bill and those in which they were the supporting feature.
70   NRS, GD289/1/1, Playhouse Ledger, weeks ending 4 March 1933; 4 February 1939; 17 August 1935.

Old Mother Riley in Paris secured the hall's highest audience of the year in 1939 (25,885, with popularity 37 per cent above the pre-war average).[71] The following year, *Old Mother Riley MP* drew an attendance across the week of 24,849, fully fifty per cent above the wartime mean. Further success followed in 1941 with *Old Mother Riley's Ghosts* which, in a supporting role to the RKO comedy *Party Girl* attracted an audience twenty six per cent above the mean, and the year after *Old Mother Riley's Circus* which exceeded the average by seventeen per cent.[72] Other comedies working to lift the performance of British films at the Capitol included the George Formby vehicles *South American George* and *Much Too Shy* (popularity scores respectively twenty three and thirty four per cent above the mean).[73] Established British stars provided reliable box-office returns at a time when British comedies more generally struggled in wartime Aberdeen. In the six years to the outbreak of war, they had provided the largest share (fourteen out of thirty seven) of British films falling short of the mean by more than twenty per cent.[74] Excluding the Lucan and Formby titles already mentioned, comedies figured on twelve programmes from 1939, but they tended to struggle, generating average audiences more than twenty two per cent below the average.[75] At Edinburgh also, the presence of a star could prove crucial to a film's chances of box-office success. Among the few British comedies to attract audiences above the norm at the Playhouse were George Formby vehicles: *Turned Out Nice Again* (+five per cent in 1944) and *Spare a Copper* (+seven per cent in April 1945), all the more impressive as both were reissues.[76]

71 CM, Capitol Cinema, Takings Book 1938–9, week commencing 2 January 1939.
72 CM, Capitol Cinema, Taking Books 1939–40, week commencing 1 January 1940; 1941–2, week commencing 21 July 1941; 1942–3, week commencing 4 May 1942.
73 CM, Capitol Cinema, Takings Book 1942–3, weeks commencing 23 March, 3 August 1942.
74 CM, Capitol Cinema, Takings Books, 1933–9.
75 CM, Capitol Cinema, Takings Books 1939–40, 1941–5.
76 NRS, GD2891/1/, Playhouse Ledger, weeks commencing 16 October 1944; 23 April 1945.

The importance of the star goes further. The war film is often credited with encouraging a more 'democratic' aesthetic, appropriate to the idea of a People's War. Yet the subjects favoured by Scottish audiences were predominantly large-budget productions, populated by familiar star names. The application of documentary techniques, so often seen as a substantial gain for British production, garnered variable support. So, Harry Watt's *Target for Tonight* (1941) about RAF Bomber Command appeared at the Playhouse in September that year, supporting the First National drama *East of the River*. If the attendance of 25,838 was six per cent above the mean, this was eclipsed the following week by the 32,516 who attended the Deanna Durbin musical *Nice Girl?*.[77] In June 1944, the attendance for *Tunisian Victory*, screened alongside a rerun of MGM's *Captain Courageous* was some ten per cent below average.[78] Mixed fortunes also awaited Ealing's dramatisation of a real-life naval drama *San Demetrio – London*, which performed well at the Capitol (audience twenty per cent above the mean in March 1944), but which generated the lowest takings at the Regent Cinema in Glasgow over that summer.[79]

Across all halls, a general decline in business for British productions was evident in the final stages of the war. Even Playhouse patrons, long well disposed to domestic efforts, were altogether less receptive to the output of home studios in 1944–5. Reflecting what *Kinematograph Weekly* detected to be a growth in demand for 'lighter films, and especially for musicals', whimsical essays in British eccentricity such as *Tawny Pipit* played well (+7.9 per cent), while the sober realism of British National's version of George Blake's novel *The Shipbuilders*, despite its Scottish setting, faltered at the box office (-twenty three per cent).[80] The trend in favour of musicals did not extend to British efforts. Although the genre had prospered at the Capitol

77 NRS, GD2891/1/, Playhouse Ledger, weeks commencing 8 and 15 September 1941.
78 NRS, GD2891/1/, Playhouse Ledger, week commencing 5 June 1944.
79 CM, Capitol Cinema, Takings Book 1944–5, week commencing 20 March 1944; SSA, 5/22/6, The Glasgow Picture House Ltd. Minute Book, 1936–49, loose insert, comparing takings in 1943 and 1944.
80 *Kinematograph Weekly*, 27 July 1944, 23; NRS, GD289/1/1, Playhouse Ledger, weeks commencing 12 June, 18 September 1944.

before 1939, enthusiasm was more muted in wartime: the Vera Lynn vehicle *Rhythm Serenade*, Butcher Films' *Variety Jubilee*, and Ealing's *Champagne Charlie*, directed by documentary veteran Alberto Cavalcanti, recorded audiences between twenty five and thirty seven per cent below the mean.[81]

Conclusion

The sum of all this is that there is no compelling evidence of a marked shift in attitude among Scottish cinema-goers that might have signalled an acceptance of broader ideas of Britishness. The trend from both before and during the conflict indicated instead enduring support for Britain as a multinational enterprise, giving due weight to the contributions of all regions and nations across the British Isles and avoiding the conflation of Britain and England. Where the latter occurred, Scottish sensibilities were immediately aroused. The film industry, despite initial failings, responded with a range of features which presented the war as a common endeavour not exclusive to one social or geographical grouping. Olivier's *Henry V*, anticipating the opening of the Second Front, made much, as *Kinematograph Weekly* noted, of the presence of 'every element of our race' in the Agincourt campaign.[82] A crucial factor mediating the efforts of London-based film producers were local cinema managers, keenly attuned to the tastes and preferences of their audiences through the signals communicated on a daily basis by the box office. This ensured frequent appearances by Arthur Lucan on the bill at the Capitol, Aberdeen, and made Leslie Howard a recurrent star in Edinburgh. An important interpretive point emerges here: the tendency to read off popular attitudes from attendance records in an uncritical way should be resisted. Cinema, as has long been recognised, was more a source

---

81   CM, Capitol Cinema, Takings Books 1943–4, week commencing 20 September 1943; 1944–5, week commencing 4 December 1944; 22 January 1945.
82   *Kinematograph Weekly*, 7 October 1943, 29.

of escape from the restrictions of everyday life than it was an extension of them. So, Eileen Crowford's political views did not map infallibly on to her taste in film: that would have required the casting of Errol Flynn in the title role in a biopic of Joseph Stalin, an unlikely but not impossible scenario in the Hollywood studio system of the 1940s. Nevertheless, the industry from producers and distributors to exhibitors had to show awareness of how audiences behaved and the choices they made in the search for entertainment and enlightenment. These extended from whether or not to go to the cinema, not too difficult a decision given the absence under wartime conditions of austerity of alternative outlets for pleasure, to the film to be seen. The fluctuations produced by the variable appeal of different subjects made predicting box-office outcomes an uncertain science, but also generated the statistical fluctuations from which posterity must judge the nature of contemporary preferences. To that extent, audience figures provide us with some insight into the broad outlines of the major taste-communities of the period. So, in Scotland an inclusive idea of Britain prevailed, sustained by a combination of large budgets and star performances. The importance of the star is a reminder that the social democratic ideals seen to have flourished in wartime Britain and to have culminated in the election of Labour in 1945 did not necessarily encompass the nation's cinema screens. Ultimately, the success of Britain's film industry rested on its ability to offer a sufficiently diverse product to satisfy the needs of audiences whose tastes often varied markedly. That role, which had developed under the protection of the quota, was maintained into wartime, making the cinema one of the most effective vehicles for the projection of a popularly accepted and inclusive Britishness.

GAVIN BOWD

'Fortify the Cheviots!': The Nazis and the Scottish Nationalists

In January 1939, Douglas Young, future leader of the Scottish National Party (SNP), wrote to his fellow poet, George Campbell Hay: 'If Hitler could neatly remove our imperial breeks somehow and thus dissipate the mirage of Imperial partnership with England etc he would do a great service to Scottish Nationalism.'[1] Young thus showed the ambivalent attitude of Scottish nationalists towards Fascism. If their movement was overwhelmingly attached to democracy, its visceral hostility to England, the 'Auld Enemy' south of the Cheviot hills, led to the downplaying of the continental Fascist threat to freedom and peace, while some extreme nationalists could be attracted to the authoritarian and xenophobic solutions offered by the *Fuhrer* and the *Duce* in the years leading up to the Second World War. The idea of 'fighting for Britain' sowed considerable disruption in nationalist ranks, who found it difficult, if not impossible, to reconcile ancestral grievances with a growing awareness of Hitler's 'big power' expansionism. At the same time, as archival documents show, the British authorities were concerned about a potential Celtic nationalist 'Fifth Column' disrupting the war effort. The Allied victory over Fascism, then the electoral triumph of Labour, may be viewed as a triumph for 'Britishness', with the creation of a pan-UK social-democratic settlement that was the fruit of what Angus Calder called the People's War.[2] However, the war years were also a catalyst for the re-organisation and eventual strengthening of the SNP, while the expansion of the Scottish Office within the framework of the UK indicated the possibility of a national resurgence north of the Cheviots.

1 National Library of Scotland (NLS), Acc. 6914/4.
2 Angus Calder, *The People's War: Britain 1939–1945* (London: Jonathan Cape, 1969).

Pre-war Fascist affinities

Before the Second World War, Scottish nationalists, like others across the political spectrum, were fascinated and attracted by the Fascist phenomenon that began in Italy. Scots Renaissance poet C.M. Grieve, alias Hugh MacDiarmid, had been a member of the Independent Labour Party since 1908, and of the Scottish Home Rule Association since 1920, when, in June 1923, after Mussolini's blackshirts marched on Rome, he called for a Scottish species of Fascism. In 'At the Sign of the Thistle: Programme for a Scottish Fascism', published in the pro-Home Rule magazine *The Scottish Nation*, he wrote:

> Scotland is not Italy and the political, social, and industrial traditions and conditions of the people of Scotland, and their psychology differ entirely from those of Italy. Nevertheless there is need for a Scottish Fascism just as there was need for an Italian Fascism – and the first plank in the programme of the former would be precisely the same as the first plank in the latter – 'Scotland First' for us as it was 'Italy First' for them.[3]

The Fascist example therefore inspired the reinvigoration of both Labour and Scottish nationalist movements. The new nationalism would incline to the Left and meet Labour half-way in the interest of 'Scotland First.' It would also create a socialism which respected or revived traditional, rural-based culture. Citing Pietro Gorgolini's *The Fascist Movement in Italian Life*, MacDiarmid claimed: 'Italian Fascism needs most urgently to be almost exactly reproduced in Scotland in so far as agrarian policy is concerned. Its agrarian policy is summed up in the maxim, *the land for those who work it*.' The entire Fascist programme could be 'readapted to Scottish national purposes and is (whether it be called Fascist or pass under any name) *the only thing that will preserve our distinctive national culture*.'[4]

---

3   Hugh MacDiarmid, 'At the Sign of the Thistle. Programme for a Scottish Fascism', *The Scottish Nation*, 5 (5 June 1923), 10 [italics in the original].
4   *Ibid.*, 10 [italics in the original].

Also in 1923, MacDiarmid declared that Mussolini represented 'an experiment in patriotic socialism' and that 'we want a Scottish Fascism which shall be ... a lawless believer in law – a rebel believer in authority.'[5] MacDiarmid eschewed the British Fascists, whose British patriotism, imperialism and anti-communism were absolute anathema. He left the Independent Labour Party (ILP) only in 1928 to join the newly formed National Party of Scotland. It can also be argued that, in 1923, the Fascist regime, as it is now historically understood, had not been fully established. Nevertheless, in the May 1929 issue of the main organ of Scottish nationalism, the *Scots Independent*, MacDiarmid unquestionably sought the type of leadership which Mussolini practised in Italy: 'What I have said about the need for aristocratic standards, for a species of fascism applies equally here. I feel we will never make any real headway till we cease to imitate English organisations by running the Party on democratic lines or wanting anything similar in organisation or programme to the English parties.'[6] In 1930, he said of a secret Scottish nationalist society, Clann Albain, to which he belonged, that 'the whole organisation is on a militaristic basis, and in this resembles the Fascist movement.'[7] This 'organisation' would, however, only count six members. That said, MacDiarmid had great plans for it. In the *Scots Independent*, he imagined the Scotland of 1979, whose path to independence had been opened by Clann Albain:

> No longer confining themselves to English precedents, [young Scots] availed themselves readily of the examples of Italy and Ireland, and, powerfully re-enforcing the transitional organisation of the Scottish Nationalist Party (up till then still deplorably liberal and Anglophile) with their militaristic neo-Fascist auxiliary Clann Albain, carried the Movement to the successful conclusion we know of by 1965, and re-established the ancient Gaelic Commonwealth in Scotland on a modern basis.[8]

---

5   Alan Bold, *MacDiarmid – Christopher Murray Grieve. A Critical Biography* (London: Paladin, 1990), 169–70.
6   *Scots Independent*, May 1929.
7   Bold, *MacDiarmid*, 274.
8   *Scots Independent*, June 1929.

In 1931, in *The Modern Scot*, a review edited by James Whyte, a nationalist newcomer from New York, MacDiarmid favourably reviewed a book on Hitler by the fascist-leaning modernist artist Wyndham Lewis. Scotland, too, needed some *Blutsgefühl* ('blood feeling').[9]

Although MacDiarmid was a maverick, whose peripatetic political journey took him in and out of the nationalist and communist movements, his pro-fascist leanings did find echoes in the mainstream nationalist movement. The *Scots Independent* also showed an ambivalent attitude towards issues of race and continental fascism. In December 1926, it had criticised the contemporary obsession, among politicians, the churches and the media, with 'the Irish menace', but only because 'the Menace to Scotland is unrestricted and excessive immigration, *whatever be the country of origin of these immigrants*.'[10] Among Scottish nationalists other than MacDiarmid, the Italian example could inspire rejuvenation: 'Mussolini points the way', headlined the *Scots Independent* of November 1928, referring favourably to *Il Duce*'s land reclamation scheme.[11]

In December 1936, as the Spanish Civil War raged unreported in the Scottish nationalist press, J.A. Russell gave a positive assessment of the Third Reich:

> Germany is held in a tight Fascist grip; Scotland is free – or will be free. Germany inclines towards militarism; Scotland is eminently pacifist. The German mind is mass-moving; that of Scotland is intensely individualistic. From these contrasting effects we might argue, therefore, that Germany is terrorised and enslaved – Scotland well-off and happy ... The strange paradox is that, in practice, it is much more the other way around. Germany under dictatorship gets things done – constructs roads, bridges, swimming-baths, strives to make its people fit and healthy, calls for sacrifices in the national interest, maintains the morale of its unemployed by local schemes of work, and uses its native resources to the fullest extent ... Germany can be said to have achieved a national spirit and unity of purpose that in many directions might well be the envy of 'free' Scotland.[12]

9   Duncan Glen, ed., *Selected Essays of Hugh MacDiarmid* (London: Jonathan Cape, 1969), 70–2.
10 *Scots Independent*, December 1926 [italics in the original].
11 *Scots Independent*, November 1928.
12 *Scots Independent*, December 1936.

Of course, admiration for Fascism and Nazism was in a minority, albeit a significant one. Thus, in May 1937, in reaction to the successes of Oswald Mosley's blackshirts, the SNP conference resolved that 'the party is alive to the significance of the growth in Fascism in England as manifested in the last County Council elections in London, and declare that unless self-government is achieved Scotland might find herself against her will forced by English votes into a British totalitarian state.'[13] But the final words of the resolution re-iterated the founding obsession of the SNP: to get rid of the English and be a nation again. The SNP asserted its opposition to conscription and refused participation in any war until there was self-government. In April 1938, in 'Scotland and Peace', the academic Archie Lamont wrote:

> Scotland cannot afford to go into a war along with England. It would mean the final destruction of our national personality. It would mean the annihilation of the Scottish National Movement, and the submersion of everything democratic and distinctively Scottish ... We must refuse to fight, refuse to pay taxes or advance loans, refuse to handle munitions, and if we are forced into the army, refuse to carry arms.[14]

However, the sacrifice of Czechoslovakia at Munich could be denounced in the name of small-nation nationalism. The November 1938 editorial of *The Scots Independent* attacked the British government which had 'abandoned the League of Nations, having exploited it. It has wrecked collective security, having used that name for electioneering purposes.' The big power behaviour of London contrasted with the 'sane neutrality' of the Oslo Powers. 'England', rather than 'Britain', was 'guiding us to war – a war of which Scotland cannot approve, if she is to be accounted sane.' The 'moment of Scotland's opportunity' had come. It was imperative to 'resist all propagandist efforts to march our people to an imperialist war in the name of those human ideals which have been betrayed.'[15]

In November 1938, John MacCormick, co-founder of the SNP (in 1934), reaffirmed 'an unwavering belief in the League of Nations and in collective security as the only possible guarantees of the safety of the small

---

13   *The Scotsman*, 19 May 1937.
14   *Scots Independent*, April 1938.
15   *Scots Independent*, November 1938.

nations and the rule of law in the world.' But the nationalist mindset allowed for all sorts of potent amalgams. The London government, MacCormick claimed, was 'casting envious eyes on Fascist methods of government, and yearning for the opportunity to introduce them at home.'[16]

In January 1939, Arthur Donaldson, leader of the Scottish Neutrality League, argued for Scotland to stay out of any future conflict: 'Everything that Hitler has done and is said to have done against humanity and democracy will be done here by our dictators within a month or two after the first gun, and worse before it is over.'[17] In April 1939, a month after Nazi troops invaded what remained of the Czech lands, destroying all illusions of 'appeasement', SNP chairman Andrew Dewar Gibb offered 'The True View' on Nationalists and war: 'Scotland has good reason to hate all this war talk, in a far deeper sense than England ... The normal Scotsman ... will be quicker to recognise in all this the revival of the spirit of Imperialist aggressiveness and empty jingoism.'[18] The visceral anti-Englishness of Scottish nationalists therefore made them averse to any 'British' war.

A visitor from the Third Reich

Given such pronounced pacifist and anti-English views, it was not surprising that, on 18 February 1939, Andrew Dewar Gibb received a very warm letter from Dr Gerhard von Tevenar, a Celtic scholar and agent of the Nazi military intelligence organisation, the Abwehr, living in Berlin.[19] In the case of von Tevenar we see the extent of Nazi penetration of Celtic nationalist movements, as well as subsequent attempts by the SNP to exculpate itself.

16   *Scots Independent*, December 1939.
17   *Scots Independent*, January 1939.
18   *Scots Independent*, April 1939.
19   NLS, Acc. 9188, 6.

Gerhard von Tevenar was born in 1912 near Danzig. In 1929, he travelled around Denmark, Hungary, Ireland and Scotland, before returning to Germany to study law. In 1934–35, he researched the problems of minorities in frontier regions. In parallel to this, he did research on Celtology and Celtic migrations. In 1936, von Tevenar was appointed correspondent of the *Berliner Borsenzeitung* in Holland and Belgium. It was then that he met Werner Best, assistant to the head of the SD intelligence service, Reinhard Heydrich, future architect of the Final Solution. Von Tevenar was then involved in developing a vast network of relationships between the numerous autonomist movements of Europe. In the 1970s, the Breton nationalist Olier Mordrel recalled 'this travelling salesman of ethnic revolution … this idealist who told us of a mystical empire of the North, which would revive in opposition to the Latin and Anglo-Saxon world the old barbarian brotherhood.'[20]

Georges Cadiou writes that 'very soon the Nazi circles in power in Berlin began to take an interest in the movements of national minorities in Western Europe. Not through sympathy as you might think but in order to use them for the expansionist politics of the Third Reich.'[21] Von Tevenar's centre for Celtic studies was linked to the information section of military espionage (Abwehr II). Dozens of agents and spies were recruited and trained in Germany before being let loose in numerous countries to fan the flames of revolt on the western periphery. Scotland was one of the nations of the Celtic race that von Tevenar visited, studied and aimed to convert to an alliance with the Third Reich. In 1936 and 1937, he visited Scotland as part of a tour of the Celtic fringe.

Von Tevenar's letter to '*Lieber Herr Professor*' displays common commitment to the nationalist cause, but without any explicit reference to subversive activity. On the other hand, the political and the cultural were never far away: 'Glasgow must have seen recently very stormy receptions of the Air Minister; on the occasion our big papers mentioned for the first

---

20   Georges Cadiou, *L'hermine et la croix gammée. Le movement breton et la collaboration* (Paris: Editions Apogée, 2006), 75.
21   *Ibid.*, 73.

time ... I would be delighted to write some book about your country and Scottish Nationalism if I can find time and rest enough this year.'[22] Von Tevenar dreamed of a return to Caledonia:

> As you know, I had the chance to drive all over Alba from John o'Groats to the Mull of Galloway and from Skye to Dunedin, and to catch some very beautiful views of land and men. I do not know if I told you that we were lucky enough to listen on some Gaelic songs which a shepherd sung while driving home his cattle, one evening near Stein (this sounds as German) on the isle of Skye. We were sitting down between some hills, covered with heather, and looking West to the thin lines of the Hebrides, with the great red sun disk behind; as the boy did not perceive us, he sang quite undisturbed – and this evening will be always one of our most beautiful impressions of the Gaelic Scotland.[23]

He recounted his continual struggle in favour of Celtic studies then turned to the prospects for the nationalist movement: 'You will certainly pardon my frankness, but I must tell you that I found amongst the young Irish more idealism and preparedness for sacrifice (*Opferbereitschaft*) than amongst the young Scotsmen.' But he concluded on a hopeful note: 'I would be delighted to discuss all this with you personally and I do regret very much that I had no chance to meet you again in August '36, after that Wallace commemoration at Elderslie.'[24] Such an encounter would, however, never come to pass. Indeed, the declaration of war against Nazi Germany seemed to finally shake Andrew Dewar Gibb out of an indulgent, appeasing attitude towards the new enemy threatening not only England but Scotland itself. In the *Scots Independent* of October 1939, Dewar Gibb tried to reconcile anti-Englishness with opposition to Nazi aggression:

> There are far more Scotsmen today who have doubts about the justice and inevitability of the war than would have had those doubts ten years ago ... The difficulty of England's is not Scotland's opportunity – not yet. If the German planes come over, Scotland, equally with England, is threatened with death and destruction. A Scottish

---

22 NLS, Acc. 9188, 6.
23 *Ibid.*
24 *Ibid.*

life was the first British casualty of the war. In the interests of Scotland we have to save what can be saved for her.[25]

In May 1940, as the Nazi threat turned towards the last remaining western democracies, Wilson MacCulluch unmasked 'Hitler's conspiracy in Scotland. The activities of Dr von T–.' According to MacCulluch, this 'intelligent and agreeable young man', an 'ardent student of Celtic affairs and culture', visited Brittany to help radicalise its separatist movement before 'studying' the IRA and the Welsh nationalist movement. He then paid a visit to Scotland, travelling about the country, questioning, meeting leading Scottish personalities, and displaying an intelligent interest in all he saw and heard. But his mission to convert the nationalists to the Nazi cause was thwarted:

> He was loud in his surprise that the Scottish Nationalist movement had not developed a 'youth movement' which was his agreeable Teutonic way of hinting at a storm troop organisation. Strange to say no Nationalist ever displayed the slightest desire to fill this lamentable gap in the movement. Scottish Nationalism remained staunchly democratic. Dr Von T must have listened to many a word of abuse of the Nazi system (of which he professed to take a detached view).

After this preliminary exploration, 'Von T' had returned to Scotland in the summer of 1937, accompanied by 'typical nazi thugs.' Sympathisers on the fringe of nationalist politics were interviewed, but 'the report to Scotland that went back to Dr Goebbels in Berlin must have been an unfavourable one. Although Scotland was not dropped entirely from the Nazi list of work in progress, the assiduous Dr Von T does not appear to have visited our shores again.'[26]

The SNP thus publicly cleansed itself of any possible compromise by the activities of this Nazi agent and stood up to the new threat. This threat was real: if Scotland may still have seemed far from the front-line and the Battle of Britain raging over the south-east coast of England, it nevertheless

25 *Scots Independent*, October 1939.
26 *Scots Independent*, October 1940.

was included in German plans.[27] In the *Scots Independent* of June 1940, E. Marischal outlined a 'Nazi Plan to Invade Scotland', involving bombs on aerodromes, small landing parties on Fife and East Lothian coasts, and small patrols in British uniforms or civilian clothes. London had to be warned: 'Until the British military authorities understand the ingenuity of the German methods, they will not be able to meet them successfully.'[28] In July, the headline was 'Fortify the Cheviots!', with the article stating that Scotland had to be made strong against invasion by the raising of a Scottish Home Defence Army, and the rapid transfer to Scotland of sufficient arms-making, planes and personnel. With Norway in the hands of the Nazis and their puppet Quisling, a 'diplomatic correspondent' of the *Scots Independent* asked: 'Who will rule the North?' The war brought possible changes to Scotland's 'living space.' Norway would take Orkney and the Shetland Islands, 'and they will be the bridle with which she holds us in her power.' Conversely, if Scotland emerged victorious from the war, it would find its place in 'a free federation of the Western Scandinavian democracies', including the Faroes and Iceland.[29] In September, the SNP compared its map of Europe with Hitler's. Those Breton nationalists, led by Olier Mordrel, who had been recruited by von Tevenar and Berlin, stood discredited: 'Herr Weyer is nominated governor-general with his capital at Rennes. This is the hideous farce in which the labours of Breton poets and dreamers have ended!' It was the 'Commonwealth idea' that would save the West for civilisation and freedom.[30] In October 1940, the *Scots Independent* described the present conflict as 'a war of nations against the would-be destroyer of nations. It is a war "for" the Commonwealth idea, the idea of a co-operation of peoples, and "against" the idea of a super-race ruling its enslaved sub-races.'[31] Some nationalists therefore attempted to

27 See Trevor Royle, *A Time of Tyrants: Scotland and the Second World War* (Edinburgh: Birlinn, 2011).
28 *Scots Independent*, June 1940.
29 *Scots Independent*, July 1940.
30 *Scots Independent*, September 1940.
31 *Scots Independent*, October 1940.

reconcile hostility to Britain with an acute awareness of the threat posed by Fascism to the very existence of Scotland.

Against the 'Fifth Column'

In Scotland, there was antipathy to any war against continental Fascism. On 25 January 1939, Douglas Young wrote to George Campbell Hay: 'To me the cold-blooded financial stranglehold of London on the coolie and semi-coolie peoples under the aegis of democratic Westminster is quite as repulsive as the hooliganism of the Nazi storm-troopers.'[32] Young expanded on these views in a letter to Hugh Seton-Watson:

> The British Empire seems to me a worse institution than the *Staatenbund* Hitler is trying to erect. We live in as it were a genteel suburb of it, but the real empire consists of Jamaica, and the rand, and the coolie *ergastula* of India and Malaya; if democracy be representative and responsible government for the benefit of the governed, then I should be prepared to maintain that Nazi Germany with all its pogroms etc. is more concretely democratic than our hoary plutocracy, and, what is near a virtue, much less hypocritical. I believe a Nazi boss, and certainly an ordinary SA man, to be a more honest creature than a typical British bourgeois; at any rate the difference is so slight as not to be worth fifty or even five million lives.[33]

Such hostility to 'imperialist war' was widespread on the far from inconsiderable margins of Scottish politics. With the Molotov-Ribbentrop Pact, the Communists had toned down, if not buried, their anti-Fascist passion of recent years. If John Ross Campbell had resigned as editor of the *Daily Worker* in protest at the Pact, the majority of the Communist Party leadership, including the erstwhile scourge of appeasement, Willie Gallacher MP, had fallen into the Comintern line.

---

32   NLS, Acc. 6914/4.
33   *Ibid.*

But gradually, under the impact of events, the leadership of the SNP moved over to a pro-war stance. If it had opposed conscription without the assent of a Scottish parliament, as war neared in May 1939 the party relaxed its stance, provided that conscripts would be used only for the defence of Britain. In October 1939, a manifesto declared Scotland's willingness to fight alongside 'England' and the Commonwealth for ideals appealing to the Scottish people. In December, the SNP conference had agreed a policy of 'acquiescence' in the war, arguing that Germany had trampled on the freedom of three small nations already, and that a free Scotland would 'inevitably' have declared war against it anyway. However, this stance caused splinters, notably with Douglas Young, still ferociously opposed to conscription, disaffiliating his Aberdeen branch. It appears that Young even entertained the possibility of collaborating with a future Nazi occupier. In August 1940, he wrote to the SNP president Roland Muirhead: 'The Germans will look around for aborigines to run Scotland, and it is to be wished that the eventual administration consist of people who have in the past shown themselves to care for the interests of Scotland.'[34]

The poetry of Hugh MacDiarmid showed how anti-Englishness and anti-imperialism – the two inextricably linked – could lead to a downplaying, if not downright denial, of the threat emanating from Berlin. In 'On the Imminent Destruction of London, June 1940', the bard of Langholm wrote:

> Now when London is threatened
> With devastation from the air
> I realise, horror atrophying me,
> That I hardly care.[35]

The poet was echoed by Harry Miller (aka J.H. Miller-Wheeler), leader of the Scottish Socialist Party, whose socialism seemed markedly shorn of internationalism. On 4 January 1941, he wrote to MacDiarmid about schemes for the mobilisation of female labour: 'The latest racket is in

---

34 NLS, Acc. 3721, Box 89/27.
35 John Manson, Dorian Grieve and Alan Riach, eds, *The Revolutionary Art of the Future: re-discovered poems* (Manchester: Carcanet, 2003), 42.

sending Scots girls to Coventry, refusal means their dole is stopped while English wenches are arriving in droves and walking into jobs. Glasgow is crawling with prostitutes from London, Birmingham and Coventry. The same thing applies to men, there seems to be a deliberate transference of population.'[36]

That same year, in his pamphlet, *Hitlerism in the Highlands*, the socialist nationalist Oliver Brown was happy to tar the English oppressor with the Fascist brush:

> You have, so far, been presented with a one-sided view of Scottish history, the 'pacification' of the Highlands, the increase of material prosperity subsequent to (although not necessarily consequent on) the Union of 1707, and the careers offered to Scotsmen through the seizure of that land now known as the British Empire. You have been diligently shown the credit column (containing some assets of dubious value), whereas little or nothing has been said about the debt side. To rectify this omission you will find listed in these pages some of the evil consequences of the *Anschluss* of 1707, whereby the former nation of Scotland was incorporated in the English Reich. It is hoped that you will thus be enabled to strike the proper balance and reach the ultimate truth of which the following facts form an indisputable and indispensable part.[37]

Brown passed on to a litany of 'Hitlerist' crimes in the Highlands: Culloden and Butcher Cumberland, the Disarming Act, the Clearances, Skye's contribution to the tears, toil and sweat of empire building, and the heartless dictatorship blighting fishing and shipfaring. The author of this legally published polemic granted that there was a considerable freedom of speech in Scotland, but this freedom was 'every day diminishing. The imprisonment by the English Government of nationalist activists Arthur Donaldson and Matthew Hamilton without charge or trial shows the danger of rousing the resentment of our London rulers ... Scotland, under the domination of a permanent English majority in the House of Commons, has no more freedom of action than Norway under Nazi occupation.'[38]

---

36   John Manson, ed., *Dear Grieve. Letters to Hugh MacDiarmid (C.M. Grieve)* (Glasgow: Kennedy and Boyd, 2011), 296.
37   Oliver Brown, *Hitlerism in the Highlands* (Glasgow: self-published, 1941), 2.
38   *Ibid.*, 12.

Indeed, the authorities had begun to move against a suspected nationalist 'fifth column' ready to undermine the 'British' war effort. They began with Matthew Hamilton. Hamilton first came to the attention of the police in August 1933, when, at a meeting of Wendy Wood's Democratic Scottish Self-Government Organisation, at the Mound in Edinburgh, he exclaimed: 'I am one who suffered and made sacrifices for England. We will have no more of it. The next sacrifice we will make will be for our own country.'[39] There was therefore no prospect of Hamilton and his compatriots waging war for another country. In 1937, when an Excise Officer called upon him and his brother to see if they had a licence to sell cigarettes at their garage, 'Hamilton ordered him off the premises quoting old Scots Law and saying that he did not require a licence or recognise English Law.'[40] Hamilton's nationalism led him to support a position of neutrality in a future war with Germany. Indeed, this stance had a racist and anti-Semitic rather than purely pacifist underpinning, for on 24 May 1939, he wrote the following letter to Rolf Hoffmann, the Nazi propaganda chief in Munich, which is worth quoting at length:

> Your 'News from Germany' is dispelling the lies against Germany propagated by the English Press in Scotland (which is controlled by Jewish freemasonry). There is a strong opposition against an English conscription in Scotland. There has already been anti-conscription disturbance in Glasgow and Cowdenbeath – recruiting offices windows smashed in, and PO van overturned – these disturbances are being carefully censored in the Press. Also police have been armed with 'concealed' revolvers. The Celtic peoples of Scotland, Ireland and Wales (who are becoming united) desire no further participation in continental wars on behalf of Jewish-controlled England. I would be pleased to have a call from any Germans who happen to be in this vicinity, as there are many things hidden politically, and, removal of Jewish, English and Ulster Orange influences (under aegis of Jewish Foreign Freemasonry) would result in a Scots-Celtic-Germano-Social and Commercial Alliance. Enclosed find historical and legal propaganda circulating in Scotland and elsewhere, which will give you an idea of the real position of Scottish Rights. We fly a string of Welsh, Irish and Scottish flags, and would like a small swastika flag to fly alongside to

---

39 The National Archives, Kew (TNA), HO45/23680.
40 *Ibid.*

show our good feeling. Wishing you every success for German Liberty and World Peace.

Yours sincerely,
For Scottish and German Rights[41]

Hamilton was also involved in what Special Branch described as the 'highly seditious and dangerous Scots Order.'[42] On 14 January 1940, again at the Mound, Hamilton described the application of the Military Service Act to Scotland as high treason, publicly burned two calling-up papers and advised his listeners to treat all such papers in this fashion. He was also suspected of getting youths liable for conscription out to the Irish Free State. According to Special Branch, 'he decries the Royal Family and objects to members of the Royal Family being evacuated to Scotland during the war.' He was 'obviously mentally unstable and utterly irresponsible ... but is not certifiably insane.'[43]

In these febrile times, Hamilton had nevertheless done enough to merit internment under Defence Regulation 18B (a measure mainly used against the British Union of Fascists) as a potential threat to national security on 3 June 1940 and sent to Peveril Camp, Isle of Man. It was there that Hamilton claimed his 'Rights to the Protection of Scots Limitations and Security Acts, 1701–47, and the Treaty of Union, Provisions 1707.' He was unsuccessful.

On 20 May 1942, the Camp Commandant, reported that the inmate's Scottish nationalist views remained as strong as ever, although he now knew Scotland could not stay out of the war. What is more, he 'has no German sympathies, dislikes Germans and is very much against Scotland being ruled by a Royal family of Hanoverian descent; his attitude to the war, if released, would be one of disinterested aloofness.'[44] In July 1942, Matthew Hamilton was released.

41 Ibid.
42 Ibid.
43 Ibid.
44 Ibid.

Police repression continued by other means. On 3 May 1941 the police carried out raids on the houses and premises of nationalists opposed to the war effort. Various items of interest were found. It was also reported that the censor was keeping an eye on C.M. Grieve [Hugh MacDiarmid]'s correspondence.[45] Another nationalist target was Harry Miller, who had taken an active role in the 'Scottish Defence Corps', which became defunct in 1936. In April 1940, he had moved from the SNP to the Scottish Socialist Party and taken part on the anti-conscription Nationalist Mutual Aid Committee. His police interrogator was particularly interested in possible links with Nazi intelligence.

The raid on Roland Muirhead seemed relatively fruitful, turning up a small pistol and some fireworks as well as a copy of a letter sent to 'Dr von Teffenar [sic], Berlin.' In Aberdeen, Douglas Young told the police: 'I certainly am a Scottish nationalist and do not recognise the Westminster government, but there is nothing subversive to be found here, nothing that would injure the war effort.'[46] The poet George Campbell Hay, on the run from the military, was in hiding in Argyllshire. At his home was found a letter from Young Nationalist Iain Haig in which he said: 'I wish more than ever now that Germany would win the war and create a hell of a change in this bloody country.' That said, the investigators could find 'nothing of a seditious or pro-German nature was contained in the correspondence.'[47]

These raids, and the detention of Arthur Donaldson in May and June 1941, were met with indignation. On 13 May 1941, James Maxton, Independent Labour MP for Glasgow Bridgeton, raised questions in the Commons, denouncing the 'melodramatic nonsense and rubbish' used by the authorities to justify their actions. On 18 May, a week after Rudolf Hess's ill-fated flight to meet the Duke of Hamilton, Miller wrote to MacDiarmid:

> Questions have been asked about stories of Scotland being ready to make a separate peace with Germany. 'Haw Haw' [William Joyce] has also made references to the position in Scotland. Needless to say there is not a chance for that outfit doing a deal

45 National Archives of Scotland (NAS), HH 55/557.
46 NAS, HH 55/558.
47 Ibid.

with Nationalists and republicans in Scotland. Funny that Hess should fly to see a member of the ruling class, the only bunch who are likely to do a deal with Hitler, and who probably will.[48]

On 25 May 1941, it was the turn of MacDiarmid to write to 'Dear Comrade' Tom Johnston, Secretary of State for Scotland:

> Neither I nor any of the Scots Republicans who have been raided have had any subsidisation from our dealings with the German Nazis – nor any subsidisation from any other foreign source. The whole thing is a base English Imperialist manoeuvre to throttle and libel the now rapidly growing Scottish Socialist Republican Movement – and to divert public attention from the pro-Nazi Fifth Column traitors who are not to be found in our ranks but in the ranks of our aristocracy, plutocracy, and the 'internment' movement itself, where there are plenty who will sell us out to Hitler if they get a chance.[49]

He protested the raids on the offices of newspapers such as *Scottish Socialist*, *Free Man*, *Scottish News* and *Comment*, the internment of Arthur Donaldson, and the treatment of Douglas Young, who had been 'raided, questioned and grossly victimised by the English Gestapo.' Moreover, the police had seized Gaelic manuscripts by great eighteenth-century Scottish poets 'simply because they are in Gaelic and *ipso facto* objects of suspicion to our ignorant English and Anglo-Scot CID people.'[50]

Radical anti-war nationalists would create the Donaldson Defence Committee, denouncing the 'arbitrary and tyrannical treatment' of this dangerous dissident. According to the security services Donaldson, was 'an extremist Scottish nationalist who has been engaged in the formation of an organisation called United Scotland which is more extremist than the SNP from which Donaldson has been expelled.'[51] He had 'made statements indicating that in his view England would be completely crushed by the early spring of this year, that the Government would leave the country and that the movement in Scotland must then be able to show the German

48 Manson, *Dear Grieve*, 307.
49 NAS, HH 55/557.
50 *Ibid.*
51 TNA, HO 45/23801.

Government that it is organised and has a clear cut policy, that it is not with England in the war and that when fire and confusion is at its height in England the movement can start in earnest.'[52] He had also suggested the introduction of a whispering campaign which would spread rumours regarding shipping losses. Furthermore, he was the organiser of 'a body called the National Aid Society which has branches in Edinburgh, Glasgow, Aberdeen and Stirling and which assists conscientious objectors on Scottish Nationalist grounds to go into hiding.' Special Branch concluded that 'it seems apparent from his activities and the above references that he is building up an organisation with a view to his assuming the function of Scottish Quisling when invasion takes place.'[53]

Donaldson had first come to the notice of Ayrshire police in April 1939 in connection with the distribution of leaflets for the Scottish Neutrality League and United Scotland. According to a police report, he was 'described as being very dogmatic and inconsistent in these matters and is regarded as eccentric.'[54] In June 1940, Donaldson was expelled from the SNP because of his militant stance on neutrality, and formed United Scotland, 'a nucleus of extreme Nationalists who would be prepared to take advantage of an opportunity for furthering Scottish Independence by violence if necessary.'[55] He was also suspected of contact with the enemy. When the *Scots Independent* denounced Gerhard von Tevenar, he was reported as having told one of his associates, Mary Ramsay: 'We have yet to meet a Nationalist of repute, particularly of the so-called "extreme" category, who ever met or knew of him.'[56] The police report remarked: 'It is, to say the least, peculiar that Donaldson should go out of his way to ridicule this story and there is a strong possibility that he himself knew Von Teffenar [*sic*], though we have no definite evidence to support this view.'[57]

52   Ibid.
53   Ibid.
54   Ibid.
55   Ibid.
56   Ibid.
57   Ibid.

His seditious activities were confirmed later that year with his involvement in the National Aid Society, which helped Scots dodge conscription: 'At least six Nationalist Conscientious Objectors are known to have gone into hiding in Inverness-shire. While "on the run", provision is made for them to use Youth Hostels, Caves, etc as hide-outs.' In addition to Roland Muirhead, 'who was a contact of Hoffmann of the German Press Bureau', Mary Ramsay, 'soap-box agitator', and Harry Miller, 'an agitator whose activities range from window-smashing to slogan-painting', his associates included Oliver Brown and Wendy Wood, both known for 'theft of explosives.'[58] He also had contacts abroad, being 'known to have been interested in Celtic Nationalism as a whole, and contributed to Breton nationalist papers.'[59] Donaldson was reported to have 'pro-Nazi and subversive views.' In February 1942, the police informant, who had now been in close contact with Nationalist circles for nearly nine months, was asked his opinion of Donaldson, and stated that he considered him 100% pro-German:

> His wife shares his views. Donaldson sees himself as a Scottish Quisling, who will come forward when invasion takes place with a complete 'New Order for Scotland' which he will present to Hitler, and which he believes will be acceptable. When invasion comes, Donaldson's aim is to use his party for spreading confusion by false reports and minor acts of sabotage such as the cutting of telegraph wires.[60]

It was therefore concluded from the above that 'Donaldson has a mind which works along National Socialist lines; he is building up an organisation which includes political extremists of all shades whose common quality is a fervent nationalism; he is influencing young men against taking part in the War effort; and he firmly believes that a German conquest of England would be to his own and Scotland's advantage.'[61] However, despite Donaldson's subversive views, there was no substantive proof of potential Quisling activity. It was instead concluded that Donaldson 'caused and may still cause a certain amount of Parliamentary trouble.' The audience

58   Ibid.
59   Ibid.
60   Ibid.
61   Ibid.

and influence of Donaldson and his associates were negligible: 'The political side only started when Maxton began asking questions in the House of Commons.'[62] Therefore, on 12 June 1941, Tom Johnston came to the conclusion that his indefinite detention was not necessary. In his memoirs, Johnston downplayed the threat posed by Scottish nationalists to Britain's security: 'When war ultimately came to our world there were no Quislings in Scotland, and but few who carried pacifist surrenderism the length of making no preparation for the relief of suffering among the civilian population.'[63] This assessment of the 'Quisling' threat is perhaps inaccurate given the documents that have recently come to light about the extent of potential nationalist 'subversion' of the British war effort.

Fortifying the Cheviots

The clemency of the authorities notwithstanding, these raids and arrests would encourage in Scottish nationalist ranks a drift away from fortifying the Cheviots against Nazi invasion to fortifying them against the Auld Enemy. Already in January 1941, the *Scots Independent* had led on Westminster's mistreatment of Scottish hill farmers and the threat from English workers coming north. The headline in May was 'Go south or starve!', as nationalists protested the 'forced drafting of Scots girls to England.'[64] Radical nationalists were now in the ascendancy. At the SNP conference of 1942, the pro-war, moderate leadership of John MacCormick was replaced by hardliners opposed to conscription and prepared to contest elections, thus breaking Britain's wartime 'united front.' At their head was Douglas Young, imprisoned for his refusal of conscription. Young was, in

62   Ibid.
63   Thomas Johnston, *Memories* (London: Collins, 1952), 134.
64   *Scots Independent*, May 1941.

the words of Richard J. Finlay, 'the most ideal embodiment of strident, aggressive and unapologetic Scottish nationalism.'[65]

The 'martyrs' for the cause would soon resume their radical activities and attract the attention of the authorities. In April 1942, Special Branch reported on a public demonstration in Glasgow to commemorate the anniversary of the Declaration of Arbroath. It was attended by 100 people. Among the orators, Harry Miller said the meeting had been called 'to commemorate an event greater than the Gettysburg speech of Abraham Lincoln, which was looked upon as the acme of democracy, and it was certainly greater than the Atlantic Charter.' Arthur Donaldson then declared that he had been put in prison because 'he was a Scotsman trying to obtain the freedom, politically, socially and economically of his country.' Hugh MacDiarmid outdid him in patriotic zeal, one observer summarising his views:

> The Declaration of Independence of their country, which they had met together to commemorate, was a great statement, far in advance of anything else at that time and also far in advance of any ideas which the English had on the subject at the present. Grieve said that he hated Fascism wherever he found it, were it in Germany, Italy, Spain or England ... The Scots people, he declared, had better be careful lest, while they were being beguiled into taking a leading role in fighting for imperialism, with the thought that they were fighting against Fascism, they found themselves in the grip of Fascism at home. German Fascism, he said, was bad but it was nothing to English fascism.[66]

These radical positions were echoed in the *Scots Independent*. In July 1942, Douglas Young contributed 'Quislings in Scotland. Review of the Fifth Column.' His evidence was a 'Statement to give expression to public opinion in Scotland in opposition to agitation for a Scottish National Parliament', published in Glasgow in 1933. The list of signatories showed 'solid vested interests', a 'roll of infamy' that included dukes, earls and Unionist chief

---

65   Richard J. Finlay, *Independent and Free: Scottish Politics and the Origins of the Scottish National Party 1918–1945* (Edinburgh: John Donald, 1994), 230.
66   NAS, HH 55/557.

whips.⁶⁷ In August 1942, when Colin Walkinshaw (pseudonym used by journalist J.M. Reid) wrote of 'Freedom or Fascism', he meant 'this planning racket' that would be 'death to Scotland' and open the road 'towards fascism.' At the end of his assault on the 'slave state', he declared: 'This is just fascism, though Fascism in a peculiarly English dress with the Old School ties taking the place of the brown or black shirt.'⁶⁸ In 1943, Young brought out a pamphlet, *'Fascism for the Highlands'? Gauleiter for Wales?*, which portrayed the British State as 'enemy' of these Celtic nations. His translation, while imprisoned, of Aristophanes's *Lysistrata* also illustrated his anti-war position.

Under Young's leadership, the SNP was therefore half-hearted at most about the struggle against continental Fascism. On 25 August 1943, the Home Office reported on a leaflet. Beginning '1314 Bannockburn 1943 ...', it noted that it was 'high time for another Bannockburn' and for the clearing out of Scotland of its worst enemy 'the London imperialist Boss Class and the English would-be *Herrenvolk*.'⁶⁹ In September 1943, the *Scots Independent* claimed that the freedom of Scotland's youth was put in peril by being corralled into 'the British *Jugend*',⁷⁰ thus associating Britishness with alien fascist oppression. In October 1944, as the allies advanced on all fronts, Young complained of 'peace, *imperfect* peace', protesting still at the 'conscript police.'⁷¹

Robert MacIntyre's victory at the Motherwell by-election of April 1945, as well as Douglas Young's strong showing in a previous by-election in Kirkcaldy, proved that there could be an audience for Scottish nationalism, although Angus Calder points out that, paradoxically, the growing tensions in the wartime coalition meant that Conservative Unionists 'must have voted heavily for MacIntyre.'⁷² After the departure of John MacCormick, the SNP, under a young and dynamic leadership, began

67   *Scots Independent*, June 1942.
68   *Scots Independent*, August 1942.
69   NAS, HH 55/557.
70   *Scots Independent*, September 1943.
71   *Scots Independent*, October 1944 [italics in the original text].
72   Calder, *The People's War*, 574.

to put together an effective electioneering machine as well as develop a distinctive, left-of-centre programme. That said, the SNP's results at the general elections of July 1945 were dismal: Labour came first in Scotland with 48 per cent, followed by the Conservatives on 40 per cent, while the SNP garnered a mere 1.3 per cent, behind the Liberals and Communists. At this moment in its history, the SNP seemed to be badly out of touch with a geopolitical dynamic which saw the Labour landslide, an overwhelming identification with Britishness, and, in Europe, the high watermark of anti-Fascism and Communism.

If Scottish nationalism made progress during the war years, it was very much thanks to Tom Johnston, a well-known Labour proponent of Home Rule. For Johnston, 'devolution – timeous devolution – was imperative if a sort of Scots Sinn Feinism was to be obviated.'[73] As Secretary of State in Churchill's War Cabinet, he felt he 'would be at the centre of things during "our finest hour" and that [he] would be given a chance to inaugurate some large scale reforms under the umbrella of a Council of State, and which reforms, if we emerged intact as a nation at the end of the war, might mean Scotia Resurgent!'[74] Johnston fought cannily and effectively for Scottish interests in the War Cabinet: the Scottish Council on Industry attracted large investment to the country, while the foundations were laid for hydro-electric generation in the Highlands. At the end of the last meeting of the Scottish Council of State, he recalled, 'we knew our experiment had worked: we were now no longer representatives of an old nation in decay, but of a young virile people lit up with the assurance that whatever men dare in unison they can do.'[75] According to Christopher Harvie, 'the growth of the Scottish Office meant that the preoccupations of Scottish politicians were increasingly contained within the country.'[76] At the same time, after Labour's landslide, the creation of the National Health Service and the National Coal Board served, in the words of Tom Gallagher, to 'reinforce

---

73 Johnston, 148.
74 *Ibid.*, 148.
75 *Ibid.*, 169.
76 Christopher Harvie, *Scotland and Nationalism: Scottish society and politics 1707 to the present* (London: Routledge, 2004), 34.

the threadbare fabric of Britishness.'[77] The Scottishness within Britain represented by Tom Johnston can therefore be seen as more representative than that promoted during the war via the SNP and its radical fringe.

Already in the late 1940s, the success of the Scottish Covenant, a cross-party petition which attracted two million signatures, including Tom Johnston's, showed that an aspiration to Home Rule had not been killed stone dead by fighting for Britain. In the words of Tom Gallagher, many now saw Scotland as a 'partner nation and not a vassal region.'[78] As for the SNP, it was setting out on a long road that would eventually lead to it posing as champion of a post-war social-democratic settlement that was the fruit of an anti-Fascist struggle with which it had been only tenuously associated.

---

[77] Tom Gallagher, *The Illusion of Freedom: Scotland under Nationalism* (London: Hurst and Co., 2009), 50.

[78] Gallagher, 51.

JESSICA THURLOW

'Total War on Spiritual Issues': English feminists, Christian national identity and gender equality in wartime Britain

Relatively little is known about the intersections between faith, religious identity and feminism during the Second World War; a lacuna in British women's history which can be traced back to assumptions that religion was antithetical to women's emancipation. Yet more recent historical scholarship by Jacqueline deVries, Sue Morgan, and others has pointed to the need for historians to 'overcome simplistic assumptions about religion's conservative influence' and shift away from viewing religion as a 'hopelessly patriarchal institution and a primary source of oppressive domestic ideology.'[1] The archival records of English feminists and organisations from the Second World War indicate a widespread interest in women's religious identity and equality and there were two significant milestones in the development of women's church work during the war: the 1942 creation of a female 'chaplaincy' to serve all women's forces, including chaplains' assistants for the Auxiliary Territorial Service (ATS), the wartime women's branch of the British army, and the 1944 ordination of the first female priest within the Anglican Communion in war-torn China.[2] Addressing the former, this chapter elucidates the way in which both gender and religious

---

1   Jacqueline deVries, 'Rediscovering Christianity after the Postmodern Turn', *Feminist Studies*, 31/1 (2005), 135–55. Here 135. Also see Sue Morgan, ed., *Women, Religion and Feminism in Britain, 1750–1900* (Houndmills: Palgrave Macmillan, 2002); Sue Morgan and Jacqueline deVries, eds, *Women, Gender and Religious Cultures in Britain, 1800–1940* (London: Routledge, 2010).
2   On 1944 ordination see Thurlow, 'The "Great Offender": Feminists and the Campaign for Women's Ordination', *Women's History Review*, 23/3 (2014), 480–99.

identities shaped what English feminists were fighting for during the war and, also, the manner in which new opportunities and exigencies created by warfare emphasised both the 'centrality of gender difference to the nation'[3] and the persistence and relevance of English Christian national identity[4] to many English in a century traditionally perceived as overwhelmingly secular. This chapter will use the female 'chaplaincy' scheme to explore how conflict, or even cooperation, between English feminists, the military, the Free Churches and the Church of England in particular highlighted women's unequal status as citizens at the same time that it emphasised the importance of Christianity to feminists' personal identities and their and others' understanding of the nation and national identity during the war.

Research by Harold Smith and Alison Oram has demonstrated the vitality of English feminism in the mid-twentieth century.[5] However, there remains little research into how feminists challenged religious institutions in the twentieth century or the way in which religious identity, or corporate identity, has shaped feminism.[6] Organisations such as the feminist Women's Freedom League perceived their nation as a 'Christian society' and wartime campaigns focusing on women's church work suggest that religion was significant to many English feminists and that their identities were shaped by a sense of shared Christian values that they felt

---

[3] Sonya O. Rose, *Which People's War?: National Identity and Citizenship in Wartime Britain 1939–1945* (Oxford: Oxford University Press, 2003), 122.

[4] See Stephen Parker, 'Reinvigorating Christian Britain: The Spiritual Issues of the War, National Identity, and the Hope of Religious Education', in Tom Lawson and Stephen Parker, eds, *God and War: The Church and Armed Conflict in the Twentieth Century* (London: Ashgate, 2012), 61–79.

[5] See Harold L. Smith, 'British Feminism and the Equal Pay Issue in the 1930s', *Women's History Review*, 5/1 (1996), 97–110; Alison Oram, '"Bombs don't discriminate!" Women's Political Activism in the Second World War' in Christine Gledhill and Gillian Swanson, eds, *Nationalising Femininity: Culture, Sexuality and British Cinema in the Second World War* (Manchester: Manchester University Press, 1996), 53–69.

[6] Jessica Thurlow, *Continuity and Change in British Feminism, c. 1940–60* (Unpublished PhD dissertation, University of Michigan, 2006).

defined their nation and being English.⁷ In that respect, post-suffrage English feminism was neither anti-religious nor militantly secular and some feminists certainly embraced a Christian feminist faith. The fight for women's equal participation in the churches was part of the wartime English feminist movement and illustrates both a continuing connection between women's religious identities and their political and social activism since the nineteenth century and the importance of religion and Christian national identity to our understanding of wartime feminist activism.

Recent studies on religion during the Second World War argue convincingly that religion – conceived broadly – mattered to those on both the battlefront and home front, as did the Church of England. Michael Snape's study of the wartime British army illuminates the significant place held by organised Christianity in the military and claims that, ultimately, the war was witness to a 'deepening of religious faith at a personal level.'⁸ His work, and that of other historians, offers important revisions to the historiography of secularisation in twentieth-century Britain and understandings of the place of religion, religious institutions, and religious identity in Britain's 'culturally Christian societ[y]' during the war.⁹ As Tom

---

7   Women's Library, London (henceforth WL), *Women's Freedom League Bulletin* (henceforth *WLFB*), Leader, 16 October 1942.
8   Michael Snape, 'War, Religion, and Revival: The United States, Canadian, and British Armies during the Second World War', in Callum Brown and Michael Snape, eds, *Secularization in the Christian World: Essays in Honour of Hugh McLeod* (London: Ashgate, 2010), 135–57. Here 151, 147, 151.
9   Snape, 'War, Religion, and Revival', 138; Michael Snape, *God and the British Soldier: Religion and the British Army in the Era of Two World Wars* (London: Routledge, 2005); Callum Brown, *Religion and Society in Twentieth-Century Britain* (London: Pearson, 2006); Callum Brown, *The Death of Christian Britain: Understanding Secularization, 1800–2000* (London: Routledge, 2009); Callum Brown and Michael Snape, 'Introduction: Conceptualizing Secularization 1974–2010: the Influence of Hugh McLeod', in Brown and Snape, eds, *Secularization in the Christian World*, 1–12; Tom Lawson and Stephen Parker, 'Introduction: God and War: A Century in the Politics of Religion', in Lawson and Parker, eds, *God and War*, 1–13; Clive Field, 'Puzzled People Revisited: Religious Believing and Belonging in Wartime Britain, 1939–45', *Twentieth Century British History*, 19/4 (2008), 446–79.

Lawson and Stephen Parker point out, it is 'increasingly accepted that Britain during the Second World War appeared outwardly Christian' and the Church was critical to 'the life of the nation' and to 'the very nature of being British.'[10] Examining English feminist (hereafter feminist) activism in light of this historiography helps to emphasise the way in which wartime feminists were often united with those around them in fighting for a Christian England even as they contested gender inequalities.

This chapter focuses primarily on English feminist activism and events surrounding the origins and work of the English-based Churches Work for Women in the Forces. While references to Britain are common in wartime discussions of Christian national identity within England, the term English Christian national identity is used here to more specifically categorise the efforts and interests of Englishmen and women within the military, churches and feminist organisations on the question of a female chaplaincy. Similarly, the Church of England's role in these decisions places these conversations in a very specific national context even while they had broader repercussions for the British military.

Feminist activism and English churches in wartime

At the beginning of the war, the Women's Freedom League (WFL), founded in 1907, had boldly declared that its work for women's rights would continue 'even in the shadow of war' so that women could 'make their full contribution in the struggle for freedom and civilization.'[11] They wanted a peace that was not 'merely the cessation of hostilities,' but 'the building of a new world where men and women alike enjoy equal ... freedom.'[12] Scholars, including Sonya Rose and Alison Oram, have found that war

10 Lawson and Parker, 'Introduction', 5, 9, 11.
11 WL, *WFLB*, 'Our 33rd Annual Conference', May 24, 1940.
12 WL, *WFLB*, Leader, 7 June 1940.

reenergised feminist activism and feminists did not cease their work.[13] Both the required registration of women with employment exchanges in 1939 and the 1941 conscription of women into the auxiliary forces, civil defence or industry encouraged feminists to argue for equal citizenship. Undeniably, protests for equal social and civil rights and a proportionate voice in politics grew as women were required to fulfil their obligations as citizens and, in some cases, do the same work as men.[14] Feminists and others campaigned throughout the war on older campaigns like equal pay and married women's nationality or started new campaigns related to the specific circumstances of warfare such as equal compensation for war injuries.[15]

Religious institutions had become a focus of feminist campaigns in the nineteenth and twentieth centuries not just because they denied women equality, but because they denied society women's spiritual leadership and women full expression of their faith and identities. Growing interest in women's church work can be traced back to the development of women's religious communities in the mid-1800s.[16] Victorian society, according to Martha Vicinus, 'assumed that religion would be the inspiration of women's work and there was widespread support for the 'creation of Protestant religious orders to train women in nursing, teaching, social work and other "womanly" tasks.'[17] Feminist interest in women's church work continued into the Second World War and, by that time, both secular and Christian feminists had been criticising the churches for decades for discrimination against women. Additionally, numerous texts had been written by pro-ordination supporters, including feminists, in the first half of the twentieth century against the

---

13   Rose, *Which People's War?*, 107–50; Oram, '"Bombs don't discriminate!"', 65; Thurlow, *Continuity*.
14   Penny Summerfield, 'Women and War in the Twentieth Century', in June Purvis, ed., *Women's History in Britain, 1850–1945* (London: UCL Press, 1995), 307–32; Oram, '"Bombs don't discriminate!"', 65.
15   Thurlow, *Continuity*, 75–128.
16   Jacqueline Field-Bibb, *Women Towards Priesthood: Ministerial Politics and Feminist Praxis* (Cambridge: Cambridge University Press, 1991), 67, 69.
17   Martha Vicinus, *Independent Women: Work and Community for Single Women, 1850–1920* (London: Virago Press Ltd., 1994), 46.

many theological, biological, and psychological arguments against women's equal ministry.[18] By the Second World War, women's position in churches had improved, but there were still vast advances to be made. Those institutions which had opened their ministry to women in England included such churches as the Baptist Union of Great Britain, the English Presbyterian Church, and the Congregational Union.[19] Women's ministry in the Church of England (hereafter Church) was not equal to men's, but there had been a number of inter-war reports years which suggested that change could be imminent. One of the more convincing pieces of evidence for this was a comment in the 1935 'The Ministry of Women' report that the 'continuous tradition' of a male priesthood rather than theological arguments was a more compelling reason for denying equal ministry.[20] Numerous British institutions had modified their 'traditions' in the preceding century in response to shifting gender roles so some sensed that the report hinted at change.

Wartime feminists found women's position in the church galling. In April 1943 Margery Corbett Ashby, a suffrage pioneer and life-long women's rights campaigner, presided over a London conference sponsored by the interdenominational Society for the Equal Ministry of Men and Women in the Church (SEM) titled 'Equality of Opportunity in Church and State.'[21] Corbett Ashby was the Society's president and focused intensively on gender inequality within churches. She believed that campaigns for equal ministry were in their 'final stage' and took this opportunity to declare a 'total war on spiritual issues.'[22] In using the term 'total war', Corbett Ashby was expressing

---

18 For example, Edith Picton Turberville, *Should Women Be Priests and Ministers?* (London: SEM, 1916).
19 Field-Bibb, *Women Towards Priesthood*, 92, 117.
20 WL, Pamphlet Collection (henceforth PC), AGOW, 'The Question of Women and Holy Orders, A Memorandum to the Committee set Up in 1963 by the Archbishops of Canterbury and York to examine the whole question of women and Holy Orders' (September 1963), 3; The Ministry of Women, *Report of the Archbishops' Commission* (London: Church Assembly Press and Publications Board, 1935).
21 WL, 'Equal Ministry in the Church', *Women in Council Newsletter*, May 1943.
22 WL, 7/AMR, Letter: Ashby to Sir/Madam, October 1948; *WFLB*, 'Society for the Equal Ministry of Men and Women in the Church (Interdenominational)', 30 April 1943.

her anger at the fact that numerous denominations continued to deny equal ministry. However, her co-option of the language of warfare and likening of the campaign to Britain's war against fascism placed her comment squarely within a specific historical moment and offers intriguing commentary on the notion of a 'common good' for which all Britons were fighting. Her suggestion that there were 'enemies' at 'home' challenged wartime rhetoric of unity against a common enemy abroad and 'unsettled the conception of Britain as an inclusive ... community'; rather, it highlighted the manner in which gender difference was central to the nation.[23] At the same time, it emphasised the importance of Christianity and Christian national identity to Corbett Ashby and her belief that it was an aspect of the nation worth preserving during a horrific war, a war perceived as a fight for 'Christian civilization' and in which there was a renewed spotlight on the Church and Christianity as a focus of national unity and culture.[24]

When the SEM renewed its work in 1942 after wartime inactivity it sought out the support of numerous women's organisations and advertised its wish in the National Council of Women's newsletter that 'many will join its ranks, recognising in the movement a factor, in the establishment of that better world, which is the aim of post-war reconstruction.'[25] That 'better world', as it pertained to England at least, was perceived as a Christian one by many feminists and one in which women could fully express their religion. Historically, Christianity was important to numerous feminists and some, like Corbett Ashby, worked with both secular and faith-based organisations or campaigns, supported women's ordination, and or preached regularly.[26] DeVries has noted that women 'realized that preaching would allow them the opportunity not only to promote social

23 Rose, *Which People's War?*, 108.
24 Lawson and Parker, 'Introduction', 2, 5.
25 WL, SWC Minutes, 22 May and 17 June 1947; Secretary, SEM, Equal Ministry in the Church, *Women in Council Newsletter*, September 1942.
26 Jacqueline DeVries, 'Transforming the Pulpit: Preaching and Prophecy in the British Women's Suffrage Movement', in Beverly Mayne Kienzle and Pamela J. Walker, eds, *Women Preachers and Prophets through Two Millennia of Christianity* (Los Angeles: University of California Press, 1988), 318–33. Here 318.

and political reform but also to critique and combat the deeply rooted cultural sources of women's subordination.'[27] Thus, women's influence within churches was seen by many as both a matter of vital national reform and a means to root out irrational prejudices against women, at the same time that it was a recognition of their strong Christian faith and identity as Englishwomen.

Female chaplains' assistants and the British military

In an effort to respond to servicewomen's spiritual wellbeing, the Churches Work for Women in the Forces (CWWF), an interdenominational organisation serving as the liaison body between the military and churches, was formed in 1940 to meet wartime needs.[28] Overseen by the Archbishop of Canterbury as the committee's president and symbolic head, the Chaplain General, Chaplain of the Fleet, Chaplain in Chief RAF, and the Federal Council of Free Churches' moderator served as vice presidents. This body and the Army Council ultimately granted approval for the War Office to hire female chaplains' assistants to serve the ATS and other female religious workers (specifically Christian ones) to work with all three branches of women's forces. While the numbers of women in these positions paled in comparison to those engaged in other forms of wartime service, the efforts to establish them illustrate the way in which the war made it possible to shift decades-long discussions about women's ministry to one of national need and highlighted a strong wartime perception on the part of English

---

27 *Ibid.*, 320.
28 Lambeth Palace, London (henceforth LP), Fisher 22, 1946 (CCWF; work of 1945–7), Letter: Chairman General, CCWF to church leaders, 17 May 1947.

churches, the military, feminists and others of England as a Christian nation and the importance of Christianity to English national identity.

Official discussions about servicewomen's spiritual welfare began under Archbishop of Canterbury, Cosmo Gordon Lang, in 1939 when a number of individuals and groups contacted him about work with national servicewomen.[29] Of particular interest was communication with Dorothea Belfield, an Anglican deaconess and then SEM honorary secretary, which highlights the institutionalisation of gender difference in the Church and how the military became a site of contestation over women's equal ministry. Belfield had had a conversation at the start of the war with YWCA representative Una Saunders about the provision of religious education for servicewomen.[30] She hoped that the mobilisation of women might lead to the opening of female lay reader positions and, also, that deaconesses would be used as both chaplains and chaplains' assistants.[31] However, Lang made it clear early on that, while he was prepared to consider how women with religious training could work with servicewomen, this was not an opportunity to re-examine women's ministry. He frequently noted in their correspondence and meetings in 1939 and 1940 that neither he nor the military would consider women in the chaplaincy.[32] Lang's opinion on the War Office's position was, in part, substantiated by a letter to then Archbishop of York, William Temple, from Chaplain General C.D. Symon detailing a meeting with Corbett Ashby and Belfield. Symon had told them that while the ATS would welcome evening religious talks on a voluntary basis 'the Army would never recognize a Woman Chaplain.'[33] When Belfield argued in a letter to Lambeth Palace that the Chaplain-Generals

---

29 On women's wartime church work, see, for example, LP, Lang 94, 1939–42 ('Ministry of Women'), Fisher 22, 1946 (CCWF), Temple 3; National Archives (henceforth TNA), AIR 19/436–7.

30 LP, Lang 94, Letter: Saunders to Lang (25 November 1939); *The Churches Work for Women in the Forces 1940–1950* (henceforth *CWWF 1940–1950*), 1.

31 LP, Lang 94, Letter: Belfield to Don, 10 January 1940; Letter: Belfield to Lang, 21 November 1939.

32 LP, Lang 94, Letter: Don to Belfield, 12 January 1940.

33 LP, Lang 94, Letter: Symons to Temple, November 1939.

Department, not the military, opposed women as chaplain's assistants, Alan Don, Lang's chaplain and secretary, responded rather evasively stating that '[The Archbishop's] difficulty is that he does not see what can be done to remedy it. He must accept the fact that the responsible army authorities are not prepared to sanction the appointment of women as Assistant Chaplains and that it is therefore no good raising the question.'[34]

Although Belfield was not content with a focus merely on religious talks, Saunders and Corbett Ashby would decide to forge ahead without her and capitalise on the clear interest within the churches, military and Lambeth Palace in support of them. To this end, organisations including the Central Council for Women's Church Work, the Anglican Group for the Ordination of Women to the Historic Ministry of the Church, the YWCA, the Church of England Moral Welfare Council and the free church women's boards met at Lambeth Palace in December 1939 to consider the issue.[35] Within a month the newly created Churches Work for Women in the Forces (CWWF) had selected twenty two women to provide talks, thus in line with Symon and Lang's interests.[36]

As the CWWF's work continued, though, important shifts occurred which facilitated a broadening of ideas about the military's religious provisions for servicewomen and the eventual development of a female chaplaincy. First, fuller discussion about servicewomen's spiritual wellbeing illustrated broader support for a women's chaplaincy of some sort. For instance, the WFL was vocal about the issue in a newsletter article titled 'War Office Bans Women Parsons with Forces.'[37] This referenced Belfield's arguments for a female chaplaincy and noted that there was some support within the Church from individuals including the Dean of St. Paul's Cathedral. Bishop of Chichester, George Bell, had in fact written to Lang in 1939 indicating that something akin to female chaplains might be needed

34 LP, Lang 94, Letter: Belfield from Don, 12 January 1940.
35 LP, Lang 94, Conference of Women, 15 December 1939; 'Conference on Work among Women attached to the Army'.
36 LP, Lang 94, First Interim Selection Board (for women serving with HMs Forces); 'Women in the Services', *Church Times*, 20 March 1942.
37 WL, *WFLB*, 26 April 1940.

to work with servicewomen as 'they would resent an outsider.'[38] Moreover, a comment from William Wedgwood Benn, Lord Stansgate, the Secretary of State for Air, noted below, illustrates that some military officials felt quite differently from Lang and Symons, believing both women's equality and spirituality in the forces to be critical and that a female chaplaincy would have a 'healthy effect on the right type of recruitment.'[39] Second, women's conscription significantly altered the numbers of service personnel the all-male chaplaincy would have to serve; approximate peak wartime numbers in the Women's Royal Naval Service (WRNS) were 74,000, the Women's Auxiliary Air Force (WAAF) 180,000 and the ATS 210,000.[40] Mobilisation helped to drive home the situation's gravity to the War Office and Church and made it possible, according to World Council of Church's member Kathleen Bliss, for the CWWF to 'convinc[e], the Secretary of State for War that the pastoral care of the very large number of women drafted into the women's forces could not be properly carried out by men chaplains alone.'[41] Certainly many church officials were also fully aware by that time that the war provided an unparalleled opportunity to make an impact on citizens and develop a stronger Christian national identity.[42]

Third, was the role that the Church and Christianity assumed during the war as evidenced by the 'strong identification of Christianity with the purpose of the war and with English character and identity' and the fact that 'Christian culture remained at the forefront of the national reaction to wartime emergencies.'[43] Brown points out that religion was a key aspect

38 LP, Lang 94, Letter: Bell to Lang, c. 1939.
39 TNA, AIR19/437, Letter: Stansgate to Alan Lascelles, 2 March 1946.
40 Lucy Noakes, 'War and Peace', in Ina Zweiniger-Bargielowska, ed. *Women in Twentieth-Century Britain* (London: Longman, 2001) 307–20. Here 307, 310; Association of WRENS website, <http://www.wrens.org.uk/history> and Women's Auxiliary Air Force Association, <http://www.waafassociation.org.uk> accessed 15 June 2014.
41 TNA, AIR19/436, CWWF Chaplain's Assistants, 1; 'Helping the Padre', *Church Times*, 7 December 1945; Bliss, *The Service and Status of Women in the Churches* (London: SCM Press Ltd., 1952), 130.
42 Parker, 'Reinvigorating Christian Britain'.
43 Parker, 'Reinvigorating Christian Britain', 78; Brown, *Religion and Society*, 165.

of the state's endeavours to maintain the war effort noting, for instance, the production of propaganda films such as *Went the Day Well?* (1942) in 'which a national Christian religion was depicted as underlying British society and as holding the nation together. [Such] films resonated with a sense that British character and the nation's identity were underscored by a religion made placid yet sturdy by long familiarity.'[44] National Days of Prayer, the 'Big Ben Minute,' and the BBC's *Children's Hour Prayers* and other religious programming also acted to 'articulate this vision of Christian identity and national unity', and 'the bond between people, Church, state, and royalty.'[45] Parker asserts that '[w]artime Britain, in many ways, was tangibly and self-consciously religious, and generally assumed itself to be Christian.'[46] The Ministry of Labour, for instance, approved the wartime training of women for church work in lieu of national service, 'in view of the importance of the work' to the nation's future.[47] Despite declining church attendance in pre-war England, 'there was a widespread perception that the war was a legitimate defence of the "Christian values" permeating the country's political, social and ethical fabric',[48] that war acted to strengthen England's 'Christian self-consciousness' and that 'Christianity remained a valid referent in the construction of individual identity.'[49] The notion of a nation united by their Christian beliefs and heritage, real or imagined, was powerful during the war.[50]

Together, these aspects of wartime England helped to create a female and specifically Christian chaplaincy that, while not equal to the men's

---

44 Brown, *Religion and Society*, 164–65.
45 Parker, 'Reinvigorating Christian Britain', 65; Lawson and Parker, 'Introduction: God and War,' 4.
46 Parker, *Faith on the Home Front: Aspects of Church Life and Popular Religion in Birmingham, 1939–1945* (Bern: Peter Lang, 2006), 60.
47 'Women Candidates for Church Work', *Church Times*, 4 December 1942.
48 Field, 'Puzzled People', 474.
49 Michael Snape and Stephen Parker, 'Keeping Faith and Coping: Belief, Popular Religiosity and the British People', in John Bourne et al., eds, *The Great World War 1914–1945*, Volume 2 (London: HarperCollins, 2001), 397–420. Here 401; Parker in Field, 'Puzzled People', 473.
50 Parker, 'Reinvigorating Christian Britain'.

in having full chaplain positions, recognised the part women could play in the military's religious services and emphasised the idea of both an English and British Christian national identity. Hence three years into the war the CWWF was entrusted to appoint a small army of religious workers all officially approved by each branch's respective chaplains. This included the first twelve Chaplains' Assistants appointed by June 1942 under Lang's successor, William Temple,[51] District Organisers and about 200 religious speakers.[52] This network was 'maintained by [a] complex system of collaboration' between, in this case, the CWWF, represented churches, and the military.[53] Chaplains were directed to 'make full use' of assistants for the Church's 'ministry among women', who were considered military personnel rather than civilians or philanthropic workers, thus emphasising that this new chaplaincy was critical to the military.[54] In his discussion of the Second World War's male chaplaincies in Britain, the U.S., and Canada, Snape asserts that 'as products of culturally Christian societies, it was inevitable that religion and religious agencies should play a significant role' in supporting soldiers.[55] In Britain, the military's support of religion was seen in a variety of ways including mandated regular worship in the army and stamping one's religion on identity discs.[56] This was, Snape argues, 'fundamentally indicative of the abiding importance of religion in contemporary British society and of the military value of religious belief in modern conflicts of unparalleled magnitude.'[57]

Chaplains' Assistants and District Organisers often did many of the exact same things as male chaplains, emphasising the importance of the

---

51   For comparison, there were approximately 1,000 RAF chaplains and triple that number in the army; '90th Anniversary brochure on RAF Chaplains, 2008, 'History of Army Chaplains', British Army website <http://www.army.mod.uk/chaplains/23350.aspx> accessed 15 June 2014.
52   'Women in the Services', *Church Times*, 20 March 1942.
53   Snape, 'War, Religion and Revival', 138.
54   TNA, AIR19/436, CWWF Chaplain's Assistants, 2.
55   Snape, 'War, Religion and Revival', 138.
56   *Ibid.*, 139, 141.
57   Snape, *God and the British Solider*, 138.

military's religious personnel. Notably, their duties included leading, or assisting with, 'Padre's Hour' which were compulsory religious instruction and discussion sessions for servicemen that were reaching millions in the army by 1942.[58] In general, the Chaplains' Assistants and District Organisers were in similar positions, yet differed in the service and regions served.[59] The latter covered large areas and worked with all three military branches whereas the former served the ATS throughout Britain (and the WAAF soon after the war's end[60]) and were assigned posts by the War Office to camps, training centres, or postings abroad in continental Europe, East Asia, the Middle East, and Africa.[61] In this respect, some aspects of the CWWF's scheme was present throughout Britain, and seven ATS Chaplains' Assistants were abroad by demobilisation, which demonstrated the importance of Christianity in the nation's wartime military.[62] The CWWF officially represented the Church of England and some English protestant denominations, including Baptists, Methodists, Congregationalists and Presbyterians. However, some churches in Northern Ireland and Scotland also expressed interest in the scheme and sought to represent regional churches and personnel, a fact which seems to suggest a wider interest throughout Britain of the relevance of Christianity to national identity.[63] Interestingly, Field's survey of religious belief and affiliation in wartime Britain indicates that the war did not push Britain further toward secularisation, rather quantitative data illustrates continuing trends of pre-war decline and limited wartime decline leading him to conclude that 'faith on the home front was remarkably resilient.'[64]

---

58   Snape, 'War, Religion, and Revival', 139.
59   'Helping the Padre', *Church Times*, 7 Dec. 1945; There were 50–60 by 1945.
60   See TNA, AIR19/436–7.
61   LP, Fisher Papers 1946, *CWWF 1940–1950*; Letter: CWWF to Fisher, 8 March 1945; 'The ATS', *Church Times*, 9 April 1943 (letter from Saunders); 'For Service Women', *Church Times*, 26 June 1942.
62   TNA, AIR19/436H, Letter: Nathan to Stansgate, 8 February 1946.
63   LP, Fisher Papers 1946, *CWWF 1940–1950*, 6–7; 'Women in the Services', *Church Times*, 20 March 1942; Bliss, *The Service*, 130.
64   Field, 'Puzzled People', 477–8.

Some extant documents provide a window into this select group of military personnel and their experiences. The women eventually chosen as Chaplains' Assistants, of whom approximately 70 percent were Anglicans and thirty per cent Free Church members, often hailed from the 'caring' or teaching professions and had backgrounds as deaconesses, welfare officers and missionaries among other employment.[65] For example, Anglican Eveline Holmes had five years of public health work experience with the London County Council and had also worked as a Church Missionary Society Training Centre tutor and London Diocese church worker.[66] Unsurprisingly, gender shaped the experiences of Chaplains' Assistants as well as perceptions of them. A *Church Times* interview about the positions with the CWWF pointed out that in order to qualify, the women 'must not be bluestocking' and 'their mouths must not be full of prunes and prisms,' derogatory references to women which characterised them as disapproving, undesirable and lacking humour because of their education and intellect.[67] Additionally, the Rev. Elsie Chamberlain, a Congregationalist minister appointed as the RAF's first woman chaplain at the end of the war (appointed as a WAAF Squadron Officer), interacted with both servicemen and women. She commented that 'in the Air Force, a few queried whether I ought to be "madre", but I was soon just padre along with the others', thereby illustrating the lack of experience people had with female church leaders.[68]

Overall, the positions were fairly well received and the scheme perceived important by the Church, the military and even some Commonwealth countries. Some chaplains reportedly 'resented their appointment and did not give them much to do', but others valued the new personnel.[69] Interestingly, Archbishop Geoffrey Fisher, Temple's predecessor, publicly

---

65   LP, Fisher 22, 1946, 'Workers Passes by Executive Committee Since July 1944'.
66   'Religion in the ATS', *Church Times*, 4 April 1944.
67   'Paragons with Personality', *Church Times*, 28 August 1942.
68   Elsie Chamberlain, 'The World in Which We Worship', in Hazel Hunkins-Hallinan, ed., *In Her Own Right: A Discussion Conducted by the Six Point Group* (London: George G. Harrap & Co., 1968), 121–32. Here 131.
69   Bliss, *The Service*, 130.

advocated for these women despite his strong opposition to women's equal ministry commenting that the 'Church could not function without relying on the trained skill and understanding of women.'[70] Additionally, in response to War Office policy prohibiting the Chaplains' Assistants from wearing khaki and battledress overseas, he was rather adamant and agreed with the CWWF that they were in an 'exceptional position which calls for special treatment.'[71] In a letter to the Chaplain General F.L. Hughes, Fisher was insistent that they should be allowed to wear khaki uniforms overseas specifically because they needed to be clearly identified as military personnel.[72] In order to make his point he emphasised that the positions were paid by the Treasury, approved by the Army Council, and supervised by the Chaplain General. Ultimately, Hughes agreed, commenting that 'It is altogether in the interest of their work that their identification with the ATS and Army should be as complete as possible.'[73] The scheme's success was also made evident by Stansgate's desire to continue it during peacetime, and attempts of Commonwealth countries to replicate it. According to Bliss, groups in New Zealand and Australia tried to create the same programme, but authorities felt there were not enough servicewomen to warrant it, while the Canadian forces appointed five Protestant women church workers to work with servicewomen.[74] Despite the lack of success or size of these schemes, these efforts suggest that Christianity was also perceived by Commonwealth countries with significant Christian populations as an integral component of wartime British imperial – now Commonwealth – identity.

Certainly two of the most significant aspects of the military's expanded chaplaincy were the state's expansion of women's church work and the manner in which wartime needs had taken precedence over various

70   LP, Fisher 22, 1946, Letter: Fisher to Stansgate, 1 December 1945; Letter: Stansgate to Fisher, 8 December 1945; 'Helping the Padre', *Church Times*, 7 December 1945.
71   LP, Fisher 22, 1946, 'Extract from Confidential Letter from the Staff Chaplain at the War Office'; TNA, AIR19/436, Letter: P.S. to Stansgate, 11 February 1946.
72   LP, Fisher 22, 1946, Letter: Fisher to Chaplain General, 18 April 1947.
73   LP, Fisher 22, 1946, Letter: Hughes to Fisher, 22 April 1947.
74   Bliss, *The Service*, 131.

churches' stances on women's ministry. Aware of the momentousness of these events, a CWWF booklet stated that 'for the first time, religious work on an interdenominational basis undertaken by women received official recognition.'[75] By widening women's religious responsibilities, the state had affirmed the importance of Christianity to the nation and its citizens' identities, at least during wartime, and of women's central roles in fostering an English Christian national identity. Additionally, by placing churches at the centre of English life the state emphasised that 'Christian civilisation' was at stake. In the aftermath of the war, Lord Stansgate, taking the women's wartime 'chaplaincy' even further, wrote a letter to the monarch providing details about a recent 'innovation' in the RAF, that of the appointment of Chamberlain as a RAF chaplain.[76] Fully aware of the significance of the event not just for the RAF, but Britain as a whole, Stansgate had also written to the prime minister stating:

> for the first time the state will be recognizing the ministry of women – though only of course among nonconformists. The appointment, therefore, may provoke opposition among… circles where women are regarded as being incapable of administering the Sacrament. My own concern is two-fold. First, the spiritual interest of the Royal Air Force, which I consider would be advantaged, and secondly, the recognition of sex equality which I believe would engage the goodwill of women in general and … of public opinion.[77]

On this significant military decision, Stansgate clearly chose to support the interests of the Air Force and servicewomen rather than the Church's antiquated views on women. Yet his letter also illustrated the importance he placed on Christian identity as a central component of being English and British by his acceptance of the church's role in the military. Like others in Britain's largely Protestant military leadership, he 'had long held religion to be an indispensable aid to military discipline and efficiency' and integral to British society.[78]

---

75 LP, *CCWF 1940–50*, 4.
76 TNA, AIR 19/436, February 1946.
77 TNA, Air 19/437; draft does not appear to have been sent.
78 Snape, 'War, Religion and Revival', 144.

Wartime feminist protest, women's citizenship and the post-war future

Wartime feminist discourse about women's citizenship and personal fulfilment emphasised the important place of Christianity in many women's lives and was intricately intertwined with discussions of a post-war world in which women would be equal citizens. For instance, the WFL's 1941 annual conference report noted under the heading 'Spiritual Equality' that 'Perhaps the most fundamental of all the requests made by women, equality in the Churches, has the full support of the Executive and members.'[79] That same year the Church was referred to as the 'great offender' at the WFL's autumn conference.[80] The conference report noted that 'the main problem facing women today is not merely to get justice or the rate for the job, it is where and how they may make their fullest contribution not only to the war effort but to the rebuilding of a world where wars may cease.'[81] The WFL repeatedly emphasised that women's 'contributions' in an egalitarian future included church work and believed that 'we who have views covering the whole life of women say that equality of opportunities and a full life for women is essential in a Christian Society. The Church should remember the women.'[82] Similarly, a 1942 article titled 'The Woman of the Future', stated optimistically that 'Women will be spiritual leaders in all the Churches; no restraint shall be imposed on their spiritual future.'[83] This expected post-war social transformation, particularly as it would impact women, was a common theme in wartime feminist documents and unsurprising given the public place of post-war discussions during the war. Naturally, feminists did

---

[79] WL, *WFLB*, 'Thirty-Fourth Annual Conference, Report of the Hon. Political Secretary', 13 June 1941.
[80] WL, 7/AMP/A1, Box 588, 'Women's Freedom League, Autumn Conference, 17 October 1942, Women's Influence in Parliament & Local Government'.
[81] WL, *WFLB*, 'Women's Freedom League Autumn Conference of Women's Organizations', 30 October 1942.
[82] WL, *WFLB*, 16 October 1942.
[83] WL, *WFLB*, 'The Woman of the Future', 2 January 1942.

not want to see a return to pre-war gender roles. Yet the emphasis above on a woman's 'full life,' 'fullest contribution' and unrestrained 'spiritual future' challenge the notion that campaigns on women's church work were merely about equality or capitalising on wartime strife, rather than a concerted focus on Christian identity and the right to an equal place in English churches that many feminists held to be central to their nation. Also noteworthy, is reference to a 'Christian Society' and that statement's suggestion that the nation's Christian heritage remained vitally relevant. For feminists to describe their nation in this way was illustrative of how some saw themselves – as Christian feminists – but also that Christianity and churches were 'valuable, and meaningful still': indeed 'British society ... remained identifiably and self-consciously Christian between 1941 and 1945 ... [and] Christian moral values continued to exert a strong and defining influence on British society.'[84] Therefore, even as English feminists battled against their national and other churches, their identity was shaped, in part, by the historic and complex relationship between Christianity and their nation and a belief that England's churches were central to their construction of Englishness.

Hence, despite the female chaplaincy's widespread support, feminist organisations protested that the churches had not gone far enough. In a 1942 article titled 'Why Not Women Chaplains?' the WFL voiced its disapproval stating:

> For nearly three years the many thousands of women in H.M. Forces have been left without the spiritual care and guidance of members of their own sex which has been available to men. Now, when the conscription of women for national service has roused the Churches to their responsibility towards them, the best to be offered to them by Authority are ministrations of a kind which would, rightly, be considered totally inadequate in the case of men ... [T]hey will be handicapped from the outset by being forced to accept a position of permanent inferiority to men, both in

---

84 Chandler, 'The Church of England and the Obliteration of Bombing of Germany in the Second World War', *The English Historical Review* 108/429 (Oct. 1993), 920–46. Here 920; Snape and Parker, 'Keeping Faith and Coping', 400–1.

status and functions, very different to the responsible place occupied by officers of all ranks in Women's Forces.[85]

The WFL's criticism about the new chaplaincy certainly held some truth. Neither Chaplains' Assistants nor District Organisers were given the same recognition as male chaplains, and evidence that women found within the Church a lack of fulfilment and responsibility could be seen, for example, in the precipitous decline from 1939 in the number of deaconesses, the highest position to which women could be ordained.[86] In general, this new chaplaincy represented the state's need for women workers and the wartime value placed on both religion and the formation of Christian national identity; nevertheless, both the state's and the Church's insistence on gender difference emphasised women's unequal citizenship.

Feminist protest was sometimes echoed by complaints from within the Church, or those closely aligned with Anglican interests, and it did not go unnoticed that the Church was losing women's work and interest due to discrimination. A wartime Central Council for Women's Church Work leaflet noted that religion was not as important in women's lives as it once was and that single women who might have considered church work in the past no longer did so because it appeared 'to be undefined, to lack professional status, to be strictly limited in opportunity, and to be insecure as regards both tenure and salary.'[87] A *Church Times* correspondent identified as a woman church worker reiterated these concerns, pointing out that women made far more as munitions workers.[88] Additionally, a 1944 *Church Times* article on returning service personnel presented a picture of the Church as both hopeful and 'anxious' about post-war opportunities.[89] The writer suggested that men and women would be 'hungry to find a set of guiding ideas and to found their lives on a secure spiritual basis' and that

---

85   WL, *WFLB*, D.B., 'Why Not Women Chaplains?', 15 May 1942.
86   WL, AGOW Papers, Ruth Adam, 'Why is an Educated Woman Denied a Place in the Anglican Ministry?', *Church of England Newspaper*, 1 August 1958.
87   'Women in the Church Alleged Lack of Status', *Church Times*, 12 February 1943.
88   'Correspondence from A Woman Church Worker', *Church Times*, 18 February 1944.
89   'When the Men Come Home', *Church Times*, 11 August 1944, 426.

the Church should be prepared to welcome them, seeming to imply that change was needed to stop declining membership.[90]

Aware that women were leaving the Church, the Bishop of Sheffield, Leslie Howard, wrote to then Archbishop of Canterbury Temple in 1942 encouraging him to re-examine the church's employment and training of women. He commented that the:

> employment of women in every branch of service since the outbreak of war is bound to result in immense social changes after the war and may also provide the church, if it cares to train and use them, with a large body of women workers. From my many contacts with the Social Services I find that the opinion is widespread and is hardening, that the Church in its attitude to the employment of women is falling further and further behind the movement of the times.[91]

In response to concerns such as these, Temple created a wartime committee on women's church work to formulate policy suggestions. Ultimately, the committee's 1943 report found that:

> The use and employment of women had been widely extended in the war and had constituted a revolution in the social life of the country, but women were not finding within the Church ... opportunities of work or service comparable with those offered to them elsewhere. Within the Church a woman is continually made aware that her sex is a handicap and a limitation.[92]

It went on to point out that 'modern society will not be won to the Christian allegiance and drawn into the fellowship of the Church by the activities, however heroic and devoted, of one sex alone.'[93] Despite these bold statements about the Church's discrimination against women, the report had, as the WFL pointed out, 'dismisse[d] in a foot-note the question of the admission of women to the priesthood as outside its terms of reference.'[94]

---

90 Ibid.
91 LP, Temple 3, Letter: Howard to Temple, 15 September 1942.
92 Quoted in Margaret J. Roxburgh, *Women's Work in the Church of England, A Consideration of the Last Hundred Years* (London: AGOW, 1958), 14.
93 Ibid.
94 WL, *WFLB*, 'Women's Work in the Anglican Church', 18 February 1944.

The WFL questioned how the Church could appeal to women who had worked alongside men during the war and argued that its 'plea of tradition' would only further alienate women.[95]

Unwilling to wait for institutions like the Church to end gender discrimination on their own, the Women's Publicity and Planning Association (WPPA), a wartime feminist organisation, had set itself the task of eliminating all remaining legislative inequalities that women faced, something which could impact women's ministry. Furious over the lengthy campaign for equal compensation for war injuries, WPPA chairman Rebecca Sieff believed that there was an urgent need for the formation of a 'true democracy.'[96] In 'Women and Self-Emancipation', Sieff stated that 'War, the extreme expression of national crisis, must either cleanse the body politic or be used to bolster up outworn prejudice and preserve present privilege.'[97] To this end, the WPPA published Dorothy Evans' 1944 Equal Citizenship (Blanket) Bill which sought to revise all legislation which embodied sex discrimination.[98] The Bill noted the Church's stance on ministry stating that, although the Church was a 'legal establishment' women were not excluded in statute law from being priests except 'perhaps by implication' and that it 'may be necessary to establish that a deaconess of the Church qualifies in the same way as a deacon does for ordination.'[99] In effect, the Bill advocated removing the Church's power to decide the extent of women's ministry. At a wartime Women for Westminster meeting, Evans argued that 'The time has come ... to establish a principle – unless women are speedily raised from this position of second class citizens there is no chance their influence will be felt in post-war planning as it should be. They are half the nation!'[100]

95 Ibid.
96 WL, PC, Sieff, 'Introduction', in Dorothy Evans, 'The Equal Citizenship (Blanket) Bill', (London: WPPA, 1944), 4.
97 WL, WPPA Papers, Sieff, 'Women and Self-Emancipation'.
98 WL, SPG Papers, SPG/B, SPG Annual Report 1943–44.
99 WL, SPG Papers, Executive Committee Meeting, 11 August 1944, Book 1943–45; WL, PC, Evans, 'The Equal Citizenship (Blanket) Bill', 4 and 39.
100 WL, SPG News Clippings, B544, 'Equal Citizenship Blanket Bill', *Harrogate Advertiser*, 18 December 1943.

English feminists' identities were not necessarily bound by national borders, but their nation mattered intensely during the war. Many identified strongly with their national culture, particularly with the political philosophy and values they believed would eventually provide the equal rights and responsibilities they sought. In 1940 following the surrender of France, Corbett Ashby had stated gravely that 'the problem ... was no longer how to force democracies logically to include women, but how to protect democracy itself ... We called on women, while fighting their own battle, to fight for all mankind and to keep alive the belief in democracy.'[101] Feminist Six Point Group member Monica Whately seconded this sentiment when in a discussion about the Equal Citizenship (Blanket) Bill she expressed hope that British citizens would 'show the whole world that democracy is not only worth fighting for but worth practicing.'[102] Even though it was ironic, feminists' campaigns against the Church illustrated just how integral it was – as central as democracy and freedom – to their sense of being English.

Conclusion

Sonya Rose has noted that the 'most powerful compelling historical memory of wartime Britain was that Britons felt that they were an integral part of a community – a national community.'[103] However, her work illustrates that even when Britain needed women, and the entire nation was mobilised for war, the reality was that they were not usually accorded the same rights or responsibilities as men; they remained, as the wartime female chaplaincy

---

101 Ashby, 'The History of the Alliance,' *Jus Suffragi* 35/1 (Oct.–Nov. 1940), 5, quoted in Karen Offen, *European Feminisms, 1700–1950: A Political History* (Stanford: Stanford University Press, 2000), 368.
102 WL, SPG News Clippings, B544, 'Women's Right to Full Equal Citizenship,' *Torquay Directory*, 12 January, 1944.
103 Rose, *Which People's War?*, 2.

makes clear, gendered, second-class citizens excluded from full participation in all aspects of British life. Thus, while the war brought important changes, even if not always lasting, to women's lives, 'awareness of their unequal status as citizens relative to men became heightened ... [and] disrupted the idea that there was a national *common* good.'[104]

Still, the creation of this female chaplaincy, even if not equivalent to the men's, offers evidence in support of the importance of religion and Christian national identity during wartime to a broad range of Englishmen and women. Feminists' support of women's religious instruction and care, as well as their desire for an equal ministry, suggests the continuing relevance for many of spirituality, religion and churches, even if not the specific nature of those institutions. Thus, although they relentlessly criticised the churches for their discrimination against women, their interest in women's spiritual wellbeing and women's roles in English churches demonstrated that some wartime feminists thought of their nation as a Christian one, fostered a Christian national identity, and fought hard to maintain that.

---

104 *Ibid.*, 108, Rose's emphasis.

WENDY WEBSTER

Transnational communities of allies

In January 1941, the novelist Rose Macaulay wrote about the consolations of war:

> The pageant of life is enormously enriched by the presence of so many foreigners in our midst ... the uniforms of Polish soldiers mingle with those of Czechs, Norwegians, Dutch and Free French ... And not only foreigners. Driving in the country, you are continually hailed by the rich accents of young men in battle-dress from Alberta or Montreal, who seldom know where they are and always want to go somewhere else. They are, as a rule, enormously charming.[1]

Macaulay was writing before America entered the war and GIs began arriving in Britain. Mollie Panter-Downes, in her regular 'Letter from London' for the *New Yorker* in June 1942, produced a similar description of the transformation of British scenes and soundscapes that encompassed their arrival:

> Londoners are beginning to get accustomed to the uniforms of American troops, who are now seen in ever-increasing numbers in the streets. Middle West and Southern accents are heard in the crowds as frequently as the French, Czech, Polish, and Norwegian which make a blackout saunter down Piccadilly a nostalgic Cook's tour.[2]

These observations draw attention to the diversity of the population in Britain during the Second World War. Unprecedented movements of people to Britain began before the war as Hitler's rise to power prompted

---

1   Rose Macaulay, 'Consolations of the War', *The Listener*, 16 January 1941, in Jenny Hartley, ed., *Hearts Undefeated: Women's Writing of the Second World War* (London: Virago, 1994), 225.
2   Mollie Panter-Downes, ed. by William Shawn, *London War Notes 1939–1945* (London: Longman, 1972), 233.

the arrival of refugees and émigrés. By the outbreak of war, some 78,000 refugees from Austria, Germany and Czechoslovakia were in Britain, the majority of them Jewish.[3] In 1940, as Germany invaded and occupied much of Europe, they were joined by other European national groups including exiled governments and civilian refugees. Six European armed forces in exile arrived in the same year – those whose uniforms were noticed by Macaulay, from Czechoslovakia, France, Holland, Norway and Poland, as well as a small contingent from Belgium. This too was completely unprecedented. Troops from the empire included not only the Canadians who hailed Macaulay, but also Africans, Australians, Indians, New Zealanders and West Indians. There was also brisk recruitment from Eire.[4] More than 100,000 war-workers travelled to Britain during the war, while estimates of the numbers of volunteers for the British armed forces from Eire vary from 42,000 to 165,000.[5] The US troops that Panter-Downes noticed in increasing numbers in 1942 continued to arrive. Nearly three million Americans disembarked in Britain between 1942 and 1945. 10 per cent of the US forces stationed in Britain were black.[6]

The wartime British media promoted a vision of a community of allies united in a common cause against a common enemy. The idea of an 'allies war' was as prominent in propaganda as the idea of a People's War, associating Britishness not only with the stoicism and courage of ordinary British citizens but also with an expansive transnational community. This chapter considers the idea of an 'allies war' and the very wide range of allies who were honoured in wartime film and broadcasting in what I call a 'culture of tribute' as well as the groups that had limited visibility. Many documentary films honouring allies in Britain were officially sponsored,

---

[3] Louise London, *Whitehall and the Jews, 1933–1948: British Immigration Policy and the Holocaust* (Cambridge: Cambridge University Press, 2000), 12.

[4] See Bernard Kelly, '"Excellent Irishmen": Irish volunteers and identities during the Second World War' in this volume.

[5] Enda Delaney, *Demography, State and Society: Irish Migration to Britain, 1921–1971* (Montreal: McGill-Queen's University Press, 2000), 130, 149.

[6] David Reynolds, *Rich Relations: The American Occupation of Britain, 1942–1945* (London: HarperCollins, 1995), 432.

but there was often considerable divergence between the public 'culture of tribute' and what policy-makers recorded confidentially.

The chapter draws on evidence from Home Intelligence (HI) and Mass Observation (MO) to look at British attitudes to different national and ethnic groups in wartime Britain. Both HI and MO, investigating the state of morale and public opinion, used methods such as eavesdropping on people's conversations which fell far short of those deployed by social scientists. Even so, their findings provide rich evidence. The chapter also draws on personal narratives – autobiography, wartime diaries and letters – to look at evidence of people in wartime Britain making transnational friendships and identifying as part of a transnational community of allies, as well as evidence of inter-allied friction and conflict. It considers what happened when the war was over as the 'culture of tribute' faded and the diversity of the population in wartime Britain was generally forgotten. Some groups who had contributed to the Allied war effort in Britain, falling outside any national memory, were doubly forgotten.

The 'allies war'

In 1940, after the fall of France, a cartoon by David Low showed a British soldier standing on a shore and shaking his fist at a sky full of Nazi planes. The caption was 'Very Well, Alone'![7] Britain standing alone – the only European nation still engaged in armed conflict with Nazi Germany – features strongly in post-war memories of 1940. But in 1940 there was a great deal of publicity for friends and allies. In January, newsreels showed Australian, Canadian and New Zealand servicemen arriving in Britain, Newfoundland lumberjacks crossing the Atlantic to fell timber in Scotland for Britain's war needs and New Zealanders living in England forming their

---

7 *Evening Standard*, 18 June 1940.

own anti-tank unit.[8] Such publicity may have shaped the response of one woman in May 1940 to the news that Belgium had surrendered: 'she did not see how England could lose with all the Australians and New Zealanders.'[9]

The media also showed Polish and Czechoslovakian troops and airmen arriving in the spring and summer of 1940. By the autumn, there was increasing publicity for their records in the Battle of Britain. In September, a newsreel showing the King's visit to Polish and Canadian airmen stationed in South East England commented: 'This Polish Squadron brought down eighty German planes in one month.'[10] *The Manchester Guardian*, reporting that Czech pilots had brought down five enemy planes in the greatest raid yet seen on London, called them 'valuable allies.'[11] A telegram to Polish airmen demonstrated a commitment to celebrating allies in Britain at the highest levels of the BBC. It came from the Director General who sent: 'warm greetings to the famous 303 Polish Squadron with lively congratulations upon its magnificent record and all best wishes for its future. You use the Air for your gallant exploits and we for telling the world of them. Long live Poland!'[12] Also in September, the BBC launched a series of programmes titled *Fights On*, featuring armed forces continuing the fight from Britain. In October a further series, *Comrades in Freedom*, chronicled 'life

---

8   'Australian Airmen Arrive', *British Paramount News*, 1 January 1940; 'Making Themselves at Home', *Universal News*, 4 January 1940; 'Australia Sends First Instalment', *British Paramount News*, 1 January 1940; 'New Zealanders Arrive', *Universal News*, 4 January 1940; 'Lumberjacks Cross Atlantic to Help', *British Paramount News*, 29 January 1940; 'Newfoundland Lumberjacks Over Here', *Universal News*, 29 January 1940; 'New Year Sees Empire Gathering of the Clans', *British Paramount News*, 4 January 1940.
9   Mass Observation (MO) TC 25 2/E, Mass Observation interview, 28 May 1940.
10 *Gaumont British News*, 30 September 1940.
11 *The Manchester Guardian*, 10 September 1940.
12 Quoted in Lynne Olson and Stanley Cloud, *For Your Freedom and Ours: The Kościuszko Squadron Forgotten Heroes of World War II* (London: Arrow Books, 2003), 142.

in Britain as seen by our allies [and] their views of what we are fighting for.' The series included Belgian, Czech, Dutch, and French speakers.[13]

Exiles in wartime Britain contributed to the vision of a transnational community of allies. Jiri Weiss, a Jewish Czechoslovakian who had fled from Prague in 1938 advocated enlarging the ideological scope of British documentary film with propaganda showing that 'Britain stands for much more than just the British Empire' and telling 'true stories of the multitude of nations which have forgotten the enmities of yesterday, and now stand side by side.'[14] Weiss went on to direct *Night and Day* (1945), which was produced by the Czechoslovakian Film Unit and showed members of the Czechoslovakian 311 squadron working for Coastal Command attacking a U-boat and blasting it out of the sea. Its commentary identified a transnational team: 'The skipper comes from Prague, the gunners from Budejovice, Brno, Hana, the navigator, once a lecturer at the University of Prague, is British.'[15]

Eugeniusz Cekalski, the Polish film-maker, scripted and directed *Diary of a Polish Airman* (1942) celebrating Polish aviators. The film traced the airman's wartime life through his diary entries before he was killed in action. As the Germans surround Warsaw, he continues the fight initially from France and then from Britain. His diary entry for 10 September 1940 honours all Polish airmen, recording that they had already shot down over 200 planes. The film ends with his death and the statement that 'we will finish this diary.' A survey of thirty six viewers found that nineteen of them 'strongly approved' of the film and seven thought it 'the best, or one of the best, MOI [Ministry of Information] films they had seen.' It was thought to show 'the courage and patriotism of Poles and their faith in victory.'[16] MO surveys often recorded admiration for Polish airmen, but if films played a role in this, it was the intense

---

13   Thomas Hajkowski, 'Friends and Allies: Representing Europe in the BBC Home Service during the Second World War', paper to 2009 British Scholar Annual Conference.
14   Jiri Weiss, 'An Allied Film Unit', *Documentary Newsletter* 2/1 (December 1941): 233.
15   National Archives (TNA), INF 6/607.
16   TNA, INF 1/293, Home Intelligence Special Report No. 28, 22 August 1942.

romanticism of *Dangerous Moonlight*, a feature film with a much wider distribution, that had more popular impact.[17] The Warsaw Concerto, composed for the film by Richard Addinsell, was particularly popular with the Royal Air Force (RAF) and the Women's Auxiliary Air Force (WAAF).[18] Within the film its composition is attributed to the Polish hero Stefan Radetsky (Anton Walbrook), an airman, composer and concert pianist. He begins the composition in Poland and completes it in neutral America, but subsequently abandons his musical career to join the RAF and continue the fight from Britain.

Airmen were also prominent in films paying tribute to American forces stationed in Britain. Initial conflicts and misunderstandings between British and American airmen in *The Way to the Stars* (1945) give way to mutual respect sealed by the death of an American airman. *I Live in Grosvenor Square* (1945) also begins with conflict between British and Americans. An American GI encountering hostility in Britain comments: 'Anyone would think we were an army of occupation or something.' By the end of the film, after an American airman has lost his life, the British pay 'deep tribute' at his funeral to 'the brave men who gave their lives for this village.' The idea of British-American alliance is endorsed in images of male comradeship in war that emphasise an equal partnership – one in which British and American men jointly secure victory.[19]

Black GIs were excluded from these celebrations of American sacrifice and rarely portrayed in British media. Black British servicemen and warworkers in Britain also had limited visibility with wartime salutes to black and Asian troops from empire mainly confined to settings overseas. But *Africa's Fighting Men* (1943) sponsored by the Ministry of Information, which showed African troops in Ceylon and Africa, incorporated shots of Peter Thomas, the first black African RAF Pilot Officer. Against shots of Thomas shaking hands with a white officer, the film ends with commentary

---

17 See, for example, responses to a 1943 survey on feelings about foreigners, MO, TC25 2/O.
18 Martin Francis, *The Flyer: British Culture and the Royal Air Force 1939–1945* (Oxford: Oxford University Press), 30–1.
19 *I Live in Grosvenor Square* (1945); *The Way to the Stars* (1945).

celebrating imperial unity: 'The colonial people ... from the beginning have shown that they are able and ready to take their place side by side with all the peoples of the empire in the battle for freedom.' *West Indies Calling* (1943), also sponsored by the Ministry of Information, similarly celebrates imperial unity showing Caribbeans serving in the RAF and working on the home front. The film emphasises a multi-ethnic Caribbean identity with friendly mixing between African-Caribbeans, Indo-Caribbeans and white Caribbeans, including interracial dancing. It shows friendships across differences of nationality and ethnicity through shots of a West Indian pilot, Jimmy Hyde, chatting with members of his squadron and the commentary explaining: 'In Hyde's squadron, there are pilots from New Zealand, Poland, Britain and Canada. Friendships are being made between people who before the war knew little or nothing about each other, and we find it impossible to believe that these friendships will just fade out when the war is won.'[20]

Private government views conflicted with this celebration of imperial unity across differences of ethnicity. In 1942 a Foreign Office official, after discussion with other government departments, noted that: 'the recruitment to the United Kingdom of coloured British subjects, whose remaining in the United Kingdom after the war might create a social problem, was not considered desirable.'[21] In the same year, the War Cabinet noted 'the serious social consequences which might arise from the demobilisation in this country of any appreciable numbers of certain classes of coloured men who are serving in His Majesty's Forces.' It also noted that black men could not be deported if they proved to be undesirable since they were British with a right of settlement and that overt discrimination in the form of a colour bar could not be accepted. In this context, covert discrimination was recommended: 'The only course open to us is to recommend very strongly that service departments should do all they possibly can by administrative action to reduce to a minimum the opportunities these men might have of

20 *West Indies Calling* (1943).
21 Reynolds, *Rich Relations*, 217.

being demobilised in this country.'[22] The Air Ministry similarly advocated covert discrimination to keep people like Peter Thomas and Jimmy Hyde out of the post-war RAF. Although the post-First World War period had seen a reversion to the pre-war policy of excluding all those who were not 'of pure European descent' there was no such reversion at the end of the Second World War. But the Air Ministry envisaged that although 'on paper coloured troops (would) be eligible for entry to the service', in practice 'the process of selection (would) eliminate them.'[23]

The merchant navy was particularly diverse by ethnicity and nationality and had a higher death rate at some 17 per cent than any of the three fighting services. There was some acknowledgement of African, Arab, Caribbean or Indian contributions in wartime government publications, but wartime film showed the merchant navy as white.[24] Tributes were paid to Chinese merchant seamen in a Ministry of Information documentary, *The Chinese in Wartime Britain* (1944), but this was designed for distribution in China, not for a domestic audience. The commentary was written and spoken by Hsiao Ch'ien who had arrived in Britain in 1939 to teach Chinese at the School of Oriental and African Studies. His script focused on Chinese merchant seamen in Britain:

> China fights not only on the land in the East, engaging huge Japanese forces, but in the West her men fight on the merchant navy front shoulder to shoulder in the greatest battle of naval history alongside their British seamen comrades. They too brave the torpedoes, bombs and mines ... making history under fire. Here in Britain, the Chinese seaman is not only doing a splendid job of work. He is getting an insight into those better conditions of labour that are a commonplace in modern Britain.[25]

---

22   TNA, AIR 20/9051.
23   Roger Lambo, 'Achtung! The Black Prince: West Africans in the Royal Air Force, 1939–46', in David Killingray, ed., *Africans in Britain* (Ilford: Frank Cass, 1994), 161.
24   Paul Davenport, 'Dangerous, Courageous, Invisible: Non-white Seafarers in the Merchant Navy of the 1940s and 1950s', *Journal of War and Culture Studies* 4/1 (2011), 51–64.
25   *Chinese in Wartime Britain* (1944), TNA, INF 6/615.

Views expressed confidentially by the government offer a different view of Chinese seamen and their conditions of labour. During the war the government had assisted the ship-owners Alfred Holt and Company to force Chinese seamen to join the *Sarpedon* despite the government's own view of this vessel: 'to describe it as a "hell-ship" from a crew point of view would be an under-statement.' When the war was over, the government planned to repatriate and deport as many Chinese seamen as possible:

> It is in the public interest that these seamen should now go back to China. They may not go willingly, but the number of recalcitrants and who they are, will not be known in advance. If compulsion proves to be necessary, deportation orders should, it is suggested, be held in readiness; otherwise there may not be time to submit them for signature before the boat on which it is proposed to accommodate the seamen (as passengers) is due to sail, and she would go partly empty.[26]

By July 1946, 1,362 Chinese seamen had been repatriated.[27]

In government discussions about repatriating Austrians and Germans who had come to Britain as refugees, there were also many reservations about accepting them for settlement when the war was over. The Home Secretary, Herbert Morrison, had forbidden them naturalisation during the war and refused to offer any guarantee of settlement, even for those serving in the forces. His views were not shared by other officials at the Home Office and the refugees began campaigning against repatriation in 1944. Morrison's reservations were effectively overruled by Churchill's two-word reply to a question in the House of Commons asking whether arrangements could be made for the immediate repatriation of Jewish refugees: 'No sir.' By 1950, the majority of Austrians and Germans who had come to Britain as refugees had applied for and been granted British naturalisation.[28]

Morrison also had reservations about Polish settlement in Britain, expressing concerns about the effect this would have on 'all those many aliens who desire to stay here and claim they have rendered assistance to

---

26   TNA, HO 213/926, Home Office minute, 22 October 1945.
27   <http://www.halfandhalf.org.uk/dr.htm> accessed 5 March 2014.
28   Anthony Grenville, *Jewish Refugees from Germany and Austria in Britain 1933–1970* (London: Vallentine Mitchell, 2010), 52–78.

the war effort.' Again Churchill intervened. On his return from the Yalta Conference which had agreed to hand over almost half of Polish territory to the Soviet Union – a decision condemned by the Polish government in exile and regarded by most Poles in Britain as a shameful betrayal – Churchill made a speech in the House of Commons, subsequently known as 'Churchill's pledge.' The speech expressed his earnest hope that Polish forces who had fought under the British flag might, if they desired, be offered citizenship of the British Empire. When the war was over, this pledge was honoured by the Labour government through the Polish Resettlement Act of 1947 which meant that Poles who did not want to emigrate to other countries or return to Poland could settle in Britain. Churchill stated: 'We should think it an honour to have such ... faithful and valiant warriors dwelling among us as if they were men of our own blood.'[29] Language that identified Europeans as people of the same 'blood' or 'stock' as Britons was characteristic of debates about refugees and immigrants in the late 1940s, assigning them a racial identity marked by approbation in contrast to official concerns to demobilise British Caribbeans back home and to deport Chinese seamen.[30]

Public and officially sponsored views expressed in the 'culture of tribute' promoted an image of British liberality and tolerance and associated Britishness with an expansive transnational community. People of non-white ethnicity who had contributed to the British war effort were nevertheless regarded as unacceptable for settlement in government discussions that demonstrate a concern to maintain geographical boundaries between black and white where black people belonged in the empire, not the metropolis. A narrow and exclusive view of who could belong in Britain was also evident in initial reluctance to allow settlement to white European groups. The eventual decision to allow this, together with post-war policies developed

---

29   Tony Kushner and Katharine Knox, *Refugees in an Age of Genocide: Global, National and Local Perspectives During the Twentieth Century* (London: Frank Cass, 1999), 221–3; *The Times*, 28 February 1945.

30   Wendy Webster, 'Britain and the Refugees of Europe 1939–1950', in Louise Ryan and Wendy Webster, eds, *Gendering Migration: Masculinity, Femininity and Ethnicity in Post-war Britain* (Aldershot: Ashgate, 2008), 35–51.

in the context of an acute labour shortage, demonstrate the government's preference for white settlement and its desire to keep out black and Asian people as far as possible when the war was over.[31]

Britishness and allies

Mid-1940 was a moment of intense anti-alienism in Britain. Many Britons supported the mass internment of enemy aliens that began in May.[32] On Italy's declaration of war in June there were violent anti-Italian riots in a number of British towns and cities.[33] Hostility was not only directed towards those of enemy nationality. In the context of expectations of an imminent invasion, many British people lumped all foreigners together as potential spies and Fifth Columnists. In May, MO reported that stories of aliens acting as Fifth Columnists in Holland meant that:

> the enemy in our midst is easily visualised. The always latent antagonism to the alien and foreigner began to flare up. Nearly everyone, as previous research has shown, is latently somewhat anti-Semitic and somewhat anti-alien. But ordinarily it is not the done thing to express such sentiments publicly. The news from Holland made it quite the done thing all of a sudden.[34]

By contrast, people from the empire were particularly valued as allies and exempt from suspicion. At the height of the Fifth Columnist scare in June an HI report from Kettering commented on the Canadian troops billeted there awakening 'true feelings of empire cooperation' and on their 'toughness

---

31 Wendy Webster, 'The Empire Comes Home: Commonwealth Migration to Britain', in Andrew Thompson, ed., *Britain's Experience of Empire in the Twentieth Century* (Oxford: Oxford University Press, 2011), 129–36.
32 MO, File Report (FR) 118, 18 May 1940; MOA, Report 276, 16 July 1940.
33 See Wendy Ugolini, *Experiencing War as the 'Enemy Other': Italian Scottish Experience in World War II* (Manchester: Manchester University Press, 2011), 118–43.
34 MO, FR 107, 14 May 1940.

and efficiency.' A report from London later in the same month noted the 'pleasure expressed at arrival of Australians' and the 'new confidence shown because of it.' On the following day HI recorded that the arrival of Empire troops was experienced in Tunbridge Wells as 'cheering.'[35] The idea of 'empire cooperation' was also apparent later in the war in responses to the prestigious BBC Sunday night *Postscript* series, broadcast after the nine o'clock news. Listener research at the BBC showed that speakers from the Dominions were 'assured of a very sympathetic audience' and regarded as contributing to the idea of fellowship within the British empire and 'friendship between each other.'[36]

How far was the idea of 'empire cooperation' confined to the white empire? Public opinion on black troops and war-workers in Britain varied, but black GIs were generally regarded as belonging to the allied community. HI reported that black American troops were referred to as a 'fine lot of men', that their courtesy drew much favourable comment in contrast to the behaviour of their white compatriots and that in the Huddersfield area, they were viewed as 'better behaved than the British troops.'[37] There were regular reports of criticism of the racial segregation of the American armed forces in Britain. Amongst diverse attitudes, one significant strand of opinion favoured interracial social mixing that demonstrated British tolerance and liberality against such segregation.[38] From the North Midlands Region, HI noted that 'the kindness meted out to coloured Americans by their British hosts is said to be resented and misunderstood by the white Americans who do not mix with them.'[39] A black GI who had been a guest in several homes in Cornwall, including one where they baked a cake for his

---

35   Paul Addison and Jeremy Crang, eds, *Listening to Britain: Home Intelligence Reports on Britain's Finest Hour* (London: Bodley Head, 2010), 72, 142, 144.
36   BBC Written Archives Centre (BBC, WAC), R9/65/1, Listener Research Report on broadcast by Major Piet Jooste, 5 November 1941.
37   TNA INF 1/292, Home Intelligence weekly report, no 104, 1 Oct 1942; Home Intelligence Monthly Review, 8 June 1944. All references hereafter to Home Intelligence Reports and Reviews are from TNA, INF 1/292, unless otherwise stated.
38   Reynolds, *Rich Relations*, Chapter 18.
39   Home Intelligence weekly report, no 92, 9 July 1942.

birthday, wrote to a friend in March 1944: 'The more I see of the English, the more disgusted I become with Americans.'[40] From the Eastern Region HI reported an incident where 'British soldiers were taken to task by those from America for fraternising with the Negroes. The British replied that as both black and white troops had come 3,000 miles to help us win the war they saw no reason to draw distinctions between one type of American and another.'[41] Such comments suggest the extent to which Britishness was defined as tolerant and liberal against American segregation.

Black troops and war-workers from empire had also travelled across the world to contribute to the allied war effort. But a Jamaican serviceman who was refused service in a pub after a game of cricket records that this prompted him to ask: 'Why have I travelled thousands of miles to be on the receiving end of such treatment?'[42] Black British, including those from empire, were not always treated as valuable allies. One black woman in the ATS was refused a new issue of shoes by her white officer on the grounds that 'at home you don't wear shoes anyway.'[43] In 1943, the Women's Land Army faced charges of operating a colour bar when Amelia King, born in Britain of Caribbean descent, was refused work on a farm.[44] In 1943, Learie Constantine, well-known between the wars as a Trinidadian cricketer who played in the Lancashire League, was refused rooms in a London hotel that he had booked in advance. But HI reported 'strong indignation' about this incident, suggestions that Constantine should be invited to lunch with the Royal Family at Buckingham Palace, and condemnation of the hotel's action as 'Hitlerism' that 'exists in this land of ours and must be rooted up.' Those who deplored discrimination were clear that black people belonged

40 Reynolds, *Rich Relations*, 342, 324.
41 Home Intelligence weekly report, no. 94, 23 July 1942.
42 Quoted in Hazel Carby, 'Becoming Modern Racialized Subjects', *Cultural Studies* 23/4 (2009), 648.
43 Peter Fryer, *Staying Power: The History of Black People in Britain* (London: Pluto Press, 1984), 363.
44 *Daily Express*, 24 September 1943.

in the allied community: 'If they are good enough to fight for us, they are good enough to live with us.'[45]

The intensity of anti-alienism against Europeans in exile waned after mid-1940. Both HI and MO reported recognition of the value of European forces in Britain that highlighted their martial prowess. Toughness, virility and bravery were qualities assigned to Czechs, Free French and Poles as well as to Australians. Polish airmen were singled out for particular admiration.[46] In contrast, British Jews were frequently considered cowardly. An HI report in 1942 detailed some of the main accusations levelled at Jews that placed them well outside any vision of a united allied community: their black market activities; their avoidance of war obligations, including military service and war work; their business methods and evasion of regulations; their evacuation to safer areas; their ostentatious spending.[47] In March 1943 in the wake of the Bethnal Green tube shelter disaster which was widely blamed on Jews – a falsehood officially repudiated in the government report on the incident – MO reported that 'some of the talk and rumours overheard were violently anti-Semitic in tone.' Conversations MO observers overheard included: 'All they think of is saving their skins'; 'Stinking lot of cowards they're (*sic*) are'; 'They lost their nerve. *You* know, like they did in the blitz. They haven't got *steadiness* like what we have.'[48] Such comments suggest how far British Jews continued to be regarded as foreigners despite their history of settlement in Britain.

The range of attitudes to different ethnic and national groups in Britain reported by HI and MO are too diverse to admit a single evaluation. Anti-alienism and anti-Semitism persisted throughout the war, although there was no recurrence of the intense anti-alienism, violence and rioting of mid-1940. After 1940, diverse national and ethnic groups in Britain were increasingly viewed as valuable allies, although such acknowledgement was mainly

---

45 Home Intelligence weekly report, no 153, 9 September 1943; no 154, 16 September 1943.
46 MO, FR 1669Q, 'Attitudes to Foreigners', April 1943; MO, FR 1094, 'Feelings About Australians', 13 February 1942.
47 TNA, INF 1/293, Home Intelligence Special Report No 1, 15 January 1942.
48 MO, FR 1648, March 1943. Emphasis in original.

for fighting men who were contributing to the allied war effort. One strand of public opinion embraced an expansive view of Britishness as a member of a diverse allied community that was fighting with or alongside them.

The community of allies

In 1940, the pilots of the First Czechoslovak Fighter Squadron in Britain wrote a statement addressed to an English comrade, John Boulton, who had been their flying instructor:

> Today, alas! we can do no more than remember you ... We waited for you all that evening – September 9th. And the next – and the next.
> You never came back.
> We will avenge you ... The six Germans that we shot down in the fight in which you fell are the first instalment of the price we shall exact for your young life. You gave it for those same ideals which are graven on our own hearts in letters of burning flame.[49]

The tribute paid by Czechs to their English flying instructor was reciprocated by Flight-Sergeant Crocker in an English tribute to the Czechoslovak Fighter Squadron:

> I'm proud to be able to work with these men who are fighting so pluckily at the side of our own pilots ... The whole world ought to know how you went into the fight, met and shot down the enemy.[50]

Such close emotional identification as part of a community of allies across differences of nationality was not uncommon. Those serving in multinational forces based in Britain often experienced a close community distinguished by friendships and solidarity which crossed differences of ethnicity

---

49 Bohuš Beneš, ed., *Wings in Exile: Life and Work of the Czechoslovak Airmen in France and Great Britain* (London: 'The Czechoslovak' Independent Weekly, 1942) 93–4.
50 *Ibid.*, 80–1.

as well as nationality. Cy Grant arrived in Britain from British Guiana to join the RAF in 1941 where he made a close relationship with his French-Canadian pilot, Alton Langille. Grant spent much of the war as a prisoner of Germany after bailing out over Holland and describes his 'happiness and joy' when Langille arrived at the prison camp.[51] Willy Hirschfeld, a German Jewish refugee who had been interned by the British in 1940 and then deported to Australia, returned to Britain in 1941 to join the Pioneer Corps. He transferred to the Royal Armoured Corps in 1943 where he worked as a tank driver with a British crew. His tank suffered a direct hit in September 1944 and he was the only survivor. He records of his crew: 'You sleep together, you work together, you eat together, it's like a family … right up to that moment we were always one team.'[52]

A sense of solidarity and friendship is particularly apparent in the term 'band of brothers' used by Bob Kellow to describe the crew in which he served in Bomber Command. Kellow was an Australian member of this crew that comprised two Australians, three English and two Canadians.

People mingled across differences of nationality and ethnicity in work places as well as in the forces. A *Picture Post* article in 1943 described a transnational community at the BBC. Its photospread, taken in the BBC canteen, featured pictures of Colin Wills and Gerry Wilmot with text explaining that they came from Australia and Canada to report the war. A picture of Una Marson was captioned: 'The Girl Who Looks After the West Indian Service. Miss Una Marson, a Jamaican journalist and author, came over here specially to take over the programmes relayed to the native population in the West Indies.' The article celebrated the people in the

---

[51] Cy Grant, *A Member of the RAF of Indeterminate Race: World War Two Experiences of a West Indian Officer in the RAF* (Bognor Regis: Woodfield Publishing, 2006), 28–35, 59.

[52] Helen Fry, *The King's Most Loyal Enemy Aliens: Germans who Fought for Britain in the Second World War* (Stroud: Sutton Publishing, 2007), 45–52; *Churchill's German Army* at <http://www.youtube.com/watch?v=SDkxq5gbR0E> accessed 6 March 2014.

BBC canteen as 'the most colourful and cosmopolitan crowd anywhere in the world today.'[53]

A transnational community was particularly evident in the Indian section of the BBC Eastern Services. A photograph taken in 1942 of a recording session for its poetry magazine series shows Venu Chitale, Narayana Menyon and Mulk Raj Anand from India, Meary Tambimuttu from Ceylon, T.S. Eliot who was born in America, Una Marson from the West Indies and Christopher Pemberton from Britain. George Orwell, who was Talks Assistant and later Talks Producer in the service, also commissioned work from Hsiao Ch'ien who had written and spoken the script for *The Chinese in Wartime Britain*. Ch'ien became good friends with Mulk Raj Anand and each wrote scripts about the other's country. Orwell commissioned Anand to broadcast a letter to a Chinese Guerilla for a series of open letters.[54] Ch'ien scripted a programme on India. Like Anand, he supported Indian independence and voiced his support for this cause, but the censors deleted the programme before it went on air. George Orwell had written to him: 'As for China's political history, you can say anything you like because so far as we are concerned there are no complications, and nothing that is likely to cause offence. As to India, it is a more prickly subject.'[55]

Mulk Raj Anand had declined an offer of work at the BBC in 1941, explaining that 'the position of Indians in this war has become very invidious' since hundreds of his compatriots in India had been interned by the British. At the same time, recognising that 'fascism would destroy all I stand for' he wrote that he was 'torn between conflicting loyalties.'[56] Noor Inayat Khan, similarly had to negotiate between her anti-fascist convictions and support for Indian independence. Khan was a woman of mixed American and Indian parentage who worked in the Special Operations Executive (SOE), a British clandestine organisation. She was executed at Dachau concentration camp. During her recruitment to the SOE she had

---

53 'At the BBC Canteen', *Picture Post*, 27 November 1943.
54 W.J. West, ed., *Orwell: The War Broadcasts* (London: Duckworth, 1985), 44.
55 Orwell to Ch'ien, 31 March 1942, in West, *Orwell*, 186.
56 Anand to Sir Malcolm Darling, 22 March 1941, in West, *Orwell*, 15.

said: 'my first loyalty is to India. If I had to choose between Britain and India I would choose India.'⁵⁷ Such conflicting loyalties suggest some of the complexities and difficulties that could be involved in any identification with a transnational community of allies, and the potential for inter-allied tensions and antagonisms.

Government censorship meant that inter-allied friction was rarely reported, especially when it involved violence. Learie Constantine, who worked during the war as a Welfare Officer for West Indian technicians in Liverpool, expressed concerns about attacks on them by white Americans. He reported one case of 'a West Indian technician who was waiting in a queue for admission to a Cinema, when some white Americans came and told him that he had no right to go into the Cinema. They attacked him and he was badly handled, but some English people came to his rescue.'⁵⁸ There is also evidence of fights between British and Canadian troops and between British and Polish troops. British-Canadian fights were attributed by Canadian censors to 'general inaction' by troops who 'would probably prefer to expend their energies on the enemy.' Violent British-Polish confrontations were often prompted by Polish men's relationships with British women.⁵⁹

It was not only British women's relationships with Poles that provoked British hostility. HI noted criticism of their relationships 'with servicemen of every available nationality and colour.'⁶⁰ By 1944 virtually all weekly reports mentioned criticism of such relationships, focusing particularly on those with both white and black American GIs and Italian prisoners-of-war. Despite censure of the racial segregation of the American armed forces and championship of mixing, British popular opinion was invariably

---

57 Shompa Lahiri, 'Clandestine Mobilities and Shifting Embodiments: Noor-un-nisa Inayat Khan and the Special Operations Executive, 1940–44', *Gender & History* 19/2 (2007), 305–23. Here 308.
58 TNA, CO 876/15, 'Relationships between American white soldiers and British coloured civilians in Liverpool', no date.
59 Reynolds, *Rich Relations*, 137; Adam Zamoyski, *The Forgotten Few: The Polish Air Force in the Second World War* (London: John Murray, 1995), 63.
60 Home Intelligence Periodical Review, 27 July 1944.

uneasy about interracial sex and marriage and frequently hostile.[61] Despite such hostility, many wartime marriages crossed boundaries of ethnicity and nationality. They included a number of interracial marriages and, by the end of the war, an estimated 4,000 British-Polish marriages, 40,000 British-Canadian and 40,000–45,000 British-American.[62]

Inter-allied friction was particularly evident between British and Americans. The most common criticism of American troops in Britain reported by both HI and MO – that they were boastful, brash and over-confident – caused particular antagonism when disparaging comments on British military prowess were involved.[63] HI reported anger at references by American troops to the 'Dunkirk Harriers' and the 'Tobruk Harriers'.[64] Postal Censorship reported anger at American claims that they were winning the war expressed in a letter from London to America:

> It makes me seethe when the American troops over here say to our fellows who have been through hell, 'It's about time you had us over to win this war for you. You should have sent for us long ago' ... Friendship between the two countries would be such a great thing but you can't expect our fellows to like them when they throw their weight about so.[65]

In February 1943, in the context of American reversals in their first battle with German forces at the Battle of Kasserine Pass, HI reported that 'the most marked reaction ... has been satisfaction, going as far as jubilation in some cases, at "the American set-back".'[66]

---

61   Wendy Webster, 'Fit to Fight, Fit to Mix: Sexual Patriotism in Second World War Britain', *Women's History Review* 22/4 (2013), 607–24.
62   Reynolds, *Rich Relations*, 420–2; Sheila Patterson, 'The Poles: An Exile Community in Britain', in James Watson, ed., *Between Two Cultures: Migrants and Minorities in Britain* (Oxford: Blackwell, 1977), 224.
63   See for example TNA, INF 1/292, Home Intelligence Weekly Report, No 112, 26 November 1942; No 144, 8 July 1943; MO, FR 2222, Panel on the Americans, Feb to March directive, 1945, March 1945.
64   Home Intelligence weekly report, no 96, 6 Aug 1942; No 125, 25 February 1943.
65   TNA, PREM 4/100/1, A Report on Home Opinion, no. 28, part 1, 4 April 1942.
66   Home Intelligence weekly report, no. 125, 25 February 1943.

Tensions spilled over into street brawls between American and British troops.[67] In 1943 HI reported 'unfriendly attitudes of British servicemen towards American troops' from five regions and as late as December 1944, after most American troops had departed, continued to report 'antagonism between British and US troops' from two regions.[68] In their turn, the British were disparaging about American martial masculinity as 'unsoldierly.' HI reported a range of criticisms – 'carry themselves badly', 'doesn't look like a soldier', 'wants a hair cut', 'overbearing and arrogant manner', 'boastfulness and throwing their weight about', 'slovenliness and lack of discipline.'[69] Black soldiers were said to be 'less sloppy than whites.'[70] Even after most Americans had departed HI was reporting: 'Some still think the Americans unsoldierly and lacking in discipline; and that they are too casual, and boisterous in attitude and manners.'[71] Such comments suggest the extent to which Britishness was defined against America: Britons were not only more racially tolerant but also better soldiers. Even so, in MO surveys asking 'How do you feel about Americans'? the yearly percentage of people responding favourably increased from 45 per cent in 1941 to 58 per cent in 1945.[72]

The unprecedented diversity of the population in wartime Britain involved a wide range of encounters across differences of nationality and ethnicity in the forces, in workplaces and in British homes where many wartime groups were billeted or invited as visitors and guests. Such mingling prompted inter-allied antagonism, sometimes extending to violence, as well as friendship and solidarity. A mix of friction and friendship is particularly apparent in verdicts delivered as the war was ending by Poles and Canadians on their experiences in Britain. Both groups had engaged

---

67 Home Intelligence weekly report, no 144, 8 July 1943.
68 Home Intelligence, Periodic Review, 25 November 1943; Monthly Review 21 December 1944.
69 Home Intelligence Periodic Review, 25 November 1943; weekly report, no. 144, 8 July 1943.
70 Home Intelligence Monthly Review, 8 June 1944.
71 Home Intelligence weekly report, no 220, 21 December 1944.
72 Paul Ward, *Britishness Since 1870* (London: Routledge, 2004), 90.

in violent conflict with the British but had evidently also enjoyed strong friendships. The war diary of one Canadian regiment for 31 August 1944, during fierce fighting in France, recorded:

> We who have spent so many years in England think and speak constantly of England and of our friends there ... even to the point of appearing disloyal to Canada. The thought of returning there on leave sometime soon alone makes life supportable at times.[73]

An editorial in the Polish Air Force magazine, reflecting on the history of the previous four years stated: 'probably no people has ever been the recipient of such moving expressions of friendship on this island as the Poles.'[74]

Post-war forgettings

In 1943, Gallup Polls conducted a public opinion survey on who was winning the war. They offered respondents a choice of four countries: America, Britain, China and Russia. The publication of their findings in the *News Chronicle* prompted Winston Churchill to write to Sir Walter Layton, who was Chairman of the *News Chronicle*: 'Nothing will more arm hostile elements in the US against us than this most mischievous publication and the publicity it is bound to attain ... This is one of the worst things that has happened in the newspaper world since the war began.'[75] Churchill's strong reaction was due to poll findings which showed 50 per cent of British respondents opting for Russia and a further 42 per cent for Britain, leaving China and the United States in single figures. The United States was at the bottom of the poll, below China, with only 3 per cent.

---

73 Reynolds, *Rich Relations*, 339.
74 Zamoyski, *The Forgotten Few*, 193.
75 TNA, PREM 4/66/2, Churchill to Layton, 17 July 1943.

The poll's findings on high esteem for Russia as the country most likely to win the war and low esteem for America as the country least likely to win chime with the findings of HI and Postal Censorship in 1942–4. In contrast to the criticisms of American martial masculinity and occasional jubilation at American setbacks, there was delight at Soviet successes and 'sincere admiration and gratitude' for the Soviet war effort. Calls for more support for the Soviet people were fuelled by awareness of their sacrifices and suffering as they bore the brunt of the fighting and contrasted with attitudes to America: 'While the public are prepared to make any sacrifices necessary to help Russia ... they have no such disposition towards America.'[76]

In *The True Glory* (1945) – an Anglo-American documentary telling the story of the allied victory in Europe from D-Day to German surrender – an American voice predicts that, as the guns stop and the war in Europe ends, the focus of attention will shift from who is winning the war to who won it:

> Now it starts. All the arguments about who won the war. Well here's what I say. That no country on earth could have won it alone. So what does that mean? That anybody who wants to take a bow by himself is not only boasting, but nuts.[77]

Many allied nations proved to be 'nuts' by these standards. *The True Glory* was one of the last films to present sound and imagery of an 'allies war' acknowledging the contributions of a wide range of allies to victory in Europe – including Americans, British, Canadians, Czechs, French, Norwegians, Poles and Russians – and incorporating American, British, Canadian and French voices. This vision and the wartime 'culture of tribute' both faded rapidly in the aftermath of war as the British, like the Americans and the Soviets, increasingly took a bow by themselves. British forgettings of Soviet successes, so much celebrated in wartime, were particularly striking. The Eastern Front scarcely featured in post-war British memories and

---

76   TNA, PREM 4/100/1, A Report on Home Opinion, no. 28, part 1, 4 April 1942; Home Intelligence weekly report, no 151, 26 Aug 1943; no 176, 17 February 1944.
77   *The True Glory* (1945).

the strong wartime admiration for the Soviet Union did not survive the onset of the Cold War.

The True Glory presents Americans discovering a transnational community of allies in Britain. Shots of servicemen and women of different nationalities walking British streets resemble the word-portraits sketched by Macaulay and Panter-Downes earlier in the war. They are intercut with shots of signs advertising the American Red Cross Services Club, Canadian Red Cross Maple Leaf Club, Catholic Services Club, Indian Forces Club, Newfoundland Caribou Club, New Zealand Forces Club and Yugoslav Relief Society. An American voice comments over them: 'Funny thing, on the way over you felt like you were the whole works ... but then all over the UK you'd see things that made you begin to realise you were just part of a hell of a big proposition.' Like the wider community of allies, this transnational community in Britain was also generally forgotten when the war was over.

Such forgetting is apparent in the experiences of West Indians who were demobilised back to the Caribbean and subsequently returned to Britain. Sam King, who had served in the wartime RAF and came back to Britain on the *Empire Windrush* in 1948, noticed a change from wartime attitudes with people 'more aggressive' and 'trying to say that you shouldn't be here.'[78] Caribbean migrants who arrived in the 1950s were often viewed as threatening Britishness. Poles were excluded from the 1946 Victory Parade in London at the request of the Soviet Union and were also subject to increasing hostility. A Gallup Poll held in June 1946 showed that while 30 per cent of those interviewed favoured allowing Poles to remain in Britain, 56 per cent favoured deporting them. Those who did return to Poland faced arrest and imprisonment. Many were shot.[79]

Other groups who had been celebrated in British wartime propaganda also fell outside any national memory and were subject to double forgettings. The dominant post-war Irish narrative of Ireland's war, where

---

78   Quoted in Mike Phillips and Trevor Phillips, *Windrush: The Irresistible Rise of Multi-Racial Britain* (London: HarperCollins, 1998), 82.
79   Zamoyski, *The Forgotten Few*, 204, 212–13.

neutrality had successfully asserted independence from Britain, maintained national unity and enjoyed widespread popular support, left no place for Irish volunteers who had worn British uniform.[80] Czechoslovakians initially received a hero's welcome when they returned to Prague in 1946, but the atmosphere changed quickly and they were increasingly labelled 'Western aviators.' Miroslav Liskutin, one of those who returned, records this change:

> The nation was now orientated towards the East and the aviators from abroad did not fit into this new situation. The aviators brought from abroad an infection of foreign ideology ... endangering the progressive development of the nation. The 'aviators from abroad' had a competing claim with the Red Army for the liberation. This was intolerable ...[81]

After the 1948 Communist Putsch Liskutin, faced with the prospect of arrest, escaped to Austria and then to Britain. Many of his fellow 'aviators from abroad' were arrested and imprisoned.

Conclusion

The wartime British media promoted a vision of a community of allies united in a common cause against a common enemy. Official views expressed privately were often at odds with this vision despite official support for propaganda that promoted it. Public opinion was intensely anti-alienist in mid-1940, but although anti-alienism and particularly anti-Semitism persisted, one strand of popular opinion came to embrace an expansive version of Britishness as a member of the transnational community of allies fighting with or alongside them. People of different nationalities also

---

80 Wendy Webster, 'Allies, Enemies and Transnational Histories: Germans, Irish and Italians in Second World War Britain', *Twentieth Century British History* 25/1 (2014), 63–86.
81 Liskutin, *Challenge*, 204.

identified with this transnational community and made close transnational friendships. Even so, there was considerable inter-allied conflict. When the war was over, allies in wartime Britain played little part in public memories of war and a range of groups were subject to double forgettings.

Nila Kantan's memories offer a different vision of people mingling and of a transnational community produced by war. He grew up in a small village in Andra Pradesh before volunteering for the Indian Army in the Second World War. He served with the Eighth Army in the North African campaign and then with the Allied advance up the Italian peninsula fought by Americans, British, Canadians, Free French, Indians, New Zealanders and Poles. He remembers his experience of Monte Cassino:

> I still can't forget the Cassino ruins. There was nothing but rubble ... I have never seen such a number of dead bodies in any battle. I counted more than 800 – then I gave it up. They were just there in the rubble, covered with a blanket. I felt very sorry. I didn't know where they were born, how they came there, whether they were enemy or our own troops – they were all mingled together. So many New Zealanders, British, Germans, Indians ... Seeing that, I felt there should never be a war again.[82]

---

82   Christopher Somerville, *Our War: How the British Commonwealth Fought the Second World War* (London: Weidenfeld and Nicolson, 1998), 237.

IAIN E. JOHNSTON

Imperial settler-regions in the Second World War: The case of British air training in southern Africa

The Second World War was a unique moment in defining and transforming Britishness around the empire. For the global British diaspora, it was reflected, in part, through large-scale participation in the British war effort by overseas Britons, a phenomenon that both cemented the immediate bonds between the metropole and its settler-regions, but also contributed to the transformation of those links during six years of wartime cooperation.[1] Membership in the 'British World' was also a factor that played into geopolitical and strategic decision-making, especially during the war – while settler-regions enjoyed a privileged status within the British Empire, this attachment to the empire, when manifested in significant military contributions, also had domestic political consequences.[2] This chapter will explore the dynamic between the UK and two of its settler-regions in southern Africa, the Dominion of South Africa and the colony of Southern Rhodesia, using the shared experience of training airmen for the RAF as a framework through which to analyse the evolving imperial bonds.

First, I will consider the factors behind the UK's decision to pursue approval from the Dominions and Southern Rhodesia for the training of

---

1   I use the term settler-regions to describe territories within the empire that contained significant numbers of British emigrants, whether Dominions or colonies.
2   For more on the British World, see Phillip Buckner and Douglas Francis, eds, *Rediscovering the British World* (Calgary: University of Calgary Press, 2005); Carl Bridge and Phillip Buckner, 'Reinventing the British World', *The Round Table: The Commonwealth Journal of International Affairs*, 368, (2003), 77–88; Carl Bridge and Kent Fedorowich, eds, *The British World: Diaspora, Culture and Identity* (London: Frank Cass, 2003).

Britons and overseas British as airmen in imperial settler-regions – not just in southern Africa, but also in the Dominions of Canada, Australia and New Zealand. This underpins the importance of these settler relationships to the UK and the special benefits that London perceived in having these regions, and a significant proportion of their populations, tied to the UK by political, military and cultural bonds. Then I will turn to the specific cases of South Africa and Southern Rhodesia, and explore the reasons why these countries pursued air training apart, not only from the other Dominions, but also from one another. I will trace the shifting perceptions of the importance of the 'British connection' to South Africa and Southern Rhodesia, a changing view that had lasting implications for the UK's imperial presence in sub-Saharan Africa. Air training is a particularly useful lens through which to assess Britishness and the relationship between these two African settler-regions because, firstly, the training schemes brought Britons and personnel from multiple settler-regions together; secondly, negotiations over air training highlighted elements of both competition and cooperation in the relations between these two African imperial settler-regions; and finally, this military role formed Southern Rhodesia's single most important contribution to the war, the only involvement by the much smaller settler-region comparable to its South African equivalent. By comparing the South African and Southern Rhodesian air training experiences, I illustrate the importance, and ultimately the limitations, of a geopolitical Britishness.

The dominions

Understanding the relationship between metropole and settler-colony requires a brief outline of the development of the Dominions. In the middle of the nineteenth century, the UK granted its settler-colonies increasing powers of self-governance, in the hope that they would not follow the USA in declaring independence from the British Empire. Canada was born from the union of several North American settler-colonies in 1867 and named a

British Dominion, as a distinction for taking a constitutional step beyond being a patchwork of self-governing colonies to a single imperial entity of significant size. Australian colonies federated in 1901. In 1907 New Zealand, having refused union with Australia, gained independent Dominion status alongside Australia, marking their constitutional development and creating a coherent Dominion group distinguishable within the framework of British imperial power. The process in South Africa was less direct: during the Boer War, 1899–1902, the two British-South African colonies fought two independent Afrikaner colonies – the imperial armies employing many thousands of men from Canada, Australia and New Zealand in the process – before British Empire forces secured control over all four territories. Out of the search for a diplomatic settlement to the strained British-Afrikaner relationship, a democratic and self-governing Union of South Africa was formed as a British Dominion in 1910.[3] Taken together, the UK and its Dominions formed the British Commonwealth of Nations, an imperial group that existed within an empire from which it often stood apart, but that functioned as a remarkably successful alliance in both world wars. Other colonies controlled by British settlers, notably Southern Rhodesia, sought to increase their white, preferably British, populations and thus be extended membership into this Commonwealth group.

To varying extents, the settler-colonies/Dominions shared key features. In their early history, they relied on financial investment and immigrants (or settlers) from the UK for economic and demographic growth. Their economies, lacking the population density and resource development for significant industrialisation, were based on agriculture and the export of primary products and raw materials back to the UK; many of the manufactured items and consumer products available in the Dominions were in turn imported from the 'mother country.' Significantly for this study, armed forces were raised by settler-regions to fight within the British imperial

---

3   Yet this was 'white' democracy and racial discrimination dictated the electorate. See Robert Ross, Anne Mager and Bill Nasson, eds, *The Cambridge History of South Africa: Volume 2, 1885–1994* (Cambridge: Cambridge University Press, 2011), specifically chapter five, Bill Freund, 'South Africa: The Union Years, 1910–1948 – Political and Economic Foundations'.

army, navy and, from the Great War, the air force as well.[4] Parliamentary systems, despite the federal nature of several Dominions, were based on the British model, and the electorate was generally restricted by a colour bar. In the late nineteenth and early twentieth century, large proportions of settler populations were 'off the boat' from the UK or had a parent or parents who were born in the British Isles. Beyond the blood ties to the UK, Britishness encompassed cultural and political identities as well, allowing some non-British European immigrants to share in British imperial citizenship and participate in building these new nations. In this regard, Britishness could be conflated with 'whiteness', although British subjecthood in its legal form extended to all citizens of British territories, regardless of race.[5] Nevertheless 'whiteness' was also a factor in determining who was recruited for specific roles within the armed forces of the UK and its settler-regions alike, and an ethnic and 'racialised' conception of Britishness is one way of understanding who London particularly counted upon to support the UK beyond the British Isles.

Many elements of the war stories of South Africa and Southern Rhodesia remain to be told. Little has been written on the experience of Southern Rhodesia in the Second World War,[6] and South Africa is the only Dominion that lacks a full series of official histories on the conflict – a striking absence, particularly when we consider that the series produced by the smallest Dominion, New Zealand, runs to forty eight volumes.[7]

---

[4] Robert Holland, 'The British Empire and the Great War, 1914–1918' in William Roger Louis and Judith Brown, eds, *The Oxford History of the British Empire. Vol. IV: The Twentieth Century* (Oxford: Oxford University Press, 1999).

[5] Kathleen Paul, *Whitewashing Britain: Race and Citizenship in the Post-war Era* (London: Cornell University Press, 1997), 10.

[6] John F. MacDonald, *The War History of Southern Rhodesia, 2 Vols.* (Salisbury, 1947–1950) remains a very useful entry point into the topic.

[7] Jeffrey Grey, '"Standing humbly in the ante-chambers of Clio": The Rise and Fall of Union War Histories', *Scientia Militaria: South African Journal of Military Studies*, 30/2 (2000), 253–66; Ian van der Waag, 'Contested Histories: Official History and the South African Military in the 20th Century' in Jeffrey Grey, ed., *The Last Word? Essays on Official History in the United States and British Commonwealth* (London, Praeger, 2003).

Imperial settler-regions in the Second World War   239

Several later attempts to produce an unofficial history series of South Africa in the Second World War, a dedicated military journal and, in particular, an increasing interest in military history in the last decade, have started to fill this gap in South Africa's historiography.[8] This chapter explores a new aspect of the conflict, furthering our understanding of the importance of southern Africa in World War II and placing this in the context of global Britishness. In addition to using documents from the National Archives in London, I mobilise the South African national and military archives to focus primarily on the periphery of empire.

The UK and air training

The training of airmen for the British war effort occurred on a global scale, in both Allied and varied imperial territories. The outcome of all these air training programmes, from the USA to the Middle East, from the Commonwealth to the empire, was the production of over 326,000 airmen. The four 'white' Dominions – Canada, Australia, New Zealand and South Africa – and Southern Rhodesia were responsible for training almost 65 per cent of the total in their own territories. The UK government had known that it could accommodate less than half of the training capacity necessary

---

8   An unofficial 'official' history series was later written, which added much to existing accounts of South Africa's contribution. See Neil Orpen, *South African Forces in World War Two (Vol. I): East African and Abyssinian Campaigns* (Cape Town: Purnell, 1968), iii–iv. Some later books, such as Ian Gleeson, *The Unknown Force: Black, Indian and Coloured Soldiers Through Two World Wars* (Rivonia: Ashanti, 1994), have also made valuable contributions to the literature on the Union's war effort. This trend towards opening up the South African experience continues to emerge through books like Neil Roos, *Ordinary Springboks: White Servicemen and Social Justice in South Africa, 1939–1961* (Aldershot: Ashgate, 2005); and articles such as Andre Wessels 'The First Two Years of War: The Development of the Union Defence Forces (UDF) September 1939 to September 1941', *Military History Journal*, 11/ 5 (2000), 165–72.

to meet its strategic needs as early as 1939. As the war progressed, this proved to be the case, and the problem this posed for strategy makers was answered mainly by imperial regions of settlement. The air training that took place in the British Empire was, however, so much more than just the relocation or creation of training facilities. Overseas white manpower provided over 40 per cent of the total trained aircrew by nationality, and astonishingly over 45 per cent of all the pilots that were finally produced by the training programmes.[9] The RAF was not just relying on training taking place abroad; it was drawing almost half of its newly trained manpower from settler-regions. This substantial settler-region contribution demonstrates the strength of the imperial pull within these territories because almost all of this manpower enlisted voluntarily. It also reveals some of the key features that underwrote this wartime unity.

The British Commonwealth Air Training Plan (BCATP) was the centrepiece of the UK's global network of air training programmes, incorporating training facilities for the RAF in Canada, Australia, New Zealand and the UK. Its success was foundational to British air strategy, and it has been described as 'the most striking, if not the greatest concerted effort which the nations of the British Commonwealth have ever made.'[10] Although negotiating the scheme in Ottawa was a difficult task for the participants after war erupted in 1939, the subsequent issues for the participants were largely limited to questions of national identity for Dominion airmen within the RAF. Air power had developed into a factor that affected virtually every field of combat in this period, including convoy protection, coastal patrols, army co-operation, home defence and reconnaissance. On 6 September 1940, Churchill announced, 'The Navy can lose us the war, but only the Air Force can win it. Therefore our supreme effort must be

---

9   The National Archives (TNA), Air Ministry papers (AIR), AIR 10/551, 2, Air Ministry, *Second World War, 1939–1945: RAF Flying Training, Policy and Planning* (London, 1952).
10 TNA, Dominions Office papers (DO), DO 35/1204, History of the War: The Empire Air Training Scheme, Caines to Stephenson, 2 June 1945.

to gain overwhelming mastery in the air.'[11] In terms of trained men, the BCATP was the central component of London's plans for air superiority.

The situation that prompted London to look to its settler-regions was critical – the UK was aware of the Luftwaffe's part in the rapid subjugation of Poland, and London recognised the limitations of the British Isles for a large air training network. The latter was a particular problem due to the UK's limited space, congested conurbations and vulnerability to enemy attack. Despite the failure of pre-war initiatives there, Canada remained the favoured location for a large training network: for proximity to the UK, for industrial potential, and for the resources of its neighbour, the USA. Moreover, the suitability of settler-regions as locations for such programmes was simply never questioned – in terms of both the military and available manpower, they were viewed as extensions of the UK itself. The initial plan conceived by the Air Staff was expanded in discussions between the Australian and Canadian High Commissioners in London – Stanley Bruce and Vincent Massey – who envisioned Canada becoming the hub of all advanced air training for the UK and the Dominions.[12] This proposal met with general approval in London, and British Prime Minister Neville Chamberlain laid the plan before his Dominion counterparts in a telegram on 26 September 1939.[13] Yet for all the urgency and preference for settler-contributions, South Africa and Southern Rhodesia negotiated separate schemes with the UK.

11 TNA, AIR 10/551, 121, Air Ministry, *RAF Flying Training*.
12 Spencer Dunmore, *Wings for Victory: The Remarkable Story of the British Commonwealth Air Training Plan in Canada* (Toronto: McClelland and Stewart, 1994), 35; Andrew Stewart, 'The British and Canadian "Empire Air Training Scheme" negotiations', *The Round Table: The Commonwealth Journal of International Affairs*, 93/377 (2004), 739–54. The RAAF narration of the scheme points specifically to the role of Stanley Bruce. See Australian War Memorial (AWM), AWM 138, 1, 2, Department of Air, 'Empire Air Training Scheme, Historical Review'; for Massey's role, see Norman Hillmer, 'Vincent Massey and the Origins of the British Commonwealth Air Training Plan', *Canadian Defence Quarterly*, 16/4 (1987), 49–56.
13 TNA, Cabinet Office papers (CAB) 21/499, Dominions: Air Training Scheme, Prime Minister to Dominions, 26 September 1939.

Why did the UK favour its imperial settler-regions as the destination for RAF training? The British Dominions, South Africa included, had relatively small air forces with which to contribute to British air power upon the outbreak of war. Training, rather than operational activities, was therefore perceived to be an ideal contribution for the Dominions: their limited air personnel could help to instruct much larger numbers of Britons and white Dominion men who would see action within the RAF; while their limited productive capacity could be devoted to producing simpler training aircraft, allowing the UK to focus on operational machines. The settler-regions comprised a significant pool of white manpower; the majority of the aircrews produced here, beyond what the small Dominion air forces could absorb, thus crucially served under British operational control, within the RAF. Although Southern Rhodesia lacked significant white manpower, the few squadrons it could muster were all incorporated within the RAF.

The existing structure of air forces in the settler-regions was a vital starting point for the training schemes. This framework allowed for much more than simply relocating RAF schools abroad, as occurred in other alliances, including the Anglo-American air training arrangement. Training schools located in, and run by, settler-regions relieved the RAF of administrative duties and of providing the total manpower requirements for everything that went with these large training establishments, such as maintenance, training personnel, construction and infrastructure development. The extent of this should not be underestimated – in Canada alone over 8,300 buildings were constructed, 2,000 miles of power lines were placed, and some 35,000,000 square yards of runway were laid.[14] Canada shouldered $1.6bn of the $2.2bn cost,[15] with the UK permitted to provide its share largely in kind: namely machines, parts and advisors

---

14   Library and Archives Canada (LAC), J.L. Ralston papers, MG 27 III B II, vol. 39, Final Report of the Chief of the Air Staff to the Members of the Supervisory Board, BCATP, 16 April 1945.
15   Stephen Hayter, 'History of the Creation of the British Commonwealth Air Training Plan', Commonwealth Air Training Plan Museum, <http://www.airmuseum.ca/bcatp.html> accessed 29 April 2011.

or staff, where required.[16] All this simply could not have happened if the countries involved had not followed RAF training methods, mainly in RAF-designated aircraft, in accordance with RAF guidelines.[17] In stark contrast, the Air Ministry complained in 1941 that the small Royal Indian Air Force had 'carried on re-organisation and formation of Air Force units without keeping the Air Ministry informed.'[18] Likewise, the USA refused to consider pooling its airmen with the Commonwealth on the grounds that each nation would 'do better work if it maintains its own national identity and fights under its own command.'[19] Although the issue of national identity proved troublesome in Anglo-Dominion relations in the British Commonwealth Air Training Plan, it was a persistent difficulty precisely because the Dominions were so willing to have their manpower subsumed within the RAF, under British command. In this sense a substantial proportion of Dominion manpower also demonstrated that it acquiesced in its dual settler-region and imperial British identity; these men were largely willing to adopt their British subjecthood to such a degree as to risk death within the UK's armed forces.

Indeed, this manpower was an important factor that led the UK to seek out settler-region cooperation specifically in the area of air power. At several points during the war, the question of finding the required levels of volunteers to keep the training programmes, and subsequently the RAF, growing at the desired pace became a serious problem. This demonstrated the successful nature of settler-region training, both in terms of organisation and popularity for settler-populations – it was developed because of a

---

16   TNA, AIR 20/340, Air Training Scheme: Report of Lord Riverdale's Mission to Canada, 'Mission to Canada in connection with the Dominion Air Training Scheme', Memorandum, 27 October, 1939.
17   TNA, AIR 10/551, 79, Air Ministry, *RAF Flying Training*.
18   TNA, AIR 2/8056, Overseas: Dominions and Colonies: Proposed use of India in Empire Air Training Scheme, 'The Air Forces in India', Jan 1941.
19   National Archives of South Africa (NASA), Department of Foreign Affairs papers, 9/4/2, Part I, Closer Co-operation between the British Commonwealth and United Kingdom in Defence Matters during the European War, S.A. Legation, Washington, to Secretary for External Affairs, Pretoria, 4 June 1942.

desperate lack of training facilities, yet reached proportions that challenged the supply of overseas white manpower available to fill the vast network that was created. The question was posed on several occasions of utilising the vast manpower reserves of the colony of India, with a population of over 300 million. The Air Ministry acknowledged that an air training scheme in the colony would be hugely popular in terms of recruitment. Yet India could not provide, at least in any serious number, what the settler-regions could: white Europeans with 'sufficient education.' Small-scale samples of Indian pupils were accommodated in training schools – eighteen Indian pilots graduated from Canadian schools and a further fifteen from UK schools – but the Air Ministry considered Indian pupils less capable, despite strategic reasons that suggested a training network in India would be desirable.[20] At most the Air Ministry allowed that there was a case for 'developing elementary facilities in India to train the white man power that was available.'[21] Of the 326,000 men trained as aircrews, estimates put the non-white contingent, comprising West Indians, West Africans and South Asians, at around 400.[22]

More than simply being white, Britishness – which, within the Commonwealth, nevertheless incorporated 'whiteness' as an inherent aspect – was perceived as a desirable quality by the Air Ministry: it retrospectively admitted that, during the war, 'the main system of recruitment depended as always for its material mainly ... [on] the white population of the Empire.'[23] As a historical framework, scholars have correctly called for Britishness to adopt a capacious cultural definition far beyond any ethnic limitations.[24] However, London conceived of overseas British populations in exclusively racial terms. This perception carried particular significance in

---

20 TNA, AIR 2/8056, Overseas: Dominions and Colonies: Proposed use of Indian in Empire Air Training Scheme, Enclosure 14A, 'Extracts Relating to India'.
21 *Ibid.*
22 Martin Francis, *The Flyer: British Culture and the Royal Air Force, 1939–1945* (Oxford: Oxford University Press, 2008), 59.
23 TNA, AIR 10/551, 65, Air Ministry, *RAF Flying Training*.
24 Saul Dubow, 'How British was the British World? The Case of South Africa', *The Journal of Imperial and Commonwealth History*, 37/1 (2009), 1–27.

times of war, when Britishness was understood to give the overseas settlers a tangible stake in the struggle, one that would improve combat performance. As one Air Ministry review of an Indian pilot asserted, by contrast to his 'British' counterparts, this airman's 'heart [was] not in the war.'[25] Nor was this policy adopted only by the UK – in one discussion, at the Ottawa Air Training Conference of 1942, when Canada considered accepting Indian pupils to its BCATP schools, Canadian officials admitted that they only agreed to the *principle* of training non-whites because they had been informed that Indians would not actually be sent to North America. Canadian officials pointed to the RAF inter-war doctrine, adopted by the Royal Canadian Air Force, that aircrew could only be 'of pure European descent', but were informed by the Air Ministry that the RAF had by this time, at least officially, 'cut that out.'[26] Despite all imperial citizens enjoying British subjecthood, this evidence points to the 'racialisation' of the empire. As Kathleen Paul has argued, there was 'a fundamental contradiction' between imperial citizenship and 'the informal notion of who really did or could belong.'[27] Such hierarchy informed the decisions of British military planners.

The view on the periphery: Air training in southern Africa

While London's strategic needs and racial views in part dictated the shape of air training, the national goals of the settler-regions were the most important factors in determining the final configuration of British air training.

---

25   TNA, AIR 2/8056, Overseas: Dominions and Colonies: Proposed use of Indian in Empire Air Training Scheme, Enclosure 37B, Report on Indian Officers now Serving with the Royal Air Force.
26   LAC, RCAF papers, RG24, vol. 5389, Air Training Conference 1942 – Conference Diary – Formal Minutes Policy Committee, 'Outstanding Points of Yesterday's Discussion: Colour Bar'.
27   Paul, *Whitewashing Britain*, xiii.

Here we turn to the South African and Southern Rhodesian air training programmes, which were separate from the arrangements made with the BCATP Dominions. Exploring the imperial dynamic through the framework of these air training schemes is revealing of the nature of the Anglo-South African and Anglo-Southern Rhodesian relationships, and of the wartime interactions between the two settler-regions. The air training programmes demonstrate that South Africa and Southern Rhodesia, as prominent settler-regions in southern Africa, perceived and expected tangible benefits in their relationships with the UK and the empire. Although this first created competition between the neighbouring countries, it also sowed the seeds of future cooperation in response to shortcomings in what the UK provided.

South Africa not only stood apart from the BCATP; it also remained relatively aloof from the whole 'Commonwealth' element of air training until the Ottawa Air Training Conference in 1942. The UK, however, was happy just to have the politically divided Dominion in the war from September 1939. Once Prime Minister Jan Smuts achieved this feat, he was in a position that virtually prohibited any dictation of policy from London; the precariousness of his political power meant that, unlike his Commonwealth counterparts, he was particularly obliged – and permitted by London – to prioritise domestic politics over imperial strategy. Under the guidance of the South African High Commissioner in the UK, Sidney Waterson, Pretoria was informed of the BCATP proposal but not invited to join. Nevertheless London made it clear that if participation was considered possible, the proposal did not preclude South African entry.[28]

The initiative flowed in the opposite direction, from periphery to centre, with Southern Rhodesia. From the outset, the colony initiated its cooperation with the UK, offering itself as a potential location for air training, and then attempted to establish links with the BCATP. In

---

28 TNA, CAB 21/499, Dominions: Air Training Scheme, DO to UK High Commissioner, Pretoria, 26 September 1939. NASA, Department of Foreign Affairs papers, vol. 57, FS1/74, Part I, Monthly Report on Dominion Participation in the War, Secretary for External Affairs, Pretoria, to South African High Commissioner, London, 30 September 1939.

South Africa, Smuts contended that the timing of such a large commitment was not right for the Union so early in the war. South Africa preferred to maintain its limited supply of airmen for domestic needs. The country was in the process of completing its own defence plans, which involved the expansion of the South African Air Force, and did not wish to divert its limited white manpower to the RAF – at least not unless this entailed significant benefits for the Union and after it had first provided for South African defence.[29] Where Southern Rhodesia sought to prove its value to the UK and empire, South Africa was more concerned with the benefits that it could receive in any imperial arrangement.

To fully understand the Union's stance, it is important to consider South Africa's home front. The main issue for the South African government was its vocal right-wing opposition. Although South Africa was not the only Dominion with a significant white population that opposed close ties with the UK, the Afrikaners in the Union outnumbered those of British origin and descent, unlike, for instance, French-Canadians in Canada. Similarly to Southern Rhodesia, disenfranchised non-whites – who made up a majority at around 80 per cent of the total population in the Union – were most often ambiguous about the war effort at best. Smuts was relatively secure with voters of British heritage, who followed the mostly pro-UK viewpoint of the other settler-regions in the British Empire and readily adopted their British subjecthood, but needed to court enough of the Afrikaner population with his inclusive vision of white South Africanism, rather than narrow Afrikaner nationalism, to maintain power.[30] The UK was acutely sensitive

---

29 NASA, Department of Foreign Affairs papers, 9/4/2, Part II, Closer Co-operation between the British Commonwealth and United Kingdom in Defence Matters during the European War, Secretary of External Affairs, Pretoria, to the Accredited Representative of the Union of South Africa, Ottawa, 13 October, 1939.

30 For more on South Africanism, see John Lambert, '"An Unknown People": Reconstructing British South African Identity', *The Journal of Imperial and Commonwealth History*, 37/4 (2009), 599–617. For the emergence of competing national and imperial South African identities, see John Lambert, 'South African British? Or Dominion South Africans? The Evolution of an Identity in the 1910s and 1920s', *South African Historical Journal*, 43/1 (2000), 197–222; and John Lambert, 'An Identity Threatened: White English-speaking South Africans, Britishness and

to Smuts' position, because his opposition supported neutrality and cutting ties with the Commonwealth. Smuts came to power narrowly in September 1939 by winning the debate over South African involvement in the war, using the benefits of the Commonwealth connection alongside the autonomy of South Africa within this structure in debates.[31] Any suggestion that South Africans were paying, or dying, for an imperial war threatened to undermine Smuts' support from moderate Afrikaners. In Southern Rhodesia, with its small settler population that was largely of British origin, a lack of visible commitment to the war effort was the larger political threat.

The public perception in South Africa that the Union was fighting in its own interests, and not for the UK's imperial position, was therefore considered crucial to maintaining Smuts' power – and South Africa's participation in the war. This meant distancing the Union from higher strategy and abiding by the publicly announced geographical limits of South Africa's participation, which began at Kenya, but by the end of the war extended as far north as Italy. Pretoria warned Waterson to guard against press reports when the South African Minister for Native Affairs and Deputy Prime Minister Colonel Deneys Reitz visited the UK in 1939, fearing that his presence 'might place him in an embarrassing situation on his return vis-à-vis the Dutch population of the Union.'[32] This was an explicit reference to one substantial portion of the Union's population that would *not* volunteer to fight for Britain, and would instead require other incentives. Furthermore, when South Africa first provided airmen for the RAF, a small number of volunteers, Waterson was cautioned against allowing the press to mention their presence in the UK. Reports that South African pilots had operated in Burma for the RAF caused the Union government 'embarrassment', but by January 1942 Waterson was forced to request that the Union acknowledge

Dominion South Africanism, 1934–1939', *African Historical Review*, 37/1 (2005), 50–70.
31   Richard Sayers, *History of the Second World War, United Kingdom Civil Series: Financial Policy, 1939–45* (London: H.M.S.O., 1956), 306–7.
32   NASA, Department of Foreign Affairs papers, vol. 57, FS1/74, Part I, Monthly Report on Dominion Participation in the War, Secretary for External Affairs, Pretoria, to South African High Commissioner, London, 14 October 1939.

the growing presence of its airmen in the UK, citing the fact that 'officers wear distinctive South African Air Force uniforms', and therefore 'do not go about unnoticed.'[33] By this time, the South African training programme with the RAF was in operation in the Union, and South Africa was willing to take this step; however, the Union's involvement with the RAF was always complicated by the potential domestic opposition that it could raise.

Despite the risks that prevented the Union from joining the BCATP in 1939, there were several factors that compelled South Africa to initially broach the possibility of an air training scheme on its own territory, even one that included the provision of South African airmen for the RAF. One of these was the lack of training facilities that existed for developing the South African Air Force (SAAF). If the RAF could be induced to fund aerodrome construction or provide training aircraft, anything to reduce the burden on South Africa and stimulate growth of the Union's air power, this would assist Pretoria's plans for SAAF expansion.[34] Whether in the form of SAAF training schools that would allow both South Africans and UK cadets to train, or alternatively by moving existing RAF schools en bloc to South Africa – in which South Africans could participate in the construction, administration and actual training – expansion of the SAAF could continue apace with British assistance. This was part of the beneficial relationship that South Africa sought to have with the UK – the RAF could provide the tools for rapid SAAF expansion and the materials for developing infrastructure, a deal which, given the UK's war emergency and the possibility of furthering South African commitment to the war effort, London was willing to make.[35]

---

33 NASA, Department of Foreign Affairs papers, 9/4/2, Part II, Closer Co-operation between the British Commonwealth and United Kingdom in Defence Matters during the European War, South African High Commissioner, London, to Secretary of External Affairs, Pretoria, 13 January 1942.
34 LAC, RCAF papers, RG24, vol. 3214, Memorandum by Air Commodore Croil, 5 September 1936.
35 National Archives of Australia (NAA), Department of Air papers, A1196, 12/501/75, Notes on Air Ministry Committee Empire Air Training Scheme, Report of the 19th Meeting of the Air Ministry Committee for the BCATP.

South Africa was less willing than the other Dominions to divert its own resources into air training, particularly on behalf of the RAF. Lacking an aircraft industry at the outbreak of war, the Union could foresee no large-scale plan of production in the first three years of the conflict. These two issues prevented the Union from cooperating with the wider BCATP and made air training in the Union a slow process when it was finally undertaken. The Union required assistance from the UK to develop a significant training effort, something that it was willing to do through its own Joint Air Training Scheme (JATS) because it could use the bilateral training programme, and all the benefits this entailed in British equipment and expenditure, first to meet its own needs, before supplying a closely monitored output of airmen for the RAF. The nature of South African airmen's participation in the RAF – as 'seconded' personnel for whom the Air Ministry compensated the Union – also separated South Africa's cooperation with the RAF from that of the other Dominions and Southern Rhodesia, and hinted at the separate conception of national and imperial citizenship within the Union. South Africans were the most anonymously absorbed airmen within the RAF, lacking the individual RAF squadrons that the other Dominions and Southern Rhodesia obtained.[36] However, the *quid pro quo* was that the Union's emphasis on developing the SAAF gave its own air force the most significant individual role in imperial air operations after the UK, particularly its actions on the African coastline and in East and North Africa. Paradoxically, the fact that the Union did not seek to distinguish its aircrews within the RAF in the same manner as the other Dominions might have reflected a greater confidence, or less insecurity, about the allegiance of South Africans to their own government.

A more pressing consideration for South Africa was the success of the Southern Rhodesian Air Training Group. Southern Rhodesia sought to mark its loyalty to the UK and stake a claim for its unique desirability as a settler-region location for emigrating Britons, indeed even as a future Dominion. Although limited in its size, due to the colony's small settler population, this scheme was negotiated with supreme speed and ease in

---

36   Francis, *The Flyer*, 192.

London, while the Ottawa negotiations were apparently foundering and before South African discussions were even mooted. This left the settler government in Southern Rhodesia with what was effectively a *carte blanche* from the British Treasury to make sure the negotiated scheme got up and running as quickly as construction allowed. The financial aspects of the agreement underlined the importance of the UK to Southern Rhodesia – the 'mother country' remained the primary source of trade, materials and, most importantly, white immigrants. Southern Rhodesia wasted no time in taking advantage of the opportunity it had secured: in May 1940, the first training school in Southern Rhodesia opened, even before the first Canadian school of the BCATP began training pupils.[37]

Southern Rhodesia, often overshadowed by neighbouring South Africa's Dominion status and larger white population, perceived its recognisable war effort as a way to distinguish its importance to the UK and empire, to establish its claim for a larger share of the relatively small amount of resources diverted to British imperial territories in Africa, and to mark its development towards Dominion status, making it an equal to the Union. Although Southern Rhodesia enjoyed a substantial economic boom through the resources received as part of the air training programme, its primary goal was to attract more British settlers.[38] Through having global British populations training in the colony and therefore experiencing its hospitality and benefits first hand, Southern Rhodesia hoped that airmen would return permanently after the war: 'It is introducing to Southern Rhodesia many thousands of young men from all over the Commonwealth of Nations, and we hope many of them will stay with us and settle down', read one communiqué.[39] Such was the success of this scheme – the white

---

37 Department of Defence Documentation Centre South Africa (DDDC), Union War Histories (UWH) 262, Bureau of Information, 18, Rhodesia – War Effort, 'Southern Rhodesia War Effort', Union Broadcast by Mr W.D. Gale, undated.

38 John Golley, *Aircrew Unlimited: The Commonwealth Air Training Plan during World War 2* (Sparkford: Patrick Stephens, 1993), 36.

39 DDDC, UWH 262, Bureau of Information, 18, Rhodesia – War Effort, 'Southern Rhodesia at War', 15 August, 1942, and 'Southern Rhodesia War Effort', Union Broadcast by Mr W.D. Gale, undated.

population was estimated to have grown from 45,000 in 1939 to 69,000 in 1942, while the air training scheme specifically was credited with increasing the numbers of settlers by over 13 per cent in the same period – that the Southern Rhodesian government proclaimed air training 'the finest immigration plan the Empire has yet had.'[40]

These developments were worrisome for South Africa. The Union considered itself the leading example of Western European civilisation in Africa, with aspirations for regional political leadership and perhaps even further territorial acquisitions in the sub-Saharan portion of the continent. Yet its northern neighbour, a mere colony – indeed a colony that had previously refused integration with the Union – was leading the British African effort in terms of air training. With a white population of under 50,000 and a propensity to portray itself as something of a proto-Dominion,[41] Southern Rhodesia's success threatened to seriously compromise South Africa's preeminent position as the only Dominion to administer the empire's needs in Africa, and as the favoured destination for British and imperial resources.

Southern Rhodesia's scheme accommodated Rhodesians, Britons, South Africans, Fijians, Greeks and Belgians,[42] and gained even further prominence when Australia agreed to send elementary trained pilots from the BCATP there for advanced training.[43] This effectively, although unofficially, linked the blossoming Southern Rhodesian scheme to that of the rest of the Commonwealth – albeit with the exception of South Africa. Unless action was taken by Pretoria, it was probable that Southern Rhodesia would be the suggested location in Africa for all training of RAF and South African airmen,

40 Ibid.
41 Ibid. See also Golley, *Aircrew Unlimited*, 35.
42 DDDC, UWH 262, Bureau of Information, 18, Rhodesia – War Effort, 'Southern Rhodesia at War', 15 August, 1942, and 'Southern Rhodesia War Effort', Union Broadcast by Mr W.D. Gale, undated.
43 NAA, 'The Shedden Collection', A5954, 236/1, EATS: Training in Rhodesia of RAAF Aircrew Péronne – War Cabinet Agendum; and NAA, Department of Air papers, A8681, 1943/2611, Public Relations Bulletin – Vital Part of EATS, Rhodesia turns out many Australian Airmen.

with the attendant money, materials and aircraft that this entailed, that the Union itself could not accommodate. One Dominions Office (DO) report warned of deep resentment in the Union, going on to conclude that if the 'Rhodesian proposal cuts South Africa out, South Africa will not like it.'[44]

The Union soon took steps to remedy the situation. First, Australian pupils who failed to qualify as pilots in Southern Rhodesia were offered air observer training in South Africa with the SAAF, free of charge, despite Pretoria's notorious haggling over every financial arrangement with the UK.[45] Smuts next suggested to the UK the possibility of South African air training for men of European descent in the Union, with the possibility of supplying personnel for the RAF shortly thereafter. London enthusiastically received the offer, and plans were made to bring the South African scheme into line with other training plans.[46] Further negotiations led to the Van Ryneveld – Brooke-Popham agreement (often abbreviated to the Van-Popham agreement), signed on 1 June 1940.[47] The terms were almost casual in construction, largely ignoring the issue of expenses.[48] After surveying suitable airfield sites and working out the detailed financial negotiations, a further agreement was arranged in June 1941.[49] At this time the Union

44 TNA, DO 35/1003/6, War-General: South Africa Cooperation, Kennedy to Dawe, 17 January 1940.
45 NAA, Prime Minister's Department papers, A1608, L17/2/2, Empire Air Scheme: Flying Training Schools in Rhodesia; and NAA, Department of Air papers, A1966/5, 324, Papers Concerning the EATS: History (Part 1).
46 NAA, Department of Air papers, A1196, 12/501/75, Notes on Air Ministry Committee Empire Air Training Scheme, Report of the 22nd Meeting of the Air Ministry Committee for the BCATP.
47 Pierre Van Ryneveld was the head of the UDF. Air Marshal Robert Brooke-Popham was a respected flying veteran of the Great War who held many diverse and important roles in British and imperial defence in the inter-war years.
48 NASA, Department of Foreign Affairs papers, vol. 125, DWS1001, Part I, Joint Air Training Scheme, Memorandum on the Expansion of Training Facilities in South Africa, 1 June 1940.
49 TNA, AIR 20/1346, Joint Air Training Scheme, South Africa: Memorandum of Agreements, Joint Air Training Scheme, South Africa: Memorandum of agreements, June 1941.

also accepted the transfer of three RAF schools en bloc to South Africa, in which Britons and South Africans would train alongside one another, demonstrating imperial solidarity, if not flattening the complexities of issues of South African and British imperial identities.

The results were initially poor. In January 1941, the UK asked about the progress of the agreed schools, but heard little or nothing back. Having already enquired about progress on 12 September and 24 December 1940, the Air Ministry now warned Pretoria that a four-month notice period was the minimum time expected between receiving information on the new schools' requirements and the delivery of essential equipment.[50] This threat struck a chord with South Africa, which now feared the material consequences of its inaction.

This allowed the UK to maintain some power in this relationship through the provision of essential personnel and material, which it recognised that the Union lacked.[51] Initially South Africa found itself competing with Southern Rhodesia for those resources that the UK made available for the African continent; much to Pretoria's annoyance, London informed the Union that it had to wait in line for equipment behind Rhodesian schools, which had been agreed upon earlier.[52] The absence of an aircraft industry was particularly problematic at this stage of the development of the JATS. It was not until 1942 that a substantial amount of equipment could be diverted to the Union, by which time the initial difficulties in South Africa, such as locating suitable aerodrome sites, had also been solved.

50 TNA, AIR 2/4551, Overseas: Dominions and Colonies: Empire Air Training Scheme: South Africa, 'Equipment Requirements for Flying Training Schools in South Africa', 7 January 1941.
51 NASA, Department of Foreign Affairs papers, vol. 125, DWS1001, Part I, Joint Air Training Scheme, Memorandum on the Expansion of Training Facilities in South Africa, 1 June 1940.
52 TNA, AIR 2/4551, Overseas: Dominions and Colonies: Empire Air Training Scheme: South Africa, Air Ministry to Brooke-Popham, Pretoria, 17 May 1940.

Imperial settler-regions in the Second World War 255

It is worth considering how successful the two southern African training schemes were, as their relative success shaped the South African and Southern Rhodesian relationship. The slow start to the JATS left South Africa lagging behind the BCATP Dominions, and it only managed to produce a training output roughly equivalent to Southern Rhodesia's by 1942. At the Ottawa Air Training Conference that year, the South African High Commissioner in Ottawa made an impromptu decision to give an opening statement at the inauguration dinner, announcing South Africa's presence by elaborating on the nature of the Union's entire war effort, a speech that stood apart in its content from the other delegations' statements.[53] South Africa was uncomfortably side-lined from Commonwealth negotiations during the conference, reflecting the peculiar position – more akin to that of a minor wartime ally during the proceedings – that its separate scheme had created within the wider imperial network.[54]

Nevertheless South Africa's training programme developed from 1942 with a striking rapidity, and retrospectively both the Southern Rhodesian Air Training Group, but more so the JATS, were genuine successes for the RAF. Table Three indicates the progression of training in southern Africa, with a comparison to the BCATP:

---

53   TNA, AIR 2/8181, Empire Air Training Scheme – Ottawa Air Training Conference, May 1942, Opening speech by the South African representative.
54   LAC, RCAF Papers, RG24, vol. 5388, Air Training Conference – May 1942 – Historical Record – Precis of Proceedings, Memorandum from Baldwin to Cumyn, 19 June, 1942. NASA, Department of Foreign Affairs papers, 9/4/2, Part II, Closer Co-operation between the British Commonwealth and United Kingdom in Defence Matters during the European War, Accredited Representative of the Union of South Africa, Ottawa, to Secretary of External Affairs, Pretoria, 3 June 1942.

Table Three: Output of Training Schemes in the Union of South Africa, Southern Rhodesia, the UK and the BCATP Dominions[55]

Country of Graduation	1939–1940	1940–1941	1941–1942	1942–1943	1943–1944	1944–1945
South Africa	–	446	3,797	6,686	7,945	7,233
Southern Rhodesia	24	856	2,365	2,548	2,450	1,864
BCATP Dominions	1,196	12,128	32,209	47,464	50,604	40,526
UK	7,830	17,424	17,870	23,864	20,805	11,437

The slow nature of the JATS's development is plainly apparent – by September 1941 South Africa had trained fewer than 500 aircrew, while the still accelerating BCATP had surpassed 12,000. In 1941–2, South Africa became the main training location in southern Africa, utilising its larger white population and the potential of the SAAF. This was also a period of rapid growth for the JATS. By the end of the war, the JATS had produced 26,107 airmen, substantially more than emerged from Southern Rhodesia. The Union therefore preserved its unique leadership role in southern Africa in this framework of air training, in addition to receiving the majority of the material benefits provided by the UK to develop air training on the entire continent. The UK retrospectively claimed that the JATS was 'a striking example of the spirit of co-operation which brought us successfully through the war.'[56] Although by comparison the Southern Rhodesian effort derived from a greater loyalty to, and cultural unity with, the UK, tensions also arose in this relationship – Rhodesians serving in RAF units wanted their significant commitment rewarded and were frustrated by their country's continued colonial status, taking small but visible actions

---

55   Statistics from TNA, AIR 10/551, Appendix No. 2, 273–8, Air Ministry, *RAF Flying Training*.
56   NASA, Department of Foreign Affairs papers, 9/4/2, Part I, Closer Co-operation between the British Commonwealth and United Kingdom in Defence Matters during the European War, Secretary of State for Dominion Affairs, London to Minister of External Affairs, Pretoria, 18 October, 1946.

of protest in defiance of the RAF and British hierarchy.[57] Even though war served to narrow the distance between settler identity and British imperial citizenship, the gap was never fully bridged and, over issues such as this, it threatened to become a chasm.

The superior size of South Africa's scheme eased tensions between the Union and Southern Rhodesia, once Pretoria felt that its privileged position as a Dominion in Africa was restored. Although the Union had been relegated behind Southern Rhodesia for air training equipment deliveries from the UK before 1942, by late 1942 South Africa had once more established its position of dominance in the region. Indeed, despite the competitive elements, links proliferated. The man who negotiated Southern Rhodesia's agreement with the RAF, Lieutenant-Colonel Charles Meredith, was a product of the SAAF. Before South African training expanded sufficiently, South African airmen were allowed to train in Southern Rhodesia; and where Southern Rhodesian facilities were lacking, trainees meant for training in the colony were later diverted to the Union. When construction materials, training equipment and especially direction from the UK in establishing facilities proved inadequate, the two settler-regions looked to one another for support and to fill the void that the UK had left.[58] This laid the foundations for future cooperation apart from the UK, and increased awareness that the countries could share interests as African neighbours, rather than as competing areas of imperial settlement.

After the conclusion of hostilities, relations were such that Smuts declared Southern Rhodesia's war effort akin to 'a fairy tale, but a fairy tale come true.' He established further common ground in his claim that RAF men who trained there should consider British southern Africa as a destination for emigration, repeating a common settler trope that these countries were 'devoid of the entanglements of an ancient society and ...

---

57   For instance, on one occasion Rhodesian flyers scraped the crown from their badges. See Francis, *The Flyer*, 58.
58   NASA, Department of Foreign Affairs papers, vol. 125, DWS1001, Part I, Joint Air Training Scheme, Construction of Air Stations – Southern Rhodesia (sub-file).

not overcrowded like the older countries.'[59] These calls from South Africa and Southern Rhodesia were ultimately successful: over 20 per cent of the UK's emigrants in 1945–8 moved to southern Africa, in part a result of the rare direct contact that air training had provided for Britons with the settler-regions of southern Africa.[60]

Conclusion: Imperial Connections and Air Training in Southern Africa

South Africa trained airmen for the RAF and SAAF in a bilateral arrangement with the UK, rather than within the wider Commonwealth scheme, due to national and regional political considerations. This placed it in competition with its northern neighbour Southern Rhodesia, which had a substantial training effort of its own, one that preceded South Africa's and was loosely connected to the major imperial initiative, the BCATP. The UK looked to its settler-regions to answer the problem of its shortage of space and manpower, which says much about how the empire was understood in London: that settler-regions were a source of substantial practical benefits, an idea that derived from the privileged place of settler-regions within the wider imperial patchwork. This privileged position, which centred on perceived Britishness – defined, in part, in racial and ethnic terms – made the settler societies attractive prospects for London and the RAF, where conceptions of an imperial ethnic hierarchy, a distinction between those British imperial subjects who truly 'belonged' and those who did not, and 'martial races' persisted through the Second World War and beyond.

---

59 DDDC, UWH 262, Bureau of Information, 18, Rhodesia – War Effort, *Rand Daily Mail*, 3 December 1945.
60 Jean P. Smith, '"Transformation to Paradise": Wartime Travel to Southern Africa, Race and the Discourse of Opportunity, 1939–50', *Twentieth Century British History*, 25/4 (2014), 1–22.

What did conceptions of Britishness explain when the periphery looked back toward the centre? In Southern Rhodesia, it drove the war effort of the colony as it sought to prove its loyalty and value to the imperial project, and the concept of British superiority echoed back to the UK in the attempt to attract emigrants and expand the colony into a Dominion with a significant white, preferably British, population. This was greatly facilitated by a settler population that deeply identified with its British subjecthood and identity. There were also signs, however, that these expressions of loyalty bred expectations of further recognition that were easily frustrated by a reticent and preoccupied 'mother country' and overshadowed by its southern neighbour. Ian Douglas Smith, himself a Southern Rhodesian airman of the Second World War and later prime minister of Rhodesia, later expanded upon this current of thought when justifying Rhodesian independence in 1965, following its 'abandonment' by the UK. This was a reminder that imperial Britishness, or what historian John Darwin terms 'Britannic sentiment',[61] did not necessarily equate with any affinity for, or obedience to, the UK.[62]

Smith's Rhodesian regime received its major support from its neighbour, South Africa. During the Second World War, Pretoria had established its own paternal role with Southern Rhodesia, transforming brief competition into cooperation, cooperation which was necessitated by the UK's inability to provide for both Dominion and colony during the war years. This mutual assistance persisted into the post-war years, even after South Africa's turn to Afrikaner nationalism, suggesting that it was built upon foundations of mutual regional concerns and shared views of racial hierarchy, rather than ties of Britishness. This nationalist swing itself was a consequence of the Union's efforts during the Second World War. Indeed, this demonstrates the limitations of Britishness as an explanation for the contributions of southern Africa's settler-regions to the war effort. South Africa's Britishness was conceived in pragmatic geopolitical terms and as

---

61 John Darwin, *The Empire Project: The Rise and Fall of the British World-System, 1830–1970* (Cambridge: Cambridge University Press, 2009), 6–8.
62 Dubow, 'How British was the British World?', 1–27.

imperial opportunity, an understandable compromise for a country balancing a significant British settler population with a larger, significantly anti-British population. Pretoria viewed the primary importance of the imperial connection to be the opportunities it provided for South Africa to expand its economy, infrastructure, and military, in addition to extending its influence in sub-Saharan Africa. All these elements are visible in the experience of air training in the Second World War. Britishness on a personal and cultural level was not without importance: unsurprisingly, a disproportionate number of British settlers enlisted in the Union's armed forces, and it has been described as the 'finest hour' for English-speaking South Africans.[63] For a government balancing two settler populations, however, it was membership in a 'British World' that provided South Africa with its own privileges and imperial prospects in southern Africa that really mattered.

---

63   Lambert, 'Unknown Identity', 599–617.

STUART ALLAN

'Some idea of our country': Scotland, Wales and Northern Ireland in early wartime documentary film

Film was a powerful tool for promoting unity and a shared sense of national identity to the British public during the Second World War. Working with the film industry in an initially tense but increasingly productive wartime relationship, the Government's Ministry of Information considered cinema to be a persuasive means of furthering British war aims, of influencing public opinion and of maintaining public morale, in tandem with the more altruistic motivation of meeting popular demand for information about the progress of the war.[1] The extent to which film propaganda constructed and imposed a sense of shared experience and commitment among the British people, or whether its output was a genuine, if heightened, reflection of how people already felt about their involvement in the conflict, is still a matter for debate. However, the imagery and tone of wartime films has remained potent as a medium for the idea of a People's War bringing together the whole British population across the divides of class, gender and national origin. Films carrying this message constitute part of the culture of nostalgia which constructs, or reinforces, understandings of the Second World War as a key moment of British national unity.[2] Whether

---

[1] The Ministry of Information's confidence in the film medium was tested through Mass Observation reports, Home Intelligence Division briefings, and the 1943 Wartime Social Survey, *The Cinema Audience*. Anthony Aldgate and Jeffrey Richards, *Britain Can Take It: the British Cinema in the Second World War* (Edinburgh: Edinburgh University Press, 1986), 3–4.

[2] The substantial historiography of British cinema in the Second World War was summarised in James Chapman, *The British at War: Cinema, State and Propaganda 1939–1945* (London: I.B. Tauris, 1998), 1–9. Later studies include Robert Murphy, *British Cinema and the Second World War* (London: Continuum, 2000) and Neil

these films are subjected to critical examination and interpretation or, as is more common, are taken at face value as historical record, the documentary, newsreel and feature films produced during the Second World War have since provided a staple of moving picture content supplying the prolific output of television documentaries and museum exhibitions which, more than seventy years later, reflect an apparently undiminished popular appetite for information about this period of British history.

The three films which form the subject of this chapter represent rare instances where the concept of wartime Britain as a multinational state was aired. In two of these films the war efforts of Scotland and Wales respectively are presented as what might be inferred to constitute national contributions in themselves, albeit within the embrace of the greater British endeavour. Although they were seen by cinema audiences in Scotland and Wales, they were principally made to educate and inform audiences in other parts of the United Kingdom, the British empire, and with a view to reaching people of allied and sympathetic nations beyond.[3] As discussed below, in tone and content they are to a large degree typical of British wartime documentary film output, but each has enough of a uniquely Scottish and Welsh perspective in it to afford some insight into how the sense of distinct nationhood was squared with the over-riding imperative of demonstrating wholehearted commitment to the sense of British common purpose. The Northern Ireland film, from the same production stable, was made specifically for the British Council for overseas screenings but was also shown in cinemas in Northern Ireland and elsewhere across the UK. Its survey of the natural and industrial resources of Northern Ireland is initially just a little less forthright than the other two in representing cultural difference based on a distinctive history. But ultimately, and if anything more pointedly, it uses something of a similar differentiating tone. All three films

---

Rattigan, *This is England: British Film and the People's War, 1939–1945* (London: Associated University Presses, 2001).

[3] Both films were made with the intention of overseas distribution. Frances Thorpe and Nicholas Pronay, with Clive Coultass, *British Official Films in the Second World War: A Descriptive Catalogue* (Oxford: Clio Press, 1980), 85, 131.

were made in 1941–2 by the commercial production company Strand, a London-based operation.

Wartime output in this field begs to be understood in the context of the longer history of the documentary film industry, and not only in relation to the immediate imperatives of the war. The British documentary movement blossomed in the 1930s, and its purposes were always, at least in part, propagandist, in as much as a good deal of its product served the concerted promotion of a positive British image overseas through government, the British Council and by commercial organisations such as the Empire Marketing Board.[4] The Strand film unit was one outlet of a group of film-makers associated with the Scotsman John Grierson who, through his work during the 1930s as a producer with the Empire Marketing Board and the General Post Office (GPO) Film Unit, later the Crown Film Unit, is widely acknowledged as the founding father of the British documentary.[5] Grierson's influential form of documentary film-making proceeded from his developed ideas about the function of the new medium, which he considered a democratic tool to be wielded in the cause of social integration. By realistically depicting the people of Britain at work and at play Grierson sought to educate and improve the whole of the British population towards his vision of a fully participative and interdependent social democratic society, where individuals, institutions and government recognised one another's inter-related roles and worked towards the common good. The job of the documentary film maker was therefore 'to inform the public about their nation and involve them emotionally with the workings of their government.'[6] Grierson's view has been recognised as one which permeated the output of the wartime film-makers whom he influenced directly

---

4   Pre-war efforts to present a modern, positive image of Britain are described in Philip M. Taylor, *The Projection of Britain: British Overseas Publicity and Propaganda, 1919–39* (Cambridge: Cambridge University Press, 1981).
5   Jeffrey Richards, 'John Grierson and the lost world of the GPO Film Unit', in Scott Anthony and James G. Mansell, ed., *The Projection of Britain: A History of the GPO Film Unit* (London: BFI/Palgrave Macmillan, 2011), 1–9.
6   Jack C. Ellis, *John Grierson: Life, Contributions, Influence* (Carbobdale and Edwardsville, IL: Southern Illinois University Press, 2000), viii.

and indirectly. These included Humphrey Jennings, whose films *Listen to Britain* and *Fires Were Started* continue to enjoy a reputation today as outstanding examples of the documentary film-maker's art.[7]

The Strand film unit's wartime output may certainly be seen to have been part of this wider socio-democratic consensus. Strand was the brainchild of Donald Taylor who, with his partner Ralph Keene, took over a former feature film-making operation and transformed it into the first of the independent units making officially sponsored documentaries. Taylor had not only been part of Grierson's stable at the Empire Marketing Film Unit and the GPO, but was also Grierson's brother-in-law twice over, courtesy of Donald Taylor's marriage to Grierson's younger sister Marion, and John Grierson's marriage to Taylor's sister Margaret, all four being film-makers working in association at the time.[8] At the outbreak of war, Strand was accustomed to working at the behest of government ministries, having produced a series of short films for the Ministry of Labour and government agencies. Indeed, in its wartime film about Wales Strand re-used footage from its 1937 production *Today We Live* for the National Council of Social Services.[9] The political context of wartime film production was not altogether extraordinary, and Strand's wartime output would have been no more subject to official control than these earlier productions. It has been suggested that censorship of British film was, if anything, somewhat more relaxed in the war years than it had been hitherto, and was mediated by a consensus between government and film-makers over the social purposes of documentary and feature film.[10] So comfortable was the meeting of minds between the liberal intelligentsia of the documentary

---

7   *Listen to Britain*, Crown Film Unit, 1942 and *Fires Were Started*, Crown Film Unit, 1943, British Film Institute National Archive (BFI) 14132 and 14073.

8   Barbara Evans, 'Job in a Million. Evelyn Spice at the GPO', in Anthony and Mansell, *The Projection of Britain*, 80–8.

9   Ministry of Information file, 'Wales – Green Mountain, Black Mountain', The National Archives (TNA), INF 6/483; *Today We Live,* Strand, 1937, BFI 12137.

10 Nicholas Pronay and Jeremy Croft, 'British Film Censorship and Propaganda Policy during the Second World War', in James Curran and Vincent Porter, eds, *British Cinema History* (London: Weidenfeld and Nicolson, 1983), 144–63.

film industry and kindred spirits at the Ministry of Information, that their wartime creative output has been interpreted as a left-wing project helping to pave the way to a Labour government in 1945.[11] The three films under consideration in this chapter, each in their subtly different ways, certainly promoted an egalitarian, democratic conception of the war effort and, by implication or explicit statement, looked forward to social and economic reconstruction within a reformed British society. What is interesting is the question of how Northern Ireland, Wales and Scotland were presented as fitting in to this picture.

The films in question are *Scotland Speaks*, produced by Alexander Shaw and directed by Jack Ellitt and released in the spring of 1941; *Ulster*, also produced by Shaw and directed by Ralph Keene, completed in late 1940 to appear in the British Council Film Department Catalogue in 1941; and *Wales – Green Mountain, Black Mountain*, produced by Donald Taylor and directed by John Eldridge, made in 1942.[12] All were produced by Strand, one of three companies which specialised at this time in producing short documentaries for the non-theatrical circuit, supplementing the less prolific but bigger-budget and more prestigious cinematic output of the Crown Film Unit.[13] Besides overseas distribution through the British Council, this type of short film was typically seen by the public in screenings provided by mobile film units from the Ministry of Information's Film Division in factories, town and village halls, church halls, schools, libraries and women's and working men's institutes. There were 120 of these mobile film units by 1942, and within their remit was the provision of structured discussions

---

11   Nicholas Pronay, 'The Land of Promise: the Projection of Peace Aims in Britain', in K.R.M. Short, ed., *Film and Radio Propaganda in World War II* (London: Croon Helm, 1983), 51–77.
12   *Scotland Speaks*, Strand, 1941, Imperial War Museum Film Archive (IWM), UKY 306; *Ulster*, Strand, 1941, British Council Film Collection http://film.britishcouncil. org/british-council-film-collection/, accessed 20 December 2013, and BFI 14546; *Wales – Green Mountain, Black Mountain*, Strand, 1942, IWM, UKY 379.
13   Strand's principal counterparts and competitors in this small industry were Realist and Verity.

to follow some of the screenings.¹⁴ By one estimate the mobile film units reached, at their peak, an audience approaching 350,000 a week.¹⁵ This impact represented only a fraction however of the estimated UK average weekly cinema attendance which reached thirty million by 1945.¹⁶ But like some other short films of their type, Strand's Scottish, Welsh and Northern Irish films also secured cinema distribution on release, appearing in cinema programmes as preludes to the main feature. So, for example, *Scotland Speaks* was screened in Edinburgh in May 1941 at the New Victoria cinema supporting the George Formby feature *Spare a Copper*, and again in September 1941 at the Dominion supporting *The Four Feathers*.¹⁷

The commercial and documentary film industries were based in London, and it was the view from the capital that prevailed in much of their creative and propaganda output. A casual conflation between London, England and Britain was characteristic of this perspective, and was a mindset which endured for decades in media, exhibition and educational material about the national experience of the war.¹⁸ But this was a tendency which government and film producers at the time were conscious of and sought to mitigate. This may be observed at the superficial level of the titling and

14 Helen Forman, 'The Non-theatrical Distribution of Films by the Ministry of Information', in Nicholas Pronay and D.W. Spring, eds, *Propaganda, Politics and Film* (London: MacMillan, 1982), 221–33.
15 Nicholas Pronay, 'The News Media at War', in Pronay and Spring, *Propaganda, Politics and Film*, 187–8.
16 Estimate from the Political and Economic Planning report, *The British Film Industry* (London: Political and Economic Planning, 1952), 83.
17 *The Scotsman* 17 May 1941, and 6 September 1941. I am grateful to Dr Trevor Griffiths, University of Edinburgh, for this reference and for his advice about the cinema distribution of short films. John Hill noted that *Ulster* was distributed in UK cinemas by General Film Distributors. John Hill, *Cinema and Northern Ireland: Film, Culture and Politics* (London: BFI, 2006), 82.
18 Assumptions about 'the natural right of England to speak for Britain' are addressed in Kenneth Lunn, 'Reconsidering Britishness: the Construction and Significance of National Identity in Twentieth Century Britain', in Brian Jenkins and Spyros A. Sofos, eds, *Nation and Identity in Contemporary Europe* (London: Routledge, 1996), 83–100.

re-titling of films, as in the case of *London Can Take It!* (1940), a GPO Film Unit documentary about the London Blitz which had been made for the US market, but which was retitled for domestic distribution as *Britain Can Take It!*[19] Similarly, there was awareness that an assumed correlation between 'England' and 'Britain', which might be automatic for overseas audiences, and unproblematic for English audiences, risked ruffling feathers in other parts of the UK. In this spirit the British National propaganda feature film *This England* (1941), which depicted centuries of life in a fictional, idealised English village, was renamed *Our Heritage* for distribution in Scotland.[20] Government-endorsed feature films frequently included Scottish, Welsh and Irish fringe characters. For his roles in films such as *The Gentle Sex* (1943) and *The Way Ahead* (1944), the actor John Laurie was well-known as the stereotyped Scotsman.[21] Gordon Jackson provided a more youthful and romantic Scottish supporting role in films such as *Millions Like Us* (1943).[22] The inclusion of such characters was part of a wider representation of the People's War ideal whereby feature film casts included characters from a variety of regional and class backgrounds.[23] But the multinational point could also be made very deliberately. In Laurence Olivier's *Henry V* (1944) Shakespeare's Welsh, Scottish and Irish captains were badged with leek, thistle and shamrock to ensure recognition.[24]

Similarly, in promoting the ideal of a united Britain through the medium of the documentary film, care was taken to profile the contribution and experience of what, to employ here an anachronistic media term of the present day, we might call the 'nations and regions.' So, a 1941 Crown Film Unit short film was made by Humphrey Jennings about the industrial cities of the English North and Midlands and titled *The Heart of Britain* (renamed for US distribution, predictably, *This Is England*), and numerous

---

19 *London Can Take It!* and *Britain Can Take It!*, GPO Film Unit, 1940, IWM, COI 943-4.
20 *This England* and *Our Heritage*, British National, 1941, BFI 48041.
21 *The Gentle Sex,* Two Cities, 1943, BFI 30654. *The Way Ahead*, Two Cities, 1944.
22 *Millions Like Us*, Gainsborough 1943, BFI 37892.
23 Rattigan, *This is England*, 161-2.
24 *Henry V*, Two Cities, 1944, BFI 32159.

films were made to document and promote particular industries, such as *Fighting Fields* (1941), a showcase for Scottish farming, in order to give the sense of a concerted UK-wide economic war effort.[25] Later, with a similar approach, there was the British Council film series made between 1944 and 1947 about the farmlands of England under the umbrella title *The Pattern of Britain*.[26] These films were not overtly war-orientated but, mindful of the unprecedented movement and inter-mixture of people which the war effort entailed, they were intended to promote understanding and recognition between the populations of different parts of the country. They were also intended to inform overseas audiences about the way of life and values of their allies, with a view to illustrating why fighting for Britain, or fighting alongside Britain, was a worthy and worthwhile cause.

Despite Grierson's Scottish background, and his early success with *Drifters* (1929), his film about the North Sea herring industry, the pre-war documentary movement had existed within that London cultural milieu which could at times casually conflate Britain with England as a matter of course.[27] Grierson's early patron was Sir Stephen Tallents, whose public relations career was launched on the back of his influential 1933 pamphlet 'The Projection of England', a manifesto for the use of film in the promotion of Britain overseas.[28] But the film-makers demonstrated sensitivity to the complex character of the British society they sought to represent, and in the years just before the war they had won business satisfying demand for a documentary perspective from constituencies outside London. Strand and its rival Realist were among contributors to seven short films made under the supervision of John Grierson for the 1938 Empire Exhibition in Glasgow.[29] Producing its wartime public information films about Wales,

---

25 *The Heart of Britain* and *This Is England*, Crown Film Unit, 1941, BFI 13856. *Fighting Fields*, Scottish Films and GB Instructional, 1941, IWM, UKY 274.
26 *The Pattern of Britain*, Greenpark, c1944–7, BFI 768610.
27 *Drifters*, Empire Marketing Board Film Unit, 1929, BFI 14679.
28 Scott Anthony, 'The GPO Film Unit and Britishness in the 1930s,' in Anthony and Mansell, *The Projection of Britain*, 10–16.
29 *The Face of Scotland*, Realist, 1938, Scottish Screen Archive (SSA), 0034; *The Children's Story*, Strand, SSA, 1059.

Northern Ireland and Scotland from London, Strand sought credibility by employing London-based Scottish, Irish and Welsh creative talent to showcase and speak for their own countries. The three documentaries may be taken to represent an accommodation between the requirement to explain and acknowledge, for the purposes of public information and morale, Scottish, Welsh and Northern Irish difference, and the need to incorporate these differences into an imagery of a united Britain at war, all approached through the agency of 'Griersonian' film-making and its associated philosophy of social integration and participative citizenship.

'A free country': *Scotland Speaks* (1941)

Behind *Scotland Speaks* were figures from the Scottish literary renaissance of the inter-war period. The script was conceived by the Scottish author and journalist A.G. Macdonell, best-known for his 1933 satirical novel *England, Their England* in which a Scotsman adrift in London researches the social manners and sporting proclivities of the English middle and upper classes. India-born and Winchester-educated, Macdonell was essentially a liberal, and might be said to have been in sympathy with the 'mild form of intellectual socialism' he ascribed to one of his colourful Home Counties fictional characters.[30] The apparent anglophilia of this his most popular work was however the affection of an outsider and was counterpoised by the rallying call to Scottish independence embodied in his 1937 memoir *My Scotland*. Macdonell exercised his frustration about the disregard for and casual denigration of his own national heritage which permeated the culture of his adopted English home.[31] The writing credits for *Scotland Speaks* were ultimately shared between Macdonell, who died suddenly in January 1941, and the Scottish writer and broadcaster George Blake, remembered today for *The*

---

30 A.G. Macdonell, *England, Their England* (London: Macmillan, 1933).
31 A.G. Macdonell, *My Scotland* (New York and London: Funk and Wagnalls, 1937).

Shipbuilders, his 1935 novel about a Clyde shipbuilding dynasty.[32] Another figure in the social realist school, Blake had already scripted government-sponsored documentary films about industry on the Clyde for Scottish Film Productions in 1938 and 1939.[33] He was an established broadcaster, having contributed to the BBC commentary at the coronation of George VI and was also someone who had represented a personal view of Scotland in print, as author of the 1934 travelogue *The Heart of Scotland*.[34]

The commentary for *Scotland Speaks* was provided by Joseph Macleod, a well-known Scottish voice at the time as newsreader and announcer for the BBC Home Service. He was also actor, theatre director and playwright, and a poet, publishing modernist work under the pseudonym 'Adam Drinan' which documented community life in the Scottish Highlands. He was a Labour Party activist and a promoter of friendly relations with the Soviet Union. At the BBC, Macleod championed Gaelic song and culture in his 'Music of Scotland' programme. In a published account of his time at the BBC, from which he resigned in 1945 under something of a cloud, Macleod recorded his frustration at the scant regard paid by the corporation to Scottish subjects.[35] His later literary work revealed overt Scottish nationalism as a strand of his socialist outlook.[36]

Macleod's Scottish tones, which perhaps sound a little forced to the twenty-first-century ear, take the audience on a tour of Scotland's urban and rural industries over a score by Cedric Thorpe Davie which pays homage to Scottish traditional music.[37] The film's refrain in imagery and commentary

---

32 George Blake, *The Shipbuilders* (London: Collins, 1935).
33 *World of Steel*, Scottish Film Productions, 1938, SSA, 0111; *River Clyde – a Survey of Scotland's Greatest River*, Scottish Film Productions, 1939, SSA, 0377.
34 George Blake, *The Heart of Scotland* (London: Batsford, 1934).
35 Joseph Macleod, *A Job at the BBC: Some Personal Reminiscences* (Glasgow: William Maclellan, 1947), 126–8.
36 James Fountain, 'Macleod, Joseph Todd Gordon [Adam Drinan] (1903–1984)', Oxford Dictionary of National Biography, Oxford University Press, 2009 <http://www.oxforddnb.com/view/article/98169> accessed 5 January 2014.
37 *Cedric Thorpe Davie, 1913–1983. Catalogue of Works and Index to Correspondence.* Compiled by Christine M. Gasgoine (St. Andrews: University Library, St. Andrews, 1988).

is the return of a Scottish soldier from the war back to family and home, a motif which the commentary relates to the centuries-old Scottish tradition of military service overseas. This particular imagined soldier's return is to rural Perthshire, which in its idyllic tranquillity, and with its soundtrack of a lone piper, seems far removed from industrial-scale warfare of the 1940s.[38] But as the *Scotland Speaks* travelogue moves on, enunciating the names of regions, counties, towns and villages on the way, we are taken on a tour of decidedly twentieth-century Griersonian activity where labour in the countryside, in the town and at sea works in inter-related harmony. Some of the settings remain traditional, and peaceful, but they are above all settings for active effort, and are interspersed with sequences of heavy industrial technology and of rhythmic working machinery, a favourite of the documentary realist style. The commentary makes clear the film's purpose: to 'give you some idea of our country', and to demonstrate how 'the men and women of Scotland are working day and night for our common victory.' Scottish endeavour is represented through sequences on lowland agriculture, forestry, heavy industry, two on Clyde shipbuilding, the prominence of which perhaps owes something to the preferences of George Blake and the availability of existing footage, on sheep-farming in the Highlands and the borders, on textile production, on the contribution of women with a focus on the Women's Land Army, on the naval and merchant naval services, and on the Scottish fishing fleets.

The makers added an extra dimension towards the end of the film, by having characters representative of earlier sequences speak directly to camera, so realising the intention implied in the film's title. These were authentic voices, not the voices of actors, or were intended to appear as such. Employing the voices of real people, albeit scripted, was a still novel technique favoured by the social realist film-makers of the 1940s. It was the essential feature of Humphrey Jennings' influential 1942 documentary *Listen To Britain* and can be seen in other Scottish examples such as *The Crofters* (1945) and *North East Corner* (1946) about agriculture and fishing

---

38   The soldier's return trope has often been given a Scottish pastoral setting, courtesy of the Robert Burns' 1793 ballad of the same name.

in Aberdeenshire.[39] In *Scotland Speaks*, a seaman, a coal-miner, a steelworker, the afore-mentioned soldier's wife (with a more polished delivery, she was possibly a professional actress), a farm manager and a shepherd are presented as the voices of Scotland. They were perhaps offered with the intention of preparing audiences unfamiliar with Scottish accents to hear them and be as ready *not* to understand them as to understand them. The contribution from the shepherd is so inscrutable to the unaccustomed ear it seems to serve no other purpose. By this method Scottish 'otherness' was demystified, celebrated, and demonstrably related to the familiar for a wide audience by incorporation into customary film propagandist constructions of the British war effort.

What is rather more surprising in the film is the manner in which the *Scotland Speaks* travelogue is introduced. The opening sequence is strident in its nationalistic tenor. Over shots of Stirling Castle, with contemporary Scottish infantry marching beneath its crags, Macleod sets out the stall of Scottish difference with a lesson in medieval history:

> These are the fields of Bannockburn. Look at them well. On these fields, at the foot of Stirling Castle, our native country of Scotland won her freedom six hundred years ago. Our ancestors faced tremendous odds, and won, and we have been a free country ever since.

The straightforward purpose of this opening statement, the drawing of an analogy between the Wars of Independence and the threat of foreign domination in the present day, was made explicit in the commentary. There is therefore no obvious discordance between the assertion of Scottish historical nationhood at the outset, and what follows in the body of the film. As a starting point for explaining Scotland to the uninitiated, history seems an uncontroversial, indeed an obvious, choice. History, moreover, was a stock in trade of the British wartime film industry; constructions of the English heritage of liberty in the past were frequently held up as an appeal to rigour in defending and extending British liberty in the present,

---

39 *Listen to Britain*, Crown Film Unit, 1942, BFI 14132; *The Crofters*, Greenpark, 1945, SSA, 0120; *North East Corner*, Greenpark, 1946, SSA, 0281.

as seen in the aforementioned *This England* and in the historical biopic *The Young Mr Pitt* (1942).[40] Scottish history had already by this point had its first airing in the documentary film format in Realist's *The Face of Scotland* (1938) which commenced its thoughtful exposition of the history and character of Scotland with the words of a Roman soldier at Hadrian's Wall, introducing the idea of the indomitability of a hardy northern land and the inhabitants it bred.[41]

But while *The Face of Scotland* alluded in passing to the wars of William Wallace and Robert Bruce, and finished predictably on the ancient ramparts of Edinburgh Castle, there seems something a little more pointed in the manner in which *Scotland Speaks* sets out from Bannockburn. The identity of the enemy there, that is of 'the Auld Enemy', England, is tactfully left unspoken. Nothing is said that would have jarred with any shade of opinion over the historical substance and present relevance of Scottish nationhood, particularly in relation to the immediate priority of winning the Second World War. But a viewing of *Scotland Speaks*, bearing in mind the tone of Macdonell's memoir, *My Scotland*, leaves the impression that there might be a subtext here. The 'free country' referred to in the opening lines of *Scotland Speaks* is the same one which was the subject of Macdonell's anxiety over the power of English cultural assimilation, expressed in print four years earlier, in his personal manifesto for Scottish Home Rule: 'I am now convinced that Scotsmen must decide in the near future whether they wish to be citizens of a free country or citizens of a rather stale music-hall joke.'[42] Implicit in the introduction to *Scotland Speaks*, and reiterated in the closing shots at Stirling Castle, where a bugler of the Argyll and Sutherland Highlanders plays under the statue of William Wallace, is an assertion of sovereign Scottish national identity – identity within Britain, but with historical roots pre-dating Britain. In this representation, Scotland as an ancient realm offers and exercises its part in the British war effort of the present

---

40 Chapman, *The British at War*, 232–48. *The Young Mr Pitt*, 1942, Twentieth Century Productions, BFI 52345.
41 *The Face of Scotland*, Realist, 1938, SSA, 0034.
42 Macdonell, *My Scotland*, ix.

day by free choice, and its efforts, documented in the body of the film, are predicated upon, perhaps even conditional upon, the maintenance of its historic difference and so of its dignity. With this interpretation *Scotland Speaks* might be taken not merely as public information, but as a reminder that Scotland's contribution to Britain ought not to be taken for granted.

'The world shall never deny them again': *Wales – Green Mountain, Black Mountain* (1942)

Parallels between *Scotland Speaks* and Strand's Welsh film of the following year are quickly apparent. *Wales – Green Mountain, Black Mountain* begins similarly with an allusion to border conflict of centuries past. Opening with shots of coastal and mountain landscapes, the medieval castles of Harlech and Conwy come into view. In its spoken evocation of Anglo-Welsh medieval conflict, the Welsh film is less circumspect than its Scottish counterpart: 'Morning mist grinds over Snowdon, over the mountains where for centuries the men of Wales fought their enemy the English, over the castles of Harlech and Conwy and Caernarfon, garrisoned by English kings in the long and faraway wild wars.' But the past is soon placed firmly in the past, and seen there to be in its proper perspective, given present exigencies: 'Morning is breaking over Wales at war. Not the long and faraway wild war of the mountain Welshmen and the English kings, but the terrible near war of England and Wales and her brothers and sisters all over the earth, against the men who would murder man.' The lyricism and rhetoric of the film's commentary, clearly delivered in Welsh voices, and supported on the traditional song and pastoral flute and harp flourishes of English composer William Aldwyn's score, reveal work of a different measure to the standard fare of British documentary script-writing.[43] This may be attributed to the

---

43 The narration was shared by actors William Griffiths and David Raymond. A Welsh language version was also made.

authorship of the screenplay and script, which were written by the poet Dylan Thomas. In the early war years Thomas's fame still lay ahead of him, but his work was already known in literary circles. Although its quality is not consistent throughout, and although Thomas later dismissed his wartime labours for Strand as 'hack work' undertaken while he applied himself to finding employment with the BBC, the script may justifiably be considered a poetic work in itself.[44]

The film consequently takes its shape as something of an accommodation between the requirements of Strand and its Ministry of Information sponsor, and Dylan Thomas's personal view of the war. With an anxious and almost physically felt abhorrence of conflict, Thomas had managed to stay out of the war, and to a large degree he kept the war out of his Welsh film. But having avoided conscription by ensuring rejection on medical grounds, and contributing instead his pen, Thomas understood his obligations in relation to the propaganda imperatives of the task and also the philosophical standpoint of British documentary film-making. Despite his stated communist sympathies, and the Marxist perspective which can be followed in his work, or perhaps because of these, Thomas at times found the Strand brand of social reformist commentary wearisome. With characteristic impatience and contrariness, he grew peevish over writing 'film scripts on Rehabilitation, Better Housing, Post-war Full Employment etc., for the socialist film department of the Ministry of Information', and quarrelled with his friend and employer Taylor.[45] Although, in David Berry's assessment of *Wales – Green Mountain, Black Mountain*, 'too many lines indicate that Thomas was operating on automatic', the work he produced

---

44   Andrew Lycett, *Dylan Thomas: A New Life* (London: Weidenfeld and Nicolson, 2004), 240. The script is reproduced in full in John Ackerman, ed., *Dylan Thomas. The Filmscripts* (London: Dent, 1995).

45   Quoted in Lycett, *Dylan Thomas*, 260. I am grateful to Dr Martin Johnes, Swansea University, for his observations about Dylan Thomas's attitudes to revolutionary socialism, for which see Victor Paananen, 'The Social Vision of Dylan Thomas', *Welsh Writing in English – a Yearbook of Critical Essays*, 8 (2003), 46–66.

for Strand was imaginative and substantial, and clearly mattered to him.[46] Other notable wartime documentary films to which he brought his heightened talents included *These are the Men* (1943), for which he wrote a script dubbed over Leni Riefenstahl's film footage of leading Nazis, and *Our Country* (1944), a film about nature regenerating a war-torn but victorious Britain.[47]

With a properly Griersonian sense of industry and modernity merging harmoniously with traditional life, Strand's *Wales* constructs, connects and reconciles the 'green mountain' of rural mid-west and north-west Wales, the Wales of the farmer and the shepherd, with the 'black mountain' of the south Wales coalfield, the Wales of the miner and the steelworker. In so doing, Strand was in competition, in conceptual terms at least, with the might of Hollywood. John Ford's Oscar-winning feature film *How Green Was My Valley* (1941), based on the 1939 novel of the same name by Richard Llewellyn, which explored the impact of modernity, in the guise of coal-mining, on the physical, social and psychological landscape of Wales during the 1890s, was also playing in British cinemas in 1942.[48] Ford's psychological drama, exploring self-doubt and the grapple with change, was arguably a complex step beyond the nostalgia and sentimentality with which it has come to be associated critically.[49] In Strand's documentary however, there was less of a place for sentimentality about the past. It offered little equivocation over what was happening, and over what needed to happen next, in Wales.

Strand's film seeks first to project a brighter future based on technology, as represented by the latest advances in agricultural science with a sequence on research at Aberystwyth University where new grasses for sheep-farming were being cultivated. Progress of this kind is presented as evolutionary rather than revolutionary, and the future promises harmony

---

46 David Berry, *Wales and Cinema: The First Hundred Years* (Cardiff: University of Wales Press, 1994), 185–8.
47 *These Are The Men*, Strand, 1943, BFI 15594; *Our Country*, Strand, 1944, BFI 18265.
48 *How Green Was My Valley*, 20th Century Fox, 1941, BFI 32963; Richard Llewellyn, *How Green was My Valley* (London: Michael Joseph, 1939).
49 For a more balanced critique see Berry, *Wales and Cinema*, 161–6.

between innovation and tradition, a contrast to Ford's tortured familial and societal strife. The science of the new grass is melded with scenes of traditional slate-quarrying at Llanberis, and there follows a paean to cultural life of the Welsh village, revolving around 'the squat grey chapel at the grey butt-end of the street.' This is a world presented as timeless, with the narration lingering over the pronunciation of village names, a tactic equivalent to that earlier employed in *Scotland Speaks*. It was Thomas's task to reconcile this imagery with that of the other, modern Wales, the Wales of the English-speaking, Labour-voting, industrial working class, and to present a picture of integration between the two to the outside world.[50] This might not have come naturally, since the 'pulpit' world of non-conformist chapel-going, Welsh-speaking, Liberal-voting rural communities, and the undiluted Welsh national identity they were held to represent, was not one with which Thomas readily identified, nor one which he had embraced within his work. Indeed, the choice of the London-dwelling, English-speaking, morally suspect Dylan Thomas as the man to speak for Wales was a prospect which reportedly ruffled some feathers. Officials at the Welsh office of the Ministry of Information in Cardiff raised questions about Thomas's 'real' Welsh credentials and the option of approaching a more suitable scriptwriter with the proper cultural connections was aired.[51]

But what really set alarm bells ringing at the British Council, which had commissioned *Wales – Green Mountain, Black Mountain* for overseas distribution, was the content and tone of the second half of the film where Thomas's eloquence over pre-war poverty and unemployment in the land of his birth elevate it into something out of the ordinary. As it begins to describe the impact of the Great Depression and its legacy of unemployment for a generation of Welsh industrial workers, Thomas's script is unflinching in its condemnation. Over newspaper headlines from the Wall Street Crash and handfuls of coins turning to mud, the imagery of tradition and

---

50   On attitudes to cinema within 'Liberal Wales' and 'Labour Wales' see Peter Miskell, *A Social History of the Cinema in Wales, 1919–1951: Pulpits, Coal Pits and Fleapits* (Cardiff: University of Wales Press, 2006), 3–4.
51   Ackerman, *Dylan Thomas*, 27.

active industry gives way to sequences of figures scavenging on slag heaps, of the dole queue and of enforced idleness in the streets, with the script turning to fully poetic cadence:

> Remember the procession of the old-young men,
> From dole queue to corner and back again,
> From the pinched, packed streets to the peak of slag
> In the bite of the winters with the shovel and bag,
> With a drooping fag and a turned up collar,
> Stamping for the cold at the ill lit corner
> Dragging through the squalor with their hearts like lead
> Staring at the hunger and the shut pit-head.
> Nothing in their pockets, nothing home to eat
> Lagging from the slag heap to the pinched, packed street
> Remember the procession of the old-young men,
> It shall never happen again.

Here at least, Thomas's talent overcame his sense of dissatisfaction with expressing Strand's world view. This was a lyrical but logical extension of the British documentary film movement's espousal of the dignity of labour, a view in which nothing could be more wasteful, more malignant, than unemployment, a state rendered by Thomas as 'sickening, deadening idleness.' Before the war, Welsh coal mining had become a favourite vehicle for documentary and feature film makers seeking to mythologise Wales as a land of heroic workers enduring economic depression, industrial strife, colliery disasters and community tension.[52] With the prospect of a world re-shaped by war, Strand's film offered redemption in the arrival of new, cleaner industries in Wales and the promise of associated reconstruction epitomised by pictures of the new Treforest industrial estate in the Rhondda valley.

---

52   The equation between mining and proletarian heroism was made again in Humphrey Jennings' celebrated documentary *The Silent Village* (1943) which transposed the murderous German reprisals of June 1942 in the mining village of Lidice, Czechoslovakia to the South Wales coal field. Berry, *Wales and Cinema*, 160–1; 191–5. *The Silent Village*, Crown Film Unit, 1943, BFI 15578.

The sense of indignation is not quite overcome however and Thomas stopped short at representing progress to be inevitable. As suggested by the last line of verse quoted above, echoed in the commentary as it turns back to prose, 'It must not happen again', the sense of a change to come was presented as an imperative rather than mere aspiration or expectation. In the key sequence of the film, Britain receives its single mention in the script, and in it the war effort of Wales is rendered conditional on the righting of past wrongs: 'Britain at war has asked these once-denied, helpless and hopeless men for all their strength and skill at the coal seam and the dockside, the foundry and the factory. The world shall know their answer and the world shall never deny them again.' This tone of demand and defiance corresponded to a growing stridency in wartime documentary film over the necessity of planned post-war reconstruction. Thomas was no Welsh nationalist, and his script did not invoke historic nationhood in its conclusion. But his mixture of national sentiment and socialist conviction threatened to disrupt the requisite task of promoting understanding of Wales and recognition of the Welsh contribution to a united British war effort. On account of the unemployment commentary, the British Council considered the film to be unsuitable for international distribution. This was not the end however. The production was taken over by the Ministry of Information and expanded into a 'two-reeler' for Home non-theatrical distribution.[53] Released intact for UK audiences, it was recommended by the British Film Institute's *Monthly Film Review*, 'for use in schools and youth clubs both as a background film and for discussion purposes.'[54] However, when the Ministry of Information commissioned a reworking of the footage in 1943 to produce a shorter film, entitled *Cymru – Wales*, the more controversial aspects were toned down.[55] Although it did not dispense with the subject of inter-war economic depression and Welsh

---

53   TNA, INF 6/483.
54   *Monthly Film Bulletin*, British Film Institute, XII, 42.
55   *Cymru – Wales*, Hanover, 1943, IWM, COI 1195. The production of shortened and reworked versions of wartime documentary was not unusual. Strand released a shortened version of *Scotland Speaks* in 1941 as *Scotland's War Effort*. Thorpe, Pronay and Coultass, *British Official Films*, 85. *Scotland's War Effort*, Strand, 1941, BFI 278486.

unemployment altogether, the second film revised script and delivery to convey a more upbeat impression. Divested of Thomas's indignation and language, the result is a rather less interesting film, one which, despite Dylan Thomas's unwillingness to conform to traditional conceptions of Welsh national identity, seems rather less genuinely Welsh in its essence than the original.

'Britain's difficulty is Northern Ireland's opportunity': *Ulster* (1941)

The remaining film in Strand's trilogy, that representing the war effort of Ulster, was subjected to critical analysis in John Hill's 2006 cultural history of the cinema and Northern Ireland.[56] Accordingly, present observations will be limited to comparison with the film's Welsh and Scottish counterparts in its efforts to present a sense of national cultural difference compatible with British wartime identity. In this case, Strand's task was complicated by the divisiveness of recent Irish history, and was subject to the specific objectives of the Government of Northern Ireland, the film's ultimate sponsor, which was to allay any doubts in mainland Britain, and to correct any misunderstanding further afield, over the loyalty of the Ulster population and their commitment to, and participation in, the prosecution of the war.

Ulster was something of a hybrid, since it was originally commissioned from Strand in 1939, before the outbreak of war, by the Ulster Tourist Development Association as a promotional film. When war intervened, and the project was suspended, the existing film was taken on and completed under the auspices of the British Council. The film betrays the change, with early sequences presenting an idealised rural community, with music by Richard Addinsell in similar romantic, traditional vein to that of the early sequences of the Scotland and Wales films and a commentary

---

56 Hill, *Cinema and Northern Ireland*, 80–105.

spoken by the actor Robert McDermot, whose Ulster-accented delivery is, if anything, more laboured than Joseph Macleod's representation of a traditional voice in *Scotland Speaks*. More war-orientated content follows, with a tour through Northern Ireland's industries, from ship-building and munitions to the less obvious contributions in textile manufacture and cigarette production. This Strand-style representation of industrial labour was found by Hill to be a new departure for the cultural depiction of Northern Ireland, whose external, media identity had previously been firmly located in the rural and small-town commercial sphere.[57]

What Hill also identified as a salient characteristic of the film is its concern with presenting Northern Ireland as being different – not so much demonstrating difference from the rest of Britain, as was the case with the Scottish and Welsh films, but rather, on the contrary, establishing difference from the rest of Ireland. The film's closing montage, with rural and urban labourers, men and women at work, marching soldiers of the Royal Ulster Rifles and other servicemen, all superimposed over a historic building, is heavy with symbolic imagery and loaded, or coded, language to this effect. Unlike the medieval castles, which Strand used to root their films in Scotland and Wales, the monument selected to stand for Ulster was the Stormont building, completed only eight years earlier as the seat of the Northern Ireland Parliament. The new Stormont, with its prominent statue of Lord Carson, was a symbol in stone of the loyalist dominance of political power in Northern Ireland, and was a statement that the partition of Ireland effected by the Government of Ireland Act of 1920, and deepened by the establishment of the independent Irish Free State in 1922, was no provisional arrangement.

Over the scene of Stormont, the film's closing commentary did not go so far as to be explicit about what Northern Ireland was not; the rest of Ireland is not alluded to. But it was less ambiguous about asserting Northern Ireland's right, as a constituent part of Britain, to play its full and proper role in the war: 'Britain's difficulty is Northern Ireland's opportunity to place all her possessions, human and material, at the service of our King. The

---

57   Hill, *Cinema and Northern Ireland*, 84.

people of Ulster have long loved and defended liberty. They will not fail to defend it now.' This was not then a matter of merely eliding the awkward complexities of Irish history for the purposes of projecting wartime unity through the remainder of the UK. Hill contended that this connecting of Ulster with the defence of liberty was a partisan rendering of Ulster identity which rested on a loyalist heritage alone and which eschewed the nationalist heritage of the minority population ostensibly also represented by the Northern Ireland parliament. The defence of liberty was an ideal with which anyone in Northern Ireland could identify in the context of the war against Nazi Germany, but the concept also linked the war effort to a specific historical narrative in which Ulster's liberty had to be defended from the dual threat of Roman Catholicism and Irish nationalism. In a similar vein, memory of the military achievements and sacrifice of Ulster Protestants in the First World War, as represented by the 36th (Ulster) Division's part in the battle of the Somme, had become an emblem of distinctive Ulster identity.[58] The present war offered a sequel whereby Northern Ireland could further enshrine its loyalty to Britain.

If this was the intention of the film, it is unclear how far it reflected Strand's commission, or rather the individual influence of Strand's chosen commentary writer, the playwright, novelist, critic and theatre manager St. John Greer Ervine. For Belfast-born Ervine, a First World War veteran of the Royal Irish Fusiliers, and, before that, a veteran of a turbulent and controversial tenure as manager of Dublin's Abbey Theatre, the promotion of an Ulster identity was one and the same thing as a total repudiation of Eire, independent southern Ireland. Ervine regarded the existence of Eire as a betrayal of everything he believed in, regarding it with a hatred which one biographer described as 'pathological.'[59] For those in the know, the first sentence from the script excerpt quoted above was an obvious play on the old Irish nationalist maxim 'England's difficulty is Ireland's opportunity.'

---

58   Keith Jeffery, *Ireland and the Great War* (Cambridge: Cambridge University Press, 2000), 55–8.
59   John Boyd in the summer 1974 issue of *Threshold*, the magazine of the Belfast Lyric Players' Theatre, quoted in John Cronin, ed., *Selected Plays of St. John Ervine* (Gerrards Cross: Colin Smythe, 1988), 15.

One can imagine Ervine enjoying the opportunity to turn the implication of the phrase on its head.[60]

What Strand's *Ulster* seems to represent is a message of assertion born of anxiety: anxiety above all over the attitude of the British government, press and public towards the existence and survival of Northern Ireland in light of Eire's 1937 constitutional claim of sovereignty over the entire island of Ireland. There was also anxiety and resentment about Westminster's unwillingness to sanction conscription in Northern Ireland, alone in that respect in the United Kingdom, due to concerns about the historic divisions within the population and the delicacy of the political and constitutional position there.

The 1940s have come to be recognised as a decade in which, on the contrary, Northern Ireland's relationship with Great Britain was strengthened. It is understood that Ulster's war record, its material contribution and its strategic significance, coupled with the British political establishment's disdain for the wartime neutrality of Eire, ultimately helped to bring about the 1949 Ireland Act consolidating Northern Ireland's constitutional future within the United Kingdom.[61] But at the time when Strand and Ervine were making their film in late 1940 and early 1941, this reassuring outcome still lay in the future. The Northern Ireland government's disquiet about lack of support, sympathy and understanding for Northern Ireland in the early war years extended beyond the rest of the United Kingdom to the wider British world and also, in particular, to the United States. It was feared that, despite the Scots-Irish element in the immigrant heritage of North America, there was little recognition of the difference between Northern Ireland and Eire, and that popular perceptions based on nationalist traditions were dominant. Hill's analysis demonstrated that the film output from and about Ulster through the later years of the war, including the Crown

---

60   This adage has been especially associated with the 1916 Easter Rising in Dublin, but appeared in print as early as 1845 in the work of Irish nationalist activist John Mitchel. Bryan P. McGovern, *John Mitchel: Irish Nationalist, Southern Secessionist* (Knoxville, TN: University of Tennessee Press, 2009), 19.
61   Philip Ollerenshaw, *Northern Ireland in the Second World War: Politics, Economic Mobilisation and Society* (Manchester: Manchester University Press, 2013), 228–9.

Film Unit's *A Letter from Ulster* (1943), directed specifically at American audiences in light of the strong US military presence in Northern Ireland from 1942, maintained this assertive and rather worried agenda.[62]

Conclusion

At first impression, Strand's three early Second World War films about Scotland, Wales and Northern Ireland conform in many ways to expectations based on the objectives and customary practices of British wartime film documentary. Their explicit purpose was to present an image of these parts of the United Kingdom as full and equal partners in the British war effort and, for the avoidance of confusion, to explain Scottish, Welsh and Northern Irish difference for the education of audiences in other parts of the UK, across the British empire and in neutral countries. In keeping with the template of pre-war documentary film-making, emphasis was placed on depicting a harmonious community of labour working towards the promise of a modernised, more egalitarian society as the reward of victory. For the Scottish and Welsh films especially, what was different about Scotland and Wales is seen to be rooted in the distant past, in history and tradition, while what was important about Scotland and Wales is the vision of a better, greater British future. For Northern Ireland, the divisiveness of the recent past, and the constitutional complexities, demanded a more straight-forward representation based, ostensibly, in the present.

Somewhere in the production process however, the creative freedom granted to such figures as Macdonell, Thomas and Ervine introduced a further element into each film, an extra message which, although it might easily be missed by the uninitiated, was there nonetheless. With the gentle inference of *Scotland Speaks*, or the poetically expressed anger in *Wales – Green Mountain, Black Mountain*, or with the insistence born of insecurity

---

62 *A Letter from Ulster*, Crown Film Unit, 1943, BFI 14285.

Scotland, Wales and Northern Ireland in early wartime documentary film 285

in *Ulster*, each in its way delivered a message of its own to the British government, and for the instruction of British audiences, which subverted, just a little, the principal objectives of the Ministry of Information. The films passed muster, with only the forthrightness of Dylan Thomas's script apparently raising any concerns. Strand fulfilled its Ministry of Information contracts and it may be assumed that if Ministry officials even noticed the subtexts of these Scottish, Welsh or Northern Irish narratives these were not considered to be distracting from the main message. Meanwhile, of course, with that casual association between Britain and England in play, no one at the Ministry of Information in 1940–1 was charging Strand with the task of making a film about the national war effort of England – England exclusively and as a whole. If ever such a film were to have been imagined or realised, that perhaps would have been the production to raise eyebrows in the corridors of power.

LINSEY ROBB

'His Own Weapons to His Own Battlefront': The civilian working man in British culture 1939–1945

In recalling her experiences of the Second World War during an oral history interview, wartime aircraft factory worker, Fiona Thomas, asserted that 'There was no men. The men were all away, and like I say 18 to 45 was the call-up age and that. Most of them were older, over 45, or some who perhaps, something, they hadn't passed the medical for the forces.'[1] In making such a statement Thomas brings to light the predominant image of the British home front during the Second World War. It is largely perceived as a feminised space in which women donned overalls and uniforms to replace the men who had left to join the armed forces. Thomas also highlights another common belief: those who were not in uniform fighting for Britain were not 'men' or, at least, were not thought manly. Generally either because of their age or ill-health, these men were considered to be sharply distanced from the British wartime masculine ideal.[2] Such an image is repeatedly drawn, and therefore reinforced, in contemporary popular culture.[3] However, this ignores the many men whose essential war work did not place them in uniform but instead saw them working in factories, fields or building sites, fighting fires or transporting goods in the Merchant

---

1   Penny Summerfield, *Reconstructing Women's Wartime Lives: Discourse and Subjectivity in Oral Histories of the Second World War* (Manchester: Manchester University Press, 1998), 121.
2   *Ibid.*, 119.
3   For example, *Goodnight Mister Tom* (1998) and the BBC series *Land Girls* (2009) reiterate the image of a civilian society peopled by women and old men. Even the children's television series *Horrible Histories* (2009) featured a song, 'The World War Two Girls Song', which emphasised that women had to replace 'our men' who were fighting.

Navy. These men were largely in reserved occupations, those deemed by the state to be irreplaceably necessary in civilian life because of their skills, and therefore ineligible for conscription or voluntary enrolment into the armed services.[4] Between four and six million men were in reserved occupations at any given point throughout the war.[5] However, despite a growing interest in wartime civilian male exploits, these men have been all but ignored by historians.[6] This chapter will, therefore, explore the cultural identities ascribed to British non-uniformed men in a wide range of popular cultures and so will extend our understandings of both wartime masculinities and Britishness itself.

As R.W. Connell explains, masculinities are experienced hierarchically.[7] In wartime Britain the uniformed man stood at the pinnacle of the masculine hierarchy. The 'soldier hero', as argued by Graham Dawson, had long been a central tenet of British national identity and a 'real man' was often depicted as one who was willing to fight, and indeed die, for his country.[8] However, the horrors of the First World War had somewhat tarnished this glorification of martial masculinity and arguably ushered in a more domestic ideal with celebration of the ordinary husband, or 'little man', becoming more frequent.[9] In light of this Sonya Rose argues for what she terms a 'temperate masculinity';[10] a mix of the traditional soldier hero

---

4   See Juliette Pattinson, Arthur McIvor and Linsey Robb, *Men in Reserve: British civilian masculinity in the Second World War* (forthcoming).
5   Angus Calder, *The People's War: Britain 1939–1945* (London: Pimlico, 1992), 505; Mark Donnelly, *Britain in the Second World War* (London: Routledge, 1999), 71.
6   For the exceptions see, for example, Sonya O. Rose, *Which People's War?: National Identity and Citizenship in Britain 1939–1945* (Oxford: Oxford University Press, 2003); Penny Summerfield and Corinna Peniston-Bird, *Contesting Home Defence: Men, Women and the Home Guard in the Second World War* (Manchester: Manchester University Press, 2007).
7   Robert Connell, *Masculinities* (Berkeley: University of California Press, 2005), 28.
8   Graham Dawson, *Soldier Heroes: British Adventure, Empire and the Imaginings of Masculinity* (London: Routledge, 1994), 1.
9   Alison Light, *Forever England: Femininity, Literature and Conservatism Between the Wars* (London: Routledge, 1991), 8.
10 Rose, *Which People's War?*, 153.

and the 'little man' masculinity.¹¹ Rose contends that the ideal masculinity in a British context, during the years of the Second World War, combined 'traditional' masculine traits such as bravery, courage, physical strength and youthful virility with more homely qualities such as a sense of humour and being a team-player from 'ordinary' origins who enjoyed the simple pleasures of family life.¹² Contemporary films, including *In Which We Serve* (1942) and *The Way Ahead* (1944), as well as many others, all focused on the war in a way which both highlighted the necessary heroism of military life as well as extolling the pleasures of the domestic. Such an ideal was also, to some extent, present in real life. Martin Francis, for example, argues in *The Flyer* that the men of the RAF continued to prize their roles as fathers and husbands.¹³ Moreover, Rose argues that the temperate aspect of the ideal masculinity was emphasised as a direct response to the notion of the Germans as unemotional and cold-hearted war machines.¹⁴ Such a depiction was prominent in wartime films, including *Went the Day Well?* (1942) which depicted an imagined invasion of Britain by Germany and shows the German soldiers as humourless, brutish thugs. Moreover British identity and British masculinity were inextricably linked in this period. Indeed, Rose suggests that Britain was a 'masculine nation' stating 'there was a rough equivalence between the structures of wartime masculinity and the World War II constructions of Englishness and Britishness. "Good citizenship" and masculinity were virtually mirror images of one another. Masculinity, in other words, was normative personhood.'¹⁵ However, while Rose argues that only the armed services were consistently presented as the pinnacle of British ideals, and that the civilian man was sharply distanced from this image, this chapter will suggest that the actuality was less neatly dichotomous and that some civilians were culturally presented as uniquely British heroes.

11 Light, *Forever England*.
12 Rose, *Which People's War?*, 160–1.
13 Martin Francis, *The Flyer: British Culture and the Royal Air Force 1939–1945* (Oxford: Oxford University Press, 2008), 96–7.
14 Rose, *Which People's War?*, 153.
15 Ibid., 153.

Civilian men in factory and field

The vast majority of men in reserved occupations were in industrial or agricultural occupations, or their allied trades, highlighting the importance of both manufacturing and foodstuffs to total warfare.[16] Some effort was made to convey this importance to the British populace. The Crown Film Unit production, *A Diary for Timothy* (1946), directed by Humphrey Jennings, documented the closing days of war, and raised questions about Britain's future. It also attempted to highlight the necessity of civilian work to the war effort:

> You see this was total war. Everyone was in it. It was everywhere. Not only on the battlefields but in the valleys where Goronwy, the coal miner, carries his own weapons to his own battlefront in scenery which isn't exactly pretty. If you looked across the countryside of England, that is beautiful, you can see Alan, the farmer, he has spent the last five years of war reclaiming the land and making it fertile. He has been fighting against the forces of nature all his life. And now with a mortal enemy on us he has to fight harder than ever. In London Bill the engine driver looks out of his cab at his battlefront. No longer taking holiday makers to the sea but taking the miner's coal, the farmer's crops, the fighting men's ammunitions to where they have to go. Goronwy, Alan and Bill are all fighting in their ways.

As James Chapman notes this focus on the pastoral is recurrent in Jennings' cinematic vision of Britain, as well as a popular focus in much of wartime culture.[17] The same imagery can be seen in the 'It's Your Britain, Fight For It Now' poster series which included one poster which featured peaceful golden countryside through which a farmer strolls herding sheep with his dog.[18] Similarly, a Mass Observation survey in 1941 asked the question 'What

---

16 Ministry of Information, *Schedule of Reserved Occupations and Protected Work*. Revision (London: HMSO, 1941).
17 James Chapman, *The British at War: Cinema, State and Propaganda, 1939–1945* (London: I.B. Tauris, 1998), 166.
18 Frank Newbould, Army Bureau of Current Affairs, 'It's Your Britain, Fight For It Now', 1942 (currently held at the Imperial War Museum, London).

does Britain mean to you?' The response was often idyllic images of the countryside.[19] As such, Rose argues that this image came to stand for what the British were fighting for.[20] Moreover *A Diary For Timothy* reflects a desire to present Britain as a unified nation, a common aim of wartime culture. Not only does Jennings highlight the contributions of both Wales and England to the war effort but also emphasises the link between the industrial world and the rural landscape to forge a sense of strong British unity. It is within this image of an idealised Britain that Jennings clearly portrays civilian men as vital cogs in the war machine by using militaristic language and suggests an equal contribution to the war effort by uniformed and non-uniformed men. As was typical of Jennings' wartime films *A Diary for Timothy* is very much a celebration of the strong British spirit. Indeed, Jeffrey Richards and Anthony Aldgate compare Jennings to George Orwell with his 'robust Socialist patriotism, a full-blooded love of England and the English centred on an unashamed admiration for the qualities of the working man.'[21] However, the film does not, or cannot, sustain this admiration for ordinary civilian workers. Injured RAF pilot, Peter, garners much greater focus and screen-time than any of the civilian workers. Moreover, later in the film, a radio broadcast is clearly heard describing the Battle of Arnhem, part of the infamous Battle of the Bulge:

> Perhaps I should remind you here that these were men of no ordinary calibre, they'd been nine days in that little space I mentioned being mortared and shelled, machine-gunned and sniped from all around. For the last three days they'd had no water, very little but small arms ammunition and rations cut to 1/6. Luckily, or unluckily, it rained and they caught the water in their capes and drunk that. These last items weren't mentioned. They were airborne weren't they? They were tough and knew it.

The audience is reminded of the hardships faced by these men when this section is repeated over sombre music played by the famed pianist Dame Myra Hess. The message is clear: men in the army are not simply tough; they are tougher than 'ordinary calibre' civilian men. As such, despite Jennings'

---

19 See Noakes, this collection.
20 Rose, *Which People's War?*, 203.
21 Anthony Aldgate and Jeffrey Richards, *Britain Can Take It: British Cinema in The Second World War* (London: I.B. Tauris, 2007), 225.

efforts, Bill, Alan and Goronwy were not true icons of the British spirit, as perhaps he intended, but instead were shown to be secondary.

Indeed, outwith state propaganda cultural depictions of those in industrial and agricultural occupations were extremely rare and the few which did appear often distanced those presented from a masculine image.[22] There were hardly any representations of civilian life which provided a legitimate reason for a young man to be out of uniform. The whole civilian population was instead generally conceptualised as singularly female. For example, the *Daily Mirror* published a cartoon in July 1944 titled 'There is no weak link.' This cartoon showed a young housewife, complete with babe in arms, holding on to chains. The links of the chain were tagged 'Army', 'Navy' and 'R.A.F.' while on her apron is written 'civilian population.'[23] This cartoon clearly reinforces the traditional gender roles of the fighting male and the civilian female: a conceptualisation which leaves little room for the non-uniformed civilian man. This could potentially have denied civilian men a legitimate reason for being on the home front. Addressing filmic representations, Antonia Lant argues, 'Most men of Home Front fictions ... diverge conspicuously from [the] ideal construction of masculinity. They are either permanently medically disqualified, wounded, A.W.O.L., draft dodgers, or beyond serving age.'[24] Indeed, the link between ideal masculinity and war became unusually pronounced during the Second World War as the entire British nation turned to one purpose. As Corinna Peniston-Bird argues, 'although hegemonic definitions are complex and fluid, during war, these phallocentric ideals are less open to competition from alternative versions of masculinity.'[25] This certainly impacted upon the depiction of the civilian workers whose occupations lacked opportunities for heroism. For the most part both

---

22   Perhaps the only workers depicted less than male industrial and agricultural workers were white collar workers who were almost invisible in wartime.
23   'There is no weak link', *Daily Mirror*, 4 July 1944.
24   Antonia Lant, *Blackout: Reinventing Women for Wartime British Cinema* (Princeton: Princeton University Press, 1991), 52.
25   Corinna Peniston-Bird, 'Classifying the Body in the Second World War: British Men In and Out of Uniform' *Body & Society*, 9/4 (2003), 31–48.

agriculture and industry were shown to be an entirely female exploit in wartime, as seen for example in such films as *Went The Day Well?*, *Millions Like Us* (1943) and *Night Shift* (1942). As such, men of these professions were largely denied an alternate masculinity which drew on skill and hard labour, two central tenets of pre-war British working-class masculinity. Instead their work was ubiquitously shown to have been overtaken by a speedily trained female labour force. Even when industrial workers, for example, were portrayed they were generally depicted as the men behind the man behind the gun. Their role, and industry was often spoken of as a homogenous entity in wartime, was evidently seen as a support to those in the armed services. Despite the pervasive rhetoric of 'all in it together' there still remained a very potent and obvious hierarchy. Wilfred Pickles, a wartime BBC newsreader specifically selected for his Yorkshire accent as the BBC attempted to more fully represent their listeners in this People's War, presented the radio programme *We Speak for Ourselves*, in which he visited war production factories.[26] In the course of one programme one male worker declared:

> Well, whether they were trying to or not, they didn't stop us working! We just go on doing as much as we ever can – everyone's got that thought well rubbed into him. And we're glad to do it too. If anyone starts having a rest, we just say 'Come on – how about those lads in khakis?' That starts 'em off again – and it has ever since Dunkirk.[27]

This suggests that those in the forces were considered to have it harder than those on the home front and so by consequence considered more important. Such statements also suggest that even the industrial man has absorbed this notion of his secondary status implying some form of internalisation of the messages presented in propaganda.

This separation from the British ideal male image was often emphasised by the focus on the advanced age of men in industrial occupations.

---

26   Charles James Rolo, *Radio Goes to War* (London: Faber and Faber Limited, 1942), 112; Sian Nicholas, *The Echo of War: Home Front Propaganda and the Wartime BBC, 1939–45* (Manchester: Manchester University Press, 1996), 2.
27   BBC Written Archive Centre, *We Speak For Ourselves: Sheffield*, 27 March 1941.

It was regularly implied that industry was staffed by women and old men while the armed services was the acceptable role for young and fit men. In a broadcast in the BBC Talks show *Working Together* in April 1941 it was stated that:

> ... women and girls hitherto occupied in commercial and clerical employment and branches of the distributive trades, or doing house work in their homes, are being registered and guided to useful war work. And all through the great fields of industry, including the most vital of munitions trades, the engineering shops, the ship yards and the aircraft factories, there is going on now a steady sifting of the labour force, for the purpose of releasing the younger fit men for service with armed forces, and the organisations of full-time Civil Defence, and filling their jobs with older men or women.[28]

No mention is made here of the necessary skill needed of men in reserved occupations, those men who had skills honed in years of apprenticeships in engineering and industrial occupations, for example, which could not be quickly replicated with the incoming labour forces. Such an omission was typical. Instead, this makes patently clear a young man's role in the war was to be in uniform and replaced on the home front by women and old men. A similar depiction was granted to the men of the Home Guard who, despite having an average age of thirty five, were consistently presented as old and unfit.[29] While age may have brought connotations of time-earned skill, youth and virility were key attributes of the British ideal of the wartime male. Men of industry, regardless of their actual age, were therefore often distanced from these valued characteristics within wartime cultural depictions.

Agricultural workers were similarly depicted in a way which undermined any attempt at a manly image. To an even greater extent than industrial workers their occupation lacked any real opportunity for wartime bravery. This, of course, separated them from the 'soldier hero' ideal. Like

---

28   BBC Written Archive Centre, *Working Together by George Gibson*, 21 April 1941.
29   Summerfield and Peniston-Bird, *Contesting Home Defence*, 183; Craig Armstrong, 'Tyneside's Home Guard Units: An Able Body of Men?', *Contemporary British History*, 22/2 (2008), 257–78.

their industrial counterparts, they were also denied an image in the mainstream which drew upon the day-to-day dangers of their occupation.[30] Moreover, on the rare occasion they were depicted they were often shown as yokels. One article on the work of farmers published in the *Daily Mirror* in 1943 for example was accompanied by a cartoon depicting a stereotypical farmer: he is portly, middle-aged and ruddy-faced.[31] He is therefore very much distanced from the strong, heroic and dashing image of the uniformed combatant. Similarly, in late 1939, *Punch* magazine published a series of cartoons depicting 'The Changing Face of Britain', one of which represented agriculture. Entitled 'The Ploughman Homeward Plods ...', it depicted two similar scenes. The top image shows a hunched old man, presumably the ploughman of the title, walking over the brow of a hill. The second of the images depicts the same scene but the stooped elderly figure is replaced by an upright and curvaceous member of the Women's Land Army watched, most probably lustily, by several soldiers.[32] The difference between the wizened old man and the youthful, and uniformed, Land Girl is stark. Again, these suggestions of old age and infirmity sharply distance the farming community from the young virile British soldier hero. This reinforces the image that the average male civilian worker was not considered vital to the war effort and so was far down the British masculine hierarchy.

Fundamentally, although repeated attempts were made by the state to show the civilian man as a crucial part of the war effort it was undermined by the irrefutable heroism and bravery of those in the military as frequently emphasised in newspapers, radio broadcasts, propaganda posters and films and which those in most civilian occupations could never achieve. Indeed, rather than an overtly masculine identity these workers were granted almost no identity at all. This may, in part, have resulted in many young men facing internalised, and much less frequently external,

---

30   Some effort was made, often by trade union publications, to draw upon these hardships to create an alternately heroic image. However, this was infrequent. Rose, *Which People's War?*, 195.
31   'Down on Vitamin – Farm', *Daily Mirror*, 6 December 1943.
32   'The Changing Face of Britain: IX-The Ploughman Homeward Plods ...', *Punch*, 11 October 1939.

pressure to enlist. For example, Douglas MacDonell, a wartime aircraft factory worker at Vickers, explained that:

> I was put on deferred service and by this time the company knew and they were tempted to stop my movement into the Royal Navy so I went in and had a long chat with them. It was a bank holiday. I said 'I'm not going to be uncooperative but I want to go in. I think I'll being doing the country a greater amount of good.' I know this sounds pious and everything but this is the way it occurred to me at the time.[33]

Many men who were in wartime reserved occupations similarly recounted strong feelings that they would have been of greater use in uniform than in their civilian capacity. While the state clearly valued their occupations, and so by derivation the individuals undertaking these roles, without the praise and admiration heaped on other male roles many men failed to see their own necessity. Instead masculinity, and national identity, in wartime Britain became almost entirely bound up with military characteristics and despite being central to British survival and victory for men who were unable to take on this identity, there was little cultural space in the national self-image.

Fighting fires and battling U-boats

Not all civilian occupations were granted the same status. In stark contrast to farmers and industrial workers, those in jobs which included some element of war-related danger, most notably the fire services and the mercantile marine, were widely celebrated. Indeed, in many ways the depiction of these occupations closely mirrored the 'temperate masculinity' which Sonya Rose conceptualises as the ideal of British masculinity more usually associated with the uniformed man. Most notably, both the fire services and the Merchant Navy were depicted in a way which emphasised their bravery

---

33   Imperial War Museum (IWM) Sound Archive, Douglas Ivor MacDonell, Interview 9259, 1986.

in difficult and dangerous situations. For the merchant service there was an overwhelming focus on the dangers they faced. While this could tend towards an emphasis on beleaguered seamen adrift at sea, notably seen in Philip Zec's infamous cartoon mocking the increase in petrol prices, the dangers seamen faced could also elevate them to a position of high praise.[34] For example in 1943, the *Daily Mirror* published a cartoon which depicted a merchant seaman striding across the sea carrying a box of ammunition and a box of food. He strolls through U-boat-infested waters, ignoring bombs as they drop around him. This image shows a pre-occupation with the dangers the seaman faced. However, the box of ammunition, with which he is literally shouldering the burden of war, is larger than the box of food and more prominently in the viewer's line of vision. Moreover, the title explicitly mentions 'ammunition' not food. This serves to connect the Merchant Navy firmly with the military war effort.[35] The message of this cartoon is clear. The merchant seaman is very obviously playing a heroic part in Britain's war effort. Similarly, in the 1944 Crown Film Unit feature film *Western Approaches* (1944) Bob, one of a group of merchant seamen stranded in a lifeboat, explains his experience of what happened when their ship was attacked:

> ... up popped Jerry and I thought 'what the hell was that?' I damn soon found out. They opened up on us ... Fellas was dropping off the ladder into the water. I seen the fellas in the boat falling down. And just then she took a heave and I must've caught my foot in something and I went down with her. I was going down and down. [...] Then the boilers must've went. I shot up to the top. I had my eyes open and I was looking up. I could see the sky getting brighter and brighter, y'know the top of the water. And I came up to the top and I thought I was an aeroplane. I bloody near came right out of the water. And I looked around me. All that was left was a few spots of oil. Not a damned soul anywhere.

Such stories of enemy attack and subsequent survival are almost indistinguishable from those experienced by the Royal Navy. Indeed, the central crew in Noel Coward's *In Which We Serve* (1942) similarly languish in a

---

34 Mark Donnelly, *Britain in the Second World War* (London: Routledge, 1999), 75.
35 'Praise the men who bring the ammunition', *Daily Mirror*, 12 April 1943.

lifeboat after an attack for much of the film, showing a parallel between the exploits of the Merchant Navy and the idealised British hero.

Moreover, while not members of the armed services, the men of the Merchant Navy were able to mirror the behaviours more readily associated with the military. The Royal Navy remained the senior service in wartime, central not only to Britain's war but its past as an island nation. Additionally, the Royal Navy had, since the beginning of the twentieth century, become firmly connoted 'not only as defenders of British interests at home and abroad but also as exemplars of Britishness and manliness.'[36] In comparison, before the war the mercantile marine were often depicted as uncouth and lecherous. Moreover, Penny Summerfield states that maritime war was essentially 'fought by the Royal Navy with its secure place in British culture and society, and suffered by the Merchant Navy.'[37] However culturally, at least, this clear distinction was somewhat lost. With their use of arms, merchant seamen were able to emulate the actions of their armed forces counterpart. For example, the central crew of *Western Approaches*, those who served on board the *Jason* who are stranded in a life-boat, are rescued not by the Royal Navy but by a fellow merchant ship, *The Leander*, as it was separated from the convoy due to its inability to maintain the necessary slow speed without damage. In responding to the stranded sailors' distress signals *The Leander* destroys a German U-boat, therefore displaying behaviour more readily associated with the Navy than the civilian merchant service. The division between the military and civilians is transgressed here. The Merchant Navy are deployed in an active military engagement as opposed to passively transporting cargo. Indeed, they are almost indistinguishable from their Royal Navy counterparts and so allied to the prestige generally given to those in uniform.

Comparable emphasis on bravery and danger was also seen in representations of the fire services, once the Blitz had begun in earnest in

36 Mary A. Conley, *From Jack Tar to Union Jack: Representing Naval Manhood in the British Empire, 1870–1918* (Manchester: Manchester University Press, 2009), 5.
37 Penny Summerfield, 'Divisions at Sea: Class, Gender, Race, and Nation in Maritime Films of the Second World War, 1939–60', *Twentieth Century British History*, 22/3 (2011), 330–353. Here 334–5.

September 1940. Before bombing had started, the fire services, and the AFS (Auxiliary Fire Service) in particular, were frequently and openly mocked for their inactivity.[38] This ceased immediately once aerial bombardment commenced. While the ordinary civilian was encouraged to shelter during air raids the men of the fire services were duty-bound to head out in to a world of burning buildings and falling bombs. Many firemen were awarded the George Cross and the George Medal, the highest honours given to civilians in wartime, and these were widely publicised in local and national newspapers.[39] Representations of the fire services often centred on their bravery and drew comparisons with the armed forces. In December 1941, for example, the *Daily Mirror* published an article entitled 'The Happy Warriors' which depicted a naval officer and an AFS firefighter receiving their Christmas presents in hospital. Both had suffered serious injuries to their legs and were depicted side by side, with their stories intertwined, therefore emphasising the parallels between the two occupations and linking the fire services with the heroic identity more commonly projected on to the armed services.[40] Moreover, two prominent films were made about the fire services in wartime to celebrate the work of Britain's firemen during the Blitz. Released first was Crown Film Unit production *Fires Were Started* (1943), made using actual firemen, which despite its fictionalised plot was very much intended as a realistic portrayal of London's firemen. *The Bells Go Down* (1943), released shortly after *Fires Were Started*, was a much more conventional Ealing comedy-drama. However, in both the firemen are shown rushing up stairs and ladders without displaying any visible hesitancy to fight fires. This is emphasised in *Fires Were Started* as director Humphrey Jennings included many shots of firemen standing with determined and resolute facial expressions with fires raging all around them. This bravery was acknowledged at the time. In a review of *Fires Were Started*, *The Times* noted: 'it is a night terror which does not

---

38   'A pump and crew must be standing by day and night ...', *Punch*, 5 June 1940; 'And here, Gentlemen, we have what is termed a fire', *Punch*, 28 February 1940.
39   For example, 'More Heroes Of The Raid', *The Times*, 30 August 1941.
40   'The Happy Warriors', *Daily Mirror*, 27 December 1941.

terrorise those whose duty it is to be abroad in it.'[41] Such 'low key, underplayed heroism', argues Robert Murphy, was typical of the way the British wished to portray themselves.[42]

Indeed, both the men of the fire services and the Merchant Navy were not just displaying bravery but a consciously British bravery. Films, especially, which depicted the military often showed the men involved shrugging off the dangers which beset them. For example, in *In Which We Serve* Captain Kinross, played by Noel Coward, informs his men very calmly after they have been torpedoed that 'we got him. I'm afraid he got us too ... I'm afraid we're going over.' Such emotional reticence, and fortitude in the face of danger, was common in depictions of the military in this period and served to underline the bravery of the military men despite the dangers which beset them. Stoicism became an idealised trait for both British civilians and the armed forces. This stoicism was common in depictions of the fire services and the Merchant Navy. For instance, in *Fires Were Started* a bomb explodes while the men are fighting a fire. In response, all the men fall flat to the floor. As they stand up one of the men, Rumbold, laughs and exclaims 'what a windy lot of bastards we are. That was a mile away.' The men even remain in high spirits the following morning after a full night fighting fires and despite having lost a colleague. After Johnny calls the canteen girl 'beautiful', one of the men, referring to Johnny's soot-blackened face, retorts 'You look pretty beautiful yourself too mate' which leads the assembled group to laugh jovially. Similarly, merchant seamen's jokes and banter became a sign of strength and, crucially, separated them markedly from depictions of the humourless Nazis. Seamen, especially on film, were often shown literally laughing in the face of danger. For example, the following light-hearted exchange between the Bosun and the gunner in *San Demetrio, London* (1943), regarding one of their glum shipmates, takes place while under fire from a German warship:

---

41 'Fires Were Started', *The Times*, 25 March 1943.
42 Robert Murphy, *Realism and Tinsel: Cinema and Society in Britain, 1939–1945* (London: Routledge, 1989), 48.

BOSUN: Ever seen him smile?
GUNNER: Did once. Course it might've just been a touch of wind.
BOSUN: Touch of wind? It'd need a whole gale.

This British stoicism is observed in the same film by the American seaman who states 'yeah they're singing alright. Here we are rolling about in the gale in the middle of the Atlantic, U-boats all around, no escort and as far as the British are concerned it still seems to be Saturday night.' As Summerfield and Peniston-Bird argue, 'the British love of self-deprecating humour was construed during the war and afterwards as "a precious gift", "the very lifeblood of democracy".'[43] Therefore, such appearances of 'smiling through' aligned these men with the idealised image of the British citizen.

Moreover, for both of these occupations, as well as a focus on bravery and heroism, there was also an emphasis on domesticity which was similarly emphasised in depictions of the armed forces. Such a depiction was central to British identity. Mary Conley shows that, from the late Victorian era onwards, men of the Royal Navy were increasingly associated with domesticity exemplifying 'respectable British manhood celebrating their duty to nation and empire and their devotion to the family.'[44] Men of the fire service were regularly depicted in domestic settings therefore cementing their 'ordinary hero' status as well as their links to British ideals. Even outwith their work, where they were frequently shown rescuing children and the elderly, these men were often represented as ordinary and kind. In *The Bells Go Down* (1943), much of the narrative is dedicated to a young fireman's marriage and first child. Bob's colleagues help to make toys for the baby and decorate his new home therefore including them in the domestic sphere. Similarly, one memorable photograph in the *Daily Mirror* shows four firemen, in full uniform and one dressed as a clown, at a tiny children's table wearing party hats surrounded by children. The accompanying article explains that these are the children of their dead colleagues. The article also explains that the men have made them toys.[45]

43 Summerfield and Peniston-Bird, *Contesting Home Defence*, 134.
44 Conley, *From Jack Tar to Union Jack*, 3.
45 'Orphan of the (tea) storm!', *Daily Mirror*, 4 July 1944.

This article neatly encapsulates both sides of Rose's conceptualisation. By emphasising the care these men have taken of the children it captures the 'ordinary' aspect of the model. However, by also focusing on their dead comrades it reminds the reader of the sacrifices made by the fire services and so reinforces the links with the British armed forces ideal.

Domestic tropes were also regularly applied to the mercantile marine. Although their families were rarely seen, given that most depictions were set at sea, there were numerous attempts to link the merchant service to the domestic world they were physically separated from. In *San Demetrio, London*, for example, the Chief Engineer, Pollard, has a daughter about to sit her scholarship exams while the Bosun's wife is pregnant. Moreover, both the BBC's programmes aimed at merchant seamen, *Shipmates Ashore* and *The Blue Peter*, featured messages from wives, girlfriends and mothers. These sections primarily broadcast domestic news including such events as mothers' operations and sisters' weddings as well as declarations of love from wives and sweethearts.[46] These references, not only to romantic love but maternal and sibling affection as well, place the merchant seamen within the 'ordinary hero' trope as explored by Sonya Rose. Again, this reinforces links with the idealised version of British masculinity as had developed in the inter-war years and also distanced them from the demonised image of the Nazis as cold-hearted war machines.

Indeed, the men of the fire services and the Merchant Navy, unlike their counterparts in industrial and agricultural trades, were very much British heroes. They were perhaps the ideal heroes for the People's War. Both were often shown to have traits readily identifiable with being ordinarily British. As Lant notes, 'Under these conditions there was an acute demand for coherent representations of the nation which could show it to be unified despite its real difference of class, nationality, culture and gender.'[47] This sense of Britishness is underlined by the inclusion of many different regional accents, a common trope in wartime films. This can also

---

46   BBC Written Archive Centre, *The Blue Peter*, 11 October 1941; BBC Written Archive Centre, *Shipmates Ashore*, 21 March 1942.
47   Lant, *Blackout*, 6.

be seen, for example, in female recruitment films such as *The Gentle Sex* (1943) and *Millions Like Us*. Summerfield and Peniston-Bird have argued, of the Home Guard, that this national inclusiveness symbolised Britain as a whole standing together.[48] The same can be argued of the Merchant Navy and the fire services. *Western Approaches* and *San Demetrio, London*, the BBC's *Shipmates Ashore*, *Fires Were Started* and *The Bells Go Down* all made an effort to include many British accents. All feature a selection of English accents as well at least one Welsh and Scottish character. They were truly British groups, not just English ones.

Their undeniable Britishness was also shown in their actions. In *San Demetrio, London*, for instance, the merchant crew reacts heartily to the prospect of a cup of tea. In order to make the tea the Chief Engineer risks blowing the ship up to light the stove, therefore highlighting its importance to the crew's morale. Moreover, one crew member points out to the American crew member that there's 'not much in your line Yank' consequently marking tea-drinking out as a specifically British past-time. Similarly, both the fire services and the Merchant Navy were shown to have a love for alcohol, especially beer, another typical British trait. In *The Bells Go Down*, for example, the majority of the off-duty scenes take place in the pub. Similarly in *Fires Were Started* the first half of the film is mainly located in the mess room as the men drink beer and play darts.[49] Likewise, one man in *San Demetrio, London* declares as he rows a lifeboat in a storm 'What wouldn't I give to be having a pint in the Old Elephant now?' Also, as they are pulling in to port at the end of the journey, and the film, another declares his intention to get 'absolutely stinking.' Again, such a portrayal suggests the men of the fire services and the Merchant Navy were ordinary British men.

Moreover, portrayals of the military often accentuated the strong bonds between the men depicted. Christine Geraghty argues that these

48 Summerfield and Peniston-Bird, *Contesting Home Defence*, 108.
49 James Chapman, 'British Cinema and "The People's War"' in Nick Hayes and Jeff Hill, eds, *'Millions Like Us'? British Culture in the Second World War* (Liverpool: Liverpool University Press, 1999), 53.

male relationships were culturally necessary to preserve a human side for men caught up in the horrific violence of warfare.[50] As well as making these men human the depiction of male bonding served to embody another praised British quality of the time; group heroism became prized above individual bravery.[51] As Rose states, the ideal man 'was a team-player with strong bonds to his mates, yet distinguished himself: individuality, not individualism was key to wartime masculinity.'[52] *The Way Ahead* (1944), for example, depicts a group of civilian conscripts as they are turned into soldiers. For much of the early part of the film they continually grouse about the conditions in the army with especial derision aimed at their sergeant. However, when on the way to Tunisia their ship is torpedoed and the sergeant becomes trapped several of the men risk their own lives aboard the flaming sinking ship to rescue him thereby highlighting their essential unity, again emphasising another recurrent trope of the People's War. Both the fire services and the Merchant Navy displayed, culturally at least, a similar sense of deep camaraderie. For example, in 1943 the *Daily Mirror* reported the death of seaman Kenneth Coleman. His shipmate told the paper that 'As I struggled in the sea trying towards a boat, it was Coleman who pulled me on board. Next day he died ... He must have been exhausted when he spent his valuable strength pulling me on board. I will never forget him. He was a man.'[53] This final sentence is particularly striking: to be considered 'a man' Coleman had displayed the attributes of gallantry, sacrifice and comradeship, attributes more usually associated with the idealised image of the British armed forces. Similarly, in both *Fires Were Started* and *The Bells Go Down* one fireman sacrifices his life to save, or in an attempt to save, one of his colleagues. In *Fires Were Started* Jacko persuades Barrett to leave him on a burning roof and save himself in spite of him knowing that there is a chance that it might result in his own

---

50   Christine Geraghty, 'Masculinity' in Geoff Hurd, ed., *National Fictions: World War Two in British Films and Television* (London: BFI Publishing, 1984), 24.
51   Jeffrey Richards, *Films and British National Identity: From Dickens to Dad's Army* (Manchester: Manchester University Press, 1997), 84.
52   Rose, *Which People's War?*, 161.
53   'One By One They Died In Lifeboat ...'. *Daily Mirror*, 15 September 1943.

death. He is killed when the roof collapses. Such an image of self-sacrifice was more generally associated with the military and so linked the fireman to the idealised military hero. Moreover, this emphasis on friendship distanced these men from the familiar portrayal of the Nazis. This difference is most obviously shown in the film *Western Approaches*. The Germans are depicted as bloodthirsty and eager for violence, whereas the British seamen only ever use violence in response to attack. The Germans use the *Jason*'s lifeboat as bait to attack the rescuer and their Captain declares lustily 'what I wouldn't give for another torpedo.' Production notes outline the story:

> The lifeboat presents him [the German Captain] with this chance. He is prepared for a patient vigil, maybe for days, in the hope that an unsuspecting rescue ship will come along for him to send to the bottom. There are no histrionics – he arrives at this decision coolly, and in a perfectly detached manner. He looks through the periscope again, and says to himself – 'the perfect decoy.'[54]

This cool and detached attitude to death and the way the captain actively seeks to destroy ships typifies the British portrayal of Germans during the war. Moreover, the Germans are shown to have no loyalty to each other. They push and shove each other out of the way in the clamour to escape their damaged submarine. The shooting script of the film describes a scene following the destruction of the German U-boat which depicts the stranded Germans helping each other to the British lifeboat and ends in the British seamen saving the shipwrecked German sailors.[55] Although the scene was probably intended to emphasise the inexorable kindness of the British it also shows the Germans caring for each other. However, this show of German humanity is missing from the final film and the fate of the damaged submarine, and its sailors, are left undeclared. Instead, the German military are depicted as bloodthirsty and selfish when compared to the selfless and peace-loving British merchant seamen. Such a depiction likens them to their counterparts in the British armed forces while simultaneously distancing them from the perceived weaknesses of the Nazi enemy.

54 National Archives (TNA), INF 1/213 pt 2.
55 *Ibid.*

Moreover, a key component of the uniquely British People's War rhetoric was the ordinariness of civilians who could make an extraordinary difference to the war effort. Such an image was conferred upon the fire services by the fact that there was an overwhelming focus on the AFS, especially on film. Despite both *Fires Were Started* and *The Bells Go Down* being released in 1943, two years after the creation of the centralised National Fire Service, both films focus on much earlier periods of the war. While this may largely have been to centre the film's narrative on the Blitz, the period in which firemen's role in the war was most crucial, it also has the effect of focusing on the AFS and the connotations of the heroics of the ordinary man which that brought. Indeed, Brian Winston notes that Jennings fictionalised many details of the firemen's lives to convey this sense of ordinariness:

> Not only names but jobs were also sometimes fictionalised. So while 'Johnny' (Fred Griffiths) was actually the one-time taxi-driver he says he was in the film, 'Barrett', supposedly an advertising copywriter, was an author. On the other hand 'Walters' (Wilson-Dickson) had worked in an advertising agency before the War. Changing the names meant losing the Wilson-Dickson hyphen; and Rey, Sansom and Gravett were replaced with 'Jacko' and 'Johnny' and other names with working class-resonances.[56]

This also appears to be something the Crown Film Unit, the film production company for *Fires Were Started*, were keen to stress although they used the firemen's real life details. Promotional materials, for example, for the film stated:

> The Cast, who as already mentioned, are all members of the fire service, were picked as representative types from every part of the country: the principal parts are played by Leading Fireman F.W. Griffiths, a cockney taxi-driver who joined the A.F.S. before the war; Leading Fireman Phillip Wilson-Dickson, previously employed in an advertising agency; Leading Fireman Loris Rey, a brilliant sculptor who has frequently exhibited at the Royal Academy; Firemen T.P. Smith, formerly a waiter; Firemen John Barker, a Manchester Business Man, and Company Officer George Gravett, a regular London Fire Brigade man.[57]

56 Brian Winston, *Fires Were Started* (London: British Film Institute, 1999), 31.
57 TNA: TNA, INF 6/986, INF 6/985.

While the claim that these men were 'representative types from every part of the country' is obvious hyperbole, with only London and Manchester being mentioned, the focus on the men's pre-war roles highlights the desire to cast them as ordinary men as well as heroes and as such places them firmly within Rose's conceptualisation of the everyday hero.

A concerted effort was also made to present the men of the merchant service as 'ordinary.' They were, for instance, continually shown to be comprised of men of a lower class than the Royal Navy. For example, *Convoy* (1940) and *Western Approaches* both depicted upper-class officers of the Royal Navy who are in stark contrast to the 'salty robustness' of the men of the merchant service.[58] The effect of this difference between the services changes as the war progresses. For example in *Convoy*, a drama focusing on a Royal Navy vessel escorting a convoy, the class hierarchy is obvious. The captain of the Royal Navy vessel, as well as continually brandishing his authority over the merchant vessels in his care, is clearly an upper-class gentleman. In comparison the merchant captain focused upon has a broad Yorkshire accent which is played for laughs when he tries to convince a German captain to free his ship by speaking 'Spanish' ('us neutrali'[sic]) therefore connoting him as a comic character. In later films, such as *Western Approaches* for example, by having somewhat realistic representations of those men who swore, drunk and took care of each other it serves to make the merchant service look like a collection of 'ordinary' people pulling together in extraordinary circumstances. This was a recurrent and key trope of the People's War.[59] This also reflects the change in the representation of the common man in film within which the representation of merchant seamen can be placed. Early in the war he was a comic foil but by the end he was the hero.[60] As well as presenting a change in the depiction of the Merchant Navy this change reflected wider societal changes in Britain. As the war progressed there was a shift away from bold jingoism

---

58   'Western Approaches (1944)', *Monthly Film Bulletin*, December 1944, 40.
59   Summerfield and Peniston-Bird, *Contesting Home Defence*, 106.
60   Robert Murphy, 'British Film Production 1939 to 1945' in Hurd, ed., *National Fictions*, 14.

and heroism towards more sober realism and celebration of the ordinary man.[61] Indeed, as the war progressed the notion that the actions of civilians could be the decisive factor in assuring victory became more prominent. As Geoff Hurd notes the war called for a huge effort on the part of all civilians which meant a 'rapid and genuine response to the aspirations and demands of subordinate groups and classes in order to win their support for economic and military mobilisations.'[62] Therefore the concept of 'we're all in it together' was seen in many films in the middle part of the war and the representation of civilians changed accordingly. Indeed, perhaps the Merchant Navy were a greater symbol of the increased valorisation of the working classes which took place in wartime than the Royal Navy, so connected, as they were, with respectable members of the middle and upper classes. This is perhaps best emphasised by the film *San Demetrio, London* which reported true events but rather than depicting the suicidal heroism of the Royal Navy it depicts the dogged tenacity of the merchant service. As Summerfield states 'Balcon [the producer] saw the story of the men of the Merchant Navy, whose technical ingenuity and hard work brought the tanker home, as more important than that of naval heroism, and decided that *San Demetrio* rather than *Jervis Bay* should be the principal subject of his film.'[63] Moreover, the film focuses on lower ranked members of the crew, the Captain having been safely rescued, and decisions were depicted as democratically made rather than dictated by the highest ranking crew members. As such, Summerfield notes, the film reflects the increasingly left-wing politics of British society and so therefore places the Merchant Navy at the heart of it making them symbols of this People's War.[64]

61   Ibid., 180; Chapman, 'British Cinema and "The People's War"', 60.
62   Geoff Hurd, 'Notes on Hegemony, the War and Cinema' in Hurd, ed., *National Fictions*, 19.
63   Summerfield, 'Divisions at Sea', 338–9.
64   Ibid., 339.

Conclusion

Through an exploration of a vast array of cultural sources this chapter has shown that occupation was central to the identities ascribed to the male civilian in Britain during the Second World War. Evidently there was a hierarchy of masculine occupations during the war years: civilian men were not an undifferentiated mass. Indeed, rather than the somewhat binary conception of wartime masculinity offered by Sonya Rose, which simply places the civilian man in dualistic opposition to the military man, the evidence reviewed here suggests the actuality was much more complex with a continuum of masculinities stretching from the home front to the battlefront. This conforms to Connell's theory of masculine hierarchies.[65] While undoubtedly the military man, and specifically the much lauded RAF pilot, was at the top of this hierarchy, some civilian occupations came close behind. While all were central to eventual victory, there were sharp distinctions between the differing groups of civilian workers and a clear hierarchy in representation. Those in agricultural and industrial occupations were clearly considered secondary and as such were denied not only an image which drew on British ideals but almost any identity at all and were virtually completely erased from the nation's wartime self-image. However, the frequent explicit comparisons to the armed forces levied at the fire services and the Merchant Navy made clear these occupations were held in high regard. Moreover, they were imbued with traits of the idealised Briton. They were depicted as not only brave and courageous but also kind and filled with humour as well as having a deep love for tea and beer, all traits which the British held up as ideals in this period. They were truly *British* heroes and, perhaps, the ideal symbols for the People's War.

---

65   Connell, *Masculinities*, 28.

Notes on contributors

STUART ALLAN is Principal Curator of Scottish Late Modern collections at National Museums Scotland. His research interests lie in the material culture of the Scottish military tradition and its relationship to national and gender identities. His publications include *Commando Country* (2007) and, with David Forsyth, *Common Cause: Commonwealth Scots and the Great War* (2014).

GAVIN BOWD is Senior Lecturer in French at the University of St Andrews, and author of *Fascist Scotland* (2013). He works mainly on aspects of modern and contemporary France. He is currently preparing a study on Jean-Joseph Rabearivelo, Charles Maurras and colonial Madagascar.

MARTIN FRANCIS is currently the Henry R. Winkler Professor of Modern History at the University of Cincinnati. He is the author of *The Flyer: British Culture and the Royal Air Force, 1939–1945* (Oxford University Press, 2008). In 2015 he will be returning to the UK to take up the position of Professor of War and History at the University of Sussex.

TREVOR GRIFFITHS is Reader in Economic and Social History and Head of History at the University of Edinburgh. His publications include *The Lancashire Working Classes, c.1880–c.1930* (2001) and *The Cinema and Cinema-going in Scotland, 1896–c.1950* (2012). He is currently undertaking research addressing the coming of sound to cinema in Scotland.

MARTIN JOHNES is Reader in History at Swansea University. He has published widely on the social and political history of modern Wales and his books include *Wales since 1939* (2012) and *A History of Sport in Wales* (2005). He is currently writing a history of Christmas in Britain since 1914.

IAIN E. JOHNSTON completed his PhD at the University of Cambridge and is currently a Visiting Student at Sciences Po. His main research interests are the British Empire and war in the twentieth century. He is a contributor to upcoming edited volumes on *The Sea and the Second World War* and *The Imperial World at War*.

BERNARD KELLY is Honorary Postdoctoral Research Fellow at the Scottish Centre for Diaspora Studies, University of Edinburgh. His research interests are British-Irish military history, post-conflict studies and twentieth-century migration. His first book *Returning Home: Irish ex-servicemen after the Second World War* was published in 2012 and he is currently writing a history of the Irish prisoner of war experience in the Second World War.

LUCY NOAKES is Reader in History at the University of Brighton. She is a social and cultural historian who researches the experience and memory of warfare in early and mid twentieth-century Britain. Her publications include *War and the British* (1998), *Women and the British Army* (2006) and (edited with Juliette Pattinson) *British Cultural Memory and the Second World War* (2013).

JULIETTE PATTINSON is a Reader in Modern History at the University of Kent. She specialises in the Second World War and has published on the French resistance, British clandestine warfare, female combatants and male reserved workers and has co-edited collections on the cultural memory of the war, male POWs and partisan and anti-partisan warfare. Her book, *Behind Enemy Lines: Gender, Passing and the Special Operations Executive in the Second World War* was published in 2007.

LINSEY ROBB is a Research Associate at the University of Strathclyde. She is currently completing a book on men in reserved occupations during the Second World War, titled *Men in Reserve: British Civilian Masculinity during the Second World War*, with Juliette Pattinson and Arthur McIvor. Additionally, her first monograph *Men at Work: the Working Man in British Culture, 1939–1945* will be published by Palgrave Macmillan in 2015.

GARY SHEFFIELD is Professor of War Studies at the University of Wolverhampton. He has previously held Chairs at King's College London and the University of Birmingham. He has published extensively on the British army in the two world wars, including *Forgotten Victory: The First World War – Myths and Realities* (2001) and *Command and Morale: The British Army on the Western Front* (2014).

JESSICA THURLOW is an Associate Professor in the Department of History at Aurora University. She is a specialist in feminist and British women's history and her dissertation *Continuity and Changes in British Feminism, c. 1940–1960* explores post-suffrage feminism.

WENDY UGOLINI is a Lecturer in British History at the University of Edinburgh. She specialises in the role of war in identity formation and her first book, *Experiencing War as the 'Enemy Other': Italian Scottish Experience in World War II*, was published in 2011. Her current research focuses on the interconnections between English and Welsh identities in the two world wars.

WENDY WEBSTER is Professor of Modern Cultural History at the University of Huddersfield. Her research interests are in questions of migration, refugee movements, gender, ethnicity, imperialism and national identity in twentieth-century Britain. She has published widely in these areas including *Imagining Home* (1998) and *Englishness and Empire* (2005). She is currently an AHRC Fellow on the 'Mixing It' project exploring national and ethnic diversity in Britain during the Second World War.

IAN S. WOOD taught History for the Open University in Scotland and also at Edinburgh Napier University. He has been a regular contributor to the Scottish newspapers on the conflict in Northern Ireland as well as on military history. His publications include *Times of Troubles: Britain's War in Northern Ireland* (with Andrew Sanders, 2012) and *Britain, Ireland and the Second World War* (2010).

Index

ABCA (Army Bureau of Current Affairs) 11
accents 7, 57, 62n.43, 76, 97, 148, 209, 272, 302–3
Addison, Paul 1, 20
Air Ministry 216, 243, 244–5, 250, 254
Allied Forces in Britain
    American xiv, 22, 81, 104, 209–10, 214, 220–1, 226–8, 230–1, 233, 242–3, 284, 303
    Belgian 213, 252
    Czechoslovakian xiv, 209–10, 212–13, 222, 223, 230, 232
    French 209–10, 213, 222, 230, 233
    Norwegian 209–10, 230
    Polish 209–10, 212, 213–14, 217–18, 222, 226–7, 229
Anderson, Benedict 31
anti-alienism 219–22, 232
anti-English prejudice 12, 166, 168, 172–3
anti-Italian riots 219
anti-Semitism 222, 232
Anzio 125–6
Army Education Corps 11
Army regiments
    38th (Irish) Infantry Brigade 98–9, 123, 125, 126, 127
    51st Highland Infantry Division 14, 51, 56, 59, 98
    53rd (Welsh) Division 51, 57
    Fusiliers 52, 55, 60, 62–4, 69, 70, 71, 77–8, 93–4, 96, 98–9, 120–1, 122, 123, 126, 128–9, 282
    Irish Guards 51, 94, 96, 98, 105, 121, 123, 124, 125, 128–9
    Light Infantry 52, 55, 57, 61
    Royal Armoured Corps 55, 224
    Royal Army Service Corps 53
    Royal Artillery 62, 70
    Royal Ulster Rifles 61, 96, 104, 120, 121, 122, 123, 128, 130, 281
    Scots Guards 51
    Welsh Guards 51, 65, 69, 73–4, 75, 78, 87n.85
ARP (Air Raid Precautions Service) 16, 117
Attlee, Clement xii, 78, 123
ATS (Auxiliary Territorial Service) 10, 102, 185, 192, 193, 195, 198, 200, 221
Australia *see* British Commonwealth

Battle of Britain xii, 1, 32, 47, 169, 212
BBC (British Broadcasting Corporation) xi, xiv, 5, 7–8, 15, 17, 77, 81, 86, 95, 140–1, 196, 212–13, 220, 224–5, 270, 275, 293, 294, 302, 303
The Bells Go Down 32, 299, 301, 303, 304, 306
Belsen 131, 134
Blitz xi, xiv, 1, 27, 32, 44, 46, 118, 119, 131, 133, 134, 144, 222, 267, 298–300, 306
The Blue Peter 302
British Commonwealth 121, 170, 172, 199–200, 237, 239, 240, 243, 244, 246, 248, 251, 252, 255, 258

Australia 21, 200, 224, 236, 237, 239–41, 252–3
Canada 21, 197, 200, 236–7, 239, 240, 241–2, 244, 245, 247, 251
New Zealand 21, 200, 236–8, 239–40
South Africa, Union of 21–2, 235–9, 241–2, 246–50, 251–7, 258–60
Southern Rhodesia 22, 235–9, 241–2, 246–59
British empire ix, x, xiv–v, 2, 3, 4–5, 7, 8, 17, 21, 30, 42, 67, 94, 116, 171, 173, 210, 213, 214–19, 220–1, 235–9, 240, 244–5, 246–60, 262, 284, 301
British Legion 105–8
Bruton, John 108–9

Calder, Angus 26, 29, 42, 47, 66–7, 161, 182
Canada *see* British Commonwealth
A Canterbury Tale xiii, 19, 33, 138
Cavalcanti, Alberto xiii, 36–7, 159
Chamberlain, Neville xi, 116, 117, 241
chaplaincy 11, 185–8, 193–7, 200–4, 207–8
Christian national identity 186–8, 191, 195, 197, 201, 204, 208
Church Times 199, 204
Churchill, Winston 8, 98, 104, 117, 119, 122–3, 133, 135, 183, 217–18, 229, 240
cinema 5, 18, 31, 67, 134, 137–60 passim, 226, 261–2, 266, 276, 280
Colley, Linda x, 4–5, 16, 19
commemoration 13, 66n.3, 105, 120, 168
communism 26, 183
conscientious objectors 82–3, 178, 179
conscription 11, 16, 29, 83, 95, 114, 116–17, 119, 122, 165, 172, 174–5, 179, 180, 189, 195, 203, 275, 283, 288
Constantine, Learie 221, 226

cosmopolitan xiii, 87, 225
Coward, Noel 155, 297, 300
Crown Film Unit 263, 265, 267, 290, 297, 299, 306
CWWF (Churches Work for Women in the Forces) 11, 188, 192, 194–5, 197–201
Cymru – Wales 279

The Dawn Guard 19, 39
de Valera, Eamon 89, 90–3, 102, 105–6, 109, 110–11, 117, 127, 128
The Demi-Paradise 151
Derry 97, 108, 122
deserters 109, 111
A Diary for Timothy 290, 291
difference ix, 14, 16, 17, 18, 24, 29, 67, 73, 76, 77, 81, 86–7, 89, 97, 110, 138, 139, 143, 186, 191, 193, 204, 215, 223–4, 228, 262, 269, 272, 274, 280, 281, 284, 302
documentary film movement 278
domesticity 301
Dominions 21, 22, 78, 96, 105, 220, 235–9, 240, 241–3, 246, 250, 251–3, 255–6, 257, 259
Dunkirk 1, 38, 122, 227, 293

Easter Rising (1916) 92, 283n.60
Eire 16, 78, 89–92, 96, 100–2, 105–7, 109–10, 121, 123, 124, 128–9, 133, 135, 210, 282–3
Empire Exhibition, Glasgow 1938 143, 268
Empire forces in Britain
Australian 210, 211–12, 220, 222, 224
Canadian 210, 211–12, 215, 219, 224, 226, 227, 228, 229, 230, 231, 233
New Zealander 210, 211–12, 215, 231, 233
West Indian 210, 215, 224, 226, 231, 244

Index

Empire Marketing Board 145, 263
England x, xii, xiii, 2, 5, 12, 15, 17–19, 21, 25–47 *passim*, 49–64 *passim*, 67–8, 69, 72, 80, 81, 82, 83–4, 86, 87, 103, 113, 121, 122, 128, 130, 133, 139, 141, 142–3, 145, 146, 159, 161, 165–6, 168, 169, 172, 174, 177, 178, 179, 180, 181, 188, 190, 191, 193, 196, 203, 211–12, 229, 266–8, 273, 274, 282, 285, 290, 291
Englishness xii, xiv, 15, 18–19, 25, 33, 38–9, 40, 44, 46–7, 49–51, 52–3, 61, 64, 142, 166, 203, 289
Equal Citizenship (Blanket) Bill 206–7
ethnicities 22
Europe xi, xii, xiii–xiv, 4, 7, 23, 36, 37, 57, 69, 130, 167, 170, 183, 198, 210, 218, 222, 230, 238, 244, 252
evacuees 34, 36, 81
Euro 96; identity 50

The Face of Scotland 145, 146, 268n.29, 273
Fascism 26, 27, 161, 162–5, 171, 181–2, 191, 225
feminism 185–7
Fifth Columnists 219
Fires Were Started 264, 299–300, 303, 304, 306
The First of the Few 138
First World War 13, 26, 32, 34, 54, 58n.32, 95, 98, 105, 108, 116, 121, 122, 216, 282, 288
Ford, John 276
The Foreman Went to France 151

The Gentle Sex 17n.76, 155, 156, 267, 303
Germany x, 6, 26, 31, 32, 38, 42, 50, 78, 103, 126, 164, 167–8, 171, 172, 174, 176, 181, 210, 211, 224, 282, 289

GPO Film Unit 145, 263, 267
Grierson, John 143–4, 145, 263–4, 268–9, 271, 276
Greene, Graham 36

Harper, Sue 141n.14, 142
Harrisson, Tom 27, 40, 41, 42–3
Heart of Britain 137, 267
The Heart of Scotland 270
Henry V 152, 153, 159, 267
Highland xiii, 14, 44, 51, 52, 55, 56, 57, 59, 60, 98, 100, 145, 173, 182, 270, 271, 273
Home Guard 16, 39, 118–19, 294, 303; *see also* LDV
Home Intelligence 211, 261n.1
How Green Was My Valley 276
hybridity xv, 22

In Which We Serve 17n.76, 138, 155–6, 289, 297–8, 300
IRA (Irish Republican Army) 16, 114, 115, 119, 134, 169
Ireland 2, 16, 44, 76, 89–111 *passim*, 121, 129, 163, 174, 231–2, 281, 282, 283
Irishness 16, 89, 99, 102–3, 104, 125

Jackson, Gordon 17, 31, 267
Jennings, Humphre xiv, 8, 20, 40, 41, 264, 267, 271, 278n.52, 290, 291, 299, 306
Johns, Mervyn 17

Kumar, Krishan 2–3, 21, 24

A Letter from Ulster 284
The Life and Death of Colonel Blimp 138, 151, 155
The Lion Has Wings 154, 155
Listen to Britain xiv, 264, 271

LDV (Local Defence Volunteers) 36, 38, 118
Lloyd George, David 69
London Can Take It! 44n.59, 267

MacDiarmid, Hugh (C.M. Grieve) 162–4, 172, 176–7, 181
Macdonell, A.G. 269, 284
Mass Observation 19, 25, 40–5, 82, 83, 87, 117, 211, 261n.1, 290
memorialisation 13
Merchant Navy 102, 216, 296, 298, 300, 302–3, 307–8
Miles, Bernard 17, 39
Millions Like Us 18n.76, 32, 267, 303
Minden Day 60
Ministry of Information 7, 20, 26, 38, 86n.84, 144, 213, 214, 215, 216, 261, 264, 265, 275, 277, 279, 285
Ministry of Labour 79, 196, 264
morale 27, 38, 58, 67, 74, 88n.88, 99, 103, 123, 211, 261, 269, 303
Morrison, Herbert 217–18

National Eisteddfod 77, 85
nationalism x, xv, 12, 20, 43, 50, 69, 70, 81, 83, 89, 138, 161, 162, 163, 165, 168, 169, 174, 179, 181, 182, 183, 247, 259, 270, 282
neutrality 89–90, 91–2, 93, 101–2, 106, 109, 111, 123, 165, 166, 174, 178, 232, 248, 283
New Zealand *see* British Commonwealth
nicknames 54, 55, 59, 89, 97–8, 110
Noakes, Lucy ix, 11, 19
Normandy 53, 56, 58, 74n.33, 128
Northern Ireland 2, 12, 13, 15, 16, 23, 27, 30, 31, 46, 78, 89, 90, 91, 95–6, 100–1, 103, 105, 107, 108, 110, 111, 113–36 *passim*, 198, 262, 265, 269, 280–4

One of Our Aircraft is Missing 17n.76, 151
Orange Order 120
Orwell, George 8, 30, 43, 225, 291
Our Heritage 143, 149, 267

Pickles, Wilfred 17, 293
Plaid Cymru 81n.63, 82–3
pluralism xv
Pocock, John ix, xv, 4, 29, 41
post-war memories 212
Priestley, J.B. 8, 17, 26n. 4, 38–9, 45
propaganda 7, 18, 20, 22, 23, 26, 37, 43, 65, 67, 78, 86, 87n.85, 103, 154, 174, 196, 210, 231, 232, 261, 266, 267, 275, 292, 293, 295

RAF (Royal Air Force) 22, 31, 70, 79, 97–8, 101, 103, 104, 108, 110, 130–1, 158, 192, 197n.51, 199, 201, 214–15, 216, 224, 231, 235, 240, 242–3, 245, 248–9, 250, 252, 253, 254, 255, 257, 258, 289, 291, 309
Randle, Frank 17, 142
recruitment 41, 54, 71, 72, 93–4, 95, 118, 119, 120, 121–2, 129, 210, 215, 225–6, 244, 303
refugees 210, 217, 218, 224
regimental traditions 73
religious identity xii, 185, 186, 187
Rose, Sonya O. ix, 8, 9, 10, 18, 35, 67, 85, 188, 207, 288–9, 291, 296, 302, 304, 307, 309
Royal Navy 94, 101, 129, 131, 296, 298, 301, 307, 308
Royal Ulster Constabulary 114, 115
rural England 19, 25, 38, 39, 43, 46–7

San Demetrio, London 158, 300–1, 302, 303, 308
Scotland 2, 5, 12, 20, 23, 27, 30, 31, 42, 46, 55, 76, 98, 122, 133, 137–60

passim, 161–84 *passim*, 198, 211, 262, 265, 266, 267, 269–74, 280, 281, 284
Scotland Speaks 20, 265, 266, 269–74, 277, 279n.55, 281, 284
Scottishness 18, 51, 64, 100, 184
SEM (Society for the Equal Ministry of Men and Women in the Church) 190, 191, 193
Settler-regions 22, 235–60 *passim*
Shipmates Ashore 302, 303
Shipyard Sally 146, 147, 148
The Silent Village 20, 278n.52
SNP (Scottish National Party) 12, 161, 165, 166, 169, 170, 172, 176, 177, 178, 180, 182, 183, 184
South Africa, Union of *see* British Commonwealth
Southern Rhodesia *see* British Commonwealth
Soviet Union 218, 231, 270
The Spy in Black 154, 155
stereotypes 49
structures of feeling 28, 40

taste communities 140, 141
territorialisation 54
This England 17n.76, 138, 143, 151, 267, 273
Thomas, Dylan 275, 277–80, 284, 285
trade union(ism) 5, 295n.30

Ulster 20, 280–5

Unionism 15, 49, 89

volunteers 12, 15, 16, 89–111 *passim*, 114, 119, 122, 123, 124, 129, 134, 210, 232, 243, 248
von Tevenar, Gerhard 166–70, 178

WAAF (Women's Auxiliary Air Force) 10, 195, 198, 199, 214
Wales 2, 5, 10, 12, 13, 15–16, 20, 23, 27, 30, 31, 32, 42, 44, 46, 65–88 *passim*, 174, 182, 262, 264, 265, 268, 274–80, 284, 291
Wales – Green Mountain, Black Mountain 20, 264n.9, 265, 274–80, 284
Ward, Paul 1, 2, 3, 20, 22
The Way Ahead 267, 289, 304
Welsh language xi, 20, 23, 67, 79, 274n.43
Welsh nationalism 81, 83
Welshness 16, 18, 65–88 *passim*
Went the Day Well? xiii, 19, 36, 196, 289, 293
Western Approaches 17n.76, 297, 298, 303, 305, 307
Women's Freedom League 186, 188
World Cup 50
WRNS (Women's Royal Naval Service) 10, 195

Zec, Phillip 297

BRITISH IDENTITIES SINCE 1707

The historiography of British identities has flourished since the mid-1970s, spurred on by increasing national consciousness in England, Scotland, Wales and Northern Ireland, and since 1997 by devolution. Historians and other academics have become increasingly aware that identities in the British Isles have been fluid and that interactions between the different parts of the British Isles have been central to historical developments since, and indeed before, the Act of Union between England and Scotland in 1707.

This series seeks to encourage exploration of identities of place in the British Isles since the early eighteenth century, including intersections between competing and complementary identities such as region and nation. The series also advances discussion of other identities such as class, gender, religion, politics, ethnicity and culture when these are geographically located and positioned. While the series is historical, it welcomes cross- and interdisciplinary approaches to the study of British identities.

'British Identities since 1707' examines the unity and diversity of the British Isles, developing consideration of the multiplicity of negotiations that have taken place in such a multinational and multi-ethnic group of islands. It will include discussions of nationalism(s), of Britishness, Englishness, Scottishness, Welshness and Irishness, as well as 'regional' identities including, for example, those associated with Cornwall, the Gàidhealtachd region in Scotland and Gaeltacht areas in Ireland. The series will encompass discussions of relations with continental Europe and the United States, with ethnic and immigrant identities and with other forms of identity associated with the British Isles as place. The editors are interested in publishing books relating to the wider British world, including current and former parts of the British Empire and the Commonwealth, and places such as Gibraltar and the Falkland Islands and the smaller islands of the British archipelago. 'British Identities since 1707' reinforces the consideration of history, culture and politics as richly diverse across and within the borders of the British Isles.

Proposals are invited for monographs and edited collections, including those that arise from relevant conferences.

Vol. 1   Ben Wellings: English Nationalism and Euroscepticism: Losing the Peace
293 pages. 2012. ISBN 978-3-0343-0204-3

Vol. 2   Catherine McGlynn, Andrew Mycock and James W. McAuley (eds): Britishness, Identity and Citizenship: The View From Abroad
362 pages. 2011. ISBN 978-3-0343-0226-5

Vol. 3   M. H. Beals: Coin, Kirk, Class and Kin: Emigration, Social Change and Identity in Southern Scotland
289 pages. 2011. ISBN 978-3-0343-0252-4

Vol. 4   Andrew Francis: 'To Be Truly British We Must Be Anti-German': New Zealand, Enemy Aliens and the Great War Experience, 1914–1919
317 pages. 2012. ISBN 978-3-0343-0759-8

Vol. 5   Shanti Sumartojo: Trafalgar Square and the Narration of Britishness, 1900–2012: Imagining the Nation
236 pages. 2013. ISBN 978-3-0343-0814-4

Vol. 6   Jeffrey Hill: Popular Politics and Popular Culture in the Age of the Masses: Studies in Lancashire and the North West of England, 1880s to 1930s
277 pages. 2014. ISBN 978-3-0343-0936-3

Vol. 7   Wendy Ugolini and Juliette Pattinson (eds): Fighting for Britain? Negotiating Identities in Britain During the Second World War
335 pages. 2015. ISBN 978-3-0343-1824-2